THE RULE OF LAW, FREEDOM OF EXPRESSION AND ISLAMIC LAW

The importance of the rule of law is universally recognised and of fundamental value for all societies. Establishing and promoting the rule of law in the Muslim world, particularly in the Middle East, North Africa, and Central Asia, has become a pressing but complicated issue. These states have Muslim majority populations, and the religion of Islam has an important role in the traditional structures of their societies. While the Muslim world is taking gradual steps towards the establishment of rule of law systems, most Muslim majority countries may not yet have effective legal systems with independent judiciaries, which would allow the state and institutions to be controlled by an effective rule of law system.

One important aspect of the rule of law is freedom of expression. Given the sensitivity of Muslim societies in relation to their sacred beliefs, freedom of expression, as an international human rights issue, has raised some controversial cases. This book, drawing on both International and Islamic Law, explores the rule of law, and freedom of expression and its practical application in the Muslim world.

The Rule of Law, Freedom of Expression and Islamic Law

Hossein Esmaeili, Irmgard Marboe
and Javaid Rehman

•HART•
OXFORD • LONDON • NEW YORK • NEW DELHI • SYDNEY

HART PUBLISHING
Bloomsbury Publishing Plc
Kemp House, Chawley Park, Cumnor Hill, Oxford, OX2 9PH, UK

HART PUBLISHING, the Hart/Stag logo, BLOOMSBURY and the Diana logo are trademarks of Bloomsbury Publishing Plc
First published in Great Britain 2017

First published in hardback, 2017
Paperback edition, 2020

A catalogue record for this book is available from the British Library.

Library of Congress Cataloging-in-Publication Data

Names: Esmaeili, Hossein, author. | Marboe, Irmgard, author. | Rehman, Javaid, author.

Title: The rule of law, freedom of expression and Islamic law / Hossein Esmaeili, Irmgard Marboe, and Javaid Rehman.

Description: Oxford [UK] ; Portland, Oregon : Hart Publishing, 2017. | Includes bibliographical references and index.

Identifiers: LCCN 2017032006 (print) | 2017035617 (ebook) | ISBN 9781782257486 (Epub) | ISBN 9781782257462 (hardback)

Subjects: LCSH: Freedom of expression (Islamic law) | Rule of law—Islamic countries. | Justice, Administration of (Islamic law)

Classification: LCC KBP2470 (ebook) | LCCKBP2470 .E86 2017 (print) | DD 342/.167085—dc23

LC record available at https://lccn.loc.gov/2017032006

ISBN: HB: 978-1-78225-746-2
PB: 978-1-50993-746-2
ePDF: 978-1-78225-750-9
ePub: 978-1-78225-748-6

Typeset by Compuscript Ltd, Shannon

FOREWORD

AWN SHAWKAT AL-KHASAWNEH[1]

The act of asking me to write a foreword to this topical and comprehensive book on *The Rule of Law, Freedom of Expression and Islamic Law* is the latest manifestation of an unfailing courtesy and kindness extended to me for over a decade by the three distinguished authors, who are also the three Co-Rapporteurs of the Committee on Islamic Law and International Law, which is now one of the longest-standing committees of the International Law Association.[2] It was in the biennial meetings of the ILA that the themes of what is now the present book were introduced and debated, and where thorny questions, often touching everyone's sensibilities and deeply-held convictions, were aired. On account of this, the debates were sometimes provocative and always thought-provoking.

In matters of religion, there is a marked propensity to dogmatism, and a mind set steeped in legalisms only enforces that propensity. The great British diplomatist Sir Harold Nicolson once remarked, not without reason, that 'missionaries, fanatics, and lawyers' are poor diplomats.[3] But this is not always the case. In Islamic history, the legalism built around texts, sacred texts to be sure, but also less sacred ones, has been tempered in practice by two factors. First, the rise of a mass movement, generically referred to as Sufism, that emphasised the inner spiritual life and experiences of individuals and saw divine love as the ultimate aim of religion(s), transcending reward and punishment (love is its own reward). It also found that the quest for epistemological knowledge of the Beloved (gnosis) is common to mankind. The wayfarers along this path found support for their school of thought in a number of Quranic *suras* addressed to mankind at large: 'we have bestowed

[1] Chair, ILA's Committee on Islamic Law and International Law; Former Prime Minister of Jordan (2011–2012); Former Judge, International Court of Justice (2000–2011); Former Vice President, International Court of Justice (2006–2009).

[2] The International Law Association (ILA), founded in Brussels in 1873, is dedicated to the study, clarification and development of international law, both public and private, and the furtherance of international understanding and respect for international law.

[3] Harold Nicolson, *Diplomacy* (Harcourt Brace 1939) 50.

dignity on the Children of Adam'.[4] Thus, for example, Ibn Arabi, one of the greatest thinkers of Islam, writes:

My heart can take on any form:

A meadow for gazelles,

A cloister for monks,

For the idols, sacred ground,

Ka'ba for the circling pilgrim,

The tables of the Torah,

The scrolls of the Quran.

My creed is Love;

Wherever its caravan turns along the way,

That is my belief,

My faith.

The second factor, indigenous to the Sharia itself, was the preponderance of the school of higher intents (*maqāsid*) of the Sharia. According to this school, the rules and prohibitions of the Sharia are all meant to preserve and enhance a number of protected interests: the preservation of the self, the mind, honour, the country, etcetera. To illustrate the point with an example, a question was once posed to a Jurist: If there is a church in the realm of Islam and if the Christian community cannot afford to provide lanterns, who should pay for the lighting? The answer was: the Muslim *waqfs* should provide for the lighting of the Church. The reasoning is interesting: because the worshippers may stumble and fall and may die, therefore this is against the higher intents (*maqāsid*) of the Sharia, ie, self-preservation. The reasoning was not based on some theory of human rights or a grand declaration, such as that which we encounter in all modern constitutions, but based on a simple and solid ground of justice and mercy.

Thus, Ibn Qayyim Al-Jawziyyah, a Thirteenth to Fourteenth Century jurist, was ready to assert:

> Islamic law is structured and founded upon wise purposes and the best interests of God's servants both in this world and the next. The Law is pure justice, pure mercy, pure benefit, pure wisdom. Hence, anything which embodies injustice rather than justice, cruelty rather than mercy, harm rather than benefit, or folly rather than wisdom does not originate from the Law, even if it happens to have been interpolated therein by means of interpretation.[5]

[4] The Quran 17:70.

[5] Quoted at pp 31–32 of this book by the authors from GE Attia, *Towards Realization of the Higher Intents of Islamic Law: Maqāsid al-Sharia: A Functional Approach* (London, The International Institute of Islamic Thought, 2007) 7.

Ultimately, the interaction of the two tendencies: the legalistic and the Sufi (which was not free of tension as evidenced by the execution of Al-Hallaj[6] and Al-Suhrawardi for blasphemy[7]) resolved itself into a mutual accommodation that lasted until the modern era when a new and more ominous challenge from an industrial and more technologically-advanced West made itself felt. The Western model with its centralised state structure that controls law-making and espouses legal positivism, liberal democracy and secularism became the universal yardstick against which other civilizations were measured. Naturally, there was a response to this intrusion into the various Islamic polities and this reaction took many forms, ranging from reform movements that sought to return to a purer form of Islam as in 19th century India (eg. Shah Waliullah of Delhi), or to accept an accommodation with the new reality and to emulate the colonial power by taking up Western methods of education (eg Syad Ahmad Khan). Similarly, in the Ottoman Empire, the *Tenzimat* reforms that were forced on the Sultan and the promulgation of the 1876 Constitution (which was prorogated two years later by Sultan Abdul Hamid II, who instead espoused a Pan Islamist policy) all evidence a perplexity in dealing with this overwhelming challenge from the West. This 'challenge and response'—in Toynbian parlance[8]—continues today and explains the reactions (or overreactions) to such incidents as the publication of the satanic verses or the Charlie Hebdo Cartoons; a civilisation that is threatened or perceives itself to be so cannot be expected to be tolerant to what it perceives as attacks on its core beliefs. The present book addresses those tensions but it does not—indeed cannot—resolve them, and it is not expected to do so. However, it addresses them with lucidity and explores ways of resolving them. But, I wish to emphasise that history provides us with examples of where inter-civilizational cross-fertilisation may flourish. In the early formative years of Islamic law, many of its concepts, institutions and methods of reasoning were taken from Roman Law and easily incorporated into it. The great codification of that law in the reign of the Eastern Roman Emperor Justinian (529–534 AD) took place less than a century before Islam; further, Syrian jurists played an important role in it[9] and it took place in *Berytus* (it is no wonder that the first legal school in Islam was also in Beirut). I mention all of this to convey the message that, first, unlike the colonial and post-colonial 'imposition' of values by one civilization over other(s), it is possible to nurture common values, and, second, to recall that there is enough in common in terms of the intellectual reservoir from which legal concepts are distilled and the sources of law to sustain truly universal legal principles that can generate a genuine sense of obligation and respect for the law.

[6] See for details, Louis Massignon, *La Passion de Hallaj* (Gallimard 1990).

[7] Shihab Al-Din Al-Suhrawadi was executed on the order of the sultan Saladin in 1191 on a charge of blasphemy; see, John L Esposito (eds), *The Oxford History of Islam* (Oxford University Press 1999) 293–94.

[8] See, Arnold Toynbee, *A Historian's Approach to Religion* (2nd edn, Oxford University Press 1979).

[9] Ulpian and Galenus are prime examples.

It is my earnest hope that the present book, which brings to a larger audience the work of the ILA Committee on International Law and Islamic Law, will contribute to a greater and much-needed understanding of Islamic Law and in reconciling differences between Islamic Law and International Law.

Awn Shawkat Al-Khasawneh
Dhu Al-Qa'dah 1438 (*Añno Hegira*)
August 2017

Chair, ILA Committee on International Law and Islamic Law; former Prime Minister of Jordan and former Judge, International Court of Justice

ACKNOWLEDGEMENTS

The idea to write this book originated from the cooperation of the three authors as Co-Rapporteurs of the International Law Association's Committee on International Law and Islamic Law. Over almost a decade, the ILA Committee produced reports about the relationship between international law and Islamic law. In so doing it was guided and inspired by the charismatic personality of its internationally renowned Chairman, the former Judge at the ICJ and former Prime Minister of his home country Jordan, His Excellency Awn Shawkat Al-Khasawneh. Due to his continuous support and that of the ILA Directors of Study, Professor Christine Chinkin and Professor Marcel Brus, the authors felt encouraged to address one of the thorniest issues of this context, the relationship between Islamic law, the rule of law and the freedom of expression. Over the years, the biannual conferences of the ILA provided the opportunity to exchange ideas and develop and refine the topic. Most importantly, the diversity of membership in the ILA enabled discussions between researchers from different backgrounds, including civil law and common law, Sunni and Shia traditions. The authors themselves reflect this diversity. This work reflects a collective effort of all three authors, although in terms of substantive writing, Hossein Esmaeili was responsible for Chapters 3 and 5, Irmgard Marboe for Chapters 2 and 4, and Javaid Rehman for Chapters 6 and 7. Chapters 1 and 8 were written jointly.

Amongst the ILA Committee members whose experience and knowledge had an important influence on this book the authors would like to highlight and thank Dr Katja Samuel, whose research on the Organisation of Islamic Cooperation formed an essential part of the Committee's reports and is also reflected in this study. Other members of the ILA Committee contributed to the research on the relationship of Islam and international law from a plurality of perspectives. Furthermore, Juliet Fussell, Secretary of the ILA, was of invaluable help in putting the past ILA reports in the correct format and publishing them in a timely manner.

In addition, the authors would like to thank the dedicated and experienced staff of Hart Publishing for expressing faith in this project at a very early stage and for their professional support. Finally, the authors are deeply indebted to their friends and families, who endured the process of researching and writing this book with patience and understanding.

Hossein Esmaeili
Irmgard Marboe
Javaid Rehman

CONTENTS

TABLE OF CASES

International

The World Court

Human Rights Committee

European Court of Human Rights

Domestic

Pakistan

United Kingdom

TABLE OF TREATIES, INSTRUMENTS AND LAWS

United Nations

Treaties

General Assembly Resolutions

General Assembly Resolutions on the Rule of Law at the National and International Levels

United Nations General Assembly Resolutions on Combating Defamation of Religions

General Assembly Resolutions on Combating Intolerance, Negative Stereotyping, Stigmatisation, Discrimination, Incitement to Violence and Violence Against Persons, Based on Religion or Belief

Reports of the United Nations Special Rapporteurs

Human Rights Commission/Human Rights Council

Human Rights Commission/Human Rights Council Resolutions on Defamation of Religions

Human Rights Council Resolutions on Combating Intolerance, Negative Stereotyping, Stigmatisation of, and Discrimination, Incitement to Violence and Violence Against Persons, Based on Religion or Belief

United Nations Human Rights Committee

Reports by the United Nations Secretary-Generals

Other Documents

Regional

Organisation of the Islamic Conference/Cooperation (OIC)

League of Arab States

Other Regional Instruments

Constitutions and Domestic Laws

Other Instruments

Part I

Introduction

1

Introduction

I. Opening Comments

Respect for the rule of law represents a quintessential prerequisite for human civilisation. Despite the varying, sometimes conflicting interpretations of the meaning and content of the rule of law,[1] its importance and value as a concept are universally recognised. Appreciation for the rule of law is not an exclusive prerogative of the 'West' but represents a synthesis of shared values highly esteemed by all civilisations, including the Muslim world.[2] As this study demonstrates, Islamic civilisations have contributed substantially towards the development of modern rule of law principles. The Quran and the Sunna–the primary sources of the Sharia and Islamic law–reaffirm the compatibility of rational approaches to and

[1] On the meaning and definition of the rule of law, see J Finnis, *Natural Law and Natural Rights* (Oxford, Clarendon Press, 1980); M Gleeson, *The Rule of Law and the Constitution* (Sydney NSW, ABC Books, 2000); R Bellamy (ed), *The Rule of Law and the Separation of Powers* (Aldershot, Ashgate, 2005); BZ Tamanaha, *On the Rule of Law: History, Politics and Theory* (Cambridge, Cambridge University Press, 2004); D Clark, 'The Many Meanings of the Rule of Law' in K Jayasuriya (ed), *Capitalism and Power in Asia: The Rule of Law and Legal Institutions* (New York, Routledge, 1999) 28–44; M Kramer, 'On the Moral of the Rule of Law' (2004) 63 *Cambridge Law Journal* 65; MJ Radin 'Reconsidering the Rule of Law' (1989) 69 *Boston University Law Review* 781; J Raz, 'The Rule of Law and Its Virtue' (1977) 93 *Law Quarterly Review* 195; C Saunders and K Le Roy (eds), *The Rule of Law* (Sydney, The Federation Press, 2003).

[2] The people of the Muslim world including political and religious leaders, intellectuals and ordinary people have been championing the rule of law for well over a century. In 1910, an Iranian intellectual and legal scholar published a book titled 'One Term' arguing 'the fundamental basis of Western civilisation is one term: "the rule of law" and all achievements in the West result from the rule of law systems'. Mirza Yusuf Mustashar al-Dawlah-yi Tabrizi, *Yek Kalameh ve yek nameh* ('One Term and One Letter'), ed. Seyyid Muhammad Sadiq Fayz (Tehran, Sabah, 1962); see also H Enayat, *Law, State, and Society in Modern Iran: Constitutionalism, Autocracy and Legal Reform, 1906–1941* (New York, Palgrave Macmillan, 2013). In 1999, Abdul Rahman Wahid, the former President of Indonesia, stated that the implementation of the rule of law was a key achievement of his establishment; see H Esmaeili, 'The Nature and Development of Law in Islam and the Rule of Law Challenge in the Middle East and the Muslim World' (2011) 26 *Connecticut Journal of International Law* 329, 333. In addition, Mohammad Khatami's 1997 campaign for the establishment of the rule of law and civil society in Iran won him the 1997 election; see generally M Khatami, *Islam, Liberty and Development* (Binghamton, Global Academic Publishing, 1998). Current member of the Afghan government and former warlord Abdul Rashid Dotsum has made public statements in favour of the rule of law, stating, '[n]ow is the time to defend ourselves not with tanks and armed corps but by the rule of law and establishing political parties'; A Davis and Mazar-I-Sharif, 'A Makeover for a Warlord' *Time* (3 June 2002) www.time.com/time/magazine/article/0,9171,1002556,00.htm.

interpretation of Islam and the various strands of the rule of law; these include inter alia equality of all before the law, transparency and political accountability.[3] Within Islamic history, there have been phases of extraordinary and remarkable examples of the implementation of rule of law principles.

However, these historic portrayals contrast poorly with the contemporary Muslim world where establishing or promoting notions of rule of law has proved challenging and problematic. While gradual steps towards the establishment of rule of law systems are undertaken, many Muslim majority states do not yet have effective, functional democracies with independent judiciaries.[4] In many cases, governmental institutions and powerful individuals continue to unduly take advantage of ineffective and inadequate legal structures to undermine the functioning of the rule of law.

In addition to the shortcomings and deficiencies at the domestic level, Muslim majority states are also challenging global policies which fully and unequivocally demand respect for the rule of law and international human rights. In this regard, some state practices and practices of Islamic organisations (for example, the Organisation of Islamic Cooperation, hereinafter, OIC) are of profound concern.[5]

A core element of the rule of law is freedom of expression, whereby citizens enjoy the protection of the law to express freely their own ideas and thoughts. Freedom of expression is the foundational stone of all societies governed by the rule of law, and the right to free expression is recognised as a fundamental right within international law and within the constitutional paradigms of modern state structures.[6] Nevertheless, it has provoked controversy and divisiveness, especially within the context of the Sharia and the limits ostensibly drawn by Islam.[7]

Muslim states and communities have proved to be sensitive with regard to the exercise of the right to freedom of expression in relation to Islamic beliefs or in response to insults, criticisms or ridicule of sacred personalities, texts and institutions. Examples abound of the political and international furore over such transgressions. The *Charlie Hebdo* terrorist attack in January 2015 which killed 14 people, including the two Islamist Jihadists, reignited the contentious debate on the boundaries of freedom of expression in the face of Muslim sensitivities.[8]

[3] See Esmaeili, 'The Nature and Development of Law in Islam and the Rule of Law Challenge in the Middle East and the Muslim World' (n 2); J Rehman and E Polymenopoulou 'Justice after Democracy in the Arab World: Islamic Law Perspectives on Accountability' (2012) 54 *German Yearbook of International Law* 53.

[4] See Pt II (Ch 2) below.

[5] See Pts III and IV below.

[6] Human Rights Committee, General Comment No 34 (Article 19: Freedom of Opinion and Expression) CCPR/C/GC/34 (12 September 2011) para 2; See Pt IV (Ch 6) below.

[7] See J Rehman, 'Freedom of Expression, Apostasy and Blasphemy within Islam' (2010) 79 *Criminal Justice Matters* 4; see Pt IV (Chs 6 and 7) below.

[8] See I Black, 'Arab cartoonists pen their response to Charlie Hebdo affair' (15 January 2015) www.theguardian.com/world/2015/jan/15/arab-cartoonists-response-charlie-hebdo-affair; see Pt IV (Ch 5) below.

Subsequent to the attack, demonstrations took place in the Muslim world in support of the freedom of expression but also postulating limitations to expression that is insensitive towards the values of Islam and the Sharia.

Such divisiveness on the subject of the freedom of expression has been a recurrent theme within the Muslim world. In September 2012, a former federal minister of Pakistan, Ghulam Ahmed Bilour, courted international controversy by issuing a proclamation calling upon Muslims to kill Nakoula Basseley Nakoula, an Egyptian Coptic Christian residing in the United States, for his role in the production of the allegedly offensive film *The Innocence of Muslims*.[9] He offered, including to members of the terrorist organisation Al-Qaeda and to the Taliban, a bounty of one million US dollars for anyone committing this murder.[10] From his statement, Bilour gained local public support and was apparently taken off the hit-list of the Taliban. Although not stating Pakistan's state policy, as a federal minister, Bilour campaigned for extra-judicial killing for the allegedly blasphemous publication with impunity.[11] Other public pronouncements of condemnation in response to allegedly offensive and crude expressions against Islam are well known, including the infamous *fatwa* issued by the late Iranian religious leader Ayatollah Khomeini against the British author Salman Rushdie in 1989,[12] the *Jyllands-Posten* cartoons controversy emergent after the publication of cartoons of Prophet Mohammad in Denmark and republished in other parts of the world,[13] international responses over Pope Benedict's quotation of a fourteenth-century Byzantine emperor's allegation that Mohammed was 'bad and inhuman' for commanding his followers to spread Islam by the sword, naming non-humans after holy personalities,[14] as well as desecration or destruction of holy scriptures or documents.[15]

[9] 'Pakistani minister offers bounty for death of anti-Islam film maker' *The Daily Telegraph* (23 September 2012). At a press conference called in Peshawar, the minister made the following assertion: 'I invite the Taliban brothers and the al-Qaeda brothers that they should join me in this sacred mission. Along with others, they should also join in the good work. And God willing, whoever is successful (in killing him) I will present one lac dollars (100,000 U.S. dollars) to him'. www.telegraph.co.uk/news/worldnews/asia/pakistan/9571190/Minister-who-offered-bounty-for-filmmaker-is-true-Muslim-says-Taliban.html.

[10] 'Minister who offered bounty for filmmaker is "true Muslim" says Taliban' *The Daily Telegraph* (27 September 2012) www.telegraph.co.uk/news/worldnews/asia/pakistan/9571190/Minister-who-offered-bounty-for-filmmaker-is-true-Muslim-says-Taliban.html.

[11] For details, see J Rehman, 'The *Sharia*, International Human Rights Law and the Right to Hold Opinions and Expression' in M-L Frick and AT Müller (eds), *Islam and International Law: Engaging Self-Centrism from a Plurality of Perspectives* (Leiden, Martinus Nijhoff, 2013) 244–68.

[12] See Pt IV (Ch 5) below; MM Slaughter, 'The Salman Rushdie Affair: Apostasy, Honor, and Freedom of Speech' (1993) 79 *Virginia Law Review* 153.

[13] See D Keane, 'Cartoon Violence and Freedom of Expression' (2008) 30 *Human Rights Quarterly* 845; 'France Boost Embassy Security after Muhammad Cartoons' *CBC News* (19 September 2012) www.cbc.ca/news/world/story/2012/09/19/france-embassies-cartoon-muhammad.html.

[14] See eg 'Reports: Sudan Arrests UK Teacher for Teddy Bear Blasphemy' *CNN* (26 November 2007) edition.cnn.com/2007/WORLD/africa/11/26/sudan.bear/index.html.

[15] See eg 'Pentagon urges controversial Florida Pastor to Stop Qur'an Burning Plans' *The Guardian* (20 April 2012) www.guardian.co.uk/world/2012/apr/20/pentagon-florida-pastor-quran-burning; 'Nigeria Teacher Dies "Over Koran"' *BBC News* (21 March 2007) news.bbc.co.uk/1/hi/6477177.stm.

II. Scope of the Study

This study aims to examine a number of key issues related to the tensions between the rule of law and freedom of expression as currently confronted by the Sharia, Islam and Muslim majority states. The study analyses the extent to which the concepts of the rule of law and freedom of expression can be discerned in Islamic law. If the rule of law and freedom of expression are, at least potentially, enshrined within Islamic law, why have modern Muslim majority states and the OIC been constrained in respecting and practising them? The study explores the challenges faced by the Muslim world in the implementation of the rule of law and freedom of expression and the prospects of overcoming these challenges.

One area of significant controversy is the legitimacy of anti-blasphemy laws existing in many states, ostensibly aiming at the protection of the religion of Islam. The practice of many of these states (both within their domestic realm and at the international level as members of the OIC) contrasts sharply with international norms on freedom of expression as propounded by the International Covenant on Civil and Political Rights (1966)[16] and interpreted by the Human Rights Committee.[17] The Committee advanced the position that religions, as ideological belief systems, cannot per se seek and secure protection by state law. This point has been reiterated and endorsed by the former Special Rapporteur on freedom of religion or belief, Asma Jahangir, who emphasised that '[f]reedom of religion primarily confers a right to act in accordance with one's religion but does not bestow a right for believers to have their religion itself protected from all adverse comment'.[18] By contrast, the OIC, since its inception in 1969, has been determined to oppose attempts to insult, ridicule or blaspheme the religion of Islam or Islam's sacred personalities. This commitment on the part of the organisation is currently reflected in the revised Charter which reiterates the common goal to 'protect and defend the true image of Islam'.[19] In exploring the boundaries of the freedom of expression, the present study will trace the shifts and turns of the position of the OIC on the subject of 'defamation of religions'. With the commencement of the so-called 'Istanbul process' in 2011,[20] the confrontational debate prevalent within the United Nations on the development of a universal norm prohibiting

[16] New York, 16 December 1966 United Nations, 999 U.N.T.S. 171; 6 I.L.M. (1967) 368; for consideration, see Ch 6 below.

[17] See Human Rights Committee, General Comment No 34 (Article 19: Freedom of Opinion and Expression) CCPR/C/GC/34 (12 September 2011) para 48; discussed in Ch 6 below.

[18] Implementation of General Assembly Resolution 60/251: Report of the Special Rapporteur on freedom of religion or belief, Asma Jahangir, and the Special Rapporteur on contemporary forms of racism, racial discrimination, xenophobia and related intolerance, Doudou Diène, further to Human Rights Council decision 1/107 on incitement to racial and religious hatred and the promotion of tolerance A/HRC/2/3 (20 September 2006).

[19] See Charter of the Organisation of Islamic Cooperation, adopted on 14 March 2008, www.oicun.org/2/24/20140324031549266.html, Art 1(12).

[20] Ch 7 below.

all forms of defamation of religions appears to have subsided. Nevertheless, deep divisions continue to resurface when drawing up boundaries between the freedom of expression vis-à-vis respect for religions or beliefs. The study will also consider the prospects and viability of the Rabat Plan of Action (2012) as an effective mechanism for combating advocacy of national, racial and religious hatred that constitutes incitement to discrimination, hostility and violence at the national and regional levels.[21]

III. Structure of the Book

The book is divided into five parts, consisting of eight chapters, including an introductory chapter and a concluding chapter. After the present introductory chapter describing the scope of the study and highlighting its key themes, Part II of the book, consisting of Chapter 2, carries out a detailed examination of the foundational principles of the rule of law. After an historical overview, it traces the origins of the doctrine of the rule of law from within the Western as well as non-Western traditions. It analyses the extent to which various traditions including Confucianism and the legalist school of thought as practised in China, the *dharma* philosophy of India and the pluralistic systems enunciated by the Islamic Sharia have contributed to developing rule of law principles. It examines the issue as to whether there are prevailing synergies between all major global traditions to make reconciliation and agreement a congenial possibility.

After this examination, Part III engages in a comparative study of Islamic law and international law. Chapter 3 provides a detailed analysis of the development of Islamic law and of Islamic legal traditions and in so doing assesses Islamic perspectives on the rule of law. The chapter reviews the origins of Islamic law, including the Arab custom and prevailing Jewish and Christian legal principles of the time which influenced the initial stage of the legal system of Islam. The chapter also analyses terms and concepts of the Sharia based on major languages of the Muslim world and English. This section is followed by a discussion of the contentious issue of the relationship between law and religion in Islam. In so doing the chapter looks at traditional and classical approaches as well as modern pursuits. It analyses the extent to which equating religion and law, as traditional Muslim

[21] Rabat Plan of Action on the prohibition of advocacy of national, racial or religious hatred that constitutes incitement to discrimination, hostility or violence: Conclusions and recommendations emanating from the four regional expert workshops organised by OHCHR, 2011, and adopted by experts in Rabat, Morocco on 5 October 2012. See UNCHR, Annual Report of the United Nations Commissioner for Human Rights, Addendum, *Report of the United Nations Commissioner for Human Rights on expert workshops on the Prohibition of incitement to national, racial or religious hatred* A/HRC/22/17/Add.4 (11 January 2013) www.ohchr.org/Documents/Issues/Opinion/SeminarRabat/Rabat_draft_outcome.pdf.

scholars support, makes legal principles sacred and immune from critical evaluation (and may lead to a rigid and inflexible legal system far from any meaningful application in the modern world). The chapter then examines ways in which a modernised and reformed version of Islamic law may accommodate a rule of law system.

Chapter 4 critically engages with an international law perspective. It takes, as its starting point, the 2004 Report of the Secretary-General of the United Nations, entitled 'The Rule of Law and Transitional Justice in Conflict and Post-Conflict Societies'.[22] In this report, the Secretary-General defines the rule of law as:

> a principle of governance in which all persons, institutions and entities, public and private, including the State itself, are accountable to laws that are publicly promulgated, equally enforced and independently adjudicated, and which are consistent with international human rights norms and standards. It requires, as well, measures to ensure adherence to the principles of supremacy of law, equality before the law, accountability to the law, fairness in the application of the law, separation of powers, participation in decision-making, legal certainty, avoidance of arbitrariness and procedural and legal transparency.[23]

The chapter examines the extent to which rule of law principles are relevant for the United Nations and the United Nations organs (in particular for the Security Council and the International Court of Justice). It also explores the applicability of rule of law within Muslim inter-governmental organisations, such as the OIC.

Part IV, consisting of Chapters 5, 6 and 7, shifts the focus to the concrete examination of the freedom of expression and opinion under Islamic law. Chapter 5 critically examines the classical and modern interpretations of Islamic laws that relate to freedom of expression. In particular, it analyses the diverse Islamic law interpretations on the subjects of blasphemy and apostasy. The chapter reviews the prevalent challenges in modern Muslim majority states and within Muslim communities in non-Muslim countries. It refers to cases such as the execution of Mahmoud Taha, convicted for the crime of apostasy in Sudan in the 1980s, and the recent possible trial of Jakarta's Christian Governor for blasphemy in Indonesia.[24] The classical Islamic law text and sources are examined in order to trace the relevant principles that may support freedom of expression and thought in Islam. In examining the various principles of the Sharia, most notably *Hisbah* and *Shura*, the chapter advances the view that notwithstanding tensions of interpretation, Islam and the Sharia are not inherently antithetical to the right to

[22] Report of the Secretary-General on 'The Rule of Law and Transitional Justice in Conflict and Post-Conflict Societies', UN Doc S/2004/616 (23 August 2004).

[23] Ibid para 6.

[24] K Lamb, 'Jakarta's Christian governor to face blasphemy trial over insult claim' *The Guardian Online* (16 November 2016) www.abc.net.au/news/2016-11-07/jakarta-governor-questioned-by-police-over-koran-comments/8003426.

freedom of expression. Chapter 6 of the study, as its title suggests, focuses on the relationship between freedom of expression and the freedom of religion or belief. This chapter, whilst highlighting the significance of the relationship between expression and the manifestation of religions, also engages with tensions and difficulties over the boundaries that are to be drawn over expression in order to protect religions from insults, defamation and blasphemy. Anti-blasphemy laws, although by no means an exclusively Muslim majority state practice, continue to be deployed in much of the Islamic world. The deployment of anti-blasphemy laws, particularly for political ends–in order to repress political opposition, curb freedom of expression and persecute human rights defenders and religious minorities–has been a preoccupation of many governments within the Islamic world. Chapter 6 exposes the flaws and serious repercussions of anti-blasphemy legislation through a detailed critical examination of the Pakistan Penal Code.

Chapter 7 presents an assessment of freedom of expression through the lens of the OIC. The OIC, as the world's largest organisation after the United Nations, is the flag-bearer and representative of the interests, values and aspirations of Muslim majority states. The chapter reviews and critically analyses the approaches of the OIC towards the right to freedom of expression. It analyses whether the substantial ideological differences and significantly fractured relationships between OIC members are an obstacle or not to a common approach on issues pertaining to freedom of expression. The practices of the organisation as well as legal instruments, such as the Cairo Declaration on Human Rights in Islam (1990), the revised OIC Charter (adopted in 2008)[25] and the Outcome Document (2015)[26] are examined closely. While the OIC has been a willing and interested party in the 'Istanbul Process', it remains to be seen as to whether there is a real possibility on the part of the OIC and its Western partners to converge towards a common understanding of the meaning and scope of the right to freedom of expression. The chapter reviews the political debates that have emerged during the enduring ideological conflicts over efforts to criminalise any defamation of religions within the United Nations. Finally, this part of the study examines the extent to which there exist elements of double standards: when OIC member states have been vociferous in campaigning against growing Islamophobia, but fail to provide protection to religious minorities within their own states. Part V, consisting of a single chapter, contains the results and concluding reflections of the study. It provides a critical assessment of the challenges that still persist with regard to the rule of law and freedom of expression both at the national and the international levels.

[25] See Organisation of Islamic Cooperation, www.oic-oci.org/oicv3/home/?lan=en.

[26] See IPHRC 8th Session: Outcome Document of Thematic Debate on 'Freedom of Expression and Hate Speech', 23 November 2015, www.oic-iphrc.org/data/sessions/8th_iphrc_thematic_debate_outcome_en.pdf. See app I.

IV. Methodology and Literature Review

This book is inspired by the ideas drawn from the work of the International Law Association's Committee on International Law and Islamic Law. At the International Law Association's biannual conferences in The Hague (2010), Sofia (2012), Washington, DC (2014) and Johannesburg (2016), the Committee submitted the following reports: *Islamic Law and International Law* (2010), *the Rule of Law and Islamic Legal System* (2012), *the Rule of Law and Freedom of Expression* (2014) and *Islamic Law and Freedom of Expression: Challenges and Prospects* (2016).[27] The Committee on International Law and Islamic Law aims to produce its conclusions and recommendatory resolutions on the subject during the forthcoming biannual conference in Sydney (2018).

As principal contributors to the aforementioned documents, the authors have developed and refined the ideas and concepts contained in the Committee's reports. The authors' research also confirmed that, despite the existing extensive scholarly literature on Islamic law (in English and in other languages) there are only a few specific works focusing on the rule of law and Islamic law. Pertinent literature on Islamic law in English can be found on constitutionalism and democracy in Islam,[28] on human rights in Islam[29] and on freedom of expression and Islamic law.[30] The specific interlinkage between the rule of law and freedom of expression in the context of Islamic law remains, so far, a relatively unexplored area of scholarly work.

[27] For the content of these reports, see International Law Association, www.ila-hq.org/en/committees/index.cfm/cid/1006.

[28] See eg R Grote and T Roder, *Constitutionalism in Islamic Countries* (Oxford, Oxford University Press, 2012); N Brown, *Constitutions in a Non-constitutional World: Arab Basic Laws and the Prospects for Accountable Government* (New York, State University of New York Press, 2001); N Hosen, *Sharia & Constitutional Reform in Indonesia* (Singapore, Institute of Southeast Asian Studies, 2007).

[29] See AE Mayer, *Islam and Human Rights* (Oxford, Westview Press, 1995, 2013); S Abul Ala Maududi, *Human Rights in Islam* (Leicester, Islamic Foundation, 1976); AA An-Na'im, *Toward an Islamic Reformation: Civil Liberties, Human Rights and International Law* (Syracuse, Syracuse University Press, 1990); AA An-Na'im (ed), *Human Rights in Cross-Cultural Perspectives: A Quest for Consensus* (Philadelphia, University of Pennsylvania Press, 1992).

[30] See A Black, H Esmaeili and N Hosen, *Modern Perspectives on Islamic Law* (Cheltenham, Edward Elgar, 2013); H Esmaeili, 'The Rule of Law in the Middle East' in JR Silkenat, JE Hickey Jr and PD Barenboim (eds), *The Legal Doctrines of the Rule of Law and the Legal State (Rechtsstaat)* (Switzerland, Springer, 2014) 315–30; Esmaeili (n 2) and H Esmaeili, 'On a Slow Boat Towards the Rule of Law: The Nature of Law in the Saudi Arabian Legal System' (2009) 26 *Arizona Journal of International and Comparative Law* 1; I Marboe, 'The Rule of Law in the Islamic Legal System' (2011) 7 *Journal of Islamic State Practices in International Law* 1; I Marboe, 'Promoting the Rule of Law: UN, OIC and ILA Initiatives Approaching Islamic Law' in Frick and Müller, *Islam and International Law* (n 11) 184 and I Marboe, 'The Role of the State to Protect Freedom of Religion' in S Hammer and F Husein (eds), *Religious Pluralism and Religious Freedom: Religions, Society and the State in Dialogue. Contributions to the Australian-Indonesian Dialogue* (Yogyakarta, Center for Religious and Cross-Cultural Studies, 2013) 61–71; J Rehman and S Berry, 'Is "Defamation of Religions" Passé? The United Nations, Organisation of Islamic Cooperation and Islamic State Practices: Lessons from Pakistan' (2012) 44 *George Washington International Law Review* 431.

The edited collection entitled *Democracy: Rule of Law and Islam*[31] appears to be one of the most relevant existing books on the issue of the rule of law in Islam. It covers a wide range of issues relating to Islamic law, such as democracy, human rights, the rights of women, and focuses on Egypt, but the specific importance of the freedom of expression is not discussed in greater detail.[32] By contrast, *Freedom of Expression in Islam* by Mohammad Hashim Kamali[33] has a relatively detailed discussion of freedom of expression from legal and moral perspectives of Islam. It is a leading scholarly text on the theoretical basis of freedom of expression in Islamic law and in its original sources. However, it is largely theoretical, and does not involve and evaluate the practice of Muslim societies in history and in modern times. Generally, the scholarly coverage of the rule of law and freedom of expression under Islamic law is rather scarce in English legal literature as well as in academic writing in other languages such as Arabic, Turkish, and Persian. The present study–although a modest effort– aims to fill this gap.

[31] E Cotran and AO Sherif (eds), *Democracy, Rule of Law and Islam* (Leiden, Brill, 1999).

[32] See HA Agrama, *Questioning Secularism, and the Rule of Law in Modern Egypt* (Chicago, University of Chicago Press, 2012).

[33] MH Kamali, *Freedom of Expression in Islam* (Cambridge, Islamic Texts Society, 1997).

Part II

Conceptualising the Rule of Law

The concept of the rule of law has developed since the early times of classical Greece and Rome with its influential philosophers Plato, Aristotle and Titus Livius.[1] The political circumstances of statehood in ancient Greece and Rome served as a model and experiment for new conceptions of governance. The role and relevance of democracy were also vividly discussed, in view of changing political circumstances. In the Middle Ages between the fifth and the fifteenth century, the ideals of rule of law and democracy were driven back by absolute powers of kings and emperors, usually with the blessing of or even closely linked with religious power.[2] It was only in the age of Enlightenment that the idea of the rule of law was taken up again by philosophers and writers, who rediscovered the need to control state power and provide general rules that are applicable to all in an equal manner in order to avoid injustice and arbitrary exercise of government.

In the present context of examining Islamic law and its relationship with the rule of law and freedom of expression the origins and the development of the rule of law shall be analysed more closely. Such an exercise may help to identify important elements and concepts relevant for legal systems and societies irrespective of social and cultural circumstances.[3] The experiences made in different historical and political contexts could provide some guidance to address the challenges of today. While Islamic law has not been part of the discourse on the rule of law for a long time, in recent years the concept, as endorsed and promoted by the United Nations, gains increasing significance for Muslim majority countries and predominantly Muslim societies in their quest for development and peaceful coexistence in a globalised and multicultural world. The internationalisation of the concept by the United Nations has led to remarkable efforts in showing how Islamic law and international law might coexist and reinforce each other.[4]

[1] On the early history and philosophy of the rule of law, see P Costa, 'A Historical Introduction' in P Costa and D Zolo (eds), *The Rule of Law: History, Theory and Criticism* (Dordrecht and others, Springer, 2007) 73–149; B Tamanaha, *On the Rule of Law: History, Politics, Theory* (Cambridge, Cambridge University Press, 2004) 7–14.

[2] The first several centuries of this period are known as the 'Dark Ages' in which the western half of the former Roman Empire entered into a long decline due to invasions by Germanic tribes, Huns and Vikings. See Tamanaha, ibid 15–31.

[3] M Sellers, 'What is the Rule of Law and Why Is It So Important?' in JR Silkenat, JE Hickey Jr and PD Barenboim (eds), *The Legal Doctrines of the Rule of Law and the Legal State (Rechtsstaat)* (Dordrecht and others, Springer, 2014) 3–13.

[4] Out of the numerous academic efforts to throw light on the debate, some of them should be specially mentioned, such as M-L Frick and A Müller (eds), *Islam and International Law: Engaging*

The most obvious common ground for the Sharia and modern state-centric law, including international law, is that both systems have an aspiration to regulate and govern in accordance with an ideal of the individual's place within a society.[5] As Anver Emon put it,

> at the heart of both Islamic law and international law lies the aim and aspiration to regulate and order, or to ensure good and right governance. The subjects of governance and the institutions of governance may change or differ across traditions, but [...] both legal traditions are mindful of governance.[6]

In this vein, the rule of law and good governance are closely intertwined.

Within the discourse about the rule of law and good governance, the role of the individuals needs to be looked at more closely. On the one hand, 'rule of law' is associated with a functioning legal system with reliable institutions operating in a non-arbitrary and transparent manner and without corruption. From this perspective, the individual is, first of all, the addressee of the law, who has to obey and fear sanctions in case of non-compliance. Such an interpretation essentially focuses on 'law enforcement'. It is similar to the approach of the 'rule by law', which reduces the concept of the 'rule of law' to a system of rules which are strictly enforced and whose contents or manner of formation are not to be questioned.[7]

On the other hand, the 'rule of law' is understood almost as the opposite, namely as the protection of the individual from the state, as a safeguard of individual freedom against state interference. This approach is in accordance with the Kantian idea of law, namely that its rationale in human society is the protection of individual freedom.[8] From this perspective, the rule of law is closely connected to the idea of human rights. A number of human rights are particularly important in the relationship between the individual and state institutions, between the governed and the governing, namely the right to assembly and association and the right to freedom of expression. Both are political human rights and have important implications and explosive potential. It is not a coincidence that governments and political leaders, even in free and democratic societies, fear these two rights most. These two rights are consequently the most important rights to safeguard the rule

Self-Centrism from a Plurality of Perspectives (Leiden, Brill/Nijhoff, 2013); AM Emon, MS Ellis and B Glahn (eds), *Islamic Law and International Human Rights Law: Searching for Common Ground?* (Oxford, Oxford University Press, 2012); J Rehman and S Breau, *Religion, Human Rights and International Law* (Leiden, Brill/Nijhoff, 2007).

[5] AM Emon, 'Sharia and the Modern State' in Emon, Ellis and Glahn, *Islamic Law and International Human Rights Law* (n 4) 52–81.

[6] Ibid 52–53.

[7] L Jenco, '"Rule by Man" and "Rule by Law" in Early Republican China: Contributions to a Theoretical Debate' (2010) 69 *Journal of Asian Studies* 181, 182; T Moustafa and T Ginsburg, 'Introduction: The Functions of Courts in Authoritarian Politics' in T Moustafa and T Ginsburg (eds), *Rule by Law. The Politics of Courts in Authoritarian Regimes* (Cambridge, Cambridge University Press, 2008) 1–22, 4; Tamanaha, *On the Rule of Law: History, Politics, Theory* (n 1) 3.

[8] I Kant, 'On the Common Saying: "This May be True in Theory, but it does not Apply in Practice"' in H Reiss (ed), *Kant. Political Writings* (Cambridge, Cambridge University Press, 1991) 61, 90.

of law and good governance as regards the core element, the accountability of governing institutions and persons. Without the freedom to criticise, individually or in the community of others, the accountability for compliance with the different elements of the rule of law, such as the supremacy of law, equality before the law, fairness in the application of the law, separation of powers, legal certainty, avoidance of arbitrariness and procedural and legal transparency, cannot be safeguarded, even in a functioning judicial system.

Not all interpretations of the 'rule of law' appreciate, however, this approach to the role of the individual and human rights, including the freedom of expression. In the historical development one can discern different justifications for the need of a system of governance based on laws and functioning institutions. The perception of the rule of law has evolved slightly differently in various legal contexts and cannot be easily transposed from one legal system to the other (in particular the common law and the civil law systems).[9] The translation of the term into other languages, such as the French *Etat de droit*,[10] the Italian *Stato di Diritto*, the Spanish *Estado de derecho* or the German *Rechtsstaat*, cannot be conducted without difficulty.[11] As regards the Islamic realm, it has been suggested to translate the term 'rule of law' as *hukm al-qanun* in the Arabic language.[12] While it is not possible to provide a comprehensive historical overview of the development of the doctrine of rule of law, Part II of this study, consisting of a single chapter, Chapter 2, aims to articulate the most pertinent aspects of the rule of law which are relevant in the present context.

[9] T Carothers, 'The Rule-of-Law-Revival' in T Carothers (ed), *Promoting the Rule of Law Abroad: In Search of Knowledge* (Washington DC, Brookings Institution Press, 2006) 3–13; R Kleinfeld, 'Competing Definitions of the Rule of Law' in Carothers, ibid 31–74.

[10] M Flory, 'Le concept d'Etat de droit au regard du droit international' in A Mahiou (ed), *L'Etat de droit dans le monde arabe* (Paris, CNRS 1997) 45 et seq.

[11] D von der Pfordten, 'On the Foundation of the Rule of Law and the Principle of the Legal State/ Rechtsstaat' in Silkenat, Hickey Jr and Barenboim, *The Legal Doctrines of the Rule of Law and the Legal State (Rechtsstaat)* (n 3) 15–28; S Kirste, 'Philosophical Foundations of the Principle of the Legal State (Rechtsstaat) and the Rule of Law' in Silkenat et al, ibid 29–44; M Krygier 'Rule of Law (and Rechtsstaat)' in Silkenat et al, ibid 45–60.

[12] See R Bahlul, 'Is Constitutionalism Compatible with Islam?' in Costa and Zola (eds), *The Rule of Law* (n 1) 515–42; see also E Cotran and AO Sherif (eds), *Democracy, Rule of Law and Islam* (Netherlands, Brill 1999).

2

Examining the Meaning and Scope of the Rule of Law

I. Introduction

The concept of the rule of law has ancient, historic roots, stretching to the time of ancient Greek and Roman philosophers. Although imbued with varied interpretations and vexed issues of implementation, the relevance of rule of law principles has been recognised in a number of different philosophical and political traditions–Western as well as non-Western. Amongst the non-Western traditions, the present chapter highlights Chinese approaches developed between Confucianism and Legalism and the *panchayat* system as practised in India in addition to Islamic traditions which represent the focus of this study. As shall be considered, within the history of Islam, both Sunni and Shia scholars have offered theories of state and law which limit the role of the caliph and the Islamic state. Ideas and principles articulated by Ghazali, Mawardi, Ibn Khaldun and Shah Wali Allah will be referred to by way of example.[1] It will be shown that several verses in the Quran contain aspects of a modern concept of the rule of law.[2] Also the Sunna of Muhammad, the Prophet of Islam, as well as the practices of the rightly guided Caliphs endorse rule of law principles. Concepts such as 'public policy' and 'expediency' contained in the Quran and the Sunna are particularly helpful in this context.[3] Additional tools of Islamic jurisprudence, such as *masaleh mursalah*

[1] See in more detail Ch 3 below.

[2] See the Quran 2:188: 'And do not consume one another's wealth unjustly or send it [in bribery] to the rulers in order that [they might aid] you [to] consume a portion of the wealth of the people in sin, while you know [it is unlawful]'. Furthermore, the Quran 6:151: 'Say, "Come, I will recite what your Lord has prohibited to you. [He commands] that you not associate anything with Him, and to parents, good treatment, and do not kill your children out of poverty; We will provide for you and them. And do not approach immoralities–what is apparent of them and what is concealed. And do not kill the soul which Allah has forbidden [to be killed] except by [legal] right. This has He instructed you that you may use reason"'. In addition, see the Quran 65:7: 'Let a man of wealth spend from his wealth, and he whose provision is restricted–let him spend from what Allah has given him. Allah does not charge a soul except [according to] what He has given it. Allah will bring about, after hardship, ease'.

[3] In addition, one could mention the concept of *shura* ('consultation'), which is also included in the Quran. See GM El-Gindy, 'The Shura and Human Rights in Islamic Law. The Relevance of Democracy' in E Cotran and M Yamani (eds), *The Rule of Law in the Middle East and the Islamic World. Human Rights and the Judicial Process* (NY, IB Tauris, 2000) 164–68.

(consideration of public interest), *urf* (custom) and *ijtihad* (personal reasoning of learned Muslim scholars), are available and can be applied with a view to implement the rule of law.[4] The present chapter then proceeds with an overview of contemporary legal systems of Muslim majority states and highlights their diversity concerning the relationship of Islamic law and the law of the state. It addresses the question to what extent the tools and concepts available under Islamic law are used and applied to ensure respect for the rule of law. The chapter continues by a critical examination of the foundational principles of the rule of law and identifies its various strands. These include the existence of sufficiently precise and publicly proclaimed legal rules, the equal application of laws, application of laws by accountable, transparent and democratic institutions, and consistency with established human rights standards.

II. The Rule of Law in Western Philosophical Thinking

Ancient Greek legal thinking is commonly regarded as the origin of the concept of the rule of law. Plato (427–346 BC) reflected on the ideal constitution of a state mainly in his works *Politikos* (Statesman), *Nomoi* (Laws) and *Politeia* (The Republic).[5] An ideal state would be ruled by a wise ruler, who has true knowledge and can commit no error.[6] The wise ruler would legislate for the majority and in a general way, whether he issues written laws or his enactments follow the unwritten traditional customs.[7] Law-making, in such a situation, would be necessary to ensure maintenance of justice and the observance of contracts,[8] but the legislator himself would not be bound by the laws and could change them, because no rule could be above wisdom and science.[9] It would be an absolute rule of a 'philosopher-king'.[10]

Plato was later criticised for expounding on this 'ideal' because it could easily be abused and lead to totalitarianism and tyranny by absolute rulers who

[4] See in more detail Ch 3 below.

[5] FD Miller, 'The Rule of Law in Ancient Greek Thought' in M Sellers and T Tomaszewski (ed), *The Rule of Law in Comparative Perspective* (Dordrecht-NY, Springer, 2010) 11–18, 13 et seq.

[6] Plato, *Statesman*, 297a. (Citation taken from *Plato. Plato in Twelve Volumes*, vol 12, trans HN Fowler, Cambridge, MA, Harvard University Press; London, William Heinemann Ltd, 1921, available at www.perseus.tufts.edu).

[7] Ibid 295a.

[8] Ibid 294e.

[9] Ibid 295e–296a, 297a; see also Plato, *Laws*, 9.875a–c; similarly, Aristotle, *Nicomachean Ethics*, 1145b 24 et seq.

[10] See Plato, *The Republic*, 6488.d–3, where he compares the ideal leader/statesman with a pilot, a master of shipcraft, who is able to master the art and the practice of the science of navigation. (Citations taken from *Plato. Plato in Twelve Volumes*, vols 5 & 6 trans P Shorey, Cambridge, MA, Harvard University Press; London, William Heinemann Ltd, 1969, available at www.perseus.tufts.edu.).

claim to embody this 'ideal'.[11] However, Plato also raises awareness that such wise statesmen are rare and that man's mortal nature would always urge him on to grasping and self-interested action, irrationally avoiding pain and pursuing pleasure.[12] Also to Plato it was necessary to find a more or less successful 'imitation' as the second best choice.[13] Plato sees it in the reliance upon ordinance and law, which discern general rules and principles.[14] There should be fixed rules subject to gradual improvement to cover more details; but as soon as they are determined sufficiently clearly, they should be difficult to change.[15] Constitutions based on fixed codes would be the best approximations of the ideal constitution. The state should be governed by those who are most obedient to the laws, not because they are wealthy or possess any other quality, such as strength or size or birth.[16] Under such constitutions, also the authorities of the state must be subject to the law in their actions.[17] The law should be the master of the government. Plato concludes that, in a state where the law is subservient and impotent, the ruin of the state is impending, but when the authorities are servants of the law, the state will be saved and blessed.[18] The underlying argument is that the law represents an objective standard which can be known and understood by reason. According to Plato, law is the embodiment of reason and serves the purpose of controlling the other qualities of human nature, the non-rational parts, such as passions and desires.[19] Reason should rule over the other human faculties to ensure order and to avoid chaos. The same should be true for the ruling of a state.[20] The contents of the law should come from convention, which differ from place to place, and not from nature.[21] On this basis, ethical standards could be developed over time. They shall ensure that justice is not maintained by force, but by legal convention.[22]

These fundamental insights provide already an important basis for the discussion on the role of government in society. While a wise 'philosopher king' could be regarded as the ideal, the reality of human beings with all their weaknesses and shortcomings requires laws to define, limit and control the powers of the leader. It is only when the leaders, be they political or religious or both, consider

[11] See most prominently K Popper, *The Open Society and Its Enemies, Volume I: The Spell of Plato* (New York, Routledge, 2002, reprint of 1945) 121 et seq.

[12] Plato, *Statesman*, 297b; see also Plato, *Laws*, 9.875a–d.

[13] Ibid. *Statesman*, 297c–e.

[14] Plato, *Laws*, 9.875d. (citation taken from *Plato. Plato in Twelve Volumes*, vols 10 & 11 trans RG Bury Cambridge, MA, Harvard University Press; London, William Heinemann Ltd, 1967 & 1968, available at www.perseus.tufts.edu).

[15] Plato, *Laws*, 6.772b–d; 12.957a–b.

[16] Ibid 4.715b–c.

[17] Ibid 12.945b–948b.

[18] Ibid 4.715d.

[19] Ibid 10.4.713e–714a; 8.835e. See also F Miller, 'Plato and the Rule of Reason' (2005) 43 *Southern Journal of* Philosophy 43, 50–83.

[20] Plato, *Republic*, 4.442d (citation taken from *Plato. Plato in Twelve Volumes*, vols 5 & 6 trans P Shorey (Cambridge, MA, Harvard University Press; London, William Heinemann Ltd, 1969, available at http://www.perseus.tufts.edu).

[21] Plato, *Laws*, 10.889e–890b.

[22] Ibid 10.890a–c.

themselves as 'ideal' and infallible, that the 'rule of law' is not accepted. This has been the case both in European history, such as Adolf Hitler and Joseph Stalin, or in the Muslim world, with Ayatollah Khomeini, who allegedly was inspired by Plato's Republic.[23]

Aristotle (384–322 BC) rejects Plato's ideal of the 'philosopher king' from the outset and introduces the important notion that the rule of law must be distinguished from the rule of man, an individual or a group, according to their mere will.[24] In his *Politeia* he discusses the theoretical foundations of the rule of law in detail and identifies several conditions for ensuring that the rule of law, and not the rule of man, is upheld.[25] Amongst those are taking turns in holding offices, laws that define the selection process, and guardians of the law to ensure that elected officials or state authorities do not transgress the law.[26] Aristotle points out that the law must be of general application and impartial. Justice can only be achieved if decisions are taken on the basis of a general rule and not on a case-by-case basis.[27] This is necessary to avoid that decisions are influenced by subjective factors, such as passion, anger and self-interest.

The Roman writer Titus Livius (59 BC–17 AD), in his work *Ab urbe condita*, highlights the importance of written laws. He describes the story of the *decemviri*, a commission of 10 men at the time of the Roman Republic in the fifth century BC who wrote down, for the first time, the laws of the state which previously had only been transmitted orally.[28] Livius sees this as a major breakthrough and an example of righteous governance which replaced the previous ad hoc and rather arbitrary decisions of the magistrates. On this basis, he argues in favour of an *imperium legum* which should replace the government of men.[29]

With the dawn of the Roman Empire, the idea of the rule of law and democracy got lost in the political struggles of power and influence in Europe, and absolute monarchs who did not accept any laws above them reigned for centuries. It was only in the times of Renaissance and Enlightenment that the ideas of the classical philosophers were rediscovered.

First, the idea that the rule *by* law, whereby a ruler exercised power in a non-arbitrary fashion, but was not himself or herself bound by law in any meaningful sense, regained attraction. This rather positivist conception of law was

[23] V Martin, *Creating an Islamic State: Khomeini and the Making of a New Iran* (London/New York, Tauris, 2003) 100 et seq.

[24] Aristotle, *Politics. A Treatise on Government*, trans W Ellis (London & Toronto, JM Dent & Sons Ltd & New York, EP Dutton & Co, first published 1912, reprinted 1919, 1923, 1928, available at www.gutenberg.org).

[25] Ibid IV.4.1292a.

[26] Ibid IV.14.1298a–1299a.

[27] Aristotle, *Politics*, III.16.1286–87; see also Aristotle, *Nicomachean Ethics*, V.6.

[28] T Livius, *Ab urbe condita*, III; M Sellers, 'An Introduction to the Rule of Law in Comparative Perspective' in Sellers and Tomaszewski, *The Rule of Law in Comparative Perspective* (n 5) 1–10, 2.

[29] T Livius, *Ab urbe condita*, II; see also MT Cicero (106-7 BC), *De Re Publica*, III, and ibid, *De Legibus.*

advocated by Thomas Hobbes (1588–1679) who regards the misery of anarchy which he had seen in England's civil war as the greatest evil that could ever happen and concluded therefrom the need for an absolute and uncontested sovereign power to rule.[30] Hobbes develops the idea that government should originate in a social contract which determines a common authority to guarantee security of all of the members of the society.[31]

This idea of the rule *by* law is closely related to the perception that some societies may not yet have been sufficiently developed in their institutions and culture and which would be better served by a ruler full of the spirit of improvement who would 'attain an end perhaps otherwise unattainable'.[32] However, critique of this approach points out that this form of absolute leadership, even when pursued with a view to pursuing the best interest of those subject to its rule, is still despotism and susceptible to all the vices of tyranny.[33]

Fighting despotism is one of the most important aims in the writings by Montesquieu (1689–1755). In his most influential work, *The Spirit of the Laws*,[34] he identifies different powers of government, the legislative, the executive and the judicial, which should be separated and controlling each other. The balance of these powers appeared to him paramount for attaining liberty in a society.[35] Even though he expresses his firm belief in the existence of natural law, and even God-given law,[36] he emphasises the need for the desacralisation of the monarchy and its normalisation as a secular enterprise.[37] In doing so, he addressed the problem that absolute power has always the potential to be exercised in an arbitrary way.[38]

Immanuel Kant (1724–1804) takes up the idea of the three powers of government (*trias politica*),[39] namely the ruling power, or sovereignty, in the person of

[30] T Hobbes, *Leviathan* (London, 1651, revised Latin edn of 1668), see English translation and edition by E Curly, *Hobbes Leviathan with Selected Variants from the Latin Edition of 1668* (Indianapolis, Hackett, 1994); see also Sellers, 'An Introduction to the Rule of Law in Comparative Perspective' (n 28) 1–10, 3; for a discussion of the problems connected with applying Hobbes' positivist theory to international law, see J Waldron, 'Are Sovereigns Entitled to the Benefit of the International Rule of Law?' (2011) 22 *European Journal of International Law* 317.

[31] D Boucher and P Kelly, 'The Social Contract and its Critics: An Overview' in D Boucher (ed), *The Social Contract from Hobbes to Rawls* (London, Routledge, 1994) 1, 13–16.

[32] Sellers (n 28) 1–10, 7.

[33] Ibid 7.

[34] C-L Montesquieu, *De L'Esprit des Loix* (1748), first English trans, *The Spirit of the Laws* (1750).

[35] C-L Montesquieu, *The Complete Works of M. de Montesquieu* (London, T Evans, 1777), 4 vols, vol 1, available at http://oll.libertyfund.org/titles/837, 240–46.

[36] See his thoughts in book 1, Chapter I, entitled: 'Of Laws in General': 'God is related to the universe as creator and preserver: the laws by which he created all things are those by which he preserves them. He acts according to these rules, because He knows them; He knows them, because He made them; and He made them, because they are relative to His wisdom and power'; ibid. 2.

[37] M Mosher, 'Monarchy's Paradox' in D Walles, M Mosher, and P Rahe (eds), *Montesquieu's Science of Politics: Essays on the Spirit of Laws* (Maryland, Rowman and Littlefield, 2001) 171.

[38] Ibid 180; see also B Kriegel, *The State and the Rule of Law* (Princeton, Princeton University Press, 1995) 67.

[39] I Kant, 'The Metaphysics of Morals' (1797) in H Reiss (ed), *I Kant, Political Writings*, 2nd edn (Cambridge, Cambridge University Press, 1991) 131, 138.

the legislator, the executive power, in the person of the individual who governs in accordance with the law, and the judicial power, which allots to everyone what is his by law, in the person of the judge (*potestas legislatoria, rectoria et iudiciaria*).[40] All of the three powers within the state are dignities, and since they necessarily follow from the general idea of a state as elements essential for its establishment (constitution), they are political dignities.[41] They must be separate and independent from each other.[42] The act by which the people constitute a state for itself, or more precisely, the mere idea of such an act, is the 'original contract'.[43] Kant himself did not use the term '*Rechtsstaat*' (state of law), but his followers in Germany spoke about the '*Schule der Rechts-Staats-Lehre*' (school of the rule of law doctrine) and created the link between Kant and the rule of law which subsequently was taken for granted.[44]

Kant bases his theory on the idea that law was necessary for the preservation of individual freedom. He thus reverses the focus from the importance of the control of law enforcement to the importance of the protection of the individual. It is this change of focus that makes him, in the eyes of many, the foundational thinker of the idea of human rights. Law, according to Kant, is 'the sum total of those conditions within which the will of one person can be reconciled with the will of another in accordance with a universal law of freedom'.[45] Yet, Kant also recognises the importance of an authority to apply coercion to anyone who infringes it in order to protect individual freedom.[46] Individuals need to live in a state of law in order to enjoy their rights. This means that they require a constitution.[47] He defines a state (*civitas*) as a union of aggregate of men under rightful laws.[48] It follows that also in the Kantian philosophy of law the 'rule of law' requires state institutions which function in a reliable and transparent manner, but this is not an aim in itself, but only a means of achieving the ultimate goal, the safeguard of individual freedom.

In England, the doctrine of the rule of law is closely connected to the leading jurist Albert Venn Dicey (1835–1922).[49] In his *Introduction to the study of*

[40] Ibid 138.

[41] Ibid 140.

[42] Ibid 142.

[43] Ibid 140.

[44] P Costa, 'Rule of Law: A Historical Introduction' in P Costa and D Zolo (eds), *The Rule of Law: History, Theory and Criticism* (Dordrecht, Springer, 2007) 73–152, 87.

[45] Kant, 'The Metaphysics of Morals' in Reiss, *I Kant, Political Writings* (n 39) 133.

[46] Ibid 134.

[47] Ibid 136.

[48] Ibid 138.

[49] Lord Bingham notes that credit for coining the expression 'the rule of law' is generally given to him, even though he did not invent the idea lying behind it. See T Bingham, *The Rule of Law* (London, Penguin, 2010) 3. Lord Bingham (1933–2010) himself was one of the most prominent figures promoting the idea of the rule of law in the United Kingdom and beyond. The Bingham Centre for the Rule of Law was established as part of the British Institute of International and Comparative Law in 2010. See http://binghamcentre.biicl.org/schools/ruleoflaw.

the Law of the Constitution[50] he identified two features that at all times since the Norman Conquest have characterised the British political institutions: first, the undisputed supremacy of the central government throughout the whole country, and, second, 'the rule or supremacy of law'.[51] The most important characteristics of a rule of law system, according to Dicey, are: (1) no one can be punished except for a distinct breach of the law established in the ordinary legal manner before the ordinary courts of the land, which contrasts with every system of government based on the exercise by persons in authority of wide, arbitrary or discretionary powers of constraint;[52] (2) no one is above the law and everyone, whatever be his rank or condition, is subject to the ordinary law and amenable to the jurisdiction of the ordinary tribunals, which embodies the ideal of legal equality;[53] and (3) rule of law results from the judicial decisions determining the rights of private persons in particular cases before the courts rather than from general constitutional principles.[54]

Dicey's first criterion singles out specific individual rights, namely the principle of no crime and no punishment without a law (*nullum crimen, nulla poene sine lege*) and the right to fair trial. He thus concentrates on criminal law and criminal procedure and the need to have 'ordinary courts'. In contrast to Kant, he does not refer to human freedom or human rights in a more general sense as a justification for the rule of law. The second criterion advanced by Dicey also addresses law enforcement aspects rather than human rights. He emphasises the role of the courts which should be entrusted with controlling the behaviour of state organs.[55] The last criterion again focuses on the rule of the courts. It reflects Dicey's provenance from the common law system with its focus on the role of the judiciary and its case law system. It can also be understood as a defence of the absence of a codified constitution in the United Kingdom which, according to other thinkers, would be one of the most important prerequisites for the rule of law. Dicey, however, elaborates that abstract principles laid down in constitutions are not useful, if they are not implemented and applied by the courts. The judiciary thus has the most important rule in safeguarding the rule of law. Dicey's reasonings are also transferrable to other legal systems, in that the role of the judiciary is paramount in upholding the rule of law, not only in common law countries.[56]

[50] AV Dicey, *Introduction to the Study of the Law of the Constitution* (London and New York, Macmillan and Co, 1885). New editions were issued by the same publisher in 1886, 1889, 1893, 1897, 1902 and 1908. The eighth edition of 1915 was the last one he prepared himself, which is the basis of several modern editions, including those published by Oxford University Press, LibertyClassics, Project Muse, Online Library of Liberty, etc.

[51] Ibid 107.

[52] Ibid 110.

[53] Ibid 114.

[54] Ibid 115.

[55] This has been regarded as being in contrast, eg, to the French system of separation of powers and its system of *droit administratif* which, according to Dicey, provides for the control of the judges by the government, instead of the reverse. See ibid 315.

[56] See eg the observations by A Zimmermann, 'Constitutions without Constitutionalism: The Failure of Constitutionalism in Brazil' in Sellers and Tomaszewski (n 5) 101–146, 141.

However, Dicey's emphasis on constitutional principles has been criticised as being too formalistic, mechanical and positivist.[57] Even though his critics may have gone too far by saying that Dicey's book 'need no longer be read',[58] his conception of the rule of law is primarily formal and not substantive. It is notable, for example, that John Stuart Mill (1806–73) and his influential essay *On Liberty*,[59] is not mentioned in Dicey's book. This indicates a relatively strict separation between the rule of law and human rights.[60]

By contrast, in the United States, safeguarding the liberty of citizens and their individual natural rights has been fundamental from the outset. For the founding fathers, the rule of law was a necessary prerequisite and an essential principle in the Declaration of Independence in 1776 and in the formulation of the Constitution of 1787.[61] A most prominent representative of the American conception of the rule of law was John Adams (1735–1826)[62] who advocated for the establishment of a government of law and not of men as the most important goal and paramount aspiration of the founding fathers.[63] It was necessary to find and define a combination of powers in society so that the citizens may constantly enjoy the benefits of them, and be sure of their continuance. The paramount question to him was what form of government would be most suitable to compel the formation of good and equal law, an impartial execution and faithful interpretation of them.[64] The rule of law should ensure that the people enjoy their fundamental and inherent rights, such as life, liberty, property ownership and the pursuit of happiness.[65] From this perspective it was necessary to institute a government which could be constrained to a very narrow remit, to protect, and not regulate or destroy, the natural rights of the people.[66] Yet, the contents of the US Constitution are not always discernible precisely owing to its partly indeterminate and general language which leaves a rather wide margin for interpretation.[67] Nevertheless,

[57] MD Walters, 'Dicey on Writing the Law of the Constitution' (2012) 32 *Oxford Journal of Legal Studies* 21, 22.

[58] WI Jennings, 'Review of *Law of the Constitution, 9th edn*' (1940) 2 *Modern Law Review* 321, 322.

[59] JS Mill, *On Liberty* (London, John Parker, 1859).

[60] As is well known, Mill advocated basic civil liberties which should be respected and safeguarded by the state, such as liberty of thought and discussion, individuality as one of the elements of well-being and the limits to the authority of society over the individual. See ibid.

[61] R Cass, *The Rule of Law in America* (Baltimore and London, Johns Hopkins University Press, 2001) 1; B Casalini, 'Popular Sovereignty, the Rule of Law, and the "Rule of Judges" in the United States' in Costa and Zolo, *The Rule of Law* (n 44) 201–36; R Charlow, 'America's Constitutional Rule of Law: Structure and Symbol' in Sellers and Tomaszewski (n 5) 89–99, 99.

[62] See J Adams, *A Defence of the Constitutions of Government of the United States of America*, vol I (London, 1787).

[63] Sellers (n 28) 1–10, 2.

[64] Ibid 2.

[65] R Gosalbo-Bono, 'The Significance of the Rule of Law and its Implications for the European Union and the United States' (2010) 72 *University of Pittsburgh Law Review*, 229, 272.

[66] Ibid. See Cass, *The Rule of Law in America* (n 61) 1.

[67] R Charlow, 'America's Constitutional Rule of Law: Structure and Symbol' in Sellers and Tomaszewski (n 5) 89–99, 96.

it has an important symbolic value and is conceived as representing the 'values' of the United States, in particular peace, freedom, tolerance, and equality.[68] In this vein, the rule of law, in addition to procedural aspects of regulating state power, has always had an important substantive scope.

III. Rule of Law and Non-Western Traditions

Questions concerning rule of law and governance have not only exercised minds in the Western tradition, but reflections about an ideal legal framework for the functioning of society have also been present in other parts of the world. The Code of Hammurabi, promulgated by the King of Babylon around 1760 BC in the area of today's Iraq, is sometimes mentioned as one of the first examples of the codification of law, presented to the public and applying to the acts of the ruler.[69] Referring to the Code of Hammurabi in his address to the General Assembly in 2004, the then UN Secretary-General, Kofi Annan, highlighted that the vision of 'a government of laws and not of men' was almost as old as civilisation itself and that the Code of Hammurabi entailed principles of justice recognised by almost every human society since that time, such as legal protection for the poor, restraints on the strong, so that they cannot oppress the weak, and law publicly enacted and known to all.[70]

Core principles of holding government authority to account and placing the wishes of the populace before the rulers, can be found amid the main moral and philosophical traditions across the Asian continent.[71] In China, the rule of law developed between Confucianism and Legalism.[72] In the ancient periods, moral values and education in accordance with Confucian philosophy were imperative and should be used to find harmonious solutions to disputes. The norms to be followed were regarded as 'rules of proper behaviour', or *li*.[73] Disputes were solved

[68] Ibid 96–99.

[69] D Charpin, *Writing, Law, and Kingship in Old Babylonian Mesopotamia* (Chicago, University of Chicago Press, 2010, trans JM Todd) 71–82.

[70] See Secretary-General's Address to the General Assembly, 21 September 2004, reprinted in D Rothwell and others (eds), *International Law. Cases and Materials with Australian Perspectives*, 2nd edn (New York, Cambridge University Press, 2014) 9; see also B Ramcharan, *United Nations Protection of Humanity and its Habitat. A New International Law of Security and Protection* (Leiden, Boston, Brill Nijhoff, 2016) 90.

[71] See for an overview A Ehr-Soon Tay, 'Asian Values and the Rule of Law' in Costa and Zolo (n 44) 565–86.

[72] L Buyun, 'Constitutionalism and China' in Y Keping (ed), *Democracy and the Rule of Law in Contemporary China* (Leiden/Boston, Brill, 2010) 197–230; X Yong, 'Several Fundamental Theoretical Issues Regarding China's Constitutional Reform', ibid 231–52.

[73] Gosalbo-Bono, 'The Significance of the Rule of Law and its Implications for the European Union and the United States' (n 65) 280.

by the 'rule by rite' or 'case law' without any written code.[74] It was an aristocratic system of government reflecting the patriarchal clan system which favoured the figure of the ruler.[75] Hierarchical relationships between the members of a family or in society played an important role.

Against this *rule by man*, the legalist school of thought demanded the *rule by law*, or *fa*.[76] Laws should be written, publicly promulgated and applied equally to all individuals regardless of their position in the family or in society. The concept of *ruling by the law* was combined with a struggle for a centralised autocratic monarchy as a political system.[77] The law was codified and supposed to be applied strictly throughout the country by public institutions to all citizens alike. However, the ruler remained the ultimate authority and his discretion was only limited by his own morality. He had the power to enact and amend the laws. Non-compliance was sanctioned with severe punishment, not only of the individual but also to judges who misapplied the law. In this sense, the *fa* regime was a harsh instrument for obtaining and maintaining political control and social order.[78] A combination of the Confucian rule by rite and the legalist rule by law then characterised the development of the legal system in China for more than 2000 years until the end of the nineteenth century, when constitutional reforms, influenced by the Western ideas on the rule of law, constitutionalism and human rights, began.[79]

During the communist period, several constitutions were enacted,[80] which were explicitly grounded on Marxism-Leninism and on Mao Zedong's ideas, thus reflecting Marxist constitutional theories on the state and law with its focus on the economy and on the class approach.[81] While China has gradually moved from planned to market economy, the Constitution has been amended several times and used as an instrument for the country's economic development.[82] In China's

[74] W Shu-Chen, 'The Chinese Legal Tradition and the European View of the Rule of Law' in Costa and Zolo (n 44) 615–32, 618.

[75] The period of 'rule by rite' or 'case law' lasted approximately from the 11th century BC until the end of the Chin-Qui period in 476 BC. See ibid.

[76] Gosalbo-Bono (n 65) 281.

[77] Shu-Chen 'The Chinese Legal Tradition and the European View of the Rule of Law' (n 74) 615–32, 618.

[78] Gosalbo-Bono (n 65) 281.

[79] A republican Interim Constitution developed by the National Party in 1912 contained popular participation through elections, democratic freedom and the doctrine of separation of powers. Shu-Chen (n 74) 615–32, 619. Yet, the period of fighting for political leadership led to the abolition of the Interim Constitution and gave way to more totalitarian control. The constitution under the power of the National Party was applicable between 1931 and 1946, before the Chinese Communist Party took control of Mainland China in 1949. L Feng, 'Modern Constitutionalism in China' in Costa and Zolo (n 44) 633–46.

[80] In 1949, 1954, 1975, 1978 and 1982. See Feng, ibid, 634–39.

[81] The class struggle has been one of the central aims of communist constitutions. Nowadays in China, the class approach is still upheld by the affirmation by the Chinese Communist Party to represent the working class. See ibid 640.

[82] Ibid 640.

efforts to strengthen the rule of law in various areas,[83] the Chinese tradition of *fa*, thus the rule by law, is still playing a dominating role. On the other hand, also the tradition of *li*, the search for harmonious solutions of conflicts, preferably through negotiations and avoiding legal dispute settlement before courts and tribunals,[84] can be explained by the Confucian tradition of Chinese legal thought.

The tradition of the philosophy of law in India is characterised by the so-called *dharma*, a concept containing eternal rules preserving the world, but also imposing duties upon the individual.[85] It differs from the concept of the rule of law as developed in the Western tradition inasmuch as moral authority is the basis for the rule of law and not its restraining power. The ultimate source of law is God or the Creator, so that the *dharma* connects the transcendental realm with the earthly world and with society.[86] The law is of divine origin and not the product of human reasoning or agreement. In classical India, legal and governmental institutions were subordinates to an ideal spiritual authority. This is not the only commonality with Plato's 'philosopher king', as the idea that the establishment of public order must go together with the establishment of order in the individual's self which requires to overcome greed, passion, and egoism, is also in line with Plato's thinking.[87]

Customary tribunals, composed of village elders, were competent to solve disputes. These so-called *panchayats* represented native Indian institutions. They fulfilled an important role in local self-government, but were not entirely immune from ethnocentricity and the furtherance of ethnical and religious conflicts. Mahatma Gandhi advocated their re-introduction at the time of India's struggle for independence, but, at the federal level, a centralised bureaucratic administration was introduced.[88] Nevertheless, *panchayats* still exist at local levels and serve as alternative means of dispute resolution in India.[89]

The jurisprudence of the *panchayat* was based on the legal rules given by the *dharma*. However, in the Indian short story 'The Voice of God', as recalled

[83] See eg the United Nations/China/APSCO Workshop on 'The Role of National Space Legislation in Strengthening the Rule of Law' 17–21 November 2014, Beijing, China, Report of the Workshop, UN Doc A/AC.105/1089 of 27 February 2015.

[84] See the position of China in the matter of the South China Sea Arbitration between the Republic of the Philippines and the People's Republic of China, PCA Case No 2013–19, Award of 12 July 2016. By contrast, China accepts the compulsory dispute settlement procedure provided for in the WTO Agreement. See M Chi, 'China's Participation in WTO Dispute Settlement over the Past Decade: Experiences and Impacts' (2012) 1 *Journal of International Economic Law* 29; MD Harpaz, 'Sense and Sensibilities of China and WTO Dispute Settlement' (2010) 6 *Journal of World Trade* 1155.

[85] A Kumar Giri, 'The Rule of Law and Indian Society: From Colonialism to Post-Colonialism' in Costa and Zolo (n 44) 587–614.

[86] Ibid 587–88.

[87] Ibid 589.

[88] R Guha, *Makers of Modern India* (Cambridge, Mass, Harvard University Press, 2011) 320.

[89] K Klock, 'Resolution of Domestic Disputes Through Extra-Judicial Mechanisms in the United States and Asia: Neighbourhood Justice Centers, the Panchayat, and the Mahalla' (2001) 15 *Temple International and Comparative Law Journal* 275.

by Gowder,[90] this does not prevent the acceptance of the idea of separation between the office and the individual.[91] A Muslim had an aunt, who called for the *panchayat* to resolve a dispute with him. When a friend of the Muslim, a Hindu, was nominated as the president, he relied on their friendship and expected an easy victory. Yet, the Hindu, after a careful cross-examination, pronounced against him and in favour of the aunt. The opportunity for revenge came a few months later, when the Hindu convened the *panchayat* to get payment of a disputed debt. This time, the Muslim was appointed as president. After hearing the evidence, he decided in favour of the Hindu. He had become aware of his duties and that, upon the assumption of the role as the president of the *panchayat*, one is no one's friend and no one's enemy, but called to dispense justice.

This story confirms that the idea of justice and the rule of law are above personal ties and sentiments. Also in non-Western and non-secular societies, people assuming a public role are called upon to safeguard the separation between office and personal attachments. Otherwise, officials would be able to use their power to avenge themselves against their enemies, to expropriate property, and to extort deferential treatment from the population at large.[92]

This example can also be used with respect to other legal systems which have their legal basis in divine sources. At first sight, the sacredness of the law is in contradiction with the concept of the rule of law as developed in the Western world.[93] However, when the law is recognised as a normative system of general application irrespective of religious beliefs and personal ties, important prerequisites of the rule of law are already fulfilled.

IV. Rule of Law and Islamic Law

Islamic law is a pluralistic system in which multiple legal traditions constitute and define the space that confers 'intelligibility to arguments of justice'.[94] While Islamic law remains part of modern Muslim majority states, it is not the sole source of law and frequently it only provides a set of principles that informs legislation.[95] Furthermore, Islamic law in itself encompasses numerous traditions and several

[90] P Gowder, *The Rule of Law in the Real World* (New York, Cambridge University Press, 2016) 12–13.

[91] The story 'Panch Parmeshwar' written by Munshi Premchand in 1916 was translated and commented by EM Foster in 1946. See JM Heath (ed), *The Creator as Critic and Other Writings by E M Foster* (Toronto, Dundurn Press, 2008) 305.

[92] Gowder, *The Rule of Law in the Real World* (n 90) 13.

[93] R Bahlul, 'Is Constitutionalism Compatible with Islam?' in Costa and Zolo (n 44) 515–42; see also A Emon, 'Sharia and the Modern State' in AM Emon, MS Ellis and B Glahn (eds), *Islamic Law and International Human Rights Law: Searching for Common Ground?* (Oxford, Oxford University Press, 2012) 52–81; A Sherif, 'Commentary: Sharia as Rule of Law' ibid, 115–22, 118.

[94] Emon, 'Sharia and the Modern State' ibid 52–81, 93.

[95] Ellis, 'Islamic and International Law: Convergence or Conflict?', ibid 91–103, 93.

schools of law.[96] In this way, the idea of the rule of law, when seen as a lens through which good governance is measured, can also apply to Islamic law. In the words of Emon, '"rule of law" provides a useful conceptual frame to illuminate how Sharia is not simply a doctrinal corpus, or catalogue of legal rules. It is, rather, both constitutive of and constituted by a view about the enterprise of governance.'[97]

There is no unitary Islamic position on the merits of rationalism or humanism as well as on constitutionalism in the Islamic world. As regards the doctrine of rule of law, the reaction of Muslims historically ranges from enthusiastic endorsement to hostile rejection:[98] the broad variety of opinions on the compatibility of democracy, human rights, and the rule of law in Muslim societies has to be taken into consideration in this respect.[99] Conservative *ulama* frequently fought constitutionalism in the name of preserving Islam because they were convinced that constitutional principles conflicted with Sharia law.[100]

The main reason for this alleged incompatibility is the focus on historic sources and traditions which stand at the beginning of the creation of Islam. Scholars have come to the conclusion that the Sharia, as it has been understood traditionally, does not offer a doctrine of 'separation of powers'.[101] Even though the caliphate could be considered to be an elective office, there is disagreement about the number of the 'electors' and the way of how they should be chosen.[102] And despite the possibility to disqualify the caliph in case of lack of justice or physical disability, it is not clear who declares and by what procedure that the ruler has become illegitimate.[103]

On the other hand, scholars have pointed out that, in the state of Medina, Prophet Mohammad actively promoted the agreement between Arabs, Jews and Muslims, formulated around 622 after his migration from Mecca and Medina, which is sometimes called the 'First Written Constitution of the World'.[104] On this basis, Muslim scholars have developed ideas on how to reconcile Islamic law with the modern concepts of the rule of law and constitutionalism. They submit that the 'Constitution of Medina' served the same purposes as modern constitutionalism and the rule of law, namely peaceful coexistence and regulating rights and obligations of the members of the community, including its rulers.[105]

[96] See Pt III (Ch 3) below.

[97] Emon, 'Sharia and the Modern State' (n 94) 52.

[98] AE Mayer, *Islam and Human Rights. Tradition and Politics* (Oxford, Westview Press, 2013) 47.

[99] Ibid.

[100] Ibid.

[101] Bahlul, 'Is Constitutionalism Compatible with Islam?' (n 93) 515–42, 531, noting, however, that 'there is no reason why contemporary Sharia thinkers cannot take up the challenge to elaborate a position with respect to the separation of the different branches of government'.

[102] Ibid 531.

[103] Ibid 531.

[104] M Hamidullah, *The First Written Constitution in the World* (Lahore, Kazi Publications, 1986) 11 et seq; see also M Berween, 'Al-Watiqah: The First Islamic Constitution' (2003) 23 *Journal of Muslim Minority Affairs* 103. For the Text of the Madina (Medina) Charter, see app IV.

[105] WM Watt, *Muhammad at Medina* (Oxford, Clarendon Press, 1956) 221–28.

The new polity that had emerged is sometimes referred to as a 'state' in the contemporary meaning of the word,[106] featuring a population, the (political) *Ummah*,[107] a defined territory,[108] a government[109] and the capacity to enter into relations with other states.[110] The Medina document defined certain basic rights and duties of the individuals and groups within the community as well as some fundamental rules of law that could be referred to by every member of the community.[111] Additionally, Prophet Mohammad, as the leader of the community, did not regard himself as standing above the law. On the contrary, numerous legal claims brought against him are witness of the attitude of the Prophet that the law needs to govern the relation of a community but also the actions of the leader.[112] At the lifetime of the Prophet, it can thus be said that Islam was rejecting the principle of 'the King can do no wrong'.[113] It follows that the concept of constitutionalism and rule of law is, at least, not alien to Islam.

However, other scholars point out that this does not mean that Islam is fully amenable to the modern concept of the rule of law.[114] It depends mainly on the way in which Islamic law is interpreted and applied in a given context. Generally, one can distinguish between historical and evolutional interpretations of the Islamic legal sources. While the Quran and the Sunna (the authentic tradition of the Prophet Muhammad) are considered as divine and immutable sources in both

[106] M Hodgson, *The Venture of Islam* (Chicago, The University of Chicago Press, 1974) 193.

[107] Baderin points out that the Medina Constitution stated in its opening parts that it was a 'document by Muhammad the Prophet, between the believers and Muslims of Qurayš and Yatrib, and those who followed them and joined them and struggled with them. [...] They are one community (*umma*) to the exclusion of all men'. Further down, the document explained that the Jews 'are one community (*umm*) with the believers. (The Jews have their religion (dīn) and the Muslims have theirs)'; M Baderin, 'Islam and Human Rights in the Constitution of African States: Agenda for Good Governance' in H Elliesie (ed), *Beiträge zum Islamischen Recht VII. Islam and Human Rights* (Frankfurt, Peter Lang, 2010) 123–53, 138.

[108] It is reported that the Prophet ordered a companion to plant some indicators to define the territorial boundaries of Medina. MT Ghunaimi, *The Muslim Conception of International Law and the Western Approach* (The Hague, Martinus Nijhoff, 1968) 54.

[109] The Medina document regulated issues of government, such as legislation, administration of justice and defence. See Baderin, 'Islam and Human Rights in the Constitution of African States: Agenda for Good Governance' (n 107) 123–53, 138; see also Ghunaimi, *The Muslim Conception of International Law and the Western Approach* (n 108) 55.

[110] This is evidenced by constitutional provisions in this regard and a number of subsequent treaty relations with other political powers in existence then. Baderin (n 107) 123–53, 138.

[111] Ghunaimi pointed out that the 'Constitution of Medina' ensured respect for individual rights, including Jews, and gave the example of Abu Bakr (succeeding Caliph after the Prophet) who, in a quarrel with a man called Pinhas, a Jewish Arab, is reported to have said that 'if it were not for the Charter between us and you, I would have cut off your head'; Ghunaimi (n 108) 57; see also Baderin (n 107) 123–53, 139. For the text of the Constitution of Medina (the Medina Pact, or the Medina Charter), see www.constitution.org/cons/medina/macharter.htm.

[112] Hamidullah, *The First Written Constitution in the World* (n 104) 12.

[113] Ibid 12.

[114] An Na'im, eg, points out that 'some interpretations of Islam are seriously problematic from a constitutional point of view, while others are at least consistent with the principle, if not positively supportive of it'. See AA An Na'im, *African Constitutionalism and the Role of Islam* (Philadelphia, University of Pennsylvania Press, 2006) 9.

interpretations, the role of *fiqh* (jurisprudence) and *ijtihad* (juristic reasoning) is regarded differently.

Under a strict historical interpretation, Islamic jurisprudence must be limited to the legal opinions of the classical jurists as recorded in the legal treatises of the classical schools of Islamic legal scholarship. However, *fiqh* was not the law of the state even though it was a source of law on a number of subjects.[115] The jurists were rather reluctant to be part of the state system. They hesitated to accept judicial positions under the caliphs so that *fiqh* developed as a private jurists' law. Jurisdiction in territorial and substantive terms was accorded by the caliphs or kings and Sultans to the *qadis* whose judgments, however, have hardly been preserved and studied. As a result, *fiqh* and state law existed in parallel. This explains why *fiqh* is not a comprehensive legal system and why differences of opinions among the jurists was possible and subsequently led to the development of several doctrinal schools of law.[116]

According to the theory of the 'closing of the gate of juristic reasoning (*ijtihad*)' around the thirteenth century, Islamic law must be understood and applied as it had been perceived in the Islamic legal schools at that time.[117] Yet, a more evolutional approach regards the rulings and practices of the classical jurists and leaders not only as an important source of jurisprudence and precedent but also emphasises the need for continual development of Islamic law by contemporary jurisprudence (*fiqh*) and the continuing process of legal reasoning (*ijtihad*).[118] This is considered to be particularly important for temporal matters pertaining to inter-human relations (*mu'āmalāt*), in contrast to matters of religious observance and acts of worship (*ibādāt*). According to this view, modern political theory and constitutional objectives, such as respect for human rights and the rule of law, fall within the realm of inter-human relations and are, therefore, amenable to evolutional interpretation.[119] A foundation for the evolutional interpretation may even be detected in some teachings of classical Islamic jurists, such as Ibn al Qayyim al-Gawziyyah of the Hanbali school of jurisprudence of the thirteenth to fourteenth century, who stated:

> Islamic law is structured and founded upon wise purposes and the best interests of God's servants both in this world and the next. The Law is pure justice, pure mercy, pure

[115] MK Masud, 'Clearing Ground: Commentary to "Sharia and the Modern State"' in Emon, Ellis and Glahn, *Islamic Law and International Human Rights Law: Searching for Common Ground?* (n 93) 104–14, 106; see also MK Masud, 'The Changing Concepts of Caliphate–Social Construction of Sharia and Ethics' in K Vogt, L Larsen and C Moe (eds), *New Directions in Islamic Thought: Exploring Reform and Muslim Tradition* (London, Tauris, 2008) 187–205.

[116] Ibid 107.

[117] On the dispute over the closing of the gate of *ijtihad*, see eg W Hallaq, 'Was the Gate of Ijtihad Closed?' (1984) 16 *International Journal of Middle East Studies* 3; S Ali-Karamali and F Dunne, 'The Ijtihad Controversy' (1994) 9 *Arab Law Quarterly* 238; Z Mir-Hosseini, 'How the Door of *Ijtihad* Was Opened and Closed: A Comparative Analysis of Recent Family Law Reforms in Iran and Morocco' (2007) 64 *Washington and Lee Law Review* 1499.

[118] Baderin (n 107) 123–53, 140.

[119] Baderin (n 107) 123–53, 141; see also A An-Na'im, 'Islam and Human Rights: Introductory Remarks and Reflections' in Elliesie, *Beiträge zum Islamischen Recht VII* (n 107) 41–47, 44.

> benefit, pure wisdom. Hence, anything which embodies injustice rather than justice, cruelty rather than mercy, harm rather than benefit, or folly rather than wisdom does not originate from the Law, even if it happens to have been interpolated therein by means of interpretation.[120]

This explains the higher intents of Islamic law (*maqāsid as-šarī'a)*, according to both the classical and contemporary Islamic jurists, namely to promote human welfare and benefit (*maslaha*) and to prevent harm (*mafsada*). Therefore, in the implementation of Islamic law in state law, these concepts can be relied upon to explain and justify the enactment and application of legal rules consistent with the concept of the rule of law.

There are various aspects of the rule of law to which Muslim scholars have found references in the sources of Islamic law. The Quran and the Sunna contain numerous references to the importance of applying justice, to the need for equality before the law and the relevance of accountability. Concerning the importance of applying justice, sura 5, verse 8, may be quoted:

> O believers! Stand firm for Allah and be witnesses in justice (apply justice), The hatred of a group shall not prevent you from justice. Apply justice; that is close to righteousness. And be conscious of Allah; indeed, Allah is well aware of what you do.[121]

With regard to equality before the law, the Quran holds, in sura 4, verse 135:

> O believe Stand firm for Allah and be witnesses in justice (apply justice), even if it is against your or your parents or your relatives and regardless (if the parties) are poor or rich: for Allah can best protect them (more than you can). Follow not the desire of ego. If you distort justice or fail to do justice surely, Allah is well aware with what you do.[122]

The concept of accountability encompasses judicial accountability and political accountability. With respect to judicial accountability, sura 4, verse 58 may be cited:

> Surely, Allah commands you to return the trust (properties) to their owners (and beneficiaries) and when you judge amongst people be just (impartial). Surely Allah gives you excellent advice for Allah is the seeing observer.[123]

As to political accountability, the acceptance speech of the first caliph after the death of the Prophet, Abu Bakr, may be quoted:

> I have been chosen as your chief although I am better than none of you. Thus, if I do good work it is incumbent on you to extend your help and support to me; if I go wrong it is your duty to put me on the right path. Truth and righteousness are trust and untruth

[120] Translation cited in GE Attia, *Towards Realization of the Higher Intents of Islamic Law: Maqāsid al-Sharia: A Functional Approach* (London, The International Institute of Islamic Thought, 2007) 7.

[121] The Quran 5:8; see also Baderin (n 107) 123–53, 149.

[122] The Quran: 4:135; see also Baderin (n 107) 123–53, 149.

[123] The Quran: 4:58; see also Baderin (n 107) 123–53, 150.

> is a breach of trust. The weak among you are strong to me unless I give them full justice, and the strong among you are weak to me unless I receive what is due from them.[124]

This quote also shows that the leader has received his authority from the fact that he was 'chosen'. It can therefore be understood as a confirmation that elections and democracy are compatible with Islamic law. Some scholars are of the opinion that democracy requires secularism, a concept which is still strongly rejected in most of the Muslim world.[125] A core problem seems to be is that democracy requires giving equal political rights to all citizens, but that to think of the possibility of a head of an Islamic state as a Christian, Jewish or atheist would strain credulity.[126] It is interesting to note that both secularist and Islamic conservatives using different types of arguments often reach the same conclusion, namely that democracy is incompatible with Islam.[127]

One of the concepts frequently advocated in favour of the compatibility of Islam and democracy is the concept of *shura*.[128] The Arabic term *shura* means picking and selecting the best thing, but also taking or giving one's opinion with due care and deliberation.[129] The Quran contains the order from God to the Prophet Mohammad to consult the believers on all matters. As the respective verses do not contain any qualifications or limitations, one could conclude that all members of a state or a community are eligible to give or request *shura*.[130] However, there is some controversy about the issue whether the Sharia contains a binding obligation to seek *shura* and whether the ruler is bound to apply the opinion reached as a result of the *shura* process.[131]

Others underline the democratic nature of the caliphate by pointing out that

> the caliphate [...] is not a right that inheres in a certain individual, or family or class. It is a right which belongs to all those who recognize divine sovereignty, and who believe in the supremacy of divine law. [...] this feature makes the Islamic caliphate democratic, in contrast to caesarism, papism, or theocracy, as known in the West.[132]

The recognition of the people's right to elect the caliph could be regarded as preparing the ground for the acceptance of the people's right to elect

[124] A Najeebabadi, *The History of Islam, vol 1* (Riyadh, Darussalam International Publications, 2000) 276.

[125] Bahlul (n 93) 515–42, 536; there are efforts by Muslim scholars to show the need for a secular state in order to enable Islam. See eg AA An-Na'im, *Islam and the Secular State: Negotiating the Future of Sharia* (Cambridge, Mass, Harvard University Press, 2008).

[126] Bahlul (n 93) 515–42, 536.

[127] This has been, however, heavily criticised by others, eg R Bahlul, 'Democracy without Secularism?' in J Bunzl (ed), *Islam, Judaism, and the Political Role of Religions in the Middle East* (Florida, Florida University Press, 2004) 99–117.

[128] El-Gindy, 'The Shura and Human Rights in Islamic Law. The Relevance of Democracy' (n 3) 164–69.

[129] Ibid.

[130] Ibid 165.

[131] Ibid 165.

[132] Mawdudi, *Al-Qanun al-Islami*, 25, quoted by Bahlul (n 93) 515–42, 532.

'representatives' with the task of voicing people's concerns, and watching over the executive powers.[133]

It follows from the above examples that reconciling aspects of the modern rule of law concept with Islamic law is possible. However, due to the variety of interpretations of the Islamic legal sources, a final conclusion on the compatibility of the rule of law with Islamic law cannot be made. It is apparent that the historical or traditional interpretation which advocates the 'closing of the gates of ijtihad' will have more difficulties with reconciliation than a more evolutional form of interpretation allowing *fiqh* and *ijtihad* to develop.

The scepticism which reform proposals are sometimes confronted with can partly be explained by the phenomenon that it is considered to be more heinous to deviate from an existing rule, for example by referring to the principle of *darura* (necessity),[134] than to question the rule as such.[135] Academic literature can help to identify sufficient authority to explain and confirm the compatibility of Islamic Law with the concept of the rule of law by the use of Islamic methods and legal concepts. However, the rule of law can only be implemented, if it is understood, supported and advocated not only by academia, but by all of the actors in society. The question of implementation is crucial which, of course, holds true not only for Muslim societies.

V. Applicability of the Rule of Law at the Domestic and International Levels

While the rule of law developed primarily as a concept at the national level, it shall be examined to what extent the rule of law is also applicable at the international level and how any international standard of the rule of law might challenge the rule of law at the national level representing divergent cultural or religious backgrounds.

It needs to be emphasised that rule of law is a concept that entails obligations for states (or other political communities), not for individuals.[136] Under international law, it is recognised that every state enjoys sovereignty and thus has the right to exercise jurisdiction over and, if needed, also coercion against natural or juridical persons. As demonstrated above, numerous legal thinkers and legal traditions have come to the conclusion that this power of coercion needs to be regulated and limited. The rule of law is thus inherently linked to the concept of states as the organiser of human beings living together.

[133] Ibid 533.
[134] W Hallaq, *An Introduction to Islamic Law* (Cambridge, Cambridge University Press, 2009) 26.
[135] See J Anderson, *Law Reform in the Muslim World* (London, Athlone Press, 1976) 36.
[136] Gowder (n 90) 25.

In today's world, Muslim societies, as well as societies in the so-called Western world, are organised and functioning in states. The concept of a state, as a sovereign and independent entity interacting with others on the basis of equality in the so-called 'Westphalian system', is not antithetical to Islamic international law, the *Siyar*. Traditionally, Islamic law referred to the *Ummah*, the community of believers, instead of 'people' or 'population' of a state. Yet, as a result of the political developments in the past centuries, also Muslim societies have adopted the concept of a 'state' as the overall organisational entity to regulate societal functioning. They generally have also adopted constitutions in which the principles and rules of the functioning of the state are laid down.

While constitutions are not solely sufficient for the implementation of the rule of law, the institutions and procedures provided by them lay down the relevant framework for its development. Several studies have already analysed constitutional law in Muslim majority states.[137] One of the key issues was to identify the role of Islamic law within the law of the state. Several categories of the different types of relationship between Islam and the state could be identified, including forms of strict separation and identity of Islamic law and state law, as well as various intermediate types in between.

The majority of member states of the OIC provide a privileged role for Islamic law in their constitutions. The notable exception is Turkey where the constitution provides that '[t]he Republic of Turkey is a democratic, secular and social State governed by the rule of law'.[138] It does not accord Islam any normative impact within the state governance. According to the Preamble to the Turkish Constitution '[a]s required by the principle of secularism, there shall be no interference whatsoever of the sacred religious feelings in State affairs and politics'.[139]

At the other end of the spectrum are states such as Iran and Saudi Arabia. The Constitution of the Islamic Republic of Iran provides that

> [a]ll civil, penal, financial, economic, administrative, cultural, military, political, and other laws and regulations must be based on Islamic criteria. This principle applies absolutely and generally to all articles of the Constitution as well as to all other laws and regulations, and the *fuqaha'* of the Guardian Council are judges in this matter.[140]

The role of Islam as the law of the state is reaffirmed by the creation of a Guardian Council '[w]ith a view to safeguard the Islamic ordinances and the

[137] See, in particular, the comprehensive comparative study by R Grote and T Röder, *Constitutionalism in Islamic Countries: Between Upheaval and Continuity* (Oxford, Oxford University Press, 2011); see also Baderin (n 107) 123–53, 126 et seq; N Abiad, *Sharia, Muslim States and International Human Rights Treaty Obligations: A Comparative Study* (London, BIICL, 2008) 32 et seq; An-Na'im, *Islam and the Secular State* (n 125) 45 et seq.

[138] Art 2 of the Turkish Constitution of 1982, www.constitution.org/cons/turkey/part1.htm.

[139] Preamble of the Turkish Constitution of 1982, see ibid. See also Abiad, *Sharia, Muslim States and International Human Rights Treaty Obligations* (n 137) 44.

[140] Art 4 of the Iranian Constitution of 1979; see www.iranonline.com/iran/iran-info/government/constitution.html; see also Adineh Abghari, *Introduction to the Iranian Legal System and the Protection of Human Rights in Iran* (London, BIICL, 2008) 163 et seq.

Constitution, in order to examine the compatibility of the legislation passed by the Islamic Consultative Assembly with Islam'.[141] The Guardian Council has the power to decide whether a law elaborated by the Islamic Consultative Assembly is contradictory to the principles, official religion of the country or the Constitution.[142] It follows that, in the hierarchy of norms, Islamic principles are positioned at the top, over other constitutional provisions and other sets of laws.[143]

The Basic Law of Saudi Arabia of 1992 declares that '[t]he Kingdom of Saudi Arabia is a sovereign Arab Islamic States with Islam as its religion; God's Book and the Sunnah of His Prophet, God's prayers and peace be upon him, are its constitution'.[144] The government derives its power from the Holy Koran and the Prophet's tradition.[145] The Basic Law provides for 'the judicial authority; the executive authority; the regulatory authority'.[146] However, '[t]he King shall be the point of reference for all these authorities'.[147] This means that a separation of powers is non-existent.[148]

Intermediate positions of Islamic Law in the constitutional system can be found in many African and Asian States. Article II of the Egyptian Constitution of 1971 (as amended) provides that 'Islam is the religion of the State and Arabic is its official language. The principles of Islamic Sharia are the main source of legislation'.[149] This formulation is the result of an amendment in 1980 and is significantly more extensive than before.[150] The formulation of Article II has been the object of highly controversial discussions in the drafting of a new Constitution in Egypt after the Arab Spring in 2011.[151] However, after a heated debate,[152]

141 Art 91 of the Iranian Constitution 1979.

142 Ibid Art 72.

143 Abiad, *Sharia, Muslim States and International Human Rights Treaty Obligations* (n 137) 45.

144 Art 1 of the Basic Law of Saudi Arabia of 1992. See the Basic Law of Governance (Promulgated by the Royal Decree No A/90 dated 27/08/1412 H, 1 March 1992).

145 Ibid Art 44.

146 Ibid.

147 Ibid.

148 FE Vogel, *Islamic Law and Legal System: Studies of Saudi Arabia* (Leiden/Boston, Brill, 2000) 170; see also Abiad (n 137) 42; P-S Agate, 'L'Arabe Saoudite: quel Etat et quell(s) droit(s)?' in A Mahiou (ed), *L'Etat de droit dans le monde arabe* (Paris, CNRS Paris 1997) 355 et seq.

149 Art 2 of the Constitution of Egypt of 1971, as amended. Constitution of Egypt of 1971, available at www.sis.gov.eg/Newvr/Dustor-en001.pdf. See also translation after C Hulsman, 'Introduction' in C Hulsman (ed), *The Sharia as the Main Source of Legislation?* (Marburg, Tectum, 2012) 13–14; see also Baderin (n 107) 123–53, 127; B Dupret "'La chari'a est la source de la législation": interprétations jurisprudentielles et théories juridiques' in Mahiou *L'Etat de droit dans le monde arabe* (n 148) 125 et seq.

150 For a detailed analysis, see P Prentice, 'Article II of the Egyptian Constitution. Background and Contrastring Opinions' in Hulsman, *The Sharia as the Main Source of Legislation?* (n 149) 153–78.

151 'Many Egyptian Christians voted "no" on constitution, fearing Islamists', http://blogs.reuters.com/faithworld/2011/03/21/many-egypt-christians-voted-no-on-constitution-fearing-islamists/; see also Hulsman, 'Example of Misrepresentation of Article II in relation to Christians in Egypt' in Hulsman (n 149) 133–52.

152 See eg C Hulsman, Nabil Ahmad Hilmi, 'A Liberal Scholar Advocating Amending Article II' in Hulsman (n 149) 207–38.

the formulation of 1980 has remained unchanged in the new text of 2011.[153] Provisions, such as 'Sharia as a source of legislation' as in the Constitution of Bahrain or of 'Islamic jurisprudence as a main source of legislation' as in the case of the Syrian Constitution mean that Islamic law constitutes just one amongst a possible variety of legislative sources.[154]

Morocco, which is generally regarded as one of the most modern states in Africa, in particular concerning the situation of human rights, provides in its Constitution that 'Islam is the religion of the State'[155] without mentioning a particular role of Islamic law in the normative hierarchy. Nevertheless, the impact of Islam as a religion of the state has important consequences for the role of Islamic law in the national legal system. One of the reasons is the position of the King, who is regarded as the 'defender of the Faith' who also 'shall ensure the respect for the Constitution'.[156] This important position of the King concerning the observation both of Islam and the Constitution shows that religion and the law are closely intertwined and that Islam directly influences the substantive law of the state.[157]

As this short overview shows, there is a variety of solutions for the relationship of Islamic law and the law of the state. The question arises as to what extent Islamic law, owing to its divine origin and sacred nature, is amenable for the implementation of the rule of law in contemporary Muslim societies. Different theoretical positions as to the possible role of Islam and Sharia in the constitution of states and legal systems have been formulated.

From a separatist theoretical perspective, the argument is that, generally, religion should have no role in modern constitutions. With the aim to ensure neutrality in the political order, religion should be completely restricted to the private sphere of individuals and not be allowed to enter the public sphere.[158] According to this view, a constitution that provides for a dominant role of one particular religion necessarily triggers discrimination of other religions and beliefs. Only a strictly secular constitutional order that is free from any religious leanings or influence can ensure a neutral politico-legal system.[159]

[153] See www.cabinet.gov.eg/AboutEgypt/ConstitutionalDeclaration_e.pdf.

[154] Abiad (n 137) 47.

[155] Art 6 of the Constitution of Morocco of 1996. For the text of the Constitution of Morocco (1996), see www.wipo.int/wipolex/en/text.jsp?file_id=180780. See M Mouaqit, 'Le movement des droits de l'homme au Maroc; du Makhzen à LEtat de droit' in Mahiou (n 148) 271 et seq; J-C Santucci. 'Etat de droit et droits de l'Etat au Maroc. Réflexions à propos du Conseil consultatif royal des droits de l'homme', ibid. 289 et seq.

[156] Art 19 of the Constitution of Morocco of 1996.

[157] Abiad (n 137) 50–51.

[158] J Hatcherd, M Ndulo and P Slinn, *Comparative Constitutionalism and Good Governance in the Commonwealth: An Eastern and Southern African Perspective* (Cambridge, Cambridge University Press, 2004) 25, fn 47.

[159] Baderin (n 107) 123–53, 133.

However, this separationist theory has been challenged by others who maintain that the strictly secular model does not provide a sufficient inspiration to mobilise the people to be engaged in public life and work for solidarity and social change. The challenge is, as one commentator put it, to

> infuse the struggles of peoples of the world for democracy, equity, and sustainability with a vision of human existence that is human-centred yet recognizes the relevance of spiritual sensibilities in the major world religions, moving us beyond a society based on reason and machines.[160]

This approach has merits insofar as it accentuates the positive role religion can play in society for promoting many goals, such as respect for human rights and dignity, education, culture and solidarity.[161] However, the challenge here is to show that this is in fact the case in states which provide a constitutional role for Islam and Islamic law.

An intermediate position emphasises that religion and religious law can be regarded as a double-edged sword that could either be utilised positively or negatively when it is given a role in the constitutions.[162] According to this view, it is necessary to contextualise the role Islam is given in a particular society.[163] In this sense, the constitutions need to reflect indigenous values of the respective society, but at the same time uphold universal principles such as respect for the rule of law.[164] It depends therefore on the concrete situation in the country, specifically its history, demography and culture, whether Islamic law may contribute positively or negatively to the society.

It is important to note that the analysis of the rule of law in the different types of constitutional systems cannot be limited to the analysis of the constitution itself but must also include an analysis of the organisation and work of the judiciary[165] and the administrative system. The rule of law is a continuum not a binary. States can satisfy it to a greater or lesser extent.[166] A state can satisfy some of the principles of

[160] R Falk, 'Religion and Global Governance: Harmony or Clash' (2002) 19 *International Journal of World Peace* (2002) 3.

[161] In this context the numerous religious NGOs should be mentioned which provide support and social services, but also engage in highly professional activities in service of those in need, such as medical assistance and education. They generally enjoy a high degree of confidence, because they are not suspected of concentrating on achievening commercial success or political power, even if this is not always entirely true.

[162] Baderin (n 107) 123–53, 135.

[163] Ibid 136.

[164] AA An Na'im, *African Constitutionalism and the Role of Islam* (Philadelphia, University of Pennsylvania Press, 2006) 99 et seq.

[165] See eg the comprehensive study on the role of the judiciary by N Brown, *The Rule of Law in the Arab World: Courts in Egypt and the Gulf* (Cambridge, Cambridge University Press, 1997); see also AO Sherif, 'The Rule of Law in Egypt from a Judicial Perspective: A Digest of the Landmark Decisions of the Supreme Constitutional Court' in E Cotran and M Yamami (eds), *The Rule of Law in the Middle East and the Islamic World. Human Rights and the Judicial Process* (New York, IB Tauris, 2000) 1–34.

[166] Gowder (n 90) 26.

rule of law, but not others, to a greater or a lesser extent. And the rule of law can be accorded to some citizens, such as certain elites, but not to others.

VI. Foundational Principles of the Rule of Law

On the basis of the historical and comparative overviews above, some of the foundational principles of the rule of law should be discussed in more detail. At the outset, it is necessary to clarify that 'law', at least in the Western understanding, means norms of general application which are binding and enforceable. They have to be distinguished from other norms, such as moral or religious norms. This is often the first misunderstanding, when 'Sharia' is translated as 'Islamic law'. Not all norms in the Sharia are meant to be binding in a legal sense and be enforceable by state authorities. Rather, the Sharia represents an all-encompassing normative system addressed to the believers in Islam. As such it also includes moral and religious norms.[167] By contrast, in the Western understanding, moral and religious norms may serve as sources of inspiration or politically influence the 'law' of a state, but they differ from the notion of law in terms of their normative basis (revelation, holy texts and scriptures, tradition, social compact) and their system of sanctions (remorse, repentance, perdition, Last Judgment, social sanctions). When we look now at the foundational principles of the rule of law, we should concentrate on the more narrow understanding of 'law' as a system of binding norms which are applied and enforced by state institutions. In essence, we are not analysing Islamic law in the abstract, as a space less and timeless religious or philosophical system, but concretely as a variant of national state law.

First, the rule of law aims at the protection from arbitrary and unpredictable decisions of rulers. In order to achieve this goal, decisions must be based on clear and understandable rules. Clarity and precision represent the first foundational principle of the rule of law. They are indispensable for ensuring to provide legal certainty. However, this does not only represent a challenge for underdeveloped societies, but also for modern and highly sophisticated legal systems. In order to be generally applicable, rules must be formulated in general terms and cannot be too specific. This inevitably leaves room for interpretation.[168] How large this room for interpretation can or must be depends on the particular norm and cannot be generalised. In the area of criminal law, the margin of interpretation must be rather small in order to safeguard the principle of '*nulla poena, nullum crimen sine lege*'. In other areas of law it can be larger. Too many and too specific

[167] See in more detail Ch 3 below.

[168] The uncertainties of inevitably unclear rules which provide room for 'marginal' cases create the 'penumbra' of a legal rule, as Hart called it. See HLA Hart, 'Positivism and the Separation of Law and Morals' (1958) 71 *Harvard Law Review* 593.

norms, for example, in administrative or in tax law, can present a similar problem for the rule of law as too few and too general norms. Conversely, if a norm is formulated too broadly and in the abstract, it can only be understood by reference to scholarly writing or jurisprudence so that a very similar problem arises. In this case, individuals cannot shape their behaviour in accordance with the law.

Secondly, the norms must be publicly known. How this can be ensured, with the appropriate degree of precision, is regarded differently in legal traditions. While in continental legal systems (in the tradition of Roman law) the need for statutory laws is regarded as an indispensable prerequisite, in common law systems this is not the case. As has been shown, even in the absence of a written constitution in the United Kingdom, safeguarding the rule of law is crucial. Similarly, rules that are based on custom or on divine revelation (such as in traditional India or in Islamic law) are not necessarily written down in codes. It will be analysed more in detail below how this criterion can be fulfilled in contemporary practice.

Thirdly, the historical and comparative overview has shown that there is agreement that, in order to comply with the rule of law premise, the law must be applied in an equal and non-discriminatory manner to all subjects. The yardstick of equality is not clearly expanded by the classical or modern jurists. Within the chronicles of history, slavery was not addressed (or addressed appropriately), women were treated differently from men, and other forms of inequality were largely ignored. These included inter alia racial discrimination or discrimination based on disability.[169] One form of discrimination, however, needs further examination, namely discrimination on religious grounds. As shall be considered in Part IV of this study, in the context of freedom of expression and freedom of religion, it is important to carve out more clearly which kind of protection the rule of law could or *should* provide.

The fourth important element of the rule of law which recurred in the historical and comparative overview above is the existence of a functioning system of legal institutions which provide for and ensure the general application of the law and which are accountable. This latter element has become particularly important in recent years, when the rule of law was discovered as a concept that is important for societal and economic development.[170] The rule of law appears to be internationally more acceptable than other concepts across nations and cultures, such as democracy and human rights. It appears politically less controversial and less moralistic or 'imperialistic' than other values of 'Western' origin.[171] Strengthening the rule of law has become a goal of several international institutions, such as the

[169] Gowder highlights and discusses in detail the difficulty of identifying the relevant criteria of distinction that are necessary for treating equal things equally and different things differently. Gowder (n 90) 30–33.

[170] Hayek supported the argument that a predictable legal system improves the rule of law because it safeguards the expectations of the individual and allows to make long-term planning and decisions. See F Hayek, *Law, Legislation and Liberty* (Chicago, Chicago University Press, 1978) 106–10; Gowder (n 90) 70.

[171] See H Esmaeili, 'On a Slow Boat Towards the Rule of Law: The Nature of Law in the Saudi Arabian Legal System' (2009) 26 *Arizona Journal of International and Comparative Law* 1, 2–4.

United Nations, the World Bank and the OECD. Each of these institutions also devoted considerable attention to the identification of the elements of the rule of law as an important factor of development.

Fifthly, the question needs to be addressed as to whether the rule of law requires that these rules themselves are designed to preserve individual rights and freedoms. It can be argued that an authoritarian regime, whose preferences and dislikes are generally known and stable for a longer period, does not necessarily limit personal freedom more than other regimes, because the citizens can foresee and plan their behaviour accordingly over time. Only unpredictable and arbitrary regimes, so-called 'sultanistic-authoritarian' regimes would severely limit personal freedom.[172] Also the Chinese perception of the rule of law, both under the traditional concept of *fa* and under communist and post-communist regimes, does not include the protection of human rights.

Not all legal thinkers and traditions mentioned above necessarily put the protection of individual rights and freedom in the focus of their definition of the rule of law. However, from a more contemporary perspective, human rights have slowly and increasingly developed into a universally recognised value system. Certainly, the extent of the individual rights and their permissible limitations remain a matter of controversy, both at the national and at the international levels. Despite the fact that 'rule of law' and 'human rights' are still understood and used as distinct concepts, they seem to have gradually merged. How separable they are remains subject of discussion.

The United Nations efforts in promoting the rule of law is an example of the increasing approximation of the rule of law and human rights. In particular, since the preparations of the World Summit of 2005, the organisation has strengthened its efforts to promote the rule of law in all of its member states and within its own activities.[173] Its concept of the rule of law is rather broad and combines both procedural and substantive elements. According to the Report of the UN Secretary-General on 'The Rule of Law and Transitional Justice in Conflict and Post-Conflict Societies', the rule of law is

> a principle of governance in which all persons, institutions and entities, public and private, including the State itself, are accountable to laws that are publicly promulgated, equally enforced and independently adjudicated, and which are consistent with international human rights norms and standards. It requires, as well, measures to ensure adherence to the principles of supremacy of law, equality before the law, accountability to the law, fairness in the application of the law, separation of powers, participation in decision-making, legal certainty, avoidance of arbitrariness and procedural and legal transparency.[174]

[172] See J Linz, *Totalitarian and Authoritarian Regimes* (Boulder, Lynne Rienner Publishers, 2000) 159; see also Gowder (n 90) 65.

[173] See World Summit Outcome, Resolution 60/1 adopted by the General Assembly on 16 September 2005, UN Doc A/RES/60/1 (24 October 2005).

[174] Report of the Secretary-General on 'The Rule of Law and Transitional Justice in Conflict and Post-Conflict Societies', UN Doc S/2004//616 (23 August 2004) para 6.

This definition makes clear that the United Nations adheres to a more comprehensive understanding of the concept as laws have to be 'consistent with human rights standards'. While the procedural aspects are present in all of the other definitions, the United Nations' focus includes substantive issues as well. This can be explained by the large scope of activities of this global organisation. Its concept of the rule of law represents a combination of two main purposes, namely 'to maintain international peace and security'[175] and to 'promote … universal respect for, and the observance of, human rights and fundamental freedoms for all without distinction as to race, sex, language or religion'.[176] The importance of the respect for human rights and fundamental freedoms for the maintenance of international peace and security has been recognised in numerous initiatives and projects of the United Nations.

In the context of the examination of the rule of law, freedom of expression and Islamic law, the broader concept which encompasses not only procedural[177] but also substantive elements seems more appropriate to address the pertinent challenges today.[178] While freedom of expression and Islamic law has so far primarily been addressed under the lens of human rights law, the present study includes considerations of the rule of law with its additional considerations on legal certainty, avoidance of arbitrariness and procedural and legal transparency. In the following, the various elements of the rule of law shall be examined more closely with a particular focus on the freedom of expression and its challenges in the realm of Islamic law.

A. Existence of Legal Rules that are Sufficiently Precise

Under the rule of law premise, state institutions are called to act upon legal rules and not upon their unfettered discretion. As legal philosopher John Rawls has pointed out, vagueness and uncertainty in the law limit personal liberty.[179] It has a chilling effect as citizens will be deterred from exercising their freedom, because they feel the risk that they might be punished for something they had thought was within their domain of choice. Vague laws on freedom of expression therefore lead to self-censorship.[180] In order to determine the competence and the scope of the decisions of state institutions, legal rules must be sufficiently precise. This means that authorities charged with the application of the law should not

[175] Art 1(1) of the Charter of the United Nations, 24 October 1945, 1 UNTS XVI.

[176] Ibid Art 55(c).

[177] According to Gowder, these elements are necessary to speak at least of a 'weak version' of the rule of law; ibid 12.

[178] This has also been the approach of the ILA Committee on Islamic Law and International Law; see Report of the Committee on Islamic Law and International Law, 75th Conference in Sofia (2012), available at www.ila-hq.org/en/committees/index.cfm/cid/1006.

[179] J Rawls, *A Theory of Justice* (Cambridge, MA, Harvard University Press, 1999) 207–10.

[180] Gowder (n 90) 63.

be conferred unfettered discretion.[181] In view of the fact that laws sometimes are imprecise, the implementing authorities should be given sufficient guidance to be able to ascertain what sorts of expression are properly restricted and what sorts are not. Recognising the impossibility of attaining absolute certainty in framing laws, and that the search for certainty may entail excessive rigidity, it is necessary to indicate with sufficient clarity the scope of the discretion and the manner of its exercise.[182] This criterion is one of the most important to avoid arbitrariness.[183]

Yet, legal rules cannot be too precise, either, to fit to every single case in the same way, because they must be formulated in a general way to make them applicable to a large variety of situations. It follows that in the interpretation and application of a legal rule, the exercise of discretion is almost always required. Yet, a 'sufficiently precise' rule is a rule whose scope of application is conceivable and can perform its role of shaping the addressee's behaviour. Individuals should be in a position to know in advance which acts and omissions are in conformity with the rule and which are not. Only this way can a rule fulfil its function, namely to guide legal subjects' behaviour. Vague rules which are open to interpretation in various ways and which are not accompanied by clear yardsticks and principles in their application do not fulfil the criterion of being sufficiently precise.

Rules that restrict the freedom of expression are amongst the most problematic in this context. As will be discussed in more detail below and in Chapters 6 and 7, the right to freedom of expression, while being recognised as one of the fundamental rights of a universal character, is subject to various restrictions. According to the practice of human rights monitoring bodies there seems to be consensus that, above all, the law must be formulated with sufficient precision to enable an individual to regulate his or her conduct accordingly.[184] The citizens should be able to foresee the exact scope and meaning of legal provisions so as to enable them to regulate their conduct.[185] This precision or foreseeability test is a crucial interpretative device.[186] The citizens should be in the position to know in advance the conditions under which any restriction of the freedom of expression will be employed. The requirement 'prescribed by law' promotes 'legal certainty' as

[181] See Human Rights Committee, General Comment No 34 (Article 19: Freedom of Opinion and Expression) CCPR/C/GC/34 (12 September 2011) para 25 [hereinafter, Human Rights Committee, General Comment No 34].

[182] See eg *Sunday Times v UK (No 2)* (1992) 14 EHRR 229 (Judgment of 26 November 1991) para 31; *Busuioc v Moldova* (2006) 42 EHRR 252 (Judgment of 21 December 2004) para 52; see also Y Arai, 'The System of Restrictions' in P van Dijk, F van Hoof, A van Rijn and L Zwaak (eds), *Theory and Practice of the European Convention on Human Rights* (Antwerp/Oxford, Intersentia, 2006) 333–50, 337.

[183] Human Rights Committee, General Comment No 27 (Article 12) Freedom of Movement, UN Doc CCRC/C/21/Rev.1/Add.9 (2 November 1999) para 14.

[184] See Human Rights Committee, General Comment No 34, para 25, *Leonardus Johannes Maria de Groot v The Netherlands*, Communication No 578/1994, UN Doc CCPR/C/54/D/578/1994 (1995) (views adopted on 14 July 1995).

[185] Arai, 'The System of Restrictions' (n 182) 333–50, 336.

[186] Ibid.

well as 'procedural and legal transparency' and is therefore an important element for the implementation of the rule of law in the context of freedom of expression.

The International Covenant on Civil and Political Rights (ICCPR) explicitly mentions as permissible limitations the 'respect of the rights or reputation of others' and 'the protection of national security or of public order (*ordre public*), or of public health or morals'.[187] However, these limitations must be prescribed by 'law'. In view of the different legal systems, including civil law, common law and Islamic law, it is not always obvious what qualifies as 'law'.

As shall be considered further below, the protection of the 'rights of others', namely their freedom of religion, and the preservation of 'public order' and/or 'public morals' has been used as a justification for enacting anti-blasphemy laws with considerable impact on the freedom of expression in many countries.[188] Generally, these laws are not particularly precise.[189] It is thus the role of the judiciary to interpret and apply them in a manner that makes their scope of application understandable and foreseeable by the general public. Unfortunately, this is not always the case and the vagueness of the prohibition of blasphemy, in combination with the threat of penal sanctions of imprisonment, fines or even the death penalty, has a negative effect from a rule of law perspective.[190]

On the other hand, complex laws can also create legal uncertainty. If laws are written in a very detailed manner and can only be understood with the help of lawyers, this can also lead to a substantial degree of citizens' uncertainty and thus lack the rule of law.[191] If a citizen not specifically trained as a legal expert cannot any more understand the law and direct his or her behaviour accordingly, an important foundational principle of the rule of law is lost.[192]

The precision of legal rules is most important in the area of criminal law. This is evident in the general law principles of *nullum crimen sine lege (certa)*, and of *nulla poena sine lege*, which enshrine the principle of legality in criminal law. Restrictions of the freedom of expression are frequently imposed by criminal law. In addition

[187] See ICCPR, Art 19, para 3(a) and (b).

[188] See Chs 6 and 7 below.

[189] See Ch 6 below. eg the formulation of the blasphemy provision in Art 295-C of the Pakistan Penal Code: 'Who ever by words, either spoken or written, or by visible representation, or by any imputation innuendo, or insinuation, directly, defiles the sacred name of the Holy Prophet Muhammad (PBUH) shall be punished with death, or imprisonment for life and shall also be liable for fine'. The scope of the provision is very wide and difficult to evaluate. eg it has been debated, whether also the rejection, in words or by deeds, is sufficient that a Muslim man must wear his facial hair long. See www.pakistanblasphemylaw.com/?page_id=15. Western laws tend to have the requirement of 'disturbing public order' built into their blasphemy provisions, which is a rather vague and unclear criterion. See eg the German Penal Code in its s 166 (prohibiting blasphemous speech or writings which are 'prone to disturb public order', or s 188 of the Austrian Penal Code (referring to 'circumstances where his behaviour is likely to arouse justified indignation'). See *Otto Preminger v Austria* App No 13470/87 (ECtHR, Judgment of 20 September 1994) Series A, paras 25, 46–48.

[190] See the more detailed discussion below in Chs 6 and 7.

[191] Gowder (n 90) 67.

[192] See Ch 6 below; Gowder (n 90) 76–77.

to the above-mentioned problem of anti-blasphemy laws, also other restrictions are contained in penal codes, such as the offences of slander and defamation. The defamation of public officials, defamation of heads of state, and defamation of the state and its symbols are other criminal offences which can be found in numerous national laws.[193]

As considered in greater detail in Chapter 3 below, within Islamic law, the crimes of apostasy, rebellion or false accusation of unchastity are to be added. These crimes are part of the category of *hudud* crimes (offences attracting prescribed *hadd* punishments), which are considered 'divine' crimes or crimes against God.[194] But also *qesas* or *ta'azir* crimes, may have a deterring effect on the freedom of expression.[195]

Hudud crimes are followed by harsh corporal punishments. Rebellion or armed robbery requires death, crucifixion, cross-amputation of the hand and foot or banishment; adultery and fornication 100 lashes respectively; false accusation of unchastity 80 lashes, and apostasy is punishable by death.[196] The hard *hudud* punishments are, however, frequently not applied in Muslim states.[197] One of the reasons is that very few Muslim states actually use Sharia in the area of criminal law.[198] In most countries, the application of Sharia is limited to private law, usually family law and inheritance law. The most notable exceptions are Iran and Saudi Arabia which apply Sharia also in criminal matters.[199] Some countries have codified criminal laws, which are inspired or influenced by the Sharia. Chapter 6 will examine in greater detail more recent research establishing that within numerous countries of the Middle East and North Africa blasphemy and apostasy continue to be criminalised.[200]

Irrespective of existing codified criminal law provisions, the principles of Islamic Sharia are sometimes adhered to outside the justice system in a disturbing manner. The death penalty for blasphemic speech or for apostasy has been 'imposed' or even 'enforced' by individuals without any legal basis or competence.

[193] See Ch 6. These are usually contained in Penal Codes, but also in Media Laws. See the database of the International Press Institute (IPI): http://legaldb.freemedia.at/legal-database.

[194] For a comprehensive analysis of hudud crimes, see AA Mansour, 'Hudud Crimes' in MC Bassiouni (ed), *The Islamic Criminal Justice System* (Oceana, London, 1982) 195–201; see also the overview below in Ch 3.

[195] See on the characteristics of Islamic criminal law H Esmaeili, 'Islamic Law Across Cultural Borders: The Involvement of Western Nationals in Saudi Murder Trials' (2001) 28 *Denver Journal of International Law and Policy* 145, 152–53; see also more in detail on Islamic criminal law below, Chs 3 and 5.

[196] Abiad (n 137) 5; R Peters, *Crime and Punishment in Islamic Law* (Cambridge, Cambridge University Press, 2005) 53–64.

[197] MJ Kelly, 'Islam & International Criminal Law: A Brief (In)Compatability Study' (2010) *Pace International Law Review Online Companion* 17–18.

[198] O Arabi, *Studies in Modern Islamic Law and Jurisprudence* (The Hague, Kluwer Law International, 2001) 189–90.

[199] Peters, *Crime and Punishment in Islamic Law* (n 196) 148–53.

[200] See below Ch 6.

Examples are the *fatwa* by Ayatollah Khomeini calling for the assassination of Salman Rushdie for his *Satanic Verses* in 1989, or the killing of politicians defending Aasia Bibi in Pakistan in 2011.[201] As this study examines, Khomeini had neither the territorial nor personal jurisdiction to impose the death penalty on a British citizen who had published a book outside the territory of Iran. The assassins of the two politicians were nothing more than misled murderers. These attacks on the freedom of expression had no legal basis whatsoever and were therefore blatant violations of the rule of law.[202]

Having said that, it has been consistently emphasised that the advent of Islam marked an improvement to the existing pre-Islamic systems.[203] The Islamic criminal system introduced a *qadi* to resolve issues where previously a tribal chief would have presided over disputes. Procedurally, rules to prove or disprove charges were introduced. The accused was held to be innocent until he was formally convicted. Torture and coercion became an unacceptable means of ascertaining the truth, and the principle of equality was implemented through various parts of the penal law, including the establishment of a uniform compensatory amount for crimes of retribution irrespective of nobility or birth.[204] All these improvements represented an important progress towards the rule of law. It follows that the underlying principles of Islamic law which helped to bring about considerable legal reform in the seventh century could be used and applied in order to continue the legal reform process. There should thus not be any inherent barrier of Islamic law to prevent it from being brought into line with contemporary requisites of the rule of law.

In relation to the need to have 'sufficiently precise' rules, both with respect to Islamic and non-Islamic law, several steps for an effective implementation of the rule of law can be identified: first, in the codification process, the legislature must address the need for a sufficiently precise formulation of legal rules. Secondly, the judiciary can be entrusted with more precisely balancing individual rights and obligations and the needs of the society as a whole. Thirdly, the administration must apply the rules in the manner they are aimed at and exercise its margin of discretion with responsibility. Fourthly, scholarly writings and comments can help to identify the scope and interpretation of the pertinent legal rules to have a better understanding of the scope and contents of the legal rules. Finally, the

[201] See in more detail Chs 3 and 5 below.

[202] In the case of Khomeini, his role as the leading politician and state official of Iran made it difficult to have his *fatwa* subject to judicial review, inter alia because of issues of jurisdiction and immunity before national courts of other states. In the Pakistani case, the national courts were competent and, indeed, convicted the murderers. However, the fact remains that Aasia Bibi, a Christian woman, was convicted to death for alleged blasphemy against Islam in 2010. In October 2016, her case was again brought before the Supreme Court of Pakistan, but eventually adjourned owing to the withdrawal of 1 judge owing to his alleged bias. See J Boone, 'Asia Bibi blasophemy appeal adjourned in Pakistan as judge pulls out' *The Guardian* (13 October 2016) www.theguardian.com/world/2016/oct/13/asia-bibi-pakistan-blasphemy-law-appeal-adjourned-judge-pulls-out.

[203] *Cf* however Kelly, 'Islam & International Criminal Law' (n 197) 10.

[204] Abiad (n 137) 5–6.

understanding of the precise content of the legal rules should, as far as possible, be known and recognised in society. The rule of law should not only be entrusted to legislators, courts and the administration, but to the population at large. This would help to avoid that the people avail themselves as self-appointed guardians of the rule of law, instead and outside of the state's legal system.

B. Publicly Promulgated Legal Rules

Another important element of the rule of law is that the 'law' is publicly promulgated. As mentioned above, the codification of previously unwritten rules by the *decemviri* in the Roman Republic or the Code of Hammurabi have been particularly praised in this regard. Montesquieu and Kant have emphasised the importance of the legislature to develop and define the legal rules which are binding upon the judiciary and the executive power.[205] Such laws must be published via appropriate means in order to be known to the citizens.

Yet, not all legal systems provide for the codification of legally binding norms. For the common law system, Dicey has pointed out that the role of the judiciary is paramount in formulating and defining the contents and scope of legal norms.[206] In order to ensure the rule of law, the judgments must be published and be accessible to the legal subjects. While it is not certain that the pertinent laws are thereby easily understood by everyone, according to the European Court of Human Rights it is sufficient that the law is accessible to the citizens, even with the advice of legal experts.[207] In the context of limitations of the freedom of expression, the Human Rights Committee emphasised that the norm must be accessible to the public which serves the purpose of enhancing 'legal certainty' and 'procedural and legal transparency'.[208] It is necessary that the respective norm is known to the citizens, or at least that it is at their reasonable disposal.[209]

In the context of Islamic law, the criterion of public promulgation poses a particular challenge. As has been pointed out above, Islamic *fiqh* has developed almost independently from any legislature by legal scholars and in academic discourse. It is not the result of legislative acts and not the result of judicial practice of courts and tribunals in one particular country. There is consequently no means of publication comparable to the civil law and common law traditions. The contents of the norms are rather to be known from textbooks and legal opinions of jurists. These are not always easy to access.

Possible means of spreading the norms of Islamic law to the general public are the *fatwas*, legal opinions by learned experts of Islamic law or Imams. However, frequently institutions or persons issuing *fatwas* are not officially recognised or

[205] See above.
[206] See above.
[207] See Arai (n 182) 333–50, 337.
[208] See Human Rights Committee, General Comment No 34, para 25.
[209] See Arai (n 182) 333–50, 337.

authorised to give an authentic interpretation of Islamic law in a particular country. They are rather regarded as providers of guidelines for orientation in the lives of Muslims living in-and outside Muslim majority countries. It can be said that *fatwas* represent a mixture of legal and religious advice. Consequently, they can generally not be regarded as representing an authoritative and authentic interpretation of Islamic law as it has to be understood by the citizens in one particular country.

Moreover, Islamic law is most frequently not the only source of law in Muslim countries, as Sharia usually exists alongside state law enacted by a legislature. In respect of this state law, the criterion of public promulgation is more easily fulfilled. Official means of publications of legal texts should normally not be a problem. In view of the diversity of Islamic law and its different schools, it helps the promotion of the rule of law, when Muslim states engage in as much codification of Islamic law as possible. This would help to identify which of the multiple schools of law is relevant in the particular state and which particular interpretation should be followed by its citizens. The competent legislature could choose and decide which interpretation should be applied and enforced under the state's jurisdiction. Such a choice and decision can then be known by the legal subjects in order to direct their actions accordingly. Such a codification would also allow development, amendment and changes of the law, as appropriate, because it would not have the nimbus of being sacred. Even in the context of the contentious blasphemy laws in Pakistan, the fact that the law was enacted by the legislature makes it amenable to change.

If a case law system is preferred, it would be necessary to define which court should have the competence as the ultimate decision-maker in Sharia matters. Furthermore, it would be helpful to identify which interpretation of Islamic law, Shia or Sunni, including their different schools of law, should be followed by the competent court. The court could then define the content of the concrete Islamic norms as authoritative for all other courts and the legal subjects in that particular country. Also in this way, the rule of law could be furthered, almost regardless of the content of the law, at least in a narrower understanding of the rule of law. The prerequisite of public promulgation is in itself vital for ensuring that important aspects of the rule of law are safeguarded, such as legal certainty, procedural and legal transparency and avoidance of arbitrariness.

C. Equal Application

Equal application of the law means that the law is applied to all citizens without discrimination. However, non-discrimination does not only mean application of the law without regard to race, colour, sex or religion,[210] it also means treating

[210] These are the 4 most basic prohibitions of discrimination as enshrined in Art 1, para 3 of the UN Charter and most relevant in the present context. For the United Nations Charter, see Charter of

equal issues equally and different issues differently.[211] The principle of equality thus requires not only the equal treatment of equals, but also consideration of differences in assessing whether different treatment is just and is geared to achieving de facto equality, not just formal equality.[212]

With regard to the freedom of expression and its limitations discussed in the present context, the existence and application of anti-blasphemy laws is again the most important issue to be examined. In view of the fact that a number of states, not only in the Middle East and in Africa, but also in North America and Europe, have enacted anti-blasphemy laws,[213] it is necessary to have a closer look at the potential discriminatory nature of these laws.

First, it is necessary to examine, whether the aim of the blasphemy law is to protect adherents of only one religion or of all religions. There is a significant difference in the laws, predominantly for historical reasons. For example, the United Kingdom's anti-blasphemy law (until its abolition in 2008)[214] only protected the Christian faith emanating from the Church of England, and not other religions or religious denominations, as confirmed by the judicial committee of the House of Lords and the European Court of Human Rights.[215] Nowadays, anti-blasphemy laws, as far as they still exist in Europe, prohibit insults against all religions and their adherents under certain conditions.[216] As regards anti-blasphemy laws in Muslim majority countries, most of them prohibit insults against the religion of Islam but not against other religions. One reason for the unequal treatment of Muslims and non-Muslims in terms of blasphemy can be seen in the fact that the state considers itself an 'Islamic' state, such as Afghanistan, Gambia, Iran, Mauretania, Pakistan[217] or Saudi Arabia.[218] While it can be argued that all

the United Nations, 26 June 1945, 59 Stat. 1031, T.S. 993, 3 Bevans 1153. Other prohibited forms of discrimination are of course also important and referred to in more detail in international human rights instruments, such as in Art 2 of the Universal Declaration of Human Rights GA Res 217A (III), UN Doc A/810 at 71 (1948) (UDHR) or Art 2 of the International Covenant on Civil and Political Rights, New York, 16 December 1966 United Nations, 999 U.N.T.S. 171; 6 I.L.M. (1967) 368 (ICCPR).

211 Aristotle, *Nicomachean Ethics*, V.3. 1131a10-b15; Politics, III.9.1280 a8–15, III. 12. 1282b18–23; see also Stanford Encyclopaedia of Philosophy, 'Equality', available at http://plato.stanford.edu/entries/equality/.

212 S Farrior, 'Equality and Non-Discrimination under International Law' in S Farrior (ed), *Equality and Non-Discrimination under International Law* (Oxford, Routledge, 2015) 2.

213 See Ch 6 below.

214 See the Criminal Justice and Immigration Act 2008 (entered into force on 14 July 2008) www.opsi.gov.uk/acts/acts2008/ukpga_20080004_en_1.

215 See *Wingrove v UK* (1997) 24 EHRR 1 (Judgment of 25 November 1996) App No 17429/90, para 28. The Court referred to the judgment in *R v Chief Metropolitan Stipendiary Magistrate, ex p Choudhury* [1991] 1 All ER 306, 318. The case related to an application for judicial review of a magistrate's refusal to issue a summons for blasphemy against Salman Rushdie and the publishers of *The Satanic Verses*.

216 The conditions are generally that the insult must be prone to cause public unrest, thus being almost equivalent to a prohibition of hate speech.

217 See the official list of names of United Nations Membership, www.un.int/protocol/sites/www.un.int/files/Protocol%20and%20Liaison%20Service/officialnamesofcountries.pdf. See Ch 6 below.

218 The Basic Law of Saudi Arabia of 1992 declares that '[t]he Kingdom of Saudi Arabia is a sovereign Arab Islamic States with Islam as its religion; God's Book and the Sunnah of His Prophet, God's prayers and peace be upon him, are its constitution'. See (n 154).

anti-blasphemy laws should equally protect insults against all religions, this would not be in line with the view of those who are of the opinion that anti-blasphemy laws are not necessary and not capable to protect their religious belief. As the then Minister of State at the Home Department of the United Kingdom, John Patten, formulated in a letter to a number of influential British Muslims in the wake of the Salman Rushdie affair:

> Many Muslims have argued that the law of blasphemy should be amended to take books such as [The Satanic Verses] outside the boundary of what is legally acceptable. We have considered their arguments carefully and reached the conclusion that it would be unwise for a variety of reasons to amend the law of blasphemy, not the least the clear lack of agreement over whether the law should be reformed or repealed. [...] an alteration in the law could lead to a rush of litigation which would damage relations between faiths. I hope you can appreciate how divisive and how damaging such litigation might be, and how inappropriate our legal mechanisms are for dealing with matters of faith and individual belief. Indeed, the Christian faith no longer relies on it, preferring to recognise that the strength of their own belief is the best armour against mockers and blasphemers.[219]

It follows from this quote that adherents of other religions might not be interested in a protection of their religion by the rule of law in any state. Equal treatment would therefore not be the solution to the problem of discrimination.

Secondly, unequal application of the law is a problem, if insults of one religion are prosecuted, but insults of another religion are not. In contrast to the first problem, the perspective here is from the persons prosecuted for blasphemy. Equal treatment would require that adherents of a religion which is not protected by the law should also not be victims of the law protecting a religion. One of the most appalling aspects of the Aasia Bibi case is that, as a Christian woman, she was convicted for blasphemy of Islam, while her own belief is not protected under the laws of Pakistan.

Finally, equal application of the law means equal law enforcement measures which do not differentiate between adherents of different beliefs. State institutions are called to protect equally places of worship of different religions and offences against adherents or religious leaders, if they are attacked.[220] Rule of law would mean that state institutions provide a safe environment for all the citizens and do not differentiate the level of protection along the lines of religious belief.

[219] Quoted by the European Court of Human Rights in *Wingrove v UK* (1997) 24 EHRR 1 (Judgment of 25 November 1996) App No 17429/90, para 29. See also the discussion of the case and its repercussion by M Paraschos, 'Religion, Religious Expression, and the Law in the European Union' in J Thierstein and Y Kamalipour (eds), *Religion, Law, and Freedom: A Global Perspective* (Westport, CT, Greenwood, 2000) 27–29.

[220] See F Magnis-Suseno, 'Pluralism Challenged: What is Happening to Religous Freedom in Indonesia?' in S Hammer and F Husein (eds), *Religious Pluralism and Religious Freedom. Religions, Society and the State in Dialogue* (Yogyakarta, Center for Religious and Cross-Cultural Studies, 2013) 55–60.

D. Application by Institutions that are Accountable

The accountability of state institutions is another important aspect of the rule of law. A reliable and functional legal system is highly important in many respects, including economic growth, investment and trade.[221] The relevant legal rules are found in national laws and regulations,[222] which have to be applied in a consistent and reliable manner.

The rule of law is closely connected to the concept of 'good governance' which has become a salient issue also in international economic law in recent years. It is based on the idea that any community needs reliable rules in order to foster long-term economic development and prosperity.[223] In this context, the protection of property rights, the right to consensually transfer property, and the normative backing of obligations have been identified as important criteria.[224] According to the World Bank's definition, the rule of law

> captures perceptions of the extent to which agents have confidence in and abide by the rules of society, and in particular the quality of contract enforcement, property rights, the police, and the courts, as well as the likelihood of crime and violence.[225]

This definition emphasises the importance of functioning institutions as an aspect of the rule of law. Commentators have criticised the World Bank's approach as a school of law promotion which aims to promote the rule of law in order to promote market reforms 'to make the world safe for capitalism'.[226] While this may be true to some extent as the primary objective of the World Bank is economic development, the World Bank has also looked more closely to the roots of poor development and concentrated on the problem of violence. The World Bank Development Report of 2011 highlighted the importance of functioning justice institutions, government effectiveness and low corruption for an effective fight

[221] N Foster, 'Islamic Perspectives on the Law of Business Organisations I: an Overview of the Classical Sharia and a Brief Comparison of the Sharia Regimes with Western-Style Law' (2010) 11 *European Business Organization Law Review* 3; ibid 'Islamic Perspectives on the Law of Business Organisations II: the Sharia and Western-style Business Organisations' 273.

[222] In this context, also the prohibition of *riba* (interest) can be discussed. See eg B Seniawski, 'Riba Today: Social Equity, the Economy, and Doing Business under Islamic Law' (2001) 39 *Columbia Journal of Transnational Law* 701.

[223] M Herdegen, *Principles of International Economic Law* (Oxford, Oxford University Press, 2013) 139; J Foundez, 'Rule of Law or Washington Consensus: The Evolution of the World Bank's Approach to Legal and Judicial Reform' in A Perry-Kessaris (ed), *Law in the Pursuit of Development: Principles into Practice?* (New York, Routledge, 2010) 180–201; S Schulte-Schlemmer, 'The World Bank's Role in the Promotion of the Rule of Law in Developing Countries' in S Schlemmer-Schulte and Ko-Yung Tung (eds), *Liber Amicorum Ibrahim F.I. Shihata: International Finance and Development Law* (The Hague, Kluwer Law International, 2001) 677–725.

[224] See Herdegen (n 223) 139 with reference to D Hume, *A Treatise on Human Nature* (London, 1739–40) Bk III, Pt II, s IV: Of the transference of property by consent.

[225] See the Worldwide Governance Indicators (WGI) Project by the World Bank and its definition of the 'rule of law': http://info.worldbank.org/governance/wgi/pdf/rl.pdf.

[226] Gowder (n 90) 169.

against violence which represents one of the biggest threats to development.[227] In accordance with this insight, the World Bank intensifies its efforts for projects on establishing 'justice' in an institutional sense.

The OECD has also emphasised the need for the promotion of development with a focus on functioning institutions. It explains the rule of law as follows:

> The principle of the rule of law refers to the authority and influence of law within a society. According to this principle, the law should govern and no one, including the government is above it. The rule of law is implemented through the existence of codified or standardised procedures and a series of mechanisms guaranteeing access, equality, predictability, reliability and accountability. It constitutes a key measure of good governance and it is crucial for maintaining peace and order, as well as fostering investment and development.[228]

Here again, the reliability of institutions which safeguard and implement the law is regarded as paramount. As the focus of the OECD is economic development, consideration of safeguarding individual freedom and/or human rights are not at the forefront of concern. Rule of law in this context is instead regarded as a degree of good governance existing in a country which can be measured and used as an indicator for economic decisions.

Several initiatives of a non-governmental character have specialised in measuring the extent to which the rule of law is implemented in different countries for the purpose of these economic aspects. The Rule of Law Index of the World Justice Project is notable in this context. This Index is based on the following definition of the rule of law:

> The WJP uses a working definition of the rule of law based on four universal principles, derived from internationally accepted standards. The rule of law is a system where the following four universal principles are upheld:
>
> 1. The government and its officials and agents as well as individuals and private entities are accountable under the law.
> 2. The laws are clear, publicized, stable, and just; are applied evenly; and protect fundamental rights, including the security of persons and property.
> 3. The process by which the laws are enacted, administered, and enforced is accessible, fair, and efficient.
> 4. Justice is delivered timely by competent, ethical, and independent representatives and neutrals who are of sufficient number, have adequate resources, and reflect the makeup of the communities they serve.[229]

The Rule of Law Index of the World Justice Project is a useful tool for politicians and entrepreneurs who are active in international economic cooperation. It can also indicate needs and prospects of the reform of justice systems. Substantive

[227] World Bank, *World Development Report 2011: Conflict, Security, and Development* (Washington, World Bank, 2012) 57.

[228] OECD, *Government at a Glance 2015* (Paris, OECD, 2015) 160–61.

[229] The World Justice Project, *Rule of Law–Index 2015* (Washington, World Justice Project, 2015) 10.

criteria are included in the measurement to the extent that the laws must be 'just' and 'protect fundamental rights, including the security of persons and property'. However, it is not clear to what extent 'fundamental rights' include the entire set of internationally protected human rights or again only rights with the particular focus of security. This focus bears the risk that individual rights are outweighed by other concerns, such as public safety and economic development.

E. Consistency with Human Rights Standards

The fullest concept of the rule of law also encompasses substantive criteria on the contents of the law. As such, legal rules may not have any contents but should be consistent with morally desirable behaviour in order to help build a civilised and humane society. The most widely accepted moral standards are internationally recognised human rights standards. In the context of the present study, we shall concentrate on the freedom of expression as one of the core human rights.

International and regional human rights instruments provide that limitations on the freedom of expression must be 'prescribed by law',[230] be 'established by law'[231] or 'within the law'.[232] The notion of 'law' includes laws of parliamentary privilege or law of contempt of court.[233] This means that restrictions on freedom of expression and information must be set down in formal legislation or an equivalent unwritten norm of common law.[234]

The limitations provided by law are only permissible if they serve one of the recognised purposes under the international and human rights documents. Most of them explicitly include the protection of the rights and the reputation of others among those purposes.[235] The 'reputation of others' reflects the human right to the protection of the personality which is, for example, protected by Article 17 of the ICCPR.[236] According to Article 17 ICCPR, states are not only entitled to

[230] ICCPR, Art 19(3); ECHR, Art 10(2) as amended.

[231] See American Convention on Human Rights, Art 13(2): 'The exercise of the right provided for in the foregoing paragraph shall not be subject to prior censorship but shall be subject to subsequent imposition of liability, which shall be expressly established by law to the extent necessary to ensure: (a) respect for the rights or reputations of others; or (b) the protection of national security, public order, or public health or morals'; American Convention on Human Rights 'Pact of San Jose, Costa Rica' (B-32) O.A.S. Treaty Series No 36, 1144 U.N.T.S. 123.

[232] See African [Banjul] Charter on Human and Peoples' Rights, Art 9: '(1) Every individual shall have the right to receive information. (2) Every individual shall have the right to express and disseminate his opinions within the law'; African [Banjul] Charter on Human and Peoples' Rights, adopted 27 June 1981, OAU Doc CAB/LEG/67/3 rev 5, 21 I.L.M. 58 (1982) (The Banjul Charter).

[233] Human Rights Committee, General Comment No 34, para 24.

[234] M Nowak, *U.N. Covenant on Civil and Political Rights. CCPR Commentary* (Kehl, NP Engel, 2005) Art 19, para 46.

[235] ICCPR, Art 19(3); ECHR, Art 10(2) (as amended); and ACHR, Art 13(2).

[236] ICCPR, Art 17 reads: '(1) No one shall be subjected to arbitrary or unlawful interference with his privacy, family, home or correspondence, nor to unlawful attacks on his honour and reputation.

restrict the freedom of expression, but even bound to provide statutory protection against intentional infringement on honour and reputation by untrue assertions.[237] Other insults, defamations or vilifications based on true assertions or not committed intentionally may be restricted by statute pursuant to Article 19(3).[238] In this context, the difference between untrue statements and value judgements plays an important role. While the existence of facts can be demonstrated, the truth of a value judgement is not susceptible to proof.[239] Limiting the expression of value judgements is therefore more difficult to justify than the prosecution of untrue assertions because it is part of the right secured by the freedom of expression itself.

Other rights which may be protected by a limitation of the freedom of expression include the freedom of religion, the prohibition of discrimination and the freedom of expression of others. The term 'others' should address other persons individually or as members of a community, ie it may refer to individual members of a community defined by its religious faith or ethnicity.[240] The relationship between the various spheres of interest is often difficult to address so that states enjoy relatively broad discretion.[241]

The protection of the rights and reputation of others may be ensured by criminal, civil and/or administrative law. The measures may be included in criminal provisions dealing with defamation, derision or slander, in compensation claims under civil law, or, most importantly, in media law.[242] However, defamation laws should be crafted with care to ensure that they do not serve, in practice, to stifle freedom of expression.[243] They should include such defences as the defence of truth and should not be applied with regard to those forms of expression that are not, of their nature, subject to verification.[244]

States may invoke legitimate aims and purposes in order to limit the freedom of expression. These aims include 'national security', 'public order', 'public health' and 'public morals'.[245] In the present context, the protection of public morals is of

(2) Everyone has the right to the protection of the law against such interference or attacks'. See also ECHR, Art 8; ACHR, Art 11; and the Banjul Charter, Art 5.

237 Nowak, *U.N. Covenant on Civil and Political Rights. CCPR Commentary* (n 234) Art 19, para 50.

238 Ibid.

239 A van Rijn 'Freedom of Expression (Article 10)' in van Dijk, van Hoof, van Rijn and Zwaak, *Theory and Practice of the European Convention on Human Rights* (n 182), 773–816, 794.

240 Human Rights Committee, General Comment No 34, para 28.

241 Nowak (n 234) Art 19, para 51. In its General Comment No 34, the Human Rights Committee also failed to appropriately address the complex and important issue of the relationship of Art 19 with Arts 17 (concerning privacy) and 18 (concerning freedom of religion or belief). See M O'Flaherty, 'Freedom of Expression: Article 19 of the International Covenant on Civil and Political Rights and the Human Rights Committee's General Comment No 34' (2012) 12 *Human Rights Law Review* 627, 652.

242 Nowak (n 234) Art 19, para 53.

243 Human Rights Committee, General Comment No 34, para 47.

244 Ibid.

245 See ICCPR, Art 19(3); ECHR, Art 10(2); and ACHR, Art 13(2)(b). As regards 'public order', the ECHR is more specific and refers, instead, to 'public safety' and 'the prevention of disorder or crime'. In addition, it includes 'territorial integrity', 'preventing the disclosure of information received

particular interest as it can represent the basis for the prohibition of blasphemous expressions or publications. However, the concept of 'public morals' is difficult to grasp because moral norms and values are different in different societies and at different times. In front of this background, human rights institutions have stated that, in the absence of a uniform standard which is universally applicable or at least accepted in a region, states enjoy a certain 'margin of appreciation' in the regulation of limitations of the freedom of expression.[246] Yet, this has been criticised as 'to perpetuate prejudice or promote intolerance'.[247] As a consequence, it has later been repudiated at the international level.[248] The Human Rights Committee now highlights that the concept of morals derives from many social, philosophical and religious traditions, and that limitations for the protection of public morals should not derive exclusively from one single tradition and should be understood in the light of universality of human rights and the principle of non-discrimination.[249]

On the other hand, the 'margin of appreciation' doctrine is still accepted on the regional level, most importantly in the framework of the ECHR. This can be explained by the greater similarities of the societies in the region and ongoing efforts of reaching greater consensus on certain common values.[250]

The protection of 'public order' has also been raised as ground for limiting the freedom of expression in anti-blasphemy laws. In order to protect public order in the context of value judgements on religions or religious leaders, states may rely on provisions aimed at combatting hate speech, racism and xenophobia, such as Article 20(2) ICCPR, Article 4 of the UN Convention on Racial Discrimination and Article 10(5) American Convention on Human Rights. In Europe, specific instruments have been adopted to ban racist and xenophobic speech.[251]

in confidence' and 'maintaining the authority and impartiality of the judiciary' in the list of legitimate public aims.

[246] *Leo R Hertzberg, Uit Mansson, Astrid Nikula and Marko and Tuovi Putkonen, represented by SETA (Organization for Sexual Equality) v Finland*, Communication No R.14/61 (7 August 1979), UN Doc Supp No 40 (A/37/40) at 161 (1982) (views adopted 2 April 1982); *Handyside v UK* (1979–80) 1 EHRR 737 (Judgment of 7 December 1976) para 48.

[247] Individual opinion by Committee members Opsahl, Lallah and Tarnopolsky in ICCPR Communication No. 61/1979. See also Nowak (n 234) Art 19, para 60.

[248] The Human Rights Committee explicitly notes that 'the scope of this freedom is not to be assessed by reference to a "margin of appreciation"'. Instead, a state party, in any given case, 'must demonstrate in specific fashion the precise nature of the threat to any of the enumerated grounds listed in paragraph 3'. Human Rights Committee, General Comment No 34, para 36.

[249] Human Rights Committee, General Comment No 34, para 32.

[250] See eg the joint effort of banning the death penalty by Protocol No 13 to the ECHR of 2002, which almost all member States of the Council of Europe have ratified (with the exception of Azerbaijan and Russia, as at the end of April 2017; Armenia signed the Protocol on 19 May 2006 but as yet has not ratified the instrument). This high level of consensus has not yet been possible to achieve at the international level. See Protocol No 13 to the Convention for the Protection of Human Rights and Fundamental Freedoms, concerning the abolition of the death penalty in all circumstance, ETS No 187.

[251] See EU Council Framework Decision 2008/913/JHA of 28 November 2008 on combating certain forms and expressions of racism and xenophobia by means of criminal law, OJ L328, 6.12.2008, 55–58; Council of Europe Recommendation No R (97) 20 of the Committee of Ministers to Member States on "Hate Speech" adopted on 30 October 1997; Additional Protocol of 2003 to the Budapest Convention

According to these provisions and instruments, advocacy of national, racial or religious hatred that constitutes incitement to discrimination, hostility or violence shall be prohibited by law. As discussed in Part IV of this study, when this threshold is reached, states are under an obligation to act.

However, limitations on the freedom of expression must be necessary to protect the legitimate and recognised aims of law and public policy. The test is generally based on three criteria: (1) they must be appropriate to achieve their protective function; (2) they must be the least intrusive instrument amongst those which might achieve the desired result, and (3) they must be proportionate to the interest to be protected.[252] These criteria taken together represent the 'principle of proportionality' which has to be respected not only in the law that frames the restrictions, but also by the administrative and judicial authorities in applying the law.[253] States should ensure that any proceedings relating to the restrictions are expeditious and that reasons for the application of restrictive measures are provided.[254]

When a state limits the freedom of expression, it must demonstrate in specific and individualised form the precise nature of the threat and establish a direct and immediate connection between the expression and the threat.[255] Laws that penalise the expression of opinions about historical facts, so-called 'Memory Laws', are acceptable if they are required by Article 20(2) ICCPR.[256] In view of the dominant position the government occupies, it must display restraint in sanctions against the freedom of expression and show prudence in choosing the measure of a less restrictive kind, in particular because of the chilling effect such measures may have in the society as a whole.[257] Even though, the ICCPR does not contain the additional requirement that the limitation must be 'necessary in a democratic society', as prescribed in Article 10(2) ECHR, the proportionality principle may lead to

on Cybercrime concerning the Criminalisation of Acts of a Racist and Xenophobic Nature Committed through Computer Systems of 28 January 2003, European Treaty Series No 189; Council of Europe Framework Convention for the Protection of National Minorities of 1 February 1995, European Treaty Series No 157.

252 Human Rights Committee, General Comment No 27 (on the freedom of movement, Article 12 ICCPR), para 14; see also, for the ECHR, *Supreme Holy Council of the Muslim Community v Bulgaria* (2005) 41 EHRR 3 (Judgment of 16 December 2004) para 97; *Incal v Turkey* (2000) 29 EHRR 449 (Judgment of 2 June 1998) para 54; *Ceylan v Turkey* (2000) 30 EHRR 73 (Judgment of 8 July 1999) para 34; *Ahmed Sadik v Greece* (1997) 24 EHRR 323 (Judgment of 15 November 1996) para 51; *Arslan v Turkey* (2001) 31 EHRR 264 (Judgment of 8 July 1999) paras 46–50; see also Arai (n 182) 333–50, 340.

253 Human Rights Committee, General Comment No 27 (Article 12) Freedom of Movement, UN Doc CCRC/C/21/Rev.1/Add.9 (2 November 1999) para 15.

254 Ibid.

255 Human Rights Committee, General Comment No 34, para 34; see also *Hak—Chul Shin v Republic of Korea* Communication No 926/2000, UN Doc CCPR/C/80/D/926/2000 (2004) (views adopted on 16 March 2004).

256 Human Rights Committee, General Comment No. 34, para 49.

257 See eg *Nikula v Finland* (2004) 38 EHRR 45 (Judgment of 21 March 2002) para 54; *Elci and others v Turkey*, App Nos 23145/93 and 25091/94 (Judgment of 13 November 2003) para 714; *Selistö v Finland* [2004] ECHR 634 (Judgment of 16 November 2004) para 53; *Cumpana and Mazare v Romania* [2005] 41 EHRR 200 (Judgment of 16 December 2004) para 114.

similar results when it comes to the safeguard of uninhibited expression in the circumstance of public debate and in the public and political domain.[258]

In the Muslim world, but also in political debates in the West, it is not always appreciated that there is a clear hierarchical relationship between the right and the limitation. Limitations are the exceptions from the rule and must therefore be interpreted and applied narrowly. Counter-terrorism measures, defamation laws and anti-blasphemy laws have to comply with the strict requirements of Article 19(3) ICCPR, including the proportionality test. With regard to prohibitions of displays of lack of respect for a religion or other belief system, including blasphemy laws, this will almost always lead to the conclusion that they are incompatible with the freedom of expression, except in the specific circumstances envisaged in Article 20(2) ICCPR.[259] However, there are instances in which appropriate measures to protect the freedom of religion do comply with the criteria on the limitation of the freedom of expression.[260] Yet, prohibitions to prevent criticism of religious leaders or commentary on religious doctrine and tenets of faith in general would not be in accordance with the principle of proportionality.[261]

The analysis of the elements of the rule of law concept in the context of the freedom of expression has shown that the elements of legal certainty and procedural and legal transparency and avoidance of arbitrariness are important prerequisites in the system of limitations of the freedom of expression under international and regional human rights documents. They are the guarantor that the freedom of expression, despite its possible limitations, can ultimately be safeguarded in different circumstances and in different societies.

VII. Conclusions

The historical and comparative overview has shown that the concept of the rule of law has developed over centuries and in many different parts of the world. Even though the scope and reach of the concept has differed in times and places the important function of the law has been twofold: to ensure that rights of individuals are safeguarded and protected, and to ensure that the exercise of power is

[258] Human Rights Committee, General Comment No 34, para 34; see also *Mr Zeljko Bodrožić v Serbia and Montenegro*, Communication No 1180/2003, UN Doc CCPR/C/85/D/1180/2003 (2006) (views adopted on 31 October 2005).

[259] Human Rights Committee, General Comment No 34, para 48.

[260] See eg a case in which a teacher who had published materials that expressed hostility towards a religious community was transferred to a non-teaching position. *Malcolm Ross v Canada*, Communication No 736/1997, UN Doc CCPR/C/70/D/736/1997 (2000) (views adopted on 18 October 2000); see also Human Rights Committee, General Comment No 34, para 33.

[261] See *Concluding observations on the United Kingdom of Great Britain and Norther Ireland—the Crown Dependencies of Jersey, Guernsey and the Isle of Man* of 27 March 2000, see UN Doc CCPR/C/79/Add. 119; see also *Concluding observations on Kuwait* of 27 July 2000, UN Doc CCPR/CO/69/KWT.

regulated and controlled. The rule of law thus helps to ensure the enforcement of the law and also to protect from arbitrary enforcement of law. While it has been rather uncontroversial that the various entities entrusted with authoritative state power should be regulated and limited by law, the submission to the rule of law by political leaders is less generally accepted. The ideal of Plato's 'philosopher king' has triggered the imagination of some that because of their fabulous qualities they would not be bound by the law. Several Western philosophers have countered this view, including Aristotle, Montesquieu and Kant, but also Islam rejects the idea that rulers are above the law. The experiences of the city of Medina with its 'First Written Constitution of the World' demonstrated that the Prophet Mohammad considered himself bound by the law. Numerous legal cases brought against him are witness of this attitude.

It is therefore not difficult to discern the possibility to reconcile the concept of the rule of law, even if the term was coined in the Western sphere, with Islamic legal thought and traditions. However, despite this insight, in many parts of the world the rule of law is far from being fully respected and implemented. The practical challenges and developments shall be discussed further in this book.

Furthermore, it has been examined as to whether and to what extent human rights form part of the concept of the rule of law. On the one hand, the two are distinct, as the rule of law can also be understood as being only concerned with the correct implementation of the law, no matter what the content of the law is. However, in a more modern understanding of the rule of law and, in fact also in the understanding of the United Nations, the observance of human rights is included in the concept of the rule of law. The rule of law analysis thus does not only limit itself on the functioning of the legal system and its institutions, but must also address the contents of the law. In this vein, the freedom of expression needs particular attention, as the concept of the rule of law may be perfectly suitable to address issues in connection with this fundamental, yet also complex human right with its various limitations.

Part III

Rule of Law and Comparative Examination

This part discusses the concept of the rule of law under Islamic law, both as a classical and theoretical legal system as well as an influential part of the legal system of a large number of contemporary Muslim majority countries and under international law. There are some similarities between Islamic law and international law in terms of development, sources of law, the nature and diversity of legal subjects and universality. However, while it is recognisable that both Islamic law and international law have significant structural differences in comparison with modern nation-state domestic legal systems, both these systems are increasingly challenged from the perspective of the rule of law.[1] Part III shall explore the extent to which the rule of law and its values are becoming recognised and implemented within these systems.

The rule of law concept, whether in its classical origin or modern versions, was implemented within domestic legal and political systems, particularly, as part of liberalism, from the late seventeenth century, predominantly in Europe.[2] Values of the rule of law, such as absence of arbitrary power and independence of the judiciary, are encompassed in constitutions and legal principles in various ways at the domestic level. This can be said to be a reflection of the idea that the rule of law is a necessary internal virtue of a functioning national legal system, without which a legal system may not exist.[3] The question here is whether Islamic law, as a classical

[1] According to James Crawford, 'International lawyers must continue to strive for the rule of law as our fundamental goal': J Crawford, 'International Law and the Rule of Law' (2003) 24 *Adelaide Law Review* 4, 12.

[2] On the definition of the rule of law, see J Finnis, *Natural Law and Natural Rights*, 2nd edn (Oxford, Oxford University Press, 2011); M Gleeson, 'The Rule of Law and The Constitution' in R Bellamy (ed), *The Rule of Law and the Separation of Powers* (Aldershot, Ashgate Publishing Limited, 2005); BT Tamanaha, *On the Rule of Law: History, Politics and Theory* (Cambridge, Cambridge University Press, 2004); D Clark, 'The Many Meanings of the Rule of Law' in K Jayasuriya (ed), *Law, Capitalism and Power in Asia: The Rule of Law and Legal Institutions* (London, Routledge, 1999) 28; M Kramer, 'On the Moral of the Rule of Law' (2004) 63 *Cambridge Law Journal* 65, 65; M Radin, 'Reconsidering the Rule of Law' (1989) 69 *Boston University Law Review* 781; J Raz, 'The Rule of Law and Its Virtue' (1997) 93 *Law Quarterly Review* 195; C Saunders and K Le Roy, 'Perspectives on the Rule of Law' in C Saunders and K Le Roy (eds), *The Rule of Law* (New South Wales, Federation Press, 2003).

[3] On this issue, see generally LL Fuller, *The Morality of Law* (New Haven, Yale University Press, 1973); MJ Detmold, 'The Unity of Law and Morality: A Refutation of Legal Positivism' (2004) *Cambridge Law Journal* 65, 98.

system as well as a coalition of the similar national systems (for example members of the OIC), and international law, as a distinct system, may engage the concept and values of the rule of law.

The nature of Islamic law and its diverse application in Muslim countries may raise the question whether it is susceptible of engaging in the values of the rule of law. Similarly, international law, as a system created through treaties and practices of states, as well as the way it is implemented by states and international institutions, is markedly different from a national legal system and hence may not engage the values of the rule of law.

Chapter 3 argues that a rule of law system, as developed and implemented in modern democratic countries, may be adopted and implemented within modern versions of Islamic law and in legal systems of Muslim majority countries. It analyses the origins of Islamic law system from its early genesis (early seventh century) up to the contemporary Muslim world. Various Islamic concepts and principles, as well as the relationship between religion and Islamic law, will be discussed. It will be demonstrated that Islamic terms and concepts are sometimes mixed within English literature and confuse English-speaking legal scholars as to the nature and principles of the legal system of Islam. The chapter also examines various traditional and modern approaches to the relationship between religion and law in Islamic countries and within the history of Islam. It then reviews various legal theories of Islamic schools of law as well as modern approaches of Muslim governments and Islamic institutions. Finally, this chapter will show that Islamic law, known as the Sharia, has developed as a pluralistic system in various and diverse Muslim territories and societies for centuries. It will address to what extent, even in the contemporary world, Islamic law is potentially open for reform and change and for adopting values of the rule of law. Some significant mechanisms, such as the concept of *ijtihad* (in interpretation of religious and legal principles), the doctrine of *shura* (consultative process), *biat* (voting and alliance) and other legal principles and concepts, may pave the way for adopting the concept of the rule of law within Muslim countries.

Chapter 4 is specifically concerned with the prevalence of the rule of law in international law and international institutions, including the United Nations, the Organisation of the Islamic Corporation (OIC) and the League of Arab States. Despite of the nature of international law and the lack of a centralised authority to make and implement law as well as of effective mechanisms to control and limit the exercise of arbitrary powers by some states, the chapter analyses the increasing trend in international law and within international organisations to promote and implement the rule of law. Various international instruments and mechanisms, which emphasise the importance and relevance of the rule of law in the international arena, are reviewed. The chapter highlights the efforts of the United Nations to strengthen the rule of law but recognises the challenges which still exist. It will also investigate the Charter of the OIC and some other instruments in order to analyse the relevance of the rule of law in relation to the operation of this organisation. Furthermore, the work of the League of Arab States, whose members are almost all Muslim majority countries, will be reviewed under the rule of law premise. In addition, some instruments of the Association of South East Asian Nations (ASEAN) will be discussed under the same premise. While this association is not per se an Islamic organisation, it should be noted that the majority of the world's Muslim population live in South East Asia (including the Indian sub-continent) and the largest Muslim country, Indonesia, is a member of the ASEAN. The chapter recognises some significant steps taken by these international and regional organisations, but observes that national interests and state sovereignty are still a powerful opponent to a more stringent implementation of the values of the rule of law and human rights.

3

Islamic Law, the Sharia and the Rule of Law

I. Introduction

In the contemporary world, common law and civil law, which are both based on European traditions, provide the foundation for most legal systems. Common law is the legal system of the United Kingdom and Ireland, and dominates the former British colonies in Asia and Africa, as well as the United States, Canada, Australia and New Zealand. Common law is also present in the Indian subcontinent, which comprises India, Pakistan, Bangladesh and Sri Lanka. Civil law is the dominant legal system of Europe and the rest of the world. There is no single legal system in the world which is not, at least partially, based on civil law or common law, or both. However, in many countries, particularly throughout Asia and Africa, elements from other legal traditions have also been integrated, such as Talmudic law, Islamic law, Hindu law and other religious or customary laws.

Given that nearly 55 Muslim majority countries, as well as some non-Muslim countries, such as India and Israel, apply Islamic law (at least in relation to personal law and family law), it can be said that Islamic law is the third major legal system in the world. Khaled Abou El Fadl provided one of the best descriptions of the current position of Islamic law when he stated, '[I]slamic law is one of the most complex and influential legal systems the world has known, but it is one of the most understudied, oversimplified, and overgeneralised systems as well'.[1]

The Islamic legal system (and it may be better to refer to it as 'Islamic legal systems') is based on four core sources, namely the Quran, the Sunna, *Ijma* and *Qias*, and a number of supplementary sources, including *Istihsan* (Equity), *Maslaha Mursalah* (consideration of public interest) and *Urf* (custom and usage).[2] However, Islamic law has been shaped over 14 centuries, by a wide range of influences, and is also based on significant elements of pre-Islamic Arabian customs

[1] KA El Fadl, 'Soul Searching and the Spirit of Shari'a: A Review of Bernard Weiss's The Spirit of Islamic Law' (2002) 1 *Washington University Global Studies Law Review* 553, 553.

[2] See MH Kamali, *Principles of Islamic Jurisprudence*, 3rd rev and enl edn (Cambridge, Islamic Texts Society, 2006) chs 11–17.

and traditions. Furthermore, it has been influenced by the cultures and customs of various Muslim societies and nations from Morocco to Indonesia, and beyond. The historic, extensive influence of Greek and European philosophies must also be taken into account, as must the more modern impact of Napoleonic civil codes and common law systems. But perhaps the most significant foreign influence on the operation of Islamic law has been the waves of modernity, globalisation and international law, particularly international human rights law, that have increased since the early twentieth century.

To understand how the rule of law can be established in the Muslim world–where Islamic law forms the dominant system, or is at least influential on the legal system–one must understand the nature and concept of Islamic law. The nature of Islamic law, its development, and its basic terms and principles will be discussed in this chapter. While there might be limited possibility of reviving a working classical Sharia law system, it shall be analysed to what extent an effective rule of law system can be established in contemporary Muslim countries which may draw on the theoretical framework of the Sharia.

II. Origins of Islamic Law

A. In Mecca (610–623 AD)

The Prophet of Islam was born in Mecca in 570 AD. At the time, the region in which the cities of Mecca and *Yathrib* (Medina), known as *Hijaz*, are located was isolated and comprised of semi-autonomous tribal regions surviving on limited trade with some Mediterranean areas, Yemen and Northern Africa. The then two powerful Roman and Persian Empires were both ignorant of this tribal region. Therefore, the powerful tribes, including the powerful merchant tribe of *Quraysh*, which incorporated the clan of the Prophet Mohammad, controlled the *Kabah* (considered the most sacred site in the Muslim world). At that time, there was no legal system operating in *Hijaz* except Arab customs and culture. This is similar to pre-1066 England, where there was no legal system except Anglo-Saxon customs and culture. At the time, a number of influential Jewish tribes lived in *Yathrib* (Medina) who followed Jewish law. There were also some Christian tribes adjacent to the *Hijaz* area, known as *Najran,* and in Yemen and Habesha (Ethiopia).

The revelation of Islam started from 610 AD. For the first 13 years, the limited number of Muslims, who were following the Prophet and living in the city of Mecca, lived in accordance with the customs and the culture of Mecca. The Quran and the Sunna of the Prophet provided limited legal principles. The chapters of the Quran, revealed during those 13 years, were concerned primarily with monotheism, beliefs, religious duties such as prayer, and fasting. The Quran, however, banned certain Arab practices of the time, such as infanticide and adultery. At this earlier stage of the development of Islam, some of the landmark Islamic legal principles, such as the prohibition of alcohol, the imposing of the *hijab*, and certain criminal punishments, had not yet formed part of the set of rules to be observed by the followers of Prophet Mohammad. On the other hand, the rituals and religious duties prescribed for Muslims, at this stage and at the later stage in the city of Medina (from 623–633 AD), preserved many existing Arab cultures of rituals, such as the *hajj* (pilgrimage and performing duties around the *Kabah*).[3]

B. In the Medina State (623–633 AD)

When the Prophet and his followers, known as *Mohajerin* (migrants), entered into the city of *Yathrib* (Medina), together with the people of the various tribes of Medina, they created a city-state which became the first Muslim state. The state of Medina extended to Mecca and the surrounding areas while the Prophet was still alive. In Medina, various Arab tribes welcomed the Prophet and converted to Islam. An agreement was concluded between the *Mohajerin* from Mecca (mainly from the tribe of the Prophet–*Quraysh*), the new converted Muslims of Medina known as *Ansar* (supporters), and the Jewish tribes of Medina. As noted in Part II above, the agreement is known as the Constitution of Medina, the Medina Pact, or the Medina Charter.[4] The Charter recognised the customs of the *Mohajerin*, the *Ansar*, who were together known as the believers, as well as the customs of the various Jewish tribes of Medina, who joined the Charter. According to a clause of the Charter, in the event of a war, the believers were to redeem their prisoners with kindness and justice. In addition, some Jewish clans were treated as one community with the believers. The Charter provided that Jews were free to apply their law and customs according to their religion. The Charter of Medina, even by modern twenty-first-century standards, was a progressive, pluralistic and a multi-religious and political pact.[5] This Charter, written at the onset of Islam's development, provides an insight into the possible reasons for the widespread and rapid expansion of this religion throughout the world.

[3] According to Joseph Schacht, 'There are four legal systems whose influence on nascent Muhammadan law and jurisprudence is at least possible: Persian Sassanian law, Roman Byzantine (including Roman provincial) law, the canon law of the Eastern churches, and Talmudic law. Outside the sphere of law proper, the far-reaching influence of Judaism and Christianity on Islamic cult and ritual, and that of Roman Byzantine and Persian Sassanian administration on Islamic political and fiscal institutions are matters of common knowledge'. See J Schacht, 'Foreign Elements in Ancient Islamic Law' in WB Hallaq (ed), *The Formation of Islamic Law* (Farnham, Ashgate Publishing Limited, 2004) 59–68, 68.

[4] See Pt II above; see also M Hamidullah, *The First Written Constitution in the World* (Chicago, Kazi Publications, 1968, first published 1941). For the Text of the Madina (Medina) Charter, see app IV; FM Denny, '*Umma* in the Constitution of Medina' (1977) 31 *Journal of Near Eastern Studies* 39; SA Arjomand, 'The Constitution of Medina: A Sociolegal Interpretation of Muhammad's Acts of Foundation of the *Umma*' (2009) 41(4) *International Journal of Middle East Studies* 555.

[5] On a commentary on the Charter, see generally, Hamidullah, *The First Written Constitution in the World* (n 4).

It should be noted that, later, the political relationship between Muslims and Jews in Medina fractured. However, the Quran contains many religious and legal principles of the Old Testament. Judaism and Christianity are the two main religions recognised as 'People of the Book', which gives them legal recognition in Muslim societies under Islamic law.[6]

During the Medina state, and its expansion into Mecca and some surrounding areas in the Arabian society, the revelation of the Quran continued gradually. During this time, in addition to religious rituals, moral and ethical principles, depending on the unfolding of events, a few legal verses of the Quran appeared. By the time of the death of Prophet Mohammad (632 AD), the Muslim state had an emerging legal system based on a number of Quranic verses revealed to him, as well as many sayings and practices of the Prophet Mohammad; both of these sources retained a significant number of existing Arabic, Jewish and Christian customs and cultures.

Significantly, new Islamic precepts, such as the prohibition of alcohol, the requirement of women to cover their hair and body (*hijab*), *hudud* offences and punishment (such as the stoning to death of adulterers) were imposed in connection with incidents which happened during the period of the Muslim state prior to the death of the Prophet. For example, the consumption of *Khamr* (alcoholic drinks) was prohibited and criminalised in different stages. First, with respect to a situation in which an intoxicated Muslim man entered the mosque the Quran banned Muslims from praying while they were drunk.[7] At this stage, *Khamr* (alcoholic drinks) was not yet prohibited, except before praying and entering the mosque. However, *khamr* was prohibited at a later stage in Medina, when two Muslim men, who were drunk, started an argument which almost escalated into a fight between the *Mohajerin* (migrants) and the *Ansar* (supporters).[8] The punishment for drinking *khamr* was added at later stage, not in the text of the Quran, but in the Sunna of the Prophet Mohammad. As a result, Islamic schools and Islamic jurists differ with respect to whether drinking alcohol is part of *hudud*

[6] 'We revealed the Torah (the Old Testament) which consisted of guidance and light': The Quran 5:44; 'We gave the *ingil* (the Bible) to Jesus, in which there was guidance and light, and confirmation of the Torah': The Quran 5:46.

[7] The Quran 4:43: 'O believers! Do not stand for performing prayers (*salat*) when you are in a drunken state, wait until you are sober and you can understand the meaning of what you utter'. According to the leading interpreter of the Quran, Mohammad ibn Jarir al-Tabari (died 923 AD), 2 early Muslim followers of the Prophet drank *khamr* and entered the mosque. Then the verse of the Quran (4:43) was revealed. See Mohammad ibn Jarir al-Tabari, *Tafsir Jami al-bayan an ta'wil ay al-Quran* (various editions in various languages have been published; originally written in the 10th century in Arabic. The Quranic verse 4:43 is interpreted in volVIII of the book; the book has 16 volumes.)

[8] The Quran 2:219: 'They ask you (the messenger) about *khamr* (alcoholic drinks) and gambling. Say, for both of these, there is a grave sin, though there are some benefits for some people in these. But the sin of these (drinking and gambling) is greater than their benefits'. Another verse of the Quran, 5:90, states 'O believers! *Khamr*, gambling, sacrificing stones (for idols), and dividing by arrows for seeking luck (a kind of gambling) are some of Satan's acts, so stay away from them, so that you may be saved'.

punishments or whether it is part of *tazirat* (discretionary) punishments.[9] The prohibition and criminalisation of drinking alcohol was (and still is) a unique feature of Islamic law. In many other areas of law, such as contract and commercial law, a large number of existing customary legal principles were adopted and amended by the emerging Muslim community. It can thus be regarded as the standard practice and procedure of the creation of Islamic law.

As noted by Anderson, '[i]t is evident that Mohammad himself made no attempt to work out any comprehensive legal system, … instead, he contented himself with what went little beyond *ad hoc* amendments to the existing customary law'.[10]

Upon the establishment of the state of Medina (623 AD), more legal verses of the Quran were revealed to the Prophet. However, only about 10 per cent of around 6600 verses of the Quran can be classified as verses providing rules (regardless of whether they are legal rules or relate to rituals) known as *ayat al-ahkam* (verses concerning rules). However, it should be noted that these 10 or less per cent of the verses of the Quran[11] include principles relating to rituals, law and even morality and ethics. Consequently, less than 100 verses of the Quran directly establish proper legal principles. These include verses relating to criminal law (*hudud* and *qisas*), inheritance, wills, marriage and divorce, the law of war, the payment of special taxes (*zakat*), property law and hunting. However, the rest of *ayat al-ahkam* are concerned with rituals (prayer, performing *hajj*, fasting etc), ethics, social etiquette (for example, not entering other people's houses without their permission)[12] and moral principles such as prohibiting the interference with others' personal affairs.[13]

By the time of the death of Prophet Mohammad (632 AD), a state had been established in Medina and Mecca, which included some of the surrendering tribes. At that stage, the structure of the societies and the city was tribal. When tribal leaders converted to Islam and joined the Prophet of Islam, their territory was added to the territory that formed the Muslim state of Medina. The legal system of Medina, headed by the Prophet, was based on the limited legal verses, the practice and sayings of the Prophet, and the existing customary law of Arab tribes in Mecca, Medina and other tribes who joined the state of Medina. It should be

[9] A al Jaziri, *Kital al Fiq Ala al Madahib al Arba'a* (*Book of Jurisprudence according to four Juristic Schools*) vol 5 (Beirut, Darelfkr, 1999) 22.

[10] JND Anderson, *The Muslim World*, vol XL (1950) 245, as discussed in SD Goitein, 'The Birth-Hour of Muslim Law? An Essay in Exegesis' in Hallaq, *The Formation of Islamic Law* (n 3) 69–76.

[11] On the number of the *ayat al-ahkam*, there are different views amongst Muslim interpreters of the Quran. eg according to Ibn al-arabi, there are more than 800 *ayat al-ahkam* in the Quran. Whereas according to Ibn al-qayyam, there are about 150 *ayat al-ahkam* in the Quran. The difference is due to the fact that some verses of the Quran are interpreted as having moral connotations only, whereas according to others, some verses are interpreted as having legal connotations only.

[12] The Quran 24:27.

[13] Since the 4th century (Islamic calendar) or the 10th century (Christian calendar), Muslim scholars have written books on *ayat al-ahkam*. See eg the book on *ayat al-ahkam* by Al-Qortbi (died 13th century AD), Abi Abdullah Al-qortbi, *Al-Jame Li Ahkam Al-Qubran, Dar Alam Al-Kitab* [*Comprehensive Verses Providing Rules*] (Riyadh, Dar Alam Al-Kitab, 2003).

noted that the state of Medina, at the time of Prophet Mohammad, was a very small territory[14] with relatively homogenous Arab tribes with similar customs and cultures.

C. Righteous Caliphate (633–661 AD)

After the death of the Prophet, his followers chose a number of caliphs from among the Prophet's companions to lead the Muslim state. The small territory of the original Muslim state expanded to include the whole Arabian Peninsula, the Persian Empire territories, as well as further territories in Africa and Asia. During the time of the Righteous Caliphate and the century following it, known as the Umayyad Caliphate (661–750 AD), Muslims were advised by the caliphs and the Prophet's companions not to write down the Prophet's sayings, in order to prevent them from being mixed with the Quranic verses. However, several small collections of *hadiths* were written during the Umayyad period.[15] From the time of the death of the Prophet, Muslims would narrate his sayings and would act upon them as a source of law, which became later known and accepted as the Sunna.

It is notable that by the time of the death of the Prophet, the majority of legal principles were based on existing customs of the Arabian society. When, during the Righteous Caliphate and the Umayyads, Islam was further expanded, legal and administrative institutions of the conquered territories (the Persians, Romans, Christians and Jewish) were also adopted and thereby modified the Islamic political and legal systems.[16]

III. Development of *Fiqh*

By the end of the Umayyad period (early eighth century), when the caliphate was weak and there was sporadic conflict between the Umayyads and the forces of the Abbasids who succeeded the Umayyads, there was a period of freedom for Muslim jurists to develop their views on many aspects of the religion of Islam, including law.

First, during the period of struggle between the two dynasties (Umayyads and Abbasid) and the creation of a free environment for scholarship and expression of

[14] The city of Medina was, at that time, as big as the current holy shrine of Medina. It was so small that around 1000 or so residents of the city were able to dig a ditch around the city within a period of a couple of months using primitive tools, although the city was surrounded by mountains from 3 directions.

[15] A Guillaume, *Islam*, 2nd edn (London, Penguin, 1954) 89.

[16] J Schacht, 'Pre-Islamic Background and Early Development of Jurisprudence' in Hallaq (n 3) 29–58, 36; U Mitter, 'Unconditional Manumission of Slaves in Early Islamic Law: A Hadith Analysis' in Hallaq (n 3) 115–52.

opinions, the Islamic religious scholars (*Foqaha*) emerged as a semi-autonomous institution beside the institution of the caliphate. Secondly, religious scholars had the opportunity to collect the sayings of the Prophet (*Ahadiths*). They laid down scholarly debates which led to the establishment of various Islamic schools of thought. This period is the genesis of Islamic jurisprudence or *fiqh*, including the foundation of the four schools of Sunni jurisprudence and the Shia school of jurisprudence. The four Sunni schools of law are known as Shafei, Hanafi, Maliki and Hanbali,[17] the Shia school included Jafari.[18]

It should be noted that the Muslim jurists at the time did not have the intention to create a specific or systematic school of thought or law. What they did was to take the opportunity of the relative freedom of opinion that existed after the collapse of the Umayyad Empire to initiate the development of the science of Islamic jurisprudence or *fiqh*. They articulated the system of inferring (*istinbat*) rules (which included legal principles) from the chief Islamic sources (the Quran and the Sunna). They used other mechanisms (such as *qiyas* or analogy) to infer rules of Islam in relation to human conduct. The jurists did not envisage to limit the Islamic schools of thought to specific, limited categories.[19] However, within the following two or three centuries, the development of Islamic jurisprudence became limited to these four Sunni schools of law and a few Shia schools, most notably, the Jafari school of thought.

From this period, the early eighth century, not only was the collection of Hadith, interpretation of the Quran and development of Islamic jurisprudence and law started gradually, also other sciences such as philosophy, *klam* (theology) and *irfan* (theosophy) were developed. The development of Islamic jurisprudence continued within the frameworks laid out by the founders of Islamic schools of thought.[20] Jurists who followed the Hanafi School based their research and scholarship on the foundations which were laid down by Imam Abu Hanifa, whereas those jurists who followed the Hanbali School based their work on the principles laid down by Imam Ahmad Ibn Hanbal. By contrast, there was no such division or schools of thought in relation to other Islamic sciences such as philosophy, theology and theosophy. As a result, from the eighth century onwards in Muslim societies (or indeed from the end of Righteous Caliphate in the late seventh century) the Muslim rulers had no religious authorities. Beside the government, the institution of *Foqaha* developed rather independently, but had significant interaction

[17] These schools are named after famous Muslim jurists of the 8th and 9th centuries AD: Imam Abu Hanifa (died in Bagdad 767); Imam Malik Ibn Anas (died in Medina 795); Imam Shafei (died in Egypt 820); Imam Ahmad Ibn Hanbal (died in Bagdad 855).

[18] Established by ImamJa'far Al-Sadiq (died in Medina 765).

[19] C Melchert, 'The Formations of the Sunni School of Law' in Hallaq (n 3) 351–66.

[20] Prior to the development of Islamic School of laws (from 8th to early 9th century), the caliphs would appoint governors (*wali*) for each Muslim territory and major towns and they would rule according to their interpretation of the Quran and oral-narrated Sunnah of the Prophet. During this period, some of the companions of the Prophet were either the caliphs or advisors to the rulers. No organised legal system existed yet.

with political authorities of Muslim societies. The institution of *Foqaha* or *Ulama* (jurists) developed based on one of the four schools of thought. However, at the same time, Islamic scholars developed theology, interpretation (of the Quran) philosophy and theosophy. Many Muslim scholars had expertise in more than one of those areas. For example, Imam Mohammad Ghazali (died 1111) was a Muslim *Faqih* but at the same time was also a theologian, philosopher and theosopher (mystic) whose ideas have influenced the Muslim world for the last millennium. However, out of various Islamic sciences, it was *fiqh* or jurisprudence which became the dominant area of scholarship within most Muslim societies up to the present day.

Fiqh generally means the study of Islam to find principles of the Sharia which includes law. Within the religion of Islam and Muslim societies, particularly from the eighteenth century, Sharia and the study of Sharia (*fiqh*) became dominant and *Foqaha* became the prominent scholars of Islam. This means that other Islamic scholars such as philosophers, theologians and theosophists, to some extent, gave way to the scholars of *fiqh*. Gradually, the pluralistic Islam of the eleventh to seventeenth centuries became a religion connected extensively with *fiqh* and legal dimension of the Sharia. This seems inconsistent with the religion which was revealed in eighth century AD. By the time of death of the Prophet, as well as according to the text of the Quran, law was a small percentage of Islam's teaching. But centuries after, *fiqh* became the dominant aspect of the religion of Islam. This is evident in the contemporary world where most other religions, such as Christianity, Buddhism and Hinduism are concerned with spiritual and personal matters of life, but Islam still has a unique and live legal system and provides rules for all aspects of human conduct. This will be discussed further below under the section on Religion and Law.

IV. Religion, *Fiqh*, Sharia and Law

A. Religion (*Din*)

The term used to refer to religion in the Quran is *din*.[21] To understand the religion of Islam one has to look at its original sources, particularly the Quran, and the experience and practice of the Prophet of Islam, his companions and followers from the early stage of Islam up to the present. As already discussed the text of the Quran, which is solely what was revealed to the Prophet Mohammed, includes very few rules relating to human conduct (less than 10 per cent). For the most part, the Quran is concerned with the divine nature of the universe (God), spirituality, rituals, creation of earth and heavens, the Day of Judgment, stories of the Prophets (similar to old testament and the Bible) and morality and ethics.

[21] The Quran 3:19, 5:3, 3:85.

In the classical term, the religion of Islam is considered to consist of two parts: *Al-Aqidah* (belief) and Sharia.[22] The belief in Islam includes *Tohid,* which means believing in only one God, the Prophethood of Prophet Mohammad and in a hereafter. The practice of the religion of Islam, since its advent in the seventh century, has developed in accordance with culture and customs of various societies who embraced this religion from Morocco to Indonesia and beyond.

In addition, *din* or religion of Islam, consists of a set of moral principles and rules known as *Akhlaq*. They are subject of a separate academic discipline and a major component of Islamic studies.[23] It includes categories such as *Akhlaq* relating to God, self, society, family, animal world and the environment. These moral and ethical principles of Islam, on which the Quran puts significant emphasis, were originally an important aspect of religion.[24] Gradually, over centuries, the Sharia and its study, the discipline of *fiqh*, became dominant in Islam, at the expense of shrinking the discipline of *Akhlaq*.

B. *Fiqh*

Fiqh is the study of that part of the religion which is concerned with rules of conduct for Muslims. This includes legal and religious duties as well as rituals. The word '*fiqh*' in Arabic means understanding. This word has been used in the Quran meaning deep understanding.[25] The Quran also refers to the understanding of the religion as *fiqh*.[26] There is also another term in Arabic known as *Usul Al-Fiqh* which refers to the methodology of Islamic jurisprudence. *Faqih* (singular of *Foqaha*) refers to a person who is an expert in *fiqh*. In English, '*fiqh*' is translated as Islamic jurisprudence and *Foqaha* is translated as Islamic jurists or Islamic scholars.

The term '*fiqh*' in Islamic scholarship refers to the study of Islam, particularly the study of the Quran, the Sunna and other secondary sources of law and religious principles, in order to infer both religious and legal principles. While religious and legal principles may overlap in most cases there may exist principles which are purely religious or legal. Examples of pure religious principles are many moral and recommended religious rules such as some of the rituals which are not mandatory but highly recommended.

[22] See eg M Shaltut, *Al-Islam, Aqida wa-Sharia* [*Islam: Belief and Sharia*], 17th edn (Cairo, Darshorouk, 2001).

[23] One of the earliest books discussing some aspects of Akhlaq was written by Imam Mohammad Ghazzali in the 11th century. It has been translated and republished in various languages and countries. See: M Gazzali, '*Kimiya-e Saadat*' [*The Alchemy of Happiness*], revised (New York, The Other Press, 2007).

[24] See eg the Quran 9:179; 49:11; 16:116; 3:180; 4:54.

[25] The Quran 63:3–7; 6:65; 6:98; 17:44.

[26] The Quran 9:122.

C. The Sharia

The Sharia, which is often referred to as Islamic law, is far more comprehensive than law. There is no exact translation of 'law' in Arabic or in the Quran. Even in modern Muslim countries, law schools are either translated as faculty of Sharia or faculty of *Hoquq*. The word *Hoquq* in Arabic means rights. The term Sharia in Arabic means, 'path to the waterhole' or the 'river'. Bernard Weiss explains the Sharia in the following words:

> The right path, the Sharia, constitutes an entire way of life. It embraces right ways of worshipping God, of interacting with fellow human beings, of conducting one's personal live, even of thinking and believing. The concept of the Sharia is the most comprehensive concept in Islam. Indeed, it forms the very core of Islam. The term Islam after all, means 'submission', and the Sharia is the divine delineation of the life of submission. To submit to God is to follow the path that God ordained, nothing more and nothing less. Even mysticism in Islam—the mysticism cultivated by Sufis—comes ultimately under the rubric of Sharia in that it represents its experimental dimension, its inner essence (*haqiqa*), its secrets (*asrar*).[27]

Generally, most Islamic jurists (*Foqaha*) divide the Sharia into three categories: *Ibadat* (rituals); *Moamilat* (commercial and personal transactions including family relations) and *Uqubat* (punishments or criminal law).[28] Therefore, Sharia has a greater meaning than Islamic law; it includes rituals such as rules relating to purity and washing, praying and fasting, and food and drink. However, as discussed below, no systematic and sharp distinction can be drawn between religion, the Sharia and law (at least in a classical sense).

D. Law

It is notable that the most significant part of the Sharia is concerned with what we categorise as legal principles. As can be seen out of four categories of topics of the Sharia, three of them are mainly concerned with modern legal matters. In classical and traditional Islamic texts on jurisprudence, the first chapters of texts known as *bab* or *kitab* are concerned with rituals followed by chapters on commercial transactions, property law, inheritance, mortgage, contracts etc. The text follows chapters on marriage, divorce and family law matters and the final chapters are generally concerned with criminal law matters.[29]

[27] B Weiss, *The Spirit of Islamic Law* (Georgia, University of Georgia Press, 2006) 17–18.

[28] According to Mohsen Kadivar, 'Islamic teachings can be divided into 4 categories namely beliefs, moralities, rituals and non-ritual Sharia, which is called jurisprudence of transactions (*fiq al Muamilat*); M Kadivar, 'Reconstruction of Wisdom: A Condition for Reconciling Religion and Human Rights' (16 May 2007) (unpublished paper presented at the Human Rights Conference, Mofid University, Qom, Iran, on file with the author.

[29] For more details on this, see WB Hallaq, *An Introduction to Islamic Law* (New York, Cambridge University Press, 2009) 29–30.

It should be noted that in the history of Muslim societies (from the seventh century up until now), there has also been a secular system operating alongside the Sharia. This secular system, known by different terms in various Muslim societies such as *qanun* or *siasah*, has been applied by various Muslim states throughout the history of Islam. For example, during the period of colonialisation of the Muslim world, colonial law operated beside the Sharia. Therefore, except in Saudi Arabia (which, owing to its significance as home to the holiest places in Islam), Sharia has often been applied alongside other legal systems and traditions. Even in Saudi Arabia, both in history (known as the Arabian Peninsula) and in the contemporary period (known as Saudi Arabia since early twentieth century), the Sharia has always been applied alongside tribal law and Arab customs. Thus, it is accurate to note that '[t]he Saudi legal and political system is based on three important components: traditional Islam (the Hanbali School of Law and the Wahhabi doctrine), tribal/monarchy structure, and modern institutions'.[30]

Therefore, as early as the time of the Righteous Caliphate (633–661 AD), when Islam expanded into the territories of the Persian and Roman Empires, the existing customs and laws of the local people blended with the principles of the Sharia. This is particularly important as many scholars of the Sharia (*Foqaha*) were not Arabs but were from surrendering societies including Persians, and others with Turkish or Indian origins. In both the Umayyad and Abassid caliphates as well as those dynasties which followed them, such as the *Mamlouks* and the Ottomans, foreign legal systems, or elements of them, were applied by the Muslim states and local authorities. The legal system of Islam borrowed many legal principles and institutions and was happy to adopt these as long as they were not inconsistent with the original principles of the Sharia concerning legal matters.

V. Law and Religion

The relationship between law and religion is one of the most controversial issues in the study of Islam. While Western legal scholarship and also parts of Islamic scholarship generally maintain that law and religion in Islam are the same, it is equally arguable that they are not. It depends mainly on the interpretation and application of Islam and on the approach to the religion of Islam in particular. In this section, various approaches to law and religion in Islam shall be reviewed.

A. Traditional and Classical Approach to Religion and Law

Western Islamic law scholars as well as traditional Islamic jurists, and many modern Islamic scholars consider law in Islam as part of a religious system (where

[30] H Esmaeili, 'On a Slow Boat Towards the Rule of Law: the Nature of Law in the Saudi Arabian Legal System' (2009) 26 *Arizona Journal of International and Comparative Law* 1, 6–38.

religious duties and legal principles are the same).[31] Within Islam, all human acts are divided into five categories. These categories are obligatory (*wajib*), recommended (*mustahabb* or *mamdouob*), permitted (*mubah*), disliked (*makrouh*) and forbidden (*haram*). The first category (obligatory) includes rituals such as praying five times a day as well as certain legal responsibilities such as maintenance of children by parents or observing the terms of contracts when individuals have entered into a contract. The second contrasting category is *haram* or forbidden acts such as drinking alcohol or breaching a contract without any good reason. Alongside these categories are two other classes. They are the classes of *mamdouob* or *mustahabb* and the class of *makrouh*. The first category includes activities which are recommended by the religion; however, they are short of being of obligatory nature, such as, respecting neighbours and helping people who are in need. Most of these activities are covered under *akhlaq* or moral principles of Islam. The second category, *markruh* or disliked, are those conducts which are not legally forbidden but are disliked by Islam, such as over-eating or too much sleeping etc. This category is also covered by the area of Islamic *akhlaq*. The fifth category includes all other activities, for which there are no rules under the Sharia and they are permitted (*mubah*). This category of conduct is legally indifferent under the Sharia.

This categorisation of all human activities and the nature of classical Sharia mean that the religion and law in Islam were, to a great extent, blended. According to Joseph Schacht,

> The central feature that makes Islamic religious law what it is, that guarantees unity in all its diversity, is the assessing of all human acts and relationships, including those which we call legal, from the point of view of the concepts of obligatory / recommended / indifferent / reprehensible / forbidden.[32]

Similarly, Noel Coulson states that in Islam, 'law is the command of God, the acknowledged function of Muslim jurisprudence and from the beginning, was simply the discovery of the terms of that command'.[33]

[31] 'Islam is a faith in the realm of the public. Sharia, the sacred law of Islam, regulates religious practice with a view of maintaining the individual's well-being though his or her social well-being. Hence, its comprehensive system deals with the obligations that humans perform as part of their relationship with the Divine Being as duties they perform as part of interpersonal responsibility. Public order must be maintained in worship, in the market place and all other areas of human interaction'; A Sachedina, 'Guidance or Governance? A Muslim Conception of "Two Cities"' (200) 68 *George Washington Law Review* 1079, 1079, quoted in H Esmaeili, 'The Nature and Development of Law in Islam and the Rule of Law Challenge in the Middle East and the Muslim World' (2011) 26 *Connecticut Journal of International Law* 329.

[32] J Schacht, *An Introduction to Islamic Law* (New York, Cambridge University Press, 1964) 200.

[33] NJ Coulson, *A History of Islamic Law* (Edinburgh, University Press, 1964) 75. According to Seyyed Hossein Nasr: 'In the Islamic perspective, Divine Law is to be implemented to regulate society and the actions of its members rather than society dictating what laws should be. The injunctions of Divine Law are permanent, but the principles can also be applied to new circumstances as they arise. But the basic thesis is one of trying to make the human order conform to the Divine norm, not vice-versa … As in Judaism, for Islam Divine Law is more central than theological thought to the religious life … Even those who have sought to go beyond the formal level, through the tariqa to the absolute Truth, which transcends all forms, have never ceased to revere the Sharia and to practice it. The greatest

B. Modern Approach to Religion and Law in Islam

Regardless of whether the comprehensive Sharia can be reintroduced in modern Muslim societies or not, there is a significant body of modern scholarship both inside and outside the Muslim world which argues that religion and law in Islam are not the same. They argue that while there are some legal elements in the Quran and other sources of Islamic law, the main objective of Islam was not to establish a legal system based on divine scripture. A number of Muslim scholars have argued that the Quran and the Sunna of the Prophet did not intend to establish a fixed legal system applicable to all societies for all time.

The earliest debate over the nature of Sharia and the Quran was started in the early ninth century by a theological Islamic group known as *Mutazila*. They argued that the Quran was not eternal but was created by God.[34] According to a contemporary Muslim commentator, the approach of *Mutazila* to religion was liberal.[35] Since then, Muslim scholars and jurists have developed various theories in relation to many aspects of religion of Islam, including the relationship between law and religion. Amongst the early Muslim jurists who adopted a rational approach to the interpretation of the Sharia where Ghazali,[36] Mawardi[37] and Ibn Khaldun.[38]

philosophers of Islam from Avicenna to Averroes practiced the sharia, so did the greatest saints and mystics'; in S Nasr, *The Heart of Islam: Enduring values for Humanity* (San Francisco, Harper, 2002) 117–19.

[34] In the history of Islam, there were a number of theological theories about the nature of God's message (*vahy*) and the Quran. They were Khavarej [Kharijits], Morjayoun [Murjiites], the Mutazili and the Asharit. The Kharijits had an extreme interpretation of religion, and their extreme interpretation faded in its early stage. The more moderate position of the Murjiites rejected any relationship between being a Muslim and committing sins. The Mutazili emphasised reason and logic, and the use of rational deduction as tools in interpretation of the Quran. During the theological debate amongst different schools of philosophical thought, the Mutazili took the position that the Quran, as the words of God, should not be considered literally. In contrast, according to Asharits, the words of the Quran were literal words of Allah and were eternal. See A Black, H Esmaeili and N Hosen, *Modern Perspectives on Islamic Law* (Cheltenham, Edward Elgar, 2013) 7. See also GC Anawati, 'Philosophy, Theology and Mysticism' in J Schacht and CE Bosworth (eds), *Legacy of Islam* (Oxford, Clarendon Press, 1974) 359–66; F Rahman, *Islam*, 2nd edn (Chicago, University of Chicago Press, 1966) ch 5; A Saeed, *Islamic Thought: Introduction* (London, Routledge, 2006) 14. For further discussion of the Mutazali, see NH Abu Zayd: *Al-Ittijah al-'Aqli fi al-Tafsir: dirasa fi qadiyyat al-magaz fi'l Quran 'ind'l Mu'tazilah [The Rational Trend in Exegesis: a Study of the Problem of Metaphor in the Quran by the Mu'tazilites]*, 4th edn (Beirut, Al-Markaz Al Thaqafi Al-Arabi, 2007).

[35] AA Engineer, 'On Developing Liberation Theology in Islam' in AA Engineer (ed), *Islamic and Revolution* (Delhi, Ajanta Publications, 1984) 15.

[36] Imam Muhammad Ghazali was a Persian theologian and Sufi who earned a place as one of the greatest Muslim scholars and had the title of the 'Renewer of Islam'. See generally WM Watt, *Muslim Intellectual: A Study of Al-Ghazali* (Cambridge, Cambridge University Press, 1963).

[37] Mawardi was a famous political theory scholar of the 11th century who laid down certain principles in relation to the function of the Islamic state and the Islamic caliphate. His famous book is titled *Al-Ahkam Al-Sultaniyeh*. See also H Mikhail, *Politics and Revelation: Mawardi and After* (Edinburgh, Edinburgh University Press 1995).

[38] Ibn Khaldun was a 14th century Muslim scholar, whose famous book is *Muqammah [The Introduction]*. He is a leading Muslim historian and sociologist who wrote on the nature of an Islamic state. See also Z Ahmad, *The Epistemology of Ibn Khaldun* (London, Routledge, 2003).

Shah Wali Allah (died 1762), an Indian Islamic scholar, attempted to reconcile Islamic legal principles with modern requirements. According to him, the Prophet of Islam never intended to universally apply a legal system that was designed for a specific society at a specific point in time (specifically, Arabia of the sixth century). Rather, he established a system and urged Muslims to follow his principles in establishing their own system of rules within the general spirit of Islam.[39] Allama Muhammad Iqbal was another great Indian Muslim scholar (1877–1938) who divided the history of human beings into two eras: a period when human beings were primarily governed by passion and instinct, and the period of experience and reason. He then argued that while passion and instinct are still part of human beings, the function of rational thinking and ideas opens up '[f]resh vistas of knowledge in the domain of man's inner experience'.[40] He viewed the Prophet of Islam as standing between the ancient and the modern worlds. He stated that the source of the revelation that the Prophet of Islam received belonged to the ancient world, but the spirit of the revelation is concerned with the modern world. According to Iqbal, as human beings have matured, the era of prophetic revelation is expired (as the Prophet Mohammed is the last Prophet of God–*khatamiat*) and humans must examine their religious experiences and shall discover the sources of knowledge, suitable to new directions.[41]

In more recent times, contemporary Muslim scholars have been debating the nature of *wahy* (revelation)[42] and the legal system of Islam. Apart from Shah Wali Allah and Iqbal, many contemporary Muslim jurists and scholars have also expressed views about the relationship between religion and more in Islam. Mahmoud Mohamed Taha argued that the portion of the Quran revealed to the Prophet in Mecca contains the real message of Islam (*iman* or faith), and should be given greater importance. He argued that the verses of the Quran revealed in Mecca, which were mainly concerned with believing in God, spiritual principles of Islam, and rituals, represented the spirit of Islam, as a faith, which should be followed by all Muslims at any time. However, the verses revealed in Medina, where the Prophet of Islam was in the process of establishing a political entity, were only applicable in their time and have no relevance in modern Islamic societies.[43]

[39] See generally M Al-Ghazali, *The Socio-Political Thought of Shah Wali Allah* (Islamabad, International Institute of Islamic Thought, 2001). See AM Iqbal, *The Reconstruction of Religious Thought in Islam* (Lahore, Institute of Islamic Culture, 1986) 136–42.

[40] Iqbal, *The Reconstruction of Religious Thought in Islam* (n 39) 101.

[41] Ibid 100–03.

[42] For a discussion of different contemporary views on the revelation of the Quran and an informative discussion of 'revelation' in Islam, see Saeed, *Islamic Thought: An Introduction* (n 34) ch 3. See also A Saeed, *Fazlur Rahman: A Framework for Interpreting the Ethico-Legal Content of the Quran* in S Taji-Farouki, *Modern Muslim Intellectuals and the Quran* (Oxford, Oxford University Press, 2004); A Gangi, *Rowshanfekriy Faqihaneh* [*Jurisprudential Intellectualism*] (unpublished manuscript) (on file with author).

[43] On Taha's doctrine, see MM Taha, *The Second Message of Islam* (Abdullahi Ahmed An-Na'im trans, New York, Syracuse University Press, 1996).

Abdullahi Ahmed An-Na'im, a contemporary Muslim scholar, sought to reconcile Islam and universal human rights, and Islam and secular states where the Sharia is not enforced coercively by states.[44] An-Na'im does not advocate the abandonment of Islamic tradition by Muslims; rather, he calls for the reformation of the religion in order to transform Islamic tradition into a viable and just culture in order to enable Muslims to exercise their human rights and the right to self-determination.[45] Mashood A Baderin summarises the Islamic legal theory of An-Na'im as follows:

> I have endeavoured to identify Abdullahi Ahmed An-Na'im's general philosophy on Islam and human rights as a three-angled philosophy, namely: (i) the philosophy for cross-cultural universality of human rights, (ii) the philosophy for internal reformation of Islamic law based on the methodology of his mentor *Ustadh* Mahmoud Mohamed Taha, and (iii) the philosophy for re-affirming secularism for Muslim states. Based on this three-angled philosophy, An-Na'im advocates a theory of interdependence between Islam, human rights and secularism through which he believes that Muslims should be able to practice their religion faithfully and at the same time enjoy the guarantees of human rights without hindrance.[46]

Khaled Abou Al-Fadhl is another contemporary Muslim scholar who tries to reconcile Islamic law and the modern challenges. Abou Al-Fadhl suggests that while God is perfect, Sharia, as understood and applied by human beings, is imperfect, contingent, and hence, should not be immune from examination and criticism. In his view, 'Sharia is not simply a collection of *ahkam* [a set of positive rules], but also a combination of principles, methodology, and a discursive process that searches for the Divine ideals. As such, Sharia is a work in progress that is never complete'.[47]

There are a number of contemporary legal scholars in Iran who strongly argue in favour of the separation of legal and religious institutions. Iran is one

[44] On An-Na'im's views, see a selection of his major works: AA An-Na'im, *Muslims and Global Justice* (Philadelphia, University of Pennsylvania Press, 2011); AA An-Na'im, *Islam and the Secular State* (Boston, Harvard University Press, 2008); AA An-Na'im (ed), *Human Rights in Cross-Cultural Perspectives: A Quest for Consensus* (Philadelphia, University of Pennsylvania Press, 1992); AA An-Na'im, *Toward an Islamic Reformation: Civil Liberties, Human Rights, and International Law (Contemporary Issues in the Middle East)* (New York, Syracuse University Press, 1996); and AA An-Na'im (MA Baderin ed), *Islam and Human Rights: Selected Essays of Abdullahi An-Na'im* (Aldershot, Ashgate Publishing Limited, 2010).

[45] AA An-Na'im, 'A Kinder, Gentler Islam?' (1991) 52 *Transition* 4, 11.

[46] An-Na'im, *Islam and Human Rights: Selected Essays of Abdullahi An-Na'im* (n 44) xxxviii.

[47] K Abou-El-Fadl, 'Islam and the Challenge of Democratic Commitment' (2003) 27(1) *Fordham International Law Journal* 2, 68. For K Abou-El-Fadl's major works, see K Abou-El-Fadl, *Rebellion and Violence in Islamic Law* (Cambridge, Cambridge University Press, 2001); K Abou-El-Fadl, *Speaking in God's Name: Islamic Law, Authority and Women* (Oxford, Oneworld Press, 2001); K Abou-El-Fadl, *The Place of Tolerance in Islam* (Boston, Beacon Press, 2002); K Abou-El-Fadl, *Islam and the Challenge of Democracy* (Princeton, Princeton University Press, 2004); K Abou-El-Fadl, *The Great Theft: Wrestling Islam from the Extremists* (New York, Harper San Francisco, 2005); K Abou-El-Fadl, *The Search for Beauty in Islam: Conference of the Books* (Lanham, Rowman & Littlefield Publishers Inc., 2006); K Abou-El-Fadl, *Reasoning with God: Reclaiming Shari'ah in the Modern Age* (Lanham, Rowman & Littlefield Publishers Inc, 2014).

of the few modern Muslim countries which have introduced a comprehensive Sharia legal system. Three notable contemporary Muslim Iranian scholars who have a modern and rational interpretation of law and religion in Islam include Abdolkarim Soroush, Mohammad Mojtahed Shabestari and Mohsen Kadivar. Soroush advocates an Islam with an emphasis on moral and ethical principles as well as spiritual strengths, and sees *fiqh* and legal aspects of the Sharia as the Prophet's historical experience in the context of the cultural, social and political environment of seventh-century Arabia.[48] Shabestari argues that the Prophet Mohammad was not a legislator, and the Quran is not a legal text.[49] According to Kadivar's approach, all principles of the Sharia must be scaled against justice and rationalism. Further, these principles must be examined and compared with other possible legal solutions, to ensure that they are the most reasonable legal principles.[50]

VI. Reviving the Sharia in Muslim Countries

It is notable that, historically, the Sharia was far from a legal system in a modern sense. As noted by Wael Hallaq, '[f]or over a millennium, and until the nineteenth century, the Sharia represented a complex set of social, economic, moral, educational, intellectual and cultural practices'.[51] For centuries, the Sharia was a pluralistic and advanced legal system, applicable in many territories in the Middle East, Africa and Asia. This was at the time when pre-common law England (before 1066) was ruled by sporadic Anglo-Saxon customs without any established legal system. However, from about the sixteenth century, and particularly by the Age of Enlightenment (early eighteenth century), the Muslim world was not advancing at the same pace as Europe in terms of philosophical thought, scientific progress, the development of political theories, the separation of church and state, and the widespread dissemination of ideas throughout society. Further, the colonisation of parts of the Muslim world, such as the Indian subcontinent and other Muslim territories in Asia and Africa, led to the sudden introduction of modern European legal systems and codes and the maintenance of only the personal law of the Sharia (such as family law, inheritance and wills) in Muslim countries. As a result, for

[48] A Soroush, *Bast Tajrobeh Nabavi* [*The Expansion of Prophetic Experience*] (Tehran, Serat Publishers 2006); English translation: A Soroush, *The Expansion of Prophetic Experience: Essays on Historicity, Contingency and Plurality in Religion* (N Mobasser ed, F Jahanbakhsh trans (Leiden, Brill Publishers, 2009).

[49] See M Mojtahed Shabestari, *Naqdi bar Qara'at Rasmi az Din* [*Examination of Prophetic Reading of Religion*] (Tehran, Tarh No, 2002); F Vahdat, 'Post-Revolutionary Islamic Modernity in Iran: The Inter-Subjective Hermeneutics of Mohamad Mojtahed Shabestari' in S Taji-Farouki (ed), *Modern Muslim Intellectuals and the Quran* (Oxford, Oxford University Press, 2004).

[50] M Kadivar, 'Human Rights and Intellectual Islam' in K Vogt, L Larsen and C Moe (eds), *New Directions in Islamic Thought: Exploring Reform and Muslim Tradition* (London, IB Tauris, 2009) 47–74.

[51] Hallaq, *An Introduction to Islamic Law* (n 29) 163.

about three centuries, the complex system of the Sharia was replaced by a narrow system of personal law, and was frozen in time without any major development. This can be explained by the situation of suppressed populations or of minorities worried about their identity and shying away from relinquishing cherished cultural traditions.

The attempts in the Muslim world since the late 1970s to revive the Sharia system, as a reaction against Western dominance, have failed. Only in Saudi Arabia, because of the location of two of the holiest shrines of the Muslim world, have foreign legal systems and codes never been imposed. However, even there, the modernisation and the development of the economy necessitated the introduction of a large body of law in relation to business and trade, administrative law, broadcasting and foreign investment, raising the question of separation of law and religion within the state.[52]

Since 1979, Iran has incorporated the application of the Sharia in its constitution. Some traditional and classical Sharia principles in areas such as criminal law, taxation and family law were introduced in the early 1980s. Since then, many Sharia principles have been the subject of reform as they have not been practically applicable. For example, for a short period, banks were required not to accept or give interest, but it soon turned out that the modern banking system of Iran needed to adapt to international practices and also operate on the basis of interest.[53] In Pakistan, the legal system went through a process of Islamisation under General Zia-ul-Haq (1979–88). As shall be considered in Chapter 6, this process created tension and impacted negatively on religious and other minorities in Pakistan and overall, politicised the legal and administrative institutions of Pakistan.[54] There have been some other limited attempts in Muslim countries such as Malaysia, Indonesia and Egypt, where some aspects of Islamic law have been revived and introduced.

While it is understandable that the Muslim world is entitled to involve the Sharia as part of its identity and rights, it seems that reviving the Sharia as a comprehensive legal, political and social system has not worked out well. To introduce traditional comprehensive Sharia, as has been attempted in a few Muslim countries, is as if European countries introduced Roman law as their legal system. There is no doubt that Roman law is the basis of continental European legal systems. However, reintroducing a classical legal system (which, at the time of its application, was glorious) may not be a promising option in a post-modern society. While

[52] See Esmaeili, 'On a Slow Boat Towards the Rule of Law' (n 30) 2; FE Vogel, *Islamic Law and Legal System: Studies of Saudi Arabia* (Leiden, Brill Publishers, 2000).

[53] See AE Mayer, 'Law and Religion in the Muslim Middle East' (1987) 35(1) *The American Journal of Comparative Law* 127; MS Khan and A Mirakhor, 'Islamic Banking: Experiences in the Islamic Republic of Iran and in Pakistan' (1990) 38(2) *Economic Development and Cultural Change* 353.

[54] See CH Kennedy, 'Repugnancy to Islam–Who Decides? Islam and Legal Reform in Pakistan' (1992) 41(4) *International and Comparative Law Quarterly* 769; R Peters, 'The Islamization of Criminal Law: a Comparative Analysis' (1994) 34(2) *Die Weld des Islams* 246; CH Kennedy, 'Islamization and Legal Reform in Pakistan, 1979–1989' (1990) 63(1) *Pacific Affairs* 62.

Islamic civilisation may still have a sense of competition with the Western world, some of the major achievements of the West in recent centuries in terms of philosophical thought, scientific progress, the development of international law and political theories, and the emergence of universal human rights principles, can be attributed to universal human achievements rather than specifically Western culture. Further, the Muslim world from the crusades period (eleventh to fifteenth centuries) up until the present time has contributed to the development of modern civilisations. Therefore, many modern legal principles, including international legal principles relating to human rights, democracy and the rule of law, are universal and may not be attributed only to the West.

Equating religion and law makes the legal principles of Islam sacred[55] and hence, immune from the evaluation and criticism which is common in modern secular legal systems through parliaments, the media and academic scholarship. Under traditional Sharia, Allah makes law, and God is the source of law-making through the Quran and the tradition of the Prophet. This means that while there would be room for interpretation of law to apply to new situations, some of the provisions contained in primary sources, such as in the Quran, for example hand amputation for robbery, cannot be evaluated, criticised and abandoned. In practice, while hand amputation, for the crime of stealing and robbery, is rarely applied in the law of Muslim countries, it is articulated in written codes of a few Muslim countries and is part of any traditional textbook of the Sharia. Furthermore, '[a]ccording to many traditional Islamic jurists (*foqaha*) rejecting or casting doubt on rules stated by the Quran or the Sunna in preference for modern positivist rules is considered an example of *kofr* (rejecting Islam by a Muslim) and is a crime under Islamic law', as noted by many contemporary Muslim jurists.[56]

The nature of societies and human interactions has changed since major religions were established. Modern societies, with the notion of the nation-state, various modern developments and the increase in populations and their diversity, are far different from the simple and homogenous societies of the past. The modern nation-state relies on the creation of legal principles and rules by the sovereign state, in accordance with day-to-day requirements of the society. Religious principles, on the other hand, are more or less fixed, and are difficult to revise and reform. In addition, the nature of religious legal principles and modern secular principles, to a great extent, are different as well. For example, *zakat* is the religious taxation in Islam. It was also applied as a state tax by Muslim states for centuries. *Zakat* as a religious donation is provided for a spiritual strengthening and divine rewards. However, as a state tax, it is imposed by the government, and humans, by nature, will try to use legal avenues to minimise their taxes. It is hardly imaginable for the government of a modern nation-state such as Iran or Saudi Arabia to operate without modern taxation systems, and instead operate solely on the notion of charitable *zakat*.

[55] Many scholars or Islamic law, including some Western Islamic law scholars, consider Islamic law as a sacred legal system. See eg Schacht, *An Introduction to Islamic Law* (n 32) 202.

[56] See eg S Al Sabiq, *Fiqh Al Sunna [The Sunni Jurisprudence]* vol 2 (Beirut, Darelfk, 1998) 304.

VII. An Islamic Perspective on the Rule of Law

A key question in the contemporary Muslim world is whether Muslim countries may be able to establish a functioning legal system based on the rule of law without abandoning core aspects of the Sharia and deviating from Islam. Within Muslim majority countries, there are not many well-established legal and political systems that incorporate an effective rule of law system in a modern sense.[57] As already discussed, Muslim scholars and jurists have developed various ideas and positions in relation to interpreting or reforming traditional Sharia principles in modern societies. Also, contemporary Muslim countries have taken various efforts to reform the Sharia and modernise their legal systems. While only Turkey has taken a strictly secular approach, in Malaysia and Indonesia, the former with a common law system and the latter with a civil law system, parliamentary democracy exists and elements of the rule of law are applicable while certain aspects of the Sharia are applicable as well. In Iran, Pakistan, Jordan, Kuwait, Egypt and the United Arab Emirates, parliamentary elections are held regularly. In Tunisia, many principles of the Sharia are reformed and interpreted in accordance with the rule of law and human rights.

However, it is necessary to recall that the modern concept of the rule of law was developed in the West as part of the doctrine of limited government, and the doctrine of separation of powers and constitutional governance.[58] As considered elsewhere in greater detail in this book, it was further articulated in the late nineteenth century, in the work of the English lawyer Albert Venn Dicey, who defined the rule of law as a system where the law is supreme against arbitrary exercise of power by influential individuals or the state.[59] Respect for the rule of law thus necessarily implies the limitation of power and discretion of the ruling elite. This is probably the best explanation for the reluctance against the effective implementation of the rule of law in some countries. Other reasons, such as the nature of Sharia law as religious law, in comparison to Western ideals of law,[60] are comparatively less convincing.

Nevertheless, it is argued here that the legal system of Islam in both theory and practice has the capacity to be reformed and interpreted in a way that would accommodate effective rule of law systems in Muslim countries.

[57] C Mallat, *Introduction to Middle Eastern Law* (Oxford, Oxford University Press, 2007); M Tessler and E Gao, 'Gauging Arab Support for Democracy' (2005) 16 *Journal of Democracy* 83, 84.

[58] I Shapiro, 'Introduction' in I Shapiro (ed), *The Rule of Law* (New York, New York University Press, 1994) 1–12.

[59] AV Dicey, *Introduction to the Study of the Law of the Constitution*, 10th edn (London, Macmillan and Co, 1964) 202.

[60] eg while traditional Sharia law is created by classical texts (the Quran and the Sunna) and through the work of Muslim jurists, law in Western tradition is produced through the process of social contracts or political process. See generally S Zifcak, 'Western and Islamic Conceptions of the Rule of Law' in A Azara and W Hudsom (eds), *Islam Beyond Conflict, Indonesian Islam and Western Political Theory* (Farnham, Ashgate, 2008) 31–40, 37.

First, Islamic jurisprudence, or *fiqh*, is a relatively well-developed system and takes a rather legalistic view of human beings and their conduct. There is generally high appreciation of the law within Muslim societies. The fact that the Sharia categorises every conduct of human beings and attempts to provide legal rules for every situation in life means that the centrality of law has a long tradition in Muslim cultures. This can be a positive aspect of the Sharia in terms of developing a rule of law system. Also, the Sharia was an effective and relatively more advanced legal system for centuries, well before the development of common law system in Europe and elsewhere. Various Islamic schools of law have developed and refined legal philosophies, jurisprudential theories and extensive legal principles for centuries.

Secondly, the Sharia, from its earliest stages of development in the seventh century, was a pluralistic system applicable in various Muslim territories and societies for centuries. Even in the contemporary world, there are over 55 Muslim majority countries in which elements of Islamic law are applicable, and a number of non-Muslim countries in which Islamic law may be applicable in certain legal spheres.

Thirdly, the fact that the Sharia evolved over centuries in various territories from Morocco to Indonesia, shows that the system is potentially open for reform and change. Indeed, *urf* or custom is a secondary source of Islamic law. Custom can be evolved and changed and hence legal principles may also be changed. The concept of *ijtihad* in Islamic jurisprudence is a suitable mechanism to enhance change and reform in Islamic law. It is a creative and comprehensive intellectual effort enabling jurists and scholars to drive legal principles on a given issue from the sources of Islamic law 'in the context of the prevailing circumstances of society'.[61] Fourthly, there is a tradition of interpretation of Islamic texts, including the Quran, within Islamic scholarship. This indicates that many principles and aspects of the Sharia may be reinterpreted in modern times. Finally, the Sharia has certain characteristics which suggest that Islamic law could accommodate at least a limited rule of law system.

As has already been analysed in Part I of this study, an important component of Islamic public law, expressly mentioned in the Quran, is the doctrine of *shura*.[62] The *shura* is a consultative process whereby the public choose their leaders and manage community affairs. The concept has been in place since the death of the Prophet Mohammad whereby *shura*, which included consultation and voting (*biat*), was used to elect early Muslim caliphs. Today, the concept of *shura* remains indoctrinated in the Iranian Constitution and provides a process for elections of both local and national governments, as well as the election of the Council of Experts who appoint the Supreme Leader. Additional Islamic concepts

[61] MH Kamali, *Shari'ah Law: An Introduction (Foundations of Islam)* (London, One World Publications, 2008) 165.

[62] The Quran 3:159 and 42:38. For further discussion of the role of *shura* in Islamic governance, see A Black, H Esmaeili and N Hosen, *Modern Perspectives on Islamic Law* (Cheltenham, Edward Elgar, 2013) 43–44.

that influence Muslim parliamentary democracies today include *ijma* (the source of law based on the consensus of Muslim jurists), *qiyas* (analogical reasoning), *irstihsan* (equity or juristic preference), *istishab* (presumptions of continuity), *sadd al-dharai* (blocking the means),[63] *maslahah* (expediency as a source of law) and *masalah mursalah* (public policy).[64] According to Ghazali, the objective of the Sharia is to protect five essential values which are religion, life, intellect, lineage (ancestry), and property and *masalah* protect those values.[65] It is notable that in the seventh century the best way to protect lineage was to prescribe civil punishment for adultery or the best way to protect property was to prescribe corporal punishment for stealing and robbery. However, in the contemporary world there are other means to protect property and to ensure lineage which are much more effective than severe punishment. Ancestry was an important element of the tribal nature of the seventh century perhaps as important as the right to citizenship in the modern world. Today, there are other methods of ensuring the right to citizenship or freedom of movement. According to the majority of Muslim scholars, the doctrine of *masalah mursalah* is a proper ground for legislation in an Islamic legal system.[66]

VIII. Conclusions

The origin of the legal system of Islam goes back to the early seventh century, but the system developed into a number of schools of law later in the mid-ninth century. Islamic law was not established as an innovative or revolutionary system. Rather, as a legal system it developed gradually and its early rules were mainly based on the then prevalent Arab, Jewish and Christian cultures of the seventh-century Arabian society. Indeed, the Prophet of Islam, and the Quran, adopted and applied some of the existing legal principles of the time based on the best available values, customs and reasons of the time. It is arguable that Islam left the law-making process to the wisdom, cultures and values of the time in each society. This means that Islam did not intend to impose the custom, values and certain laws of seventh-century Arab societies to the rest of the world for ever.

Later, the system was developed predominantly by the works of Muslim jurists, and was applied in Muslim territories as the dominant legal system. This

[63] The doctrine of *Sadd al-dharai* allows Muslim jurists or Islamic authorities to prohibit certain acts that may lead to crimes and corruption (preventative measures). In practice, this doctrine can be used in expanding the powers of the state, but it may give flexibility in making and un-making of Islamic legal rules. For further discussion of the principles and other principles mentioned here, see MH Kamali, *Principles of Islamic Jurisprudence* (Cambridge, The Islamic Texts Society, 2003) ch 16.

[64] J Esposito, 'Practice and Theory' in KA El Fadl et al (eds), *Islam and the Challenge of Democracy* (Princeton, Princeton University Press, 2004) 93–100, 96.

[65] AH Mohammed Ghazali, *Al Mustafa Min Ilm Al-Usul [Principles]* vol 1, (Cairo, al-Maktabah al-Tijariyyah, 1937) 139–40.

[66] Kamali, *Principles of Islamic Jurisprudence* (n 63) 352.

continued until the start of the colonial period in the nineteenth century, when colonial law (both civil law and common law systems) entered Muslim territories and, to a great extent, replaced the ailing Islamic law systems.

In Western literature, Islamic law and the Sharia are used frequently interchangeably. However, the terms 'Islam', 'Sharia' and 'Islamic Law' have different meanings. 'Sharia' refers to the system of Islamic beliefs, rituals and law. *Fiqh,* which is translated into English as 'Islamic Jurisprudence', refers to the study of sources of the Sharia in order to infer principles of Islam in relation to rituals, beliefs and law. There is, nevertheless, the issue of the relationship between law, beliefs and rituals (law and religion) in Islam.

The relationship between law and religion in Islam involves complex considerations both in terms of theory and practice. While in many areas, law and religion may overlap, the nature, methodology and application of the rules may not be the same. Numerous Muslim scholars have made proposals of how to explain and to apply the distinction between legal and religious norms in Islam. There is therefore no obstacle, in principle, for the practice of states to introduce legal systems in which religion and law are not identical.

While there are elements of democracy and the rule of law in many Muslim countries, the majority of Muslim states lack effective rule of law systems where governments and powerful individuals are subject to clear and effective legal principles. However, this study has argued that for the reasons discussed above, the rule of law systems can be recognised in a modernised and reformed Islamic legal system.

4

The Rule of Law and International Law

I. Introduction

The concept of the rule of law, as discussed in Part I above, emanates from the establishment of ideal governance models. The hierarchical structure between the ruler and the citizenry gains significance as does the issue of exercise of state power in relation to its citizens. The primary question investigated in this chapter is whether the rule of law is also applicable within international law–a system which operates without hierarchical structures and centralised authorities: since the Peace of Westphalia, all states have been recognised as being sovereign and equal, linked to each other via horizontal legal relationships. With regard to these characteristics, one might prima facie suggest the absence of the rule of law in international law.

However, it would be tantamount to denying the existence of public international law as such to assert that states can act arbitrarily at their own will and that they are not bound by any legal obligation.[1] Furthermore, it has to be noted that international law has diverged from its focus on state sovereignty and has shifted its focus towards strengthening the protection of the individual. It increasingly requires of states that authority is exercised in a way that preserves human dignity and fundamental human rights.[2] Yet, monitoring and enforcing these obligations remains a challenge in view of the horizontal structure of international relations and of the defective observance of human rights in almost all countries.[3]

In the present context, analysing the rule of law in international law is warranted for several interesting similarities with Islamic law. Both are prima facie not easily amenable for adopting this concept.[4] The similarities include the

[1] HLA Hart, *The Concept of Law*, 3rd edn (Oxford, Clarendon Press, 2012) 211–37.

[2] MS Ellis, 'Islamic and International Law: Convergence of Conflict?' in AM Emon, MS Ellis and B Glahn (eds), *Islamic Law and International Human Rights Law: Searching for Common Ground?* (Oxford, Oxford University Press, 2012) 91–103, 92.

[3] H Corell, 'Commentary to Sharia and the Modern State and Narrating Law' in Emon, Ellis and Glahn. Ibid 82, 83.

[4] MK Masud, 'Clearing Ground: Commentary to "Sharia and the Modern State"' in Emon, Ellis and Glahn. Ibid 104–14, 112.

question as to who has the authority to legislate, enforce, and adjudicate. Both systems are decentralised, and the separation of powers is incomplete. In the case of international law, treaties (conventions, agreements), customary law and general principles of law represent the primary sources of law. In the case of the Sharia, in addition to the Quran and the Sunna, the consensus amongst jurists, mostly in the form of schools of law (*madhab*), plays an important role. As regards authorities to enforce and adjudicate, the situation is not clearer. Plurality and variety of institutions with sometimes overlapping or parallel competences are characteristic in both areas of law. Finally, both have in common that legal obligations are binding, but not necessarily enforceable. It follows that both, international law and Islamic law, face considerable challenges when measured against the criteria developed in Part I above. In front of this background it shall be examined to what extent, as one commentator put it, '[i]nternational law today is [...] a "rule of law" project. Similarly, Sharia is also a "rule of law" concept.'[5]

II. Application of the Rule of Law within International Law and International Organisations

One of the early references to the rule of law in international relations can be found in the Preamble of the 1970 Declaration on Principles of International Law concerning Friendly Relations and Co-operation among States, which emphasised the importance of 'promoting the rule of law among nations'.[6] In the 2000 Millennium Declaration, the members of the United Nations resolved to 'strengthen respect for the rule of law in international as in national affairs'.[7] They called in particular, 'to ensure compliance by Member States with the decisions of the International Court of Justice, in compliance with the Charter of the United Nations, in cases to which they are parties'.[8] That the rule of law henceforth should be a guiding principle for the work of the United Nations, in particular in post-conflict scenarios, was explained in detail in the UN Secretary-General's Report on 'The rule of law and transitional justice in conflict and post-conflict societies' in 2004.[9] This report emphasised that 'the maintenance of peace in the long term cannot be achieved unless the population is confident that redress for grievance can be

[5] Ibid 112.

[6] Declaration on Principles of International Law Concerning Friendly Relations and Co-operation Amongst States in Accordance with the Charter of the United Nations (1970) GA Res 2625 (XXV) (1970).

[7] United Nations Millennium Declaration (2000) GA Res 55/2, UN Doc A/55/2 (2000), para 9.

[8] Ibid.

[9] Report of the Secretary-General on 'The Rule of Law and Transitional Justice in Conflict and Post-Conflict Societies', UN Doc S/2004//616 (23 August 2004).

obtained through legitimate structures for the peaceful settlement of disputes and the fair administration of justice'.[10]

The official definition of the concept of the rule of law by the United Nations contains both formal and substantive aspects which a system of law should respect and implement.[11] The United Nations World Summit in September 2005 then underlined the need for 'universal adherence to and implementation of the rule of law at both the national and international levels' and reaffirmed its commitment to

an international order based on the rule of law, which is essential for peaceful coexistence and cooperation among States'.[12] The member states recognised that rule of law was equally essential 'for sustained growth, sustainable development and the eradication of poverty and hunger.[13]

The United Nations joins forces in promoting the rule of law at the national and international levels by its Rule of Law Coordination and Resource Group.[14] It aims to assist national efforts to re-establish the rule of law in conflict and post-conflict societies drawing on existing staff within the United Nations system.[15] In this context, establishing respect for the rule of law is regarded as fundamental for achieving a durable peace in the aftermath of conflict, to the effective protection of human rights, and to sustained economic progress and development.[16] The principle that everyone–from the individual right up to the state itself–is accountable to law that is publicly promulgated, equally enforced and independently adjudicated, is accentuated as 'a fundamental concept'.[17]

The General Assembly declared that the 'rule of law', as well as 'human rights' and 'democracy' belong to the 'universal and indivisible core values and principles of the United Nations'.[18] The 2006 report of the Secretary-General about the United Nations' support for the rule of law emphasised the normative foundation for the United Nations' assistance, namely the Charter of the United Nations, together with the 'four pillars of the modern international legal system–international human rights law, international humanitarian law, international

[10] Ibid para. 2.

[11] See the definition in the 2004 Report of the Secretary-General (n 23) para 6.

[12] World Summit Outcome, Resolution 60/1 adopted by the General Assembly on 16 September 2005, UN Doc A/RES/60/1 (24 October 2005) para 134.

[13] Ibid para 11.

[14] See www.un.org/ruleoflaw/un-and-the-rule-of-law.

[15] See the Secretary-General's proposal in his report 'In Larger Freedom: Towards Development, Security and Human Rights for All'. UN Secretary-General 'In Larger Freedom: Towards Development, Security and Human Rights for All' (21 March 2005) UN Doc A/59/2005 para 137.

[16] See www.un.org/en/ruleoflaw.

[17] Ibid.

[18] See The Rule of Law at the National and International Levels adopted on 4 December 2006, GA Res 61/39 (4 December 2006) UN Doc A/RES/61/39; see also The Rule of Law at the National and International Levels adopted on 6 December 2007 GA Res 62/70 (6 December 2007) UN Doc A/RES/62/70; The Rule of Law at the National and International Levels adopted on 11 December 2008, GA Res 63/128 (11 December 2008) UN Doc A/RES/63/128; The Rule of Law at the National and International Levels adopted on 6 December 2010 GA Res 65/32 (6 December 2010) UN Doc A/RES/65/32.

criminal law and international refugee law–and the wealth of the United Nations human rights and crime prevention and criminal justice standards'.[19]

In his report of 2008, the Secretary-General emphasised that '[s]trengthening the rule of law is a difficult, complex and long-term task, the success of which depends on the commitment of the national communities with whom the United Nations works'.[20] He pointed out that no rule of law programme could be successful in the long term if imposed from the outside and that political will on the part of national authorities was essential.[21] As regards concrete support at the national level, the Secretary-General underlined that the United Nations worked to support legal frameworks, such as a constitution or its equivalent; a clear and consistent legal framework, and implementation thereof; strong institutions of justice, governance, security and human rights that are well-structured, financed and equipped; transitional justice processes and mechanisms; and a public and civil society that contributes to strengthening the rule of law and holding public officials and institutions accountable. These were the norms, policies, institutions and processes that form the core of a society in which individuals felt safe and secure; where disputes were settled peacefully and effective redress was available for harm suffered, and where all who violate the law, including the state itself, were held accountable.[22]

In his 2011 report on the rule of law, the Secretary-General referred explicitly to the profound political changes that have occurred in the Middle East and North Africa in response to popular calls for greater accountability, transparency and the rule of law.[23] This threw into sharp relief the importance of United Nations engagement in an ongoing process to promote the rule of law at the national and international levels. The report pointed out that the United Nations meanwhile provided rule of law assistance in over 150 member states[24] but that it faced considerable challenges in this endeavour. It highlighted the need to foster the political will and leadership necessary to make rule of law a national priority and advance reform efforts; and the lack of overall coordination among relevant national and international actors.[25] The report is complemented by a number of statements of member states, including Islamic states, which express their commitment towards the rule of law and tell about their achievements as regards compliance with those premises.[26]

[19] Report of the Secretary-General on 'Uniting Our Strengths: Enhancing United Nations Support for the Rule of Law' (14 December 2006) UN Doc A/61/636–S/2006/980, para 12.

[20] Report of the Secretary-General on 'Strengthening and Coordinating United Nations Rule of law Activities' (14 October 2008) UN Doc A/63/226, para 19.

[21] Ibid.

[22] Ibid.

[23] Report of the Secretary-General on 'Strengthening and Coordinating United Nations Rule of Law Activities' (8 August 2011) UN Doc A/66/133, para 1.

[24] Ibid para 2.

[25] Ibid para 4.

[26] See eg the statements submitted by the governments of Oman, Qatar and Turkmenistan, 50–51, 67–70.

The latest report of the Secretary-General on the rule of law of 2015 highlighted the role of multilateral treaties in promoting and advancing the rule of law.[27] It pointed out that institutional structures, such as conferences or meetings of the parties, treaty secretariats or other bodies, created by multilateral treaties, were increasingly involved in the interpretation and application of treaties. In this context, the important role of international human rights treaties, in particular the acceptance of the individual complaints procedure, and the work of the human rights treaty bodies, including their publications of General Comments, was emphasised.

With respect to international courts and tribunals, the Secretary-General referred to his ongoing campaign to increase acceptance of the compulsory jurisdiction of the International Court of Justice, which aims at bringing attention to its special role in international dispute resolution.[28] The report also highlighted the work of international and hybrid criminal courts and tribunals in the prosecution of international crimes and grave human rights violations.[29] In this respect, it also underlined the work of the United Nations High Commissioner for Human Rights (OHCHR) to support commissions of inquiry or to conduct investigations of allegations of serious violations of human rights and international humanitarian law.[30] The United Nations also actively engaged in support for the rule of law at the national level and sought to enhance member states' capacities in implementing international norms and standards.[31]

This brief overview highlighting developments concerning the efforts of the United Nations with regard to the strengthening of the rule of law shows that there is a general consensus in the United Nations and its members that the rule of law is a vital concept for the well-being of states, societies and individuals. It is referred to as an essential element for their independence and prosperity at the national and at the international levels and for achieving justice and peace. Nevertheless, the implementation of and compliance with the above-mentioned principles, both at the national and at the international level, remains a major challenge. A lot of effort by the UN institutions and national actors is necessary in order to address them.[32]

[27] Report of the Secretary-General on 'Strengthening and Coordinating United Nations Rule of Law Activities' (27 July 2015) UN Doc A/70/206, paras 2–20.

[28] Ibid para 22.

[29] Ibid paras 24–28.

[30] Ibid para 29.

[31] Ibid para 32.

[32] This includes, in particular, the UN Security Council as is pointed out by the Final Report of the Austrian Initiative to examine the role of the Security Council in strengthening a rules-based international system. S Chesterman, *The Role of the Security Council in Strengthening a Rules-based International System. Final Report and Recommendations from the Austrian Initiative*, 2004–2008 (Austrian Federal Ministry for European and International Affairs, Vienna, 2008)https://www.researchgate.net/publication/30505404_The_UN_Security_Council_and_the_Rule_of_Law.

III. Rule of Law and Specific UN Organs

The need for adherence to the rule of law in the activities of the United Nations has for a long time concentrated on the principle of legality in criminal matters. Considering that the Tribunals of Nuremberg and Tokyo of 1945 were regarded as problematic in this respect, the ad hoc criminal tribunals established by the UN Security Council for the former Yugoslavia in 1991 and Rwanda in 1994 have not remained unchallenged, either. The challenges were specifically based on the rule of law concepts of *nullum crimen sine lege* and *nulla poena sine lege* and had already been spelled out clearly by the Permanent Court of International Justice in an Advisory Opinion when it had to deal with the 'Creation of Law by the Application of Penal Laws by Analogy', which the Court rejected outright as not in line with the '*Rechtsstaat*, State governed by the rule of law'.[33]

It is therefore understandable that in the first report on 'The Rule of Law and Transitional Justice in Conflict and Post-Conflict Societies' of 2004,[34] the Secretary-General pointed out how the United Nations itself could strengthen the rule of law in the activities mandated or endorsed by its organs, including ad hoc and hybrid criminal tribunals and the International Criminal Court. The Secretary-General highlighted that 'United Nations norms and standards have been developed and adopted by countries across the globe and have been accommodated by the full range of legal systems of Member States, whether based in common law, civil law, Islamic law, or other legal traditions'.[35] These norms and standards therefore had legitimacy which could not be denounced as exported national models. The United Nations must comply with these standards in its own activities, which means, in particular:

> These standards also set the normative boundaries of United Nations engagement, such that, for example, United Nations tribunals can never allow for capital punishment, United Nations-endorsed peace agreements can never promise amnesties for genocide, war crimes, crimes against humanity or gross violations of human rights, and, where we are mandated to undertake executive or judicial functions, United Nations-operated facilities must scrupulously comply with international standards for human rights in the administration of justice.[36]

With regard to peace operations, several missions, most importantly transitional missions in Kosovo and Timor-Leste, but also the more recent United Nations Mission in Liberia and the Stabilisation Mission in Haiti, had important rule of

[33] *Consistency of Certain Danzig Legislative Decrees with the Constitution of the Free City of Danzig*, Permanent Court of International Justice, Advisory Opinion of 4 December 1935, Series A/B No 65, at 54.

[34] See Report of the Secretary-General on 'The Rule of Law and Transitional Justice in Conflict and Post-Conflict Societies' (n 9).

[35] Ibid para 10.

[36] Ibid.

law components reflecting and re-enforcing the organisation's emphasis on this aspect. The Secretariat included support for rule of law and transitional justice aspects of peace operations in mission planning, selection and deployment of specialised staff and provision of guidance.[37] However, owing to time constraints and limited personal and financial resources, these challenges were not always easy to meet and would have needed more support from member states.[38]

As regards the Security Council, compliance with the ideal of the rule of law seems to be even more difficult to achieve. With respect to the debate on the new concept of 'Responsibility to Protect' in the 2005 World Summit Outcome document,[39] the question was raised whether this would introduce a legal duty 'not to veto' in the Security Council in case national authorities were manifestly failing to protect their populations from genocide, war crimes, ethnic cleansing and crimes against humanity. While some academic commentators have identified such a legal duty,[40] in reality, voting behaviour in the Security Council continued to be regarded as a political and sovereign matter. The Security Council therefore still appears to enjoy almost unfettered discretion.[41] Nevertheless, in its solemn declaration on '[t]he promotion and strengthening of the rule of law in the maintenance of international peace and security' of 2014, the Security Council emphasised 'the importance of the rule of law as one of the key elements of conflict prevention, peacekeeping, conflict resolution and peace building'.[42] This can signify that, as a matter of principle, the Security Council does not consider itself above the law, but instead as forming an integral part of the rule of law efforts and considerations when it comes to the protection and maintenance of international peace and security within the framework of the United Nations. This means that, at least, well-reasoned decisions can be expected which explain its interpretation and application of the rule of law at the international level.[43]

The promotion of the rule of law by the United Nations naturally lies also in the hands of the International Court of Justice. As is well known, the jurisdiction of the Court is subject to the consent of the respective UN members. In the 2005 World Summit Outcome Document, under the title of 'Rule of Law', the heads of state and government recognised 'the need for universal adherence to and

[37] Ibid para 12.

[38] Ibid para 13.

[39] World Summit Outcome (n 11) para 139.

[40] See eg A Peters 'Humanity as the A and Ω of Sovereignty' 20 *European Journal of International Law* (2009) 513; see also J-F Thibault, 'La Responsabilité de Protéger: Une Dette pour la Communauté Internationale?' in U Mathis-Moser (ed), *Responsibility to Protect. Peacekeeping, Diplomacy, Media, and Literature Responding to Humanitarian Challenges* (Innsbruck, Innsbruck University Press, 2012) 35–51; A Blätter and P Williams, 'The Responsibility Not to Veto' (2011) 3 *Global Responsibility to Protect* 301.

[41] K Keith, 'The International Rule of Law' (2015) 28 *Leiden Journal of International Law* 403, 411.

[42] See eg 'Statement by the President of the Security Council' (2014) UN Doc S/PRST/2014/5.

[43] In this sense, see also Peters, 'Humanity as the A and Ω of Sovereignty' (n 40) 543–44; Keith, 'The International Rule of Law' (n 41) 416.

implementation of the rule of law at both the national and international levels' and also recognised

> the important role of the International Court of Justice, the principal judicial organ of the United Nations, in adjudicating disputes among States and the value of its work, call upon States that have not yet done so to consider accepting the jurisdiction of the Court in accordance with its Statute and consider means of strengthening the Court's work […].

However, as of 2016, only 72 out of the 193 member states have accepted the compulsory jurisdiction of the Court.[44] Only one of them is a permanent member of the Security Council, the United Kingdom, even though all of them have an unwritten right to nominate one of the 15 judges.[45] This can be regarded as a decline of the acceptance of the rule of law at the international level in comparison to 1948, when 60 per cent of the membership, including four of the five permanent members were among the acceptances.[46]

It follows from the above that, while the United Nations has strengthened its efforts in the conceptual development and operative promotion of the rule of law, these efforts are primarily directed towards the national level and the implementation of justice by local courts and administrations, in particular in post-conflict and transitional situations. In various programmes, projects, initiatives and operations, the rule of law has become a new focus. It is regarded as a necessary complement to the promotion of human rights and democracy. Yet, when it comes to the application of the rule of law to the United Nations organs themselves, the development does not follow at the same pace. To the contrary, some aspects, such as the acceptance of the competence of the International Court of Justice, have even developed in the opposite direction. This shows that the rule of law still faces considerable challenges in decentralised systems characterised by political and cultural diversity.

IV. Rule of Law and the Organisation of Islamic Cooperation

The Organisation of Islamic Cooperation was founded in 1969 and currently operates under the new Charter of 2008.[47] As an international organisation with currently 57 member states it has accepted and adopted the concept of sovereign

[44] See International Court of Justice, Declarations Recognizing the Jurisdiction of the Court as Compulsory, www.icj-cij.org/jurisdiction/index.php?p1=5&p2=1&p3=3.

[45] Although there is no entitlement to membership on the part of any country, the Court has always included judges of the nationality of the permanent members of the Security Council. See International Court of Justice, Members of the Court, www.icj-cij.org/court/index.php?p1=1&p2=2.

[46] Keith (n 41) 407, referring to the *Yearbook of the International Court of Justice* of 1948–49, 138–48.

[47] The Charter of 2008 was the result of a reform process launched by the 'Ten Year Programme of Action', see further below.

states which cooperate on the basis of equality and international law.[48] The need to accommodate the realities of international relations made it necessary to adapt the traditional concept of the unified Muslim constituency, the *umma*, which constituted one community bound by only one law, the sacred law of the Sharia.[49] The OIC Charter provides in its Preamble:

> In the name of Allah, the most Compassionate, the most Merciful We the Member States of the Organisation of the Islamic Conference, determined:
>
> [...] to be guided by the noble Islamic values of unity and fraternity, and affirming the essentiality of promoting and consolidating the unity and solidarity among the Member States in securing their common interests at the international arena;
>
> to adhere our commitment to the principles of the United Nations Charter, the present Charter and International Law;
>
> [...] to promote human rights and fundamental freedoms, good governance, rule of law, democracy and accountability in Member States in accordance with their constitutional and legal systems [...][50]

These references to Islamic principles, the United Nations, international law and the rule of law in the same document show that, as a matter of principle, the member states of the OIC do not see a problem of combining Islamic values with the concept of the rule of law. Their commitment in this respect is reaffirmed in Chapter 1 on 'Objectives and Principles', where Article 2, paragraph 7, asks the member states to 'uphold and promote, at the national and international levels, good governance, democracy, human rights and fundamental freedoms, and the rule of law'.[51]

A number of member states of the OIC appear very supportive of the concept of the rule of law. The statement provided by the government of Oman in the context of the UN Secretary-General's Report of 2011 on the rule of law is particularly pronounced in this respect:

> The Government of Oman would like to express its thanks and appreciation for the efforts made by the United Nations, and all of the committees, to instil the principle of the rule of law at the national and international levels. The Government would like to take this opportunity to affirm that the rule of law is one of its top priorities at the national level. This principle is an essential cornerstone of the legislation currently in force, and guides the authorities responsible for applying the law and the judicial authorities responsible

[48] The acceptance of the 'Westphalian system' consisting of a plurality of sovereign states is not rooted in Islamic law where the *umma* (the world community of Muslims) has traditionally been regarded as the original and ideal polity for Muslims. Today, the Muslim world has accepted and adopted the system of a plurality of sovereign states and supports, in particular, the related principles, such as the principle of non-intervention and of sovereignty over natural resources. See M Khadduri 'Islam and the Modern Law of Nations' (1956) 50 *American Journal of International Law* 358.

[49] According to Khadduri, the emergence of Muslim national states after the break-up of the Ottoman Empire and the dissolution of the caliphate in 1924 was probably the most significant landmark in the development of Islamic polity since its formative period. Ibid 370.

[50] See the website of the OIC: www.oic-oci.org/page/?p_id=53&p_ref=27&lan=en.

[51] Ibid.

> for prosecuting offenders. At the international level, Oman, just as all other countries in the world, strives to make the rule of law one of the principles that govern its relations with other States and with regional and international organizations. It should be noted that Oman considers international instruments, which are the primary source of international law, as having the force of law once they have been ratified by His Highness the Sultan, in accordance with Constitutional requirements (article 75 of the Basic Law of the State). Should Omani law conflict with a duly ratified international instrument, the latter has priority, making such instruments subordinate only to the Basic Law.
>
> Oman agrees with those countries that call for universal adherence to the rule of law and for its application at the international and national levels, whether in time of conflict or in post-conflict situations, because that is indispensable to achieving the noble goals to which the international community aspires, including stability, which lays the ground for economic growth, sustainable development, combating crime, eradicating poverty, hunger and disease and diminishing the effects thereof, and mitigating the impact of wars and armed conflicts. Oman believes that, in order for there to be justice for all, everyone must be equal before the law. It further believes it is essential that the rule of law not be used as an instrument of political blackmail because such use would surely bring about results that are contrary to the rule of law.[52]

Similarly, the government of Qatar declared:

> Qatar strives to foster the rule of law at the national and international level, both in the context of the United Nations and through bilateral or multilateral cooperation with Member States. The principle of the rule of law is affirmed in the Constitution and criminal laws of Qatar; it is also applied by the competent courts.[53]

Supportive of the United Nations and its initiatives on the rule of law, the government of Turkmenistan also included an overview over its ongoing legislative reform:

> In line with Turkmenistan's programme of radical reform and transformation, President Gurbanguly Berdimuhamedov has proclaimed as one of the Government's priority tasks the improvement of the legal framework of the State and the alignment of the country's law with universally recognized international standards. The process of updating the relevant legislation of Turkmenistan is currently in progress.[54]

V. The Independent Commission on Human Rights (IPHRC)

In order to implement the concept of the rule of law in the various OIC member states, a close interaction with domestic law and politics is necessary. In

[52] See Report of the Secretary-General on 'Strengthening and Coordinating United Nations Rule of Law Activities' (n 23) 50.

[53] Ibid 50.

[54] Ibid 67.

Muslim majority states, Islam has to be considered as an important factor in this interaction.[55] The implementation of the rule of law at the national level hinges on the question to what extent it is accepted and understood by the population at large. The citizens in Muslim states are the main addressees as beneficiaries and actors; without their support and agency, the rule of law cannot be implemented despite solemn declarations by their governments.

In 2005, the OIC, in order to meet the challenges of the twenty-first century, called upon member states to take joint actions 'to revive the Muslim Ummah's pioneering role as a fine example of tolerance and enlightened moderation and a force for international peace and harmony' and adopted its 'Ten-Year Programme of Action'.[56] Despite its size as the second largest organisation after the United Nations, the OIC had not succeeded in being recognised and established as an important player at the international scene for a long time. The reasons included its very diverse membership which resulted in conflicting interests, the lack of political will, the lack of an independent executive, and financial difficulties.[57] The 'Ten-Year Programme of Action' aimed at the reform and modernisation of the organisation. It introduced a clear focus on universal human rights and the importance of mainstreaming them into all programmes and activities.[58]

The first visible outcome was the establishment of 'The Independent Permanent Commission on Human Rights' (IPHRC), the main scope and objectives of which are contained in Article 15 of the revised OIC Charter of 2008:

> The Independent Permanent Commission on Human Rights shall promote the civil, political, social and economic rights enshrined in the organisation's covenants and declarations and in universally agreed human rights instruments, in conformity with Islamic values.[59]

The new commission was entrusted with the promotion of human rights 'in conformity with Islamic values'. Whether this should be a restriction or, on the contrary, an affirmation of the aforementioned human rights is not entirely clear and needs interpretation. The enumeration of various human rights texts, on the one hand, OIC's covenants and declarations and, on the other, the universally agreed human rights instruments, without any order of priority does not provide a unequivocal answer to this question.

[55] M Baderin, 'Introduction' in M Baderin (ed), *International Law and Islamic Law* (Aldershot, Ashgate 2008) i–xxxvi, xiv.

[56] See Ten-Year Programme of Action to Meet the Challenges Facing the Muslim Ummah in the 21st Century, www.oic-iphrc.org/en/data/docs/legal_instruments/OIC%20Instruments/TYPOA-%20AEFV/TYPOA-EV.pdf.

[57] KLH Samuel, *The OIC, the UN, and Counter-Terrorism Law-Making: Conflicting or Cooperative Legal Orders* (Oxford, Hart Publishing, 2013).

[58] T Kayaoglu, *The Organization of Islamic Cooperation: Politics, Problems, and Potential* (Copenhagen, The Danish Institute for Human Rights, 2015) 2.

[59] Charter of the Organisation of Islamic Cooperation, adopted on 14 March 2008, www.oic-oci.org/page/?p_id=53&p_ref=27&lan=en.

The statute of the IPHRC, adopted in 2011 in Astana, Kazakhstan, did not provide a better understanding of this question but also referred in its Preamble to the Cairo Declaration on Human Rights in Islam of 1990 and the relevant international instruments, charters and conventions.[60] It therefore depends mainly on the Commission itself, its self-definition and its practice when it comes to assessing the relationship between the various normative frameworks.

In the first years after its creation, the IPHRC appeared to favour an interpretation of human rights documents which could be described as a combined and universalist approach, focusing on the compatibility of Islamic and international human rights. The then Secretary-General Ekkmeledin İhsanoğlu stated at the Commission's first session that the establishment of the IPHRC 'reflects the ongoing process of "moderation and modernization" at the Organization'.[61] He noted that Islam was being wrongly associated with human right violations and as being inherently incompatible with international human rights norms and standards. Yet, according to his 'firm belief', exactly the opposite was true:

> Islam is not incompatible with human rights standards.
>
> [It provided for] 'hukook ul ibad' or 'rights of the people' centuries before the Human Rights acquired currency in contemporary human existence. The concept of 'ijtehad' lends a dynamism that is unparalleled. Islam in fact has the normative potential to add to the modern values and standards and push for better implementation, both at the social and political levels.[62]

This interpretation of the relationship between Islam and international human rights can be regarded as a 'moderate universalist' approach, which argues for the compatibility of Islamic and universal human rights, but prioritises universal human rights and is willing to interpret Islamic value in a way to make them conform to universal rights in case of conflict.[63] In this direction went also İhsanoğlu's vision for the first years of the Commission's work. He noted that the Commission would be complementary to the existing human rights mechanisms and would provide an added value by bridging gaps. The Commission should use its expertise also to review and update OIC instruments, including the Cairo Declaration and the Covenant on the Rights of the Child in Islam.[64] In a similar vein, the

[60] Statute of the OIC Independent Human Rights Commission, adopted by the 38th Session of the Council of Foreign Ministers (CFM) held in Astana, Kazakhstan, on 28–30 June 2011, www.oic-iphrc.org/en/data/docs/about/Statute/IPHRC%20Statute%20EV.pdf.

[61] Opening Statement by Secretary-General İhsanoğlu at the OIC at the First Session of the OIC IPHRC, 20 February 2012, www.oic-iphrc.org/data/sessions/SG%20Statement%20-%20IPHRC%20-%201st%20Session%20-%20Jakarta%20-%20EV.pdf.

[62] Ibid.

[63] See T Kayaoglu, *The OIC's Independent Permanent Human Rights Commission: An Early Assessment* (Copenhagen, The Danish Institute for Human Rights, 2015). The categorisation is based on J Donnelly, *Universal Human Rights in Theory and Practice* (Ithaca, NY, Cornell University Press, 2003). Kayaoglu notes, however, that, according to Ann E Mayer, İhsanoğlu's human rights messages were not always consistent with universal human rights. Ibid 13.

[64] Opening Statement by the Secretary-General of the OIC at the First Session of the OIC IPHRC (n 61).

appointment of the first chairwoman of the IPHRC, Siti Ruhaini Duhayatin, a university professor and human rights activist from Indonesia,[65] also seemed to underscore the universality of human rights, in particular in relation to women's rights.[66]

Yet, more recent developments seem to point to a different direction. The subsequent OIC Secretary-General, Iyad Ameen Madani, at the opening of the 4th session of the IPRC in 2014, referred to the 'Western values' upon which current human rights law was based.[67] He noted that, while many OIC countries had willingly adopted international human rights norms, a number of issues 'go beyond the normal scope of human rights and clash with Islamic teachings.'[68] In relation to 'freedom of expression' he remarked that despite repeated incidents of hatred and violence resulting from discrimination based on stereotyping and stigmatisation of individuals, communities and religions, some countries refused any limitations or responsible use of this right. On the other hand, Muslim countries enacting laws to ensure respect for the sanctity and reputation of religious values, scriptures and personalities for promotion of peace in society, were blamed for limiting this freedom through blasphemy laws.[69]

Under the leadership of the subsequent OIC Secretary-General, Yousef bin Ahmad Al-Othaimeen, in office since November 2016, the fight against Islamophobia seems to have regained high priority. The OIC Islamophobia Observatory celebrated its first decade of existence in April 2017 dedicated to the 'recent rise in Islamophobia phenomenon'.[70] The General Secretariat as well as the OIC relevant institutions and offices were encouraged to work harder towards ensuring the well-being of Muslim minorities, where Islamophobia was flagrant.

The controversies between alleged abuses of the freedom of expression and the protection of Islam against defamation has occupied the OIC since the inception of the organisation. The challenges posed by the subject of defamation of Islam shall be considered in greater depth in Chapter 7 of this study. Nonetheless, defamation and the ensuing controversies is representative of the challenges the work of the IPHRC will be facing. In addition, all references to human rights in the OIC documents stipulate that they should be applied in accordance with the member states' constitutional and legal systems. This shows a rather traditional understanding of the role of state sovereignty in relation to human rights.

[65] According to her CV on the OIC's website, Prof Siti Ruhaini Duhayatin is the Vice-Rector for Student and External Relation Affairs and senior lecturer on the Sociology of Law in the Faculty of Syariah and Law at the Islamic State University 'Sunan Kalijaga' Yogyakarta, Indonesia. In 1994, she initiated the First Women' Crisis Center in Indonesia. See www.oic-iphrc.org/data/cvs/18.pdf.

[66] Kayaoglu, *The OIC's Independent Permanent Human Rights Commission* (n 63) 13.

[67] Statement of His Excellency Iyad Ameen Madani Secretary-General of the Organisation of Islamic Cooperation at the Fourth Session of the OIC Independent Permanent Human Rights Commission (IPHRC), 2 February 2014, quoted by Kayaoglu (n 63) 14.

[68] Ibid.

[69] Ibid.

[70] OIC, 'OIC Hosts Meeting of Experts to Evaluate the First Decade of the OIC Islamophobia Observatory', Information of 4 April 2017, www.oic-oci.org//topic/?t_id=13370&t_ref=5838&lan=en.

To submit universal human rights to Islamic teachings and/or the constitution of states has been qualified as a 'relativist' approach.[71]

A preliminary assessment of the achievements of the IPHRC raised some doubts whether it lived up to the promise of a modern and moderate picture of Islam. Some recommendations to improve this situation were discussed by international human rights experts and presented to the IPHRC. They included:

> Recognition by Commissioners that OIC member states are bound by international human rights obligations.
>
> Agreement among Commissioners that international human rights treaties constitute minimum standards and that regional human rights instruments must always meet or exceed these minimum standards.
>
> Agreement among Commissioners to use only international human rights law as the benchmark in assessing all human rights issues, and clarification of the status of the Cairo Declaration to this end.
>
> Review of existing member states' reservations to international human rights treaties, and an elaboration of recommendations to remove reservations that undermine the object and purpose of the treaty in question.
>
> Affirmation of Sharia as consistent with international human rights law by rejecting interpretations of Sharia that violate or undermine international human rights law and by elaborating alternative interpretations that respect and further international human rights law.[72]

The IPHRC could foster a human rights discourse by increased coordination and cooperation with international and regional governmental and non-governmental human rights institutions. This could also help to move away from the traditional focus on the situation of Muslim minorities in non-OIC countries, such as in Palestine, Myanmar and in Western countries, to more introspection.[73]

From the rule of law perspective, it would be important to ensure that the IPHRC were truly independent and had a mandate allowing it to address existing human rights problems also within OIC member countries. As regards independence and objectivity, the statute of the IPHRC does not contain any reference. Yet, its Rules of Procedures provide:

> Rule 6—Independent status of Commissioners
>
> 1. Commissioners shall act in their personal capacity and shall express their own convictions and views.

[71] Kayaoglu (n 63) 14.

[72] In September 2013, the Danish Institute for Human Rights invited a group of international human rights researchers to a conference focused on the IPHRC which also formulated a number of recommendations for the Commission. Kayaoglu (n 63) 20–21.

[73] See MJ Petersen, 'Islamic or Universal Human Rights? The OIC's Independent Permanent Human Rights Commission' (Copenhagen, DIIS Report 2012:03) 31 et seq.

2. In exercising their function, commissioners shall at all times uphold utmost professionalism, truthfulness, independence, impartiality and integrity whilst enhancing their moral authority and credibility, free from any kind of extraneous influence.
3. Commissioners shall not receive instructions from any state, including their own, or any other third party.[74]

True independence and impartiality would be necessary to achieve progress in examination of the human rights situation in OIC countries. In its current composition, the Commission consists of people with different human rights backgrounds: diplomats, university professors, lawyers and human rights practitioners. The nomination by governments and the election by the Council of Ministers in and of themselves do not prevent independence. On the contrary, once the members of the Commission are elected they are protected by their office and in principle free and flexible to raise issues they find important themselves. They could take the chance and inspire themselves by the practice of other regional human rights monitoring bodies, such as the former European Commission on Human Rights[75] or the Inter-American Commission on Human Rights.[76]

So far, however, the mandate of the Commission is rather limited. The Statute confines the IPHRC largely to a consultative body for the Council of Ministers,[77] which does not have the right to receive complaints by states or individuals or to request reports from member states. The current situation is thus far from being comparable to existing regional human rights institutions, such as the European Court of Human Rights or the Inter-American Court of Human Rights. Yet, the Council may assign to the Commission particular other tasks,[78] which leaves the possibility open to define the mandate more broadly and also to gradually develop in the direction of other regional human rights institutions.

A limitation to its independence might be its mandate to support 'the OIC's position on human rights at the international level',[79] if this is meant to be

[74] Rules of Procedure of the OIC Independent Permanent Human Rights Commission (IPHRC) www.oic-iphrc.org/en/data/docs/about/IPHRC%20-%20RULES%20OF%20PROCEDURE%20-%20FINAL/IPHRC%20-%20Rules%20of%20Procedure%20-%20Final%20-%20Adopted%20by%2039th%20CFM%20-%20EV.pdf.

[75] The European Commission of Human Rights (until its abolition by Protocol No 11 to the European Convention on Human Rights in 1998) was composed of independent experts, which decided on the admissibility of state and individual applications and assisted with friendly settlements. In case of admissibility, it issued reports, which could be referred to the European Court of Human Rights by the Commission or a state with a recognised interest, or, if the respondent state was a party to Protocol No 9, by the individual applicant. If no such reference was made, the case was decided by the Committee of Ministers of the Council of Europe. See D Harris et al (eds), *Law of the European Convention on Human Rights*, 3rd edn (Oxford, Oxford University Press, 2014) 6, 103. See Protocol to the Convention for the Protection of Human Rights and Fundamental Freedoms, ETS No 009, 213 U.N.T.S. 262 and Protocol No 11 to the Convention for the Protection of Human Rights and Fundamental Freedoms, ETS No 155.

[76] J Cavallaro and S Brewer, 'Reevaluating Regional Human Rights Litigation in the Twenty-First Century: The Case of the Inter-American Court (2008) 102 *American Journal of International Law* 768, 778–80.

[77] See Art 12 of the Statute of the IPHRC (n 60).

[78] Ibid.

[79] Ibid Art 13.

a lobbying mandate, despite the independent opinion of the commissioners themselves. As regards its activities within the OIC, the Commission shall provide technical cooperation in the field of human rights and awareness-raising about these rights in the OIC countries, and offer consultancy on human rights issues.[80] It shall promote and support the role of national institutions and civil society organisations active in the area of human rights[81] and shall conduct studies and research on priority human rights issues.[82]

While in the first years, the majority of the Commission's topics addressed countries outside the OIC,[83] topics relevant within OIC member countries have come to be the focus of its work rather recently.[84] Furthermore, cooperation with international human rights institutions has increased. Commissioners regularly attend the meetings of the Human Rights Council, and human rights experts from UN institutions are invited to participate in events organised by the IPHRC. With regard to the topic of freedom of expression, the IPHRC organised a Thematic Debate on 'Freedom of Expression and Hate Speech' in November 2015. In this Thematic Debate also the UN Special Rapporteur on Freedom of Expression (although only through video link) and the former UN Special Rapporteur on Racism participated.[85]

The Outcome Document on freedom of expression carries substantial value in the context of the present study. Various aspects of it will be the subject of focused analysis in Chapter 7. The present brief observations shall highlight the perspective adopted by the IPHRC on a subject that is critical to the propagation and development of rule of law within the OIC. The Outcome Document provides an insight into the state of affairs with regard to the interpretation of freedom of

[80] Ibid Art 14.

[81] Ibid Art 15.

[82] Ibid Art 16.

[83] The first 6 sessions of the Commission were dominated by discussions on Islamophobia, human rights violations in the occupied Palestinian territories, the situation of the Rohingyas Muslim minority in Myanmar, the situation of Muslims in the Central African Republic and of other Muslim minorities, as well as the impact of unilateral economic sanctions on member states. It had only 1 agenda item relating to human rights issues within the OIC, namely the agenda item relating to civil, political, economic, social and cultural rights in OIC Member States. See IPHRC 'The Independent Permanent Human Rights Commission Closes its 3rd Regular Session in Jeddah Decides to visit Palestine and Myanmar to assess human rights situation', Press Communiqué, 31 October 2013; IPHRC, 'OIC Independent Permanent Human Rights Commission (IPHRC) concludes its 4th Session, Press Release, 6 February 2014; IPHRC, 'OIC Independent Permanent Human Rights Commission (IPHRC) concludes its 5th Regular Session', Final Communiqué, 5 June 2014; and IPHRC, 'OIC Independent Permanent Human Rights Commission (IPHRC) concludes its 6th Regular Session in Jeddah held from 1–6 November, 2014', Final Communiqué, 6 November 2014, www.oic-iphrc.org/en/sessions/.

[84] At the seventh session, new issues of 'high priority level' were raised on which the Commissioners would start preparing studies, namely: Women's Rights in Islam and in the Member State's Laws and Legislations; Combating Terrorism and Extremism; Respect for Cultural and Religious Diversity; The Phenomenon of Islamophobia; Inheritance Rights; The Rights of Minorities in Islam. See IPHRC, Press Communiqués, 19 and 21 April 2015, www.oic-iphrc.org/en/sessions/.

[85] IPHRC '8th Session: Outcome Document of Thematic Debate on "Freedom of Expression and Hate Speech"', 23 November 2015, www.oic-iphrc.org/data/sessions/8th_iphrc_thematic_debate_outcome_en.pdf; for text, see app I.

expression and the broader understanding of fundamental rights in the context of the rule of law analysis. The Document commences by acknowledging that freedom of expression is a key human right, which is vital for development of stable, peaceful and progressive democratic societies.[86] At the same time, it emphasises that the freedom of expression is not 'absolute' but that its exercise is subject to 'special duties and corresponding responsibilities' based on 'avoidance of harm to others' to ensure societal cohesion. It points out that also in Islam freedom of expression is guaranteed, but that Islam 'makes distinction between criticism or constructive discussion and sheer disrespect, defamation, insult and negative stereotyping that fall into the category of inciting religious hatred'.[87]

There is emphasis on 'hate speech motivated by racism, xenophobia and intolerance, coupled with impunity for perpetrators'[88] which create a climate of fear and social exclusion of the targeted persons and groups. Yet, this condemnation is not only directed against Western countries, but also against terrorist groups, such as Da'esh and Boko Haram, who use incitement to hatred and discrimination based on race or religion resulting in devastating and despicable killings of non-Muslims. However, in the same sentence, 'the printing of senseless caricatures of Prophet Mohammad (PBUH)' is also condemned and thereby arguably put on the same level as the killings by Da'esh and Boko Haram.[89]

As regards Resolution 16/18 of the Human Rights Council, the Outcome Document expresses its

> confidence in OIC sponsored HRC Resolution 16/18 (entitled Combating intolerance, negative stereotyping and stigmatization of, and discrimination, incitement to violence and violence against persons based on religion or belief), repeatedly adopted by the Human Rights Council and UN General Assembly by consensus, which includes substantive, administrative, political and legislative actions to be taken at the national and international levels to address the concerns relating to incitement to religious hatred and discrimination.[90]

The member states are urged to address the implementation gaps and provide regular reports on its implementation to the Human Rights Council, as well as rededicate to the agreed ideals in a comprehensive manner involving inclusive approaches provided in the Rabat Plan of Action on the prohibition of advocacy of national, racial or religious hatred that constitutes incitement to discrimination, hostility or violence.

The subject of 'defamation of religions' and the subsequent 'Istanbul Process' as well as the nature of involvement of the OIC is considered in great depth in Chapter 7 of this study. For the present purposes it nevertheless needs to be noted

86 Ibid.
87 Ibid.
88 Ibid.
89 Ibid (for elaboration on Da'esh, see Ch 6 below).
90 Ibid.

that the emphasis on limitations on freedom of expression in this very recent document appears striking. This is of particular concern as the Outcome Document is not an official statement of OIC governments, but the result of a Thematic Debate under the auspices of the IPHRC. From the perspective of safeguarding freedom of expression this raises the question whether the Commission exercises its function in an independent and impartial manner and whether it is eventually ready to engage in introspection. Independence and impartiality would be all the more necessary as limitations of freedom of expression are often implemented by governments to limit critical opinions by citizens. It would be an important role for the Commission to analyse carefully the different purposes and means of limiting free speech and their compatibility with human rights standards, in particular also in OIC member states.

As regards the prospects of enhancing the rule of law in the area of freedom of expression, there are also some promising outlooks which engender hope for a standardised and rationalised approach. For example, the Outcome Document recommends that the OIC commissions a study that analyses the existing legal practices used to combat hate speech and incitement to hatred in different parts of the world. This should be done with a view to suggesting parameters for hate speech and incitement to hatred based on one's race or religion as well as practical steps, in accordance with international human rights law. A comparative analysis of national laws through the lens of international human rights contains the potential to show the differences and rationalise their bases and goals.

Furthermore, the Council of Ministers at its 42nd Meeting in 2015 requested the IPHRC to review the Cairo Declaration on Human Rights in Islam against existing universal human rights instruments and make suggestions for its improvement, if and where necessary.[91] The Commission constituted a committee that met in February 2016 for the first time and formulated preliminary suggestions. With this new mandate, a perspective is taken up again that has been formulated by the former Secretary-General İhsanoğlu, when he inaugurated the first session of the IPHRC, and alluded to the human rights expertise gathered in the Commission which should be used to review and update OIC instruments, including the Cairo Declaration and the Covenant on the Rights of the Child in Islam. It remains to be seen to what extent this new mandate will be taken up to consolidate the formulations of Article 22 of the Cairo Declaration with the formulation of the freedom of expression in Article 19 of the ICCPR and in several regional human rights documents which currently do not appear to be congruent, as will be analysed in more detail in Chapter 7 below.

[91] See Resolution No 1/42–Legal Follow-Up and Coordination of Action in the Field of Human Rights, OIC/CFM-42/2015/LEG/DR.RES.1, 27–28 May 2015, para 12.

VI. The Arab League

Another regional organisation in the Islamic realm has recently begun to address human rights issues. Even though the development is quite young, it may be instructive to have a closer look at it and compare it with the endeavours of the OIC mentioned above. The League of Arab States is a regional organisation with currently 22 member states in the Middle East.[92]

The Arab Human Rights Committee was established in 2011 pursuant to Article 45 of the Arab Charter on Human Rights (ACHR). It consists of nationals of the states parties who must be highly experienced and competent in the area of human rights. The members of the Committee serve in their personal capacity and shall be fully independent and impartial. The Committee considers reports by states parties that are submitted on the measures they have taken to give effect to the rights and freedoms recognised in the Charter and on the progress made towards their enjoyment. While the first version of the Arab Charter on Human Rights of 1994 has never been accepted by members of the League of Arab States,[93] after an update and amendment by the Arab summit in Tunis in 2004, which was part of an effort to modernise the League of Arab States, it was ratified by a sufficient number of member states and entered into force in 2008.[94] The Arab Charter on Human Rights only contains scarce references to the Sharia. Yet, in its Article 3(3) it provides that '[m]en and women are equal in respect of human dignity, rights and obligations within the framework of positive discrimination established in favour of women by the Islamic Sharia, other divine laws and by applicable laws and legal instruments'. This has been criticised as making the enjoyment of rights contingent upon interpretation of Islamic Sharia.[95]

[92] The League of Arab States was founded in Cairo in 1945 by Egypt, Iraq, Lebanon, Saudi Arabia, Syria, Jordan and Yemen. See Charter of the League of Arab States, 22 March 1945, www.refworld.org/docid/3ae6b3ab18.html.

[93] Only Iraq signed the 1994 Charter on Human Rights, no member state ratified it. The reasons were manifold. On the one hand, the Charter entailed rights which were not existent in the member states, such as the right to strike. On the other hand, it was criticised for falling short of international standards. eg the Charter did not contain a right to appeal to a higher tribunal, including cases where the death penalty was imposed. It did not provide for a right to political organisation and participation. Furthermore, an extremely broad and vague exception clause provided for limitations or restrictions on all rights under the Charter, if necessary for the protection of national security and economy, public order, health, morals and the rights of others. In procedural aspects, the Charter was criticised for not providing a meaningful monitoring mechanism and only for a committee of human rights experts which should examine reports submitted by the states parties. See A An-Na'im, 'Human Rights in the Arab World: A Regional Perspective' (2001) 23 *Human Rights Quarterly* 701, 714–5; M Rishmawi, 'The Revised Arab Charter on Human Rights: A Step Forward?' (2005) 5 *Human Rights Law Review*, 361, 361

[94] In the meantime, a Sub-Commission on Human Rights, upon recommendation by the Arab Commission on Human Rights, had been created in 2006 entrusted with preparing studies and drafting treaties. Council of Ministers Resolution No 6705 of 6 September 2006. See M Rishmawi, 'The Arab Charter on Human Rights and the League of Arab States: An Update' (2010) 10 *Human Rights Law Review* 169, 177.

[95] Ibid 171.

Furthermore, the then UN High Commissioner of Human Rights criticised that the death penalty for children under 18 was not excluded, and several economic rights, such as the right to work, the right to free basic health care and the right to free education at the primary and basic levels, were only granted to citizens, and not to all persons under the jurisdiction of the state.[96] In addition, Zionism is referred to as 'an impediment to human dignity and a major barrier to the exercise of the fundamental rights of all peoples'[97] which has been criticised as being in contradiction with UN General Assembly Resolution 46/86 of 16 December 1991 which revoked UN General Assembly Resolution 3379 of 10 November 1975 stating that 'Zionism is a form of racism and racial discrimination',[98] and by NGOs which have called for reference to universal values rather than focusing on particular ideologies.[99]

Otherwise, the Arab Charter on Human Rights contains a rather restrictive 'emergency clause' which allows derogation from the obligation of the Charter only in situations that threaten the life of the nation and the existence of which is officially proclaimed, to the extent strictly required by the exigencies of the situation, provided that such measures are not inconsistent with their other obligations under international law and do not involve discrimination solely on the grounds of race, colour, sex, language, religion or social origin.[100] With regard to freedom of expression, the Arab Charter on Human Rights provides:

> Article 32
>
> 1. The present Charter guarantees the right to information and to freedom of opinion and expression, as well as the right to seek, receive and impart information and ideas through any medium, regardless of geographical boundaries.
>
> 2. Such rights and freedoms shall be exercised in conformity with the fundamental values of society and shall be subject only to such limitations as are required to ensure respect for the rights or reputation of others or the protection of national security, public order and public health or morals.

While emphasising the importance of the freedom of expression, the limitations are expounded in a manner that mirrors the formulations contained in international and other regional human rights treaties, most importantly Article 19 ICCPR, Article 10 ECHR and Article 13 ACHR, namely by formulating the right to freedom of expression separately from its limitation. This already provides an indication that in its interpretation and application the hierarchy of 'rule–exception'

[96] L Arbour, 'The Arab Charter on Human Rights is Incompatible with International Standards' *International Humanist and Ethical Union* (11 March 2008) http://iheu.org/arab-charter-human-rights-incompatible-international-standards-louise-arbour/. See also Rishmawi, 'The Arab Charter on Human Rights and the League of Arab States: An Update' (n 94) 171.

[97] Art 2 of the Arab Charter on Human Rights (2005) 12 *International Human Rights Reports* 893.

[98] Arbour, 'The Arab Charter on Human Rights is Incompatible with International Standards' (n 96).

[99] Rishmawi, 'The Revised Arab Charter on Human Rights' (n 93).

[100] ACHR, Art 4(1).

will be respected. Also the substantive wording of possible limitations is closely related to the comparable provisions in the other human rights documents. Yet, it is noteworthy that the Arab Charter on Human Rights does not contain a provision similar to Article 20 ICCPR directed against 'hate speech'.

Interestingly enough, though, Article 32(2) does not require that the limitation must be 'prescribed by law'. Nevertheless, the restrictive formulation 'subject only to such limitations as are required' leaves room for an application of the same principles as developed by the other human rights bodies on the international and regional level. It cannot be discerned yet, whether the Arab Human Rights Committee will develop a similar criterion in its practice and what influence the Islamic Sharia will have therein.

The Arab Human Rights Committee makes reference to international standards in its work.[101] A remarkable provision is contained in Article 43 of the Charter which even explicitly submits the interpretation and application of the Charter under international and regional human rights instruments which the states parties have adopted or ratified, including the right of women, the right of the child and the rights of persons belonging to minorities.[102] The mandate of the Arab Human Rights Committee is so far, however, limited to discussing the state reports, to commenting thereon and to making the necessary recommendations in accordance with the aims of the Charter through the intermediary of the Secretary-General.[103] It does not accept complaints by states or by individuals, such as the European Court of Human Rights or the Inter-American Commission of Human Rights. Yet, some further progress might be observed once the Arab Court of Human Rights will be established, which was decided at the 2013 Doha Summit.[104] The similarity of formulations and approaches in the Arab Charter on Human Rights with its regional counterparts, for example in Europe, raises high expectations. Yet, there is concern that, if the Arab League does not provide adequate resources to the Arab Human Rights Committee, it may become increasingly dependent on donations. This may affect the stability of the Committee's work, its durability, and importantly, its independence.[105]

VII. The Association of Southeast Asian Nations (ASEAN)

The Association of Southeast Asian Nations (ASEAN) established the ASEAN Intergovernmental Commission on Human Rights to promote human rights in

[101] M Rishmawi, 'The League of Arab States. Human Rights Standards and Mechanisms' (2005) *Open Society Foundations and Cairo Institute for Human Rights Studies* 43.

[102] ACHR, Art 43.

[103] Ibid Art 48.

[104] See the website of the League of Arab States: www.lasportal.org/en/Pages/default.aspx.

[105] Rishmawi, 'The League of Arab States. Human Rights Standards and Mechanisms' (n 101).

its member countries, in addition to its goal of regional economic integration.[106] Following the example of the European Union, the Association became increasingly aware of the need to address human rights issues to foster comprehensive development. As important Muslim majority states, such as Brunei, Indonesia and Malaysia, are members,[107] the Association's approach to the rule of law is relevant for the present study. Furthermore, the debate on the so-called 'Asian values',[108] which are allegedly putting more emphasis on community values than on individuals' rights and freedoms, is worth further analysis.[109] After the Commission's establishment in 2009, its first task was to draft an ASEAN Human Rights Declaration.[110] This Declaration was eventually presented to the ASEAN member countries in Phnom Penh and unanimously adopted in 2012. As a Declaration it is non-binding and only a first step towards a more effective mechanism for the protection of human rights. The fact that it had been elaborated with little involvement of civil society organisations was criticised, as were some principles and articles that could weaken and erode universal human rights.[111] Concerning freedom of expression, Article 23 of the ASEAN Human Rights Declaration provides that '[e]very person has the right to freedom of opinion and expression, including freedom to hold opinions without interference and to seek, receive and impart information, whether orally, in writing or through any other medium of that person's choice'.

This broad formulation reflects the words of Article 19 of the Universal Declaration on Human Rights. Yet, some general provisions and principles may limit and qualify its applicability. In particular, Article 6, under the heading of 'General Principles', raises some concern:

> The enjoyment of human rights and fundamental freedoms must be balanced with the performance of corresponding duties as every person has responsibilities to all other individuals, the community and the society where one lives. It is ultimately the primary responsibility of all ASEAN Member States to promote and protect all human rights and fundamental freedoms.

[106] ASEAN was founded in 1967 to promote economic growth, social progress and socio-cultural evolution. See also the amended version of the Charter of the Association of Southeast Asian Nations of 2007, http://asean.org/asean/asean-charter/charter-of-the-association-of-southeast-asian-nations/.

[107] The member states of ASEAN are Brunei, Cambodia, Indonesia, Laos, Malaysia, Myanmar, Philippines, Singapore, Thailand and Vietnam.

[108] See B Kausikan, 'Asia's Different Standard' (1993) 92 *Foreign Policy* 24; B Kausikan, 'An Asian Approach to Human Rights' (1995) 89 *Proceedings of the American Society of International Law* 146; R Peerenboom, 'Beyond Universalism and Relativism: The Evolving Debates about "Values in Asia"' (2003–04) 14 *Indian International and Comparative Law Review* 1.

[109] H Quane, 'The Significance of an Evolving Relationship: ASEAN States and the Global Human Rights Mechanisms' (2015) 15 *Human Rights Law Review* 283, 292–95, 300–03.

[110] See ASEAN Human Rights Declaration (adopted 18 November 2012) www.asean.org/storage/images/ASEAN_RTK_2014/6_AHRD_Booklet.pdf.

[111] See the statement by UN High Commissioner for Human Rights, Navi Pillay, of 19 November 2012, OHCHR 'Statement by UN High Commissioner for Human Rights Navi Pillay' (19 November 2012) www.un.org/apps/news/story.asp?NewsID=43536#.V0ysUEbBFv1.

This principle seems to condition the enjoyment of human rights on the performance of duties. In addition, it also appears to indicate that the individual rights and freedoms might be dependent on domestic laws. This has been identified as another attempt to use the concept of 'cultural relativism' to suggest that international human rights do not apply everywhere and that individual rights might be subject to group veto.[112]

In the framework of international human rights monitoring bodies, such as the UN Human Rights Council, the extent to which ASEAN members are respecting the freedom of expression has been a point of disagreement.[113] Generally, states did not contest the existence of the right, but disagreed on the assessment of whether a human rights violation had occurred in the light of all the relevant circumstances. This shows the need for an independent monitoring mechanism with a mandate to review whether state interference with the right was justifiable on the basis of permissible limitations and in the light of all the facts.[114] The validity of human rights restrictions and the legitimacy of claims made in the name of regional and national particularities need clear rules and an effective monitoring body in order to ensure that the rule of law is upheld with regard to the freedom of expression.

However, as regards monitoring the implementation of the rights contained in the Declaration, the ASEAN Intergovernmental Commission on Human Rights is rather weak. It is composed of state representatives, not of independent experts, and has to respect the principle of non-interference in the internal affairs of ASEAN member states.[115] It cannot hear individual complaints, unlike the European and Inter-American human rights monitoring institutions. While it has the responsibility to protect and to promote human rights, its limited mandate rather shows that the emphasis is on promotional activities.[116]

It remains to be seen to what extent the ASEAN Intergovernmental Commission on Human Rights will include the discussion of the issue of freedom of expression in its work in the future. It is notable that in the Five-Year Work Plan 2016–2020, this topic is not explicitly mentioned, for example as an issue on which thematic studies shall be prepared.[117]

[112] V Nuland, 'ASEAN Declaration on Human Rights', Press Statement of 20 November 2012, US Department of State, https://2009-2017.state.gov/r/pa/prs/ps/2012/11/200915.htm www.state.gov/r/pa/prs/ps/2012/11/200915.htm.

[113] Quane, 'The Significance of an Evolving Relationship' (n 109) 292.

[114] Ibid.

[115] Art 2 of the ASEAN Intergovernmental Commission on Human Rights (2009) 48 *International Legal Materials* 1165.

[116] Quane (n 109) 287.

[117] See the AICHR Five-Year Work Plan 2016–2020 (adopted on 15 June 2015) endorsed at the 48th AMM on 3 August 2015, http://aichr.org/documents/.

VIII. Conclusions

The above analysis has shown that the rule of law, as a matter of principle, is highly valued in international law and in the statutes of international and regional organisations. However, the concept of sovereignty, to a certain extent, still represents an obstacle to an unequivocal acceptance by states that 'the law' is above them, despite the fact that public international law, in fact, is 'law' and that states have to comply with it. When it comes to monitoring bodies or institutions, these obstacles become apparent. In the United Nations, acceptance of the compulsory jurisdiction of the International Court of Justice is limited to one third of the UN membership. This percentage has decreased since the foundation of the organisation which in the early years of its existence has, in the Universal Declaration on Human Rights, solemnly declared that 'it is essential, if man is not to be compelled to have recourse, as a last resort, to rebellion against tyranny and oppression, that human rights should be protected by the rule of law'. Also in the Security Council, acceptance of the rule of law binding upon sovereign states with regard to their voting behaviour, in particular by the permanent members, is hardly recognised. It follows that the United Nations' joint efforts to strengthen the rule of law are primarily addressed to the national level. At this level, the consensus seems to be unfettered that promoting the rule of law is essential to achieve peace, security, and sustainable development.

Regional organisations in the Islamic, Arab and Asian realm are not more advanced in this respect. While in other regions, human rights monitoring institutions, such as the European Court of Human Rights, the Inter-American Commission of Human Rights or the Inter-American Court of Human Rights, are recognised judicial institution with the competence to assess the actions of state from a higher level, sovereignty and non-interference still play a predominant role within the group of Islamic or Arab countries, sharing Muslim tradition, culture and law. The limited mandates of human rights monitoring bodies are witness of the reluctance of the respective states to accept scrutiny of their acts by independent experts. The lack of independent organs represents an important obstacle to the full implementation of the rule of law within the respective organisations. It remains to be seen whether awareness will increase that accepting the rule of law as a yardstick of state actions will not only ensure the protection of human rights but also, in a broader sense, peace, security, and sustainable economic development.

Part IV

The Sharia and Islamic Law: Rule of Law and the Application of Freedom of Expression

Part III of the study examined and explored the relationship between rule of Law, the Sharia and Islamic Law. It also analysed the role of rule of law and freedom of expression in international law and within various international organisations. The aim of Part IV is to bring into focus the implications of freedom of expression upon rule of law as developed and articulated within the Muslim world: this part assesses the subject of free expression both within the classical Islamic law and its modern application in the constitutional framework of Muslim majority nation-states. Chapter 5, whilst examining the position of freedom of expression within Islamic law, highlights the underlying jurisprudential complexities. Freedom of expression is a vexed subject in Islam with difficult jurisprudential interpretations of apostasy and blasphemy. Some aspects of the *Fiqh* forcefully suggest the death penalty for apostates and blasphemers. However, modern jurisprudence has tended to find congenial sources of compatibility between human rights law and Islamic law on the right to freedom of expression. In terms of the modern interpretation and application of the right to freedom of expression and opinion, Chapter 5 illustrates that, regrettably, a vast majority of the Muslim world continues to be dominated by totalitarian and dictatorial governments. These regimes regularly violate fundamental rights including the right to free expression. In order to block political opposition and repress dissenting voices, religious doctrines of blasphemy and apostasy are frequently invoked. The execution of Mahmoud Muhammad Taha in Sudan for the crime of apostasy and the contemporary reliance on anti-blasphemy laws in Pakistan represent unfortunate examples of abuse of religious doctrines for achieving political ends. As demonstrated by Chapter 6 of this part, anti-blasphemy laws have tragic results for the religious minorities of Pakistan. These laws breach norms of natural justice and their arbitrary interpretation and application have led to grave injustices including extra-judicial killings

[1] See the International Commission on Jurists on Pakistan's Blasphemy law and the Commission's recommendation, *On Trial: The Implementation of Pakistan's Blasphemy Laws* (ICJ Geneva, Switzerland, 2015).

of members of the minority communities.[1] The application of these laws has also injected violence and intolerance within the fabric of the entire society in which all vulnerable groups–women, children and religious minorities–continue to suffer.[2]

Freedom to form opinions and to articulate expressions is of critical significance for the sustenance of religions. Similarly, religious values and their manifestation represent important segments of human emotions and expressions. Thus, the right to freedom of expression and the right to freedom of religion are both heavily interdependent and reliant upon each other. Yet, the boundaries between the two rights are fussy, especially in relation to defamation or insulting of religions.

As exemplified in Chapter 7, the struggles over 'defamation of religions' was played out within the corridors of the United Nations for well over a decade. Sponsored by members of the OIC, the resolutions on 'defamation of religions' were adopted by the United Nations Human Rights Commission and its successor the United Nations Human Rights Council as well as the United Nations General Assembly. Attempts to deploy the cover of international human rights to protect religions and, in particular, Islam, became the subject of considerable criticism of human rights experts and UN mandate holders.

The sponsors of the resolutions aimed at introducing a prohibition on any form of insult and adverse comment against Islam in the form of an international norm, directly analogous to national anti-blasphemy laws. Members of the OIC were well aware of the exceptional nature of the concept of 'defamation of religions' and the consequent undesirability of introducing such a discourse within international human rights law. Furthermore, in light of the obvious difficulties in persuading the international community towards establishing an international crime of defamation of Islam, a strategic path was devised to conflate issues of discrimination against Muslim minorities in the west, 'Islamophobia', with hate speech against Islam.

As Chapter 7 of the study explores, efforts to prohibit defamation of religions has been on hiatus since the adoption of the Human Rights Council Resolution 16/18 entitled 'Combating intolerance, negative stereotyping and stigmatization of, and discrimination, incitement to violence and violence against, persons based on religion or belief'.[3] There thus commenced the 'Istanbul Process' aimed at refocusing on the issues of the right to freedom of belief including the protection of the believer (as opposed to the protection of the religions or beliefs per se). The 'Istanbul Process' has produced only mixed results, with the veneer of consensus over defamation of religions proving short-lived. Serious disagreements have

[2] See All Parties Parliamentary Group for International Freedom of Religion or Belief, *Freedom of Religion or belief in Pakistan and UK Governmental Policy: Parliamentary Inquiry*, https://freedomdeclared.org/in-parliament/pakistan-report/, 47.

[3] HRC Resolution, 'Combating intolerance, negative stereotyping and stigmatization of, and discrimination, incitement to violence, and violence against persons based on religion or belief', A/HRC/RES/16/18 (adopted 24 March 2011, without a vote).

resurfaced in recent years over the permissible boundaries between expressions of ideas and 'advocacy' of 'religious hatred' that formed 'incitement' to violence. It is unclear as to the extent to which additional initiatives such as the Rabat Plan of Action (2012)[4] and the more recent Beirut Declaration on 'Faith for Rights' (F4R)[5] would support the international community in establishing acceptable limits to free speech.

[4] Rabat Plan of Action on the prohibition of advocacy of national, racial or religious hatred that constitutes incitement to discrimination, hostility or violence: Conclusions and recommendations emanating from the four regional expert workshops organised by OHCHR, 2011, and adopted by experts in Rabat, Morocco on 5 October 2012. See UNCHR, Annual Report of the United Nations Commissioner for Human Rights, Addendum, *Report of the United Nations Commissioner for Human Rights on expert workshops on the Prohibition of incitement to national, racial or religious hatred* A/HRC/22/17/Add.4 (11 January 2013) www.ohchr.org/Documents/Issues/Opinion/SeminarRabat/Rabat_draft_outcome.pdf.

[5] See the document as published by the OHCHR on 29 March 2017, www.ohchr.org/Documents/Press/21451/BeirutDeclarationonFaithforRights.pdf, reprinted in app III below.

5

Islamic Law and Freedom of Expression

I. Introduction

Freedom of expression is a fundamental human right, and (as examined in Parts II and III of this study) represents a critical aspect of the rule of law. The idea of freedom of expression, as it is now articulated under international law and in the legal systems of modern nation-states in Europe and elsewhere, is part of the political theory of liberalism, which was born in Europe in the late seventeenth century. Freedoms of expression and belief are rights that have different versions within modern liberal systems; various arguments have been put forward to justify the principle of free speech. These arguments have been considered in greater depth in this part of the study and include inter alia the importance of discovering truth, free speech as an aspect of self-fulfilment, the argument from citizens' participation in a democracy, and suspicion of government.[1]

John Stuart Mill's essay *On Liberty* argues for the doctrine of liberty and that there should exist significant spheres where individuals are free from government coercion. According to him 'the struggle between liberty and authority is the most conspicuous feature in the portions of history with which we are earliest familiar with'.[2] According to Mill's ideal of a free society, 'liberty of conscience in the most comprehensive sense; liberty of thought and feeling; absolute freedom of opinion and sentiment on all subjects, practical or speculative, scientific, moral, or theological' is amongst the most important liberty rights.[3] He then argues that the freedom of expression and publishing opinions is as important as the liberty of thought, hence inseparable from it.[4] According to Mill, the only purpose for which individual liberties may be limited is to prevent harm to others.[5] However, liberty of opinion and expression is entitled to a greater degree of protection from government regulation compared to other forms of conduct that may cause similar

[1] E Barendt, *Freedom of Speech* (Oxford, Oxford University Press, 2005) 6–23; see also Ch 6 below.
[2] JS Mill, *On Liberty* (first published 1859) (Kitchener, Batoche Books, 2001) ch 1, para 2.
[3] Ibid.
[4] Ibid.
[5] ibid ch 1, para 9.

harms.[6] Nevertheless, as considered in Chapter 6 below, in modern times significant debates in liberal democratic countries and other countries exist in relation to the scope of the freedom of speech.[7]

Freedom of expression has found protection in constitutions as well as in international instruments. The Universal Declaration of Human Rights, Article 19, prescribes that 'Everyone has the right to freedom of opinion and expression; this right includes freedom to hold opinions without interference and to seek, receive and impart information and ideas through any media and regardless of frontiers'.[8] Article 18 of the International Covenant on Civil and Political Rights (ICCPR) guarantees 'freedom of thought, conscience, and religion'.[9] The scope of freedom of expression from the perspective of both international law and under national legal systems varies between countries. There are public debates in various societies in relation to principles under which freedom of speech may be limited. As considered in Chapter 6, there are questions as to how far the expression of certain issues relating to commerce, religion, pornography, media, hate speech and privacy can be protected. However, it is now a well-established international and constitutional principle that freedom of expression (as developed during the nineteenth and twentieth centuries in international law and under major legal systems in the world) deserves a significant degree of protection.

The Sharia, or the legal system of Islam, traditionally recognises certain rights of the individual, including the right to life, the right to justice and equality and the right to property ownership and inheritance. The rights of freedom of expression and thought may not have been highlighted under traditional sources of Islam. Nevertheless, they are endorsed in a number of sources of law and in Islamic jurisprudence. Like in many other areas of law, Sharia, and its sources can be interpreted in various ways. Rational interpretations of the Sharia can make it compatible

[6] Barendt, *Freedom of Speech* (n 1) 1.

[7] See eg J Raz, 'Free Expression and Personal Identification' (1991) 11 *Oxford Journal of Legal Studies* 303; B Hepple, 'Freedom of Expression and the Problem of Harassment' in J Beatson and Y Cripps, *Freedom of Expression and Freedom of Information: Essays in Honour of Sir David Williams* (Oxford, Oxford University Press, 2002) 177–96; Barendt (n 1) ch 3.

[8] UNGA, Universal Declaration of Human Rights, 10 December 1948, 217 A (III), GA Res 217A (III), UN Doc A/810 at 71 (1948), Art 19. See also Art 18 of the ICCPR, New York, 16 December 1966 United Nations, 999 U.N.T.S. 171; 6 I.L.M. (1967) 368.

[9] ICCPR, Art 18 states:

1. Everyone shall have the right to freedom of thought, conscience and religion. This right shall include freedom to have or to adopt a religion or belief of his choice, and freedom, either individually or in community with others and in public or private, to manifest his religion or belief in worship, observance, practice and teaching.
2. No one shall be subject to coercion which would impair his freedom to have or to adopt a religion or belief of his choice.
3. Freedom to manifest one's religion or beliefs may be subject only to such limitations as are prescribed by law and are necessary to protect public safety, order, health, or morals or the fundamental rights and freedoms of others.
4. The States Parties to the present Covenant undertake to have respect for the liberty of parents and, when applicable, legal guardians to ensure the religious and moral education of their children in conformity with their own convictions.

with certain principles of free speech; however, traditional Sharia law may seem inconsistent with modern and international free speech principles. Islamic criminal law does prescribe punishment for blasphemy and apostasy. Therefore, these concepts can be interpreted strictly or broadly.

Islam, as a religion and legal system, and Muslims as communities of people, are extremely diverse. There are various sub-religions (*Madhhab*), sects, schools and traditions within Islam. Muslim societies are diverse in almost every Muslim country and in many non-Muslim countries. The fact that Muslim peoples, Muslim nations and Islam and its legal system are all diverse shows that some kind of freedom of thought and expression can exist within Muslim societies and in the legal system of Islam.

Under Islamic law there are proponents of the strict application of apostasy and blasphemy law amongst most traditional Islamic scholars. These scholars support punishing blasphemy and apostasy as it is commonly practised in Egypt, Saudi Arabia, Malaysia, Iran and Pakistan. Similarly, there are scholars (both traditional and modern) who consider apostasy as an offence only if it has elements of treason in a modern context.

In this chapter, the issue of freedom of expression under Islamic law will be discussed in four sections. First, the challenges in modern Muslim state practice and Muslim communities in non-Muslim countries will be reviewed. Secondly, classical Islamic law texts and sources will be examined to find their positions with respect to freedom of expression. Thirdly, modern interpretations of Islamic law and the views of contemporary modern intellectuals in relation to freedom of expression will be discussed. Finally, suggestions will be made in relation to freedom of expression and speech under Islamic law and Muslim state practice.

II. Challenges in Modern Muslim State Practices and in Muslim Communities

The status of freedom of opinion and expression and more generally the status of human rights in the Middle East and the wider Muslim world is not satisfactory by modern international law standards. While some protection of human rights and freedom of expression is protected by the constitutions and other legal documents in the Muslim world in practice many Muslim countries suffer significant restriction on freedom of expression. Various human rights reports by international organisations and human rights institutions put the Middle East and North Africa and some other Muslim countries amongst the regions and countries where freedom of expression is significantly restricted.[10]

[10] Freedom House (report by J Dunham), 'Press Freedom in 2015: The Battle of the Dominant Message' (2016); Reporters Without Borders, '2016 World Press Freedom Index', https://rsf.org/en/ranking.

In analysing the issue of freedom of expression in the Muslim world, three points must be considered. First, most Middle Eastern and many other Muslim majority states are ruled by unelected, sometimes totalitarian governments and the lack of freedoms including freedom of expression can largely be attributed to this factor. Secondly, Muslim societies whether in the Middle East or elsewhere including Muslim communities in Europe and other Western Countries generally have a traditional culture where religion plays a significant role in shaping their culture, attitudes and values. Thirdly, within the legal system of Islam, or Sharia, blasphemy and apostasy are known to be criminalised.

Although the issues of blasphemy and apostasy under Islamic law and punishing perpetrators of these offences in Muslim societies,[11] and in other societies, existed for many centuries (and continues to exist),[12] a number of high-profile cases since 1985 have attracted the attention of the media and legal and political scholars in the West and elsewhere.

Perhaps the first significant international case was the execution of Mahmoud Muhammad Taha, convicted of the crime of apostasy in Sudan on 18 January 1985. Taha was the leader of the Sudanese Republican Party or the Republican Brotherhood in the 1940s. Taha was imprisoned by the British colonial administration a couple of times. After his release from the prison he developed a theory of legal interpretation of the Quran and published his significant work, *The Second Message of Islam.*[13]

The doctrine of Taha was not unprecedented in the Islamic world.[14] The core of his ideas was that the essence of Islam was stated in the sections of the Quran which were revealed to the Prophet in Mecca from 610 to 623. These included Islamic principles in relation to God, worship, beliefs and moral principles. During this

[11] According to PEW Research Centre, as of 2012, laws restricting apostasy and blasphemy are most common in the Middle East and North Africa where 14 out of 20 nations penalised blasphemy and 12 out of 20 provided criminal sanction for apostasy. The Muslim countries with laws against apostasy and blasphemy include Saudi Arabia, Iran, Pakistan, Afghanistan Bahrain, Qatar, the UAE, Oman, Yemen, Syria, Jordan, Kuwait, Somalia, Comoros, Mauritania, Nigeria, Malaysia and the Maldives.

[12] According to PEW Research Centre as of 2012, 22% of world countries and territories have anti-blasphemy laws or policies and 1 in 10 (11%) had laws or policies penalising apostasy. See Pew Research Centre, Report on Apostasy Laws 2012, www.pewresearch.org/fact-tank/2014/05/28/which-countries-still-outlaw-apostasy-and-blasphemy.

[13] MM Taha, *The Second Message of Islam (Contemporary Issues in the Middle East)* trans AA An Na'im, rev edn (New York, Syracuse University Press, 1996).

[14] One example of a Muslim jurist who, for the first time in Islamic history, attempted to reconcile Islamic legal principles with modern requirements is the 18th-century Muslim jurist from India, Shah Wali Allah. Shah Wali Allah argued that the Prophet of Islam was never intended to universally apply a legal system that was designed for a specific society at a specific point in time (specifically, Arabia of the 6th century). Rather, Shah Wali Allah established a system, and encouraged Muslims to follow his principles in establishing their own system of rules within the general spirit of Islam. See generally M Al-Ghazali, *The Socio-Political Thought of Shah Wali Allah* (Islamabad, The International Institute of Islamic Thought, 2001). Shal Wali Allah's position on legal theory was observed and accepted by many Muslim jurists and philosophers such as Allama Muhammad Iqbal in his notable book. See generally, M Iqbal, *Six Lectures on the Reconstruction of Religious Thought in Islam* in MS Sheikh (ed), (Lahore, Institute of Islamic Culture, 1996).

period, there were not many legal principles articulated in the verses of the Quran. Because of his doctrine, Taha opposed the introduction of traditional Islamic law by the then-President of Sudan, Jafar Nomeiri (President between 1969–1985). The government of Sudan prosecuted Taha for apostasy, and sentenced him to death based on the *hadd* of *rida* (*irtidad*).[15] The Court took the position that Taha was guilty based on his sayings and 'deviationist views',[16] which were known to the public. Further, the Court held that the doctrine of Taha, which stated that the Sharia, as practised during the time of the Prophet Mohammad, was not capable of solving the problems of the twentieth century, was akin to heresy.[17]

Although Nomeiri's execution of Taha was based on rivalry and competition between the two of them, the fact that Taha was prosecuted and executed for the crime of apostasy raised many questions in the Muslim world and elsewhere.[18]

The second high-profile international case involving Islamic law and blasphemy was the Salman Rushdie affair. Rushdie published his novel, *The Satanic Verses*, in 1988. In this book the Prophet of Islam, his wives, his companions and the Quran are all subjected to ridicule. The publication of the book caused violent demonstrations in several Muslim majority countries including Pakistan, Bangladesh, Malaysia and Iran and included other countries with sizable Muslim populations (eg India). On 14 February 1989, Ayatollah Khomeini of Iran issued a *fatwa*[19] sentencing Salman Rushdie to death for insulting the Prophet of Islam and the Quran. The death sentence of a British national by a religious leader and the highest political leader of another country raised significant tensions between Iran and the West in international relations for at least 10 years. The book remains

[15] For further discussion on *irtidad*, see various resources on Islamic criminal law, and *hudud* in Islam, particularly AA An-Na'im, 'The Islamic Law of Apostasy and its Modern Applicability' (1986) 16 *Religion* 197.

[16] The Court decided that Mahmoud M Taha was guilty both by his sayings and deviationist views which were known to everybody, and by his deeds, such as the fact that he did not pray. More specifically, the Court decided that Taha's views (which claimed that the sharia) as known and practised during the time of Prophet Muhammad, was incapable of solving the problems of the 20th century, should be taken as sheer heresy. See D O'Sullivan, 'The Death Sentence for Mahmoud Muhammad Taha: Misuse of the Sudanese Legal System and Islamic Sharia Law?' (2001) 5 *International Journal of Human Rights* 45, 53–54.

[17] See AS Sidahmed, 'Freedom of Religion, Apostasy and Human Rights: An Appraisal' (2000) 4 *The Mediterranean Journal of Human Rights* 139.

[18] For some analysis and comments on Taha's case, see: O'Sullivan, 'Freedom of Religion, Apostasy and Human Rights' (n 16) 45–70; M Mahmoud, 'Mahmud Muhammad Taha and the Rise and Demise of the Jumhuri Movement' (2001) 23 *New Political Science* 65.

[19] *Fatwa* is a juristic opinion on any area of the Sharia. It may be related to rituals or any other human conduct and it must be based on interpretation of sources of the Sharia. An innovative interpretation of Islamic sources may result in creation of new legal principles. However, legal verdicts are to be issued by courts and a judge (*Qadhi*). There is no centralised or international priestly hierarchy in Islam and hence there may be various *muftis* and *fatwas* in different parts of the Muslim world. A *fatwa* is usually binding for the followers of a *mufti* only. A *mufti* is a person who issues the fatwa. Such a person is a qualified high status Muslim scholar. On *fatwa* and *mufti*, see MK Masud et al, *Mufties, Fatwas, and Islamic Legal Interpretation* (Boston, Harvard University Press, 1996).

banned in most Muslim majority states and in many other states including India.[20]

Another high-profile case attracting international legal and political scholarship was that of Taslima Nasrin of Bangladesh. In this affair, Taslima Nasrin a Bangladeshi woman writer, published a book in 1993 entitled *Lajja* ('Shame'). The book contained materials which were found to be blasphemous by Islamists groups and organisations in Bangladesh and elsewhere. Nasrin was threatened with the death sentence and reward was provided for her head. Unlike the Taha and Salman Rushdie cases where the death sentence was issued by states (in Salman Rushdie's case by a head of another state against a citizen of another state without any court proceedings), Taslima Nasrin was threatened and sentenced to death by Islamist organisations in Bangladesh and India.[21] Nasrin left Bangladesh and India and she lives in Europe and the United States where she writes and publishes her works.

One of the most important recent cases where the issue of academic freedom, freedom of thought and expression, and particularly the modern application of the concept of apostasy in Muslim countries, was raised was that of Nasr Hamid Abu Zayd of Egypt (1943–2010). Unlike the Taha and Salman Rushdie incidents where rivalry in politics and international relations were involved and unlike the Taslima Nasrin case where a group of fundamentalist Muslim organisations threatened Nasrin to death for blasphemous writings, Abu Zayd's case involved proper legal procedures based on the constitution and other legislation without the involvement of political leaders in a Muslim country where the judiciary is relatively independent. Not only was his case heard before the courts, appropriate processes were followed involving expert evidence from both the University of Cairo (where Abu Zayd was a senior academic) and Al-Azhar University to evaluate Abu Zayd's writings.

Again unlike the other cases, Abu Zayd's writings were purely academic and did not involve any blasphemous remarks. As a scholar of the Arabic language and Islamic studies and as a Quranic thinker, while not denying that the Quran was of divine origin, he projected a humanistic and historical interpretation of the Quranic hermeneutics.[22] He argued that when the Quran was revealed to the

[20] For further study on Salman Rushie affairs and the basis of the *Fatwa* and the dissenting opinions of other Muslim jurists, see LV Levy, *Blasphemy: Verbal Offences against the Sacred: from Moses to Salman Rushdie* (Chapel Hill, University of North Carolina Press, 1993); M Slaughter, 'The Salam Rushdie Affair: Apostasy, Honour and Freedom of Speech' (1993) *Virginia Law Review* 153; P Chakravorty, 'Rushdie Incident as Law-and-Literature Parable' (1995) 104 *Yale Law Journal* 2213; A Chase 'Legal Guardians: Islamic Law, International Law, Human Rights Law, and the Salman Rushdie Affair' (1996) 11 *American University Journal of International Law and Policy* 375.

[21] SM Shamsul Alam, 'Women in the Era of Modernity and Islamic Fundamentalism: The Case of Taslima Nasrin of Bangladesh' (1998) 23 *University of Chicago Press* 429.

[22] Similar to Abu Zayd, Mohammad Mojtahed Shabestari, an Iranian clergy and professor of Islamic studies at the University of Tehran, has involved the hermeneutic approach in interpretation of the Quran. Although Shabestari was forced to retire upon reaching the age of retirement during the government of Mahmood Ahmadinejad (2007), he published his famous work in 1996 entitled *Hermenutik, Kitab va Sunnat [Hermeneutics, the Book (the Quran) and Tradition]*.

Prophet through the Revelation (*wahy*), the moment it was revealed to the Prophet it acquired a human existence which was different from its divine nature.[23] In 1992, Abu Zayd applied for a promotion to the position of a professor at Cairo University. During the process of academic promotion comments were made in relation to his views about revelation and the Quran, creating a high-profile legal case before the Egyptian courts. A lawsuit was filed with the Giza Personal Status Court in Cairo demanding the nullification of his marriage due to his apostasy. On 14 June 1995, Cairo's Appeal Court ruled that Abu Zayd was an apostate according to Islamic law and ordered a forced divorce from his wife. The decision of the Appeal Court was upheld by the Supreme Court of Egypt.[24]

Unlike those cases where Muslim thinkers and authors were accused of apostasy and blasphemy the Prophet Mohammad cartoons controversy of the Danish Newspaper, *Jyllands-Posten*, was of a different nature. In this, case a number of cartoons were published by a newspaper in a Western country, Denmark, with a tradition of high tolerance for freedom of speech and expression. The publication of the cartoons printed on 30 September 2005 led to the worst foreign policy crisis in Denmark since the Second World War. The publication triggered an international crisis, where violent demonstrations took place around the world particularly in some Muslim countries. Many Muslim countries and Islamic societies boycotted Danish and Norwegian products. There were also hundreds of death threats and some violent incidents including a car bomb explosion outside the Danish embassy in Islamabad, Pakistan killing eight people. The cartoon's controversy resulted in significant academic debates in relation to freedom of expression and its scope.[25]

The murders of 12 people at the site of the French satirical newspaper, *Charlie Hebdo*, is the latest in a series of incidents relating to freedom of speech where Muslim faith is somehow involved. In this incident, two gunmen entered the office of *Charlie Hebdo* and murdered a number of people involved in the publication

[23] These are some of the excerpts the prosecutors read in court and which were accepted as evidence of Abu Zayd's apostasy: 'From the moment the text was revealed and read by the Prophet, it was transformed from being divine text and became human understanding because it had immediately changed from tanzil (revelation) to ta'wil interpretation). The Prophet's interpretation of the text represents the initial stage in the text's interaction with the human mind contrary to the claim of the proponents of religious thought that the Prophet's interpretation of the test corresponds to the text itself, a claim which leads to a form of Sharak (polytheism), since it suggests conformity between the absolute and the relative, between the permanent and the unchangeable, a conformity between divine intention and the human understanding, which claim would mean attributing divine qualities to the prophet sanctifying him by concealing his human nature and consequently the fact that he was only a Prophet' (Abu Zayd, *Naqd al Katab al-dini*, 93–94 as discussed in GN Sfeir, 'Basic Freedoms in a Fractured Legal Culture: Egypt and the Case of Nasr Hamid Abu Zayd' (1998) 53 *The Middle East Journal* 402, 410–11.

[24] For further discussion on this case, see FM Najjar, 'Islamic Fundamentalism and the Intellectuals: The Case of Nasr Hamid Abu Zayd' (2000) 27 *British Journal of Middle Eastern Studies* 177.

[25] See L Lasse et al, 'The Muhammad Cartoons Controversy in Comparative Perspective' (2009) 9 *Ethnicities* 291; L Eko and D Berkowitz, 'Le Monde, French Secular Republicanism and the Mohammed Cartoons Affair' (2009) 71 *The International Communication Gazette* 181; T Modood et al, 'The Danish Cartoon Affair: Free Speech, Racism, Islamism and Integration' (2006) 44 *International Migration* 3.

of the newspaper, which had previously published cartoons about the Prophet Mohammad. After the attack, there was a massive demonstration of people in Paris, with many world political leaders in attendance, condemning the attacks on the French publication and supporting freedom of speech.[26]

A very recent case arose in Indonesia when the elected Governor of Jakarta was accused of blasphemy, which led to large peaceful protests and occasional violent protests in Indonesia. Blasphemy allegations were raised when the Christian Governor of Jakarta referred to a verse of the Quran which implied Muslims should not choose a non-Muslim leader. The Governor apologised for the remarks insisting that his criticism was directed against those who used the Quran to attack him but not the Quran itself.[27] The Indonesian Attorney General's office is charging the Governor with blasphemy.[28]

Apart from these high-profile international incidents, there have always been national cases in various Muslim countries where people have been accused, charged and convicted of apostasy, blasphemy, and in citing sacred principles of the religion of Islam. A number of the cases shall be examined in Chapter 6 of this study.[29]

III. Freedom of Expression in the Quran

A. General Quranic Principles

In a number of places in the Quran, there are verses which can be interpreted as recognising aspects of freedoms of religion and expression. Generally, the spirit of the Quran is not inconsistent with freedom of thought and expression.

[26] See A Porter, 'Words Can Never Hurt Me? Sticks, Stones and Section 18C' (2015) 40 *Alternative Law Journal* 86, RE Howard-Hassmann, 'The Charlie Hebdo Murders and Freedom of Speech' (2015) 2 *The Indonesian Journal of International & Comparative Law* 467; S Juss, 'Burqua-Bashing and the *Charlie Hebdo* Cartoons' (2015) 26 *King's Law Journal* 27; P Sturges, 'Limits to Freedom of Expression? The Problem of Blasphemy' (2015) 41 *International Federation of Library Associations and Institutions* 112.

[27] S Hawley, 'Jakarta Governor Purnama questioned by police over allegations he insulted the Koran' *ABC News Online* (7 November 2016) www.abc.net.au/news/2016-11-07/jakarta-governor-questioned-by-police-over-koran-comments/8003426.

[28] K Lamb, 'Jakarta's Christian governor to face blasphemy trial over insult claim' *The Guardian Online* (16 November 2016) https://www.theguardian.com/world/2016/nov/16/jakarta-christian-governor-to-face-blasphemy-trial-over-islam-insult-claim; N Rayda, 'Blasphemy trial threat looms for Jakarta governor Ahok' *The Australian Online* (1 December 2016) www.theaustralian.com.au/news/world/jakarta-governor-ahok-to-face-insulting-religion-trial-in-weeks/news-story/64dcfbbffb59de0de0e8de00bf72c1fc.

[29] See D O'Sullivan, 'Egyptian Cases of Blasphemy and Apostasy Against Islam: Takfir al-Muslim' (2011) 7 *The International Journal of Human Rights* 97; DF Forte, 'Apostasy and Blasphemy in Pakistan' (1994) 10 *Connecticut Journal of International Law* 27; DE Arzt, 'Religious Human Rights in Muslim States in the Middle East and North Africa' (1996) 10 *Emory International Law Review* 139; MA Crouch, 'Law and Religion in Indonesia: The Constitutional Court and Blasphemy Law' (2012) 7 *Asian Journal of Comparative Law* 1.

In the view of Muslims, the Quran is revelation (*wahy*) where the Prophet of Islam was connected to the most important, eternal, non-material existent of the universe (God). According to the Muslim belief, the Quran is the book of guidance (*hedayah*) from darkness to light and salvation.[30] Such a book, with its significant effect on the creation and development of one of the most significant human civilisations, would not block freedom of expression and fearless exchange of information and thoughts.

One of the most important verses relating to freedom of expression in the Quran is the verse 256 of the second chapter of the Quran (Baqarah), which clearly declares that

> there shall be no compulsion in religion, verily the truth has become distinct from falsehood, so whoever disbelieves in Taught and believes in Allah has grasped the most trustworthy handhold with no break in it. And Allah is hearing and knowing.

This verse clearly gives people the choice in choosing the right or the false path. According to a famous thirteenth-century Muslim jurist, compelling people to Islam is not possible as confession to Islam, which is the first significant pillar of faith, cannot be achieved by compulsion.[31] Nevertheless, the Quran suggests the right way, is to believe in Allah and rejecting the Satan (The Quran, 2:256).

In another verse, the Quran orders the Prophet that 'say this book (The Quran) is from your Lord so let whoever wills believe, whoever wills disbelieve' (18:29).

Another important verse of the Quran, which maintains freedoms of religion and thought, is in chapter 10, which was revealed to the Prophet in Mecca. The verse questions any attempts by the Prophet of Islam to compel people against their will to believe in Allah. The Quran states 'if God wished everyone on the face of the earth to be believers, are you then compelling the people to become believers?' (The Quran, 10:99). Further, the Quran has allocated one chapter, albeit a short chapter, to explain freedom of religion. The chapter is titled *Al-kafirun* ('Non-believers'): 'In the name of God, the merciful, the compassionate, say all non-believers, I do not worship what you worship and you do not worship Allah that I worship. … So unto you, your religion, and unto me, my religion' (The Quran: 109). According to some scholars, freedom of expression is further confirmed by the Quran where it states (55:1–4) 'God is the most gracious, who taught the divine texts (The Quran), created humans, and taught them the speech (expression)'.[32]

[30] 'Allah is the Protector of those who have faith: from the depths of darkness Allah will lead them forth into light': The Quran 2:257.

[31] 'It is not permissible to compel a disbeliever into professing Islam. If, for example, a non-Muslim citizen (*dhimmi*) or a person of protected status (*musta'man*) is forced to accept Islam, he is not considered a Muslim unless it is established that his confession is a result of his own choosing. If the person concerned dies before his consent is known, he will be considered a disbeliever … The reason for the prohibition of duress here are the words of God Most High that there shall be 'no compulsion in religion': Ibn Qudamah, *Al-Mughni*, vol VIII, 144.

[32] MA Baderin, *International Human Rights and Islamic Law* (Oxford, Oxford University Press, 2003) 126.

Finally, chapter 39 of the Quran provides:

> [Give the good news to] [t]hose who listen [to different views and perspectives (*qual*)], and follow the best [of those views] ... [that] those are the ones that God has guided, and those are the ones who are indeed people of wisdom (*ulul al-bab*).[33]

B. The Doctrine of *Hisbah*

One of the Quranic principles of Islam requires every individual Muslim to command good and forbid evil conduct by other members of the society, including the state. The principle is known also as the principle of *Hisbah*. This means that in a Muslim society, individuals are required to express their views in relation to things that seem good or things that must be forbidden. This can be done through acts, silence or denunciations. According to a Muslim commentator, freedom of expression 'is of central importance to the concept of *Hisbah*'.[34]

The Quran, at least in 10 verses, refers to the principle of *Hisbah*, or *Amr be al-Marouf v Nahy an al-Monkar*. A leading verse is in *Surah al Imran*, which provides that 'there should be from among you a community of people (*Ummah*) who call others to good and enjoin others to right conduct and forbid what is wrong'.[35] In the same chapter of the Quran, another verse provides that 'you are the best community of people who command good and forbid others from committing evil and wrong conducts'.[36] In another verse, the Quran describes the believer as those who believe in Allah and the after-world, and also commands others to do good and forbid evil.[37] In another chapter (*al-araf*), the Quran introduces the prophet of Islam as a messenger who enjoins people to what is good and forbids them from what is evil.[38]

It should be noted that this principle can be used in a modern Muslim majority state as a justification for freedom of expression, and as a tool for members of the community to express their concern with how the government conducts its duties and responsibilities. However, in the history of Islam, and in modern Islamic societies such as Saudi Arabia, Iran and Pakistan, the principle has been used by Muslim majority states to interfere with individual freedoms. For example, in the case of Hamid Abu Zayd of Egypt, discussed above, those people who initiated proceedings, a group of Islamists led by the former state official, filed an order to force divorce but they had no personal interests in the case. To justify their involvement they argued the principle of *Hisbah*. While the Giza Personal Status Court initially rejected the case, holding that the plaintiffs had no direct personal interest

33 The Quran 39: 17–18.
34 MH Kamali, *Freedom of Expression in Islam* (Cambridge, Islamic Texts Society, 1997) 28.
35 The Quran 3:104.
36 The Quran 3:110.
37 The Quran 3:114.
38 The Quran 7:157. See also 9:71; 9:12; and 22:41.

in the matter, the Cairo Court of Appeal reversed the lower court's decision in favour of the plaintiffs. It should be noted that the principle of *Hisbah* is included in the regulations governing the Sharia courts in Egypt.[39]

In spite of the doctrine of *Hisbah* being used by Muslim majority states and Islamic groups imposing rigid regulations on members of the society, the principle itself indicates that the Sharia has a well-established tradition of encouraging members of society to express their views. As stated by Kamali, 'without freedom of expression, it would be inconceivable to command good or to forbid evil'.[40] According to a hadith,

> If [anyone] sees something evil, he should set it right with his hand; if he is unable to do so, then with his tongue, and if he is unable to do even that, then (let him denounce it) in his heart. But this is the weakest form of faith.[41]

One important question in relation to commanding good and forbidding evil may be the meaning and scope of good and evil for the purpose of *Hisbah.* Individual Muslims have different views in relation to what is right and what is wrong. If they have the authority to command others or forbid them from certain activities that they think are good or bad, society may descend into anarchism and irregularity. In Islamic jurisprudence and texts, Muslim scholars have discussed the concept and scope of the principle of *Hisbah* in detail. In most cases, they believe that good (*Marouf*) means what is obligatory under Islam, such as prayer and fasting, and evil (*Munker*) means what is forbidden or *haram*, such as drinking alcohol. A better interpretation may be that Muslims have a duty to command the observation of the rule of law and forbidding breaches of the law by other members of society.

According to the philosophy of *Motezalah*, a branch of Islamic theology, of the eighth to tenth centuries, the doctrine of *Hisbah* is part of Islamic politics where members of the Muslim societies can express their views in relation to the rulers, and vice versa.

In the modern Muslim world, in many Muslim majority states, *Hisbah* is institutionalised in various forms. In Saudi Arabia, *Hisbah* is institutionalised as the Commission for the Promotion of Virtue and the Prevention of Vice (*Hayat al-Amre be al-Marouf v Nahy An al-Monkar*). The Commission is indeed a religious police, which enforces Sharia law, particularly in the public sphere. Members of the police force patrol the streets and take an active role in enforcing dress codes, enforcing the strict separation of men and women, prayer during prayer times, and other behaviour that is required by Islam.[42]

In Iran, there is legislation regulating the principle of *Hisbah*, or *Amr be al-Marouf v Nahy an al-Monkar,* known as the Act for Protection of those Who

[39] Regulations of *Sharia* Court Organization 1931 (Egypt) Arts 89 and 110.

[40] Kamali, *Freedom of Expression in Islam* (n 34) 28.

[41] Muslim, *Mukhtasar Sahih Muslim,* 16, *Hadith* no 34.

[42] See General Presidency of the Promotion of Virtue and the Prevention of Vices, www.saudi.gov.sa/wps/portal/SaudiPages/Pages/organizationDetails/organization-AC041/?gadCode=organization-AC041.

Command Virtue and Forbid Vices.[43] The Act provides for the protection of those who intend to command the application of Islamic principles, largely in public arenas. The provisions are more or less similar to what the Saudi Arabian Commission does, or intends to do. Section 14 of the Act, however, refers to non-governmental institutions which are established for the purpose of *Hisbah.*

In some other Islamic countries, such as Pakistan, Malaysia and Indonesia, some type of *Hisbah* exists or efforts are being made to develop similar initiatives.[44]

It seems that in those Muslim majority states where the principle of *Hisbah* is institutionalised (chiefly Saudi Arabia and Iran) the emphasis is on the state agencies and individuals' empowerment to help the observance of certain, mainly superficial, aspects of the Sharia in public arenas. While there is nothing wrong with individuals or regulated institutions observing certain principles of the Sharia, Muslim governments and societies do well if they encourage the development of non-governmental organisations where these organisations may observe the application of virtue and the prohibition of vice, particularly against the states and powerful individuals and institutions. The Quranic principle of *Hisbah* is a great institution where freedom of expression, particularly the freedom to criticise and engage with governments by members of the society, can be encouraged.

IV. Apostasy and Blasphemy in the Quran

It is notable that there is no reference to the *hadd* punishments prescribed in Islamic law for blasphemy and apostasy in the Quran. In other words, the Quran does not prescribe a penalty for those offences. Generally, there are six *hadd* punishments prescribed under Islamic law. Four of the punishments are set by the Quran: (5:41) (hand amputation for theft); (5:32) (death penalty for armed robbery); (24:2) (100 lashes for fornication or *zina*); (24:4) (80 lashes for slander or false imputation of adultery). The remaining punishments are set by the Sunna, which are lashes for drinking alcohol and the death penalty for apostasy. Blasphemy is generally overlapped with apostasy, and for this, the death penalty is prescribed under traditional Islamic law.

The lack of a specific punishment prescribed in the Quran has led to differences of opinion among some Muslim jurists and Islamic schools of jurisprudence in relation to the extent of criminalising apostasy and blasphemy.

[43] Ghanoun Hemayat az Ameran be marouf v nahian az monkar (Act for Protection of those Who Command Virtue and Forbid Vices) (2014).

[44] See F Saleh, 'The Institution of *Hisbah:* Its Roles in Nurturing Fair and Just Economic System in Islam' (National Seminar on Islamic Economics: Towards Strengthening and Understanding of Islamic Economic System Application in Malaysia, 2009); R Yates, 'Aceh's Sharia Police Get Extended Powers' *The Diplomat* (18 April 2014) http://thediplomat.com/2014/04/acehs-sharia-police-get-extended-powers/.

V. Consultation (Shura)

One of the Quranic doctrines which has significant importance in Islamic law, particularly public law, is the principle of *Shura*, or consultation. The principle of *Shura* is so significant that the Quran places it alongside some of the most important pillars of the faith of Islam, namely believing in God, prayer, and giving charitable taxes (*Alms*). The Quran provides that 'those people who respond to the call of their Lord and perform their prayers and run their affairs through consultations of others among themselves and spend what we have given them as sustenance'.[45] According to a leading modern Muslim scholar, in this verse of the Quran, 'the fact that consultation occurs side by side with the three pillars of faith has been taken to mean that it is an obligation of a similar order'.[46] While this verse is concerned with individual Muslims consulting each other in running their affairs, some other verses of the Quran specifically order the Prophet as the Head of State, to consult people in running their political affairs.[47]

It has been argued that the principle of *Shura*, established in various verses of the Quran, and applied by the Prophet of Islam and his successors, proves that the legal and political system of Islam has certain elements of modern democracies, and can be adjusted to include elements of the rule of law concerning election and representative governments.[48] There have been extensive scholarly debates in relation to the nature of *Shura* in Islam. According to some leading Muslim scholars, the concept of *Shura* in Islam is only advisory in nature.[49] By contrast, many other scholars believe that a *Shura* council has a more important role, and may provide 'mutual advice, through mutual discussions, on an equal footing'.[50]

Whatever the nature of *Shura* is, this significant Quranic principle shows that Islamic law, both in texts and in practice, did not have any intention to shut down the principle of freedom of expression and encouraging the diversity of views and opinions of the community of Muslims (*Ummah*).

[45] The Quran 42:38.

[46] Kamali (n 34) 41.

[47] 'Therefore it is a favour from Allah that you were graceful and gentle to those people. If you have been harsh on them, they would surely have dispersed away from you. Therefore forgive them, and seek pardon for them from Allah, and consult them in the community affairs. When you reach a decision, then trust in God and implement the decision': The Quran 3:159.

[48] A Belén Soage, '*Shura* and Democracy: Two Sides of the Same Coin?' (2014) 8 *Religion Compass* 90; U Shavit, 'Is *Shura* a Muslim Form of Democracy? Roots and Systemisation of a Polemic' (2010) 46 *Middle Eastern Studies* 349; A Black, H Esmaeili and N Hosen, *Modern Perspectives on Islamic Law* (Cheltenham, Edward Elgar, 2013) 38–61.

[49] See the leading work of the famous Muslim public law jurist, AA Maududi, *Political Theory of Islam* (Lahore, Islamic Publications, 1985).

[50] F Rahman, 'The Principle of Shura and the Role of Umma in Islam' in M Ahmed (ed), *State, Politics, and Islam* (Illinois, American Trust Publications, 1986) 90–91.

VI. Freedom of Expression in the Sunna

Sunna means the sayings and the practice of the Prophet of Islam (the tradition of the Prophet of Islam). The collection, interpretation and evaluation of the Sunna of the Prophet are an important area of Islamic jurisprudence. Sunna includes a large number of sayings of the Prophet Mohammad as well as his practice. Sunna, along with the Quran, is the main textual source of Islamic law. A *hadith* is referred to as a tradition emanating from the sayings, actions and practices of Mohammad, the Prophet of Islam.

Similar to the Quran, there are various saying and practices of the Prophet Mohammad, and his companions and successors, which place emphasis on certain areas relating to freedom of expression, such as the doctrines of *Hisbah* and *Shura*. The leading *hadiths* in relation to the doctrine of *Hisbah* is where the Prophet said that if anyone sees some evil conduct by others (presumably including the state authorities), they should set it right with their hands, if unable to do so, then by their tongue, and if this is not possible, then they may denounce and dislike it in their heart. But this is the weakest form of faith.[51] These *hadiths*, and many other sayings of the Prophet, besides various verses of the Quran which require members of the Muslim community to command good and forbid evil conduct, require that individuals must have the freedom to express their views and to be involved in public affairs of their community.

Again, there are many sayings and examples of the practice of the Prophet in relation to consultation and expressing both advisory and political opinion by individual Muslims. It is narrated from one of the Prophet's companions saying that 'I have not seen anyone more diligent in consulting his companions than the prophet himself'.[52]

It is notable that the source of legal principles relating to punishment for apostasy and blasphemy are found in the Sunna. There is a well cited *hadith* from the Prophet which states 'Kill anyone who changes their religion'.[53] It is also reported

> Allah's Apostle never killed anyone except in one of the following three situations: (1) A person who has killed somebody unjustly, was killed (in *Qisas*), (2) a married person who committed illegal sexual intercourse, and (3) a man who fought against Allah and his Apostle.[54]

Traditional Muslim scholars cite a few historical events where the Prophet Mohammad punished those who changed their religion and deserted Islam. However, it must be noted that there are historical events where the Prophet did not punish those who were accused of apostasy and blasphemy. The obvious example

[51] Muslim, *Mukhtasar Sahih Muslim*, 16, *Hadith* no 34.
[52] Al-Tirmidhi, *Sunan al-Tirmidhi*, IV, 213.
[53] Bukhari 52:260.
[54] Bukhari 83:37; see also Bukhari 9:85 and 9:58.

is the case of Abdulla Ibn Abi Sarh, the half-brother of the third caliph, Othman, who was forgiven by the Prophet on the request of Othman immediately after Mecca was conquered by Muslims. Further, occasional punishment prescribed for apostates at the very early stage of the evolution of Muslim Society was based on the fact that the existence of early Muslim society was under threat from apostasy and blasphemy. However, as Islamic society has developed further and the Islamic state has expanded in large parts of the world, including in Africa and Asia, there are no further reasons for punishment of those who change their views and religious beliefs. This means that there is a reasonable space for supporting an interpretation of the Sunna which does not condone capital or severe punishment for apostasy and blasphemy.

VII. Freedom of Expression in the *Fiqh*

There are a number of legal principles and developments under the Sharia which are related to the issue of freedom of expression. Prohibition of apostasy and criminalising blasphemy are the most important areas of Islamic *fiqh*, which put some limitations on freedom of expression in a modern sense. However, there are some other legal principles, albeit not well developed, that are potentially significant rules that may be considered to support freedom of expression in modern Muslim societies. These include the freedom to criticise (*Hurriyyat al-Muaradah*) and the freedom of expression (*Hurriyyat al-Ra'y*). The following discussion shall examine inter alia apostasy and blasphemy under Islamic jurisprudence (*fiqh*), freedom to criticise and freedom of expression, as well as some restrictions provided under the Sharia, which may limit the scope of freedom of expression.

A. Apostasy and Blasphemy

Islamic jurisprudence or *fiqh* has developed a number of legal principles in relation to limiting freedom of opinion and expression. Muslim jurists have developed the aforementioned legal principles based on the Quran, the Sunna and some other sources of law in Islam. This means that Islamic Law (unlike common law and civil law systems) is largely developed by juristic opinions of Muslim scholars. As a result, Islamic law has not been developed by state legislation or by judicial decisions of superior courts. Consequently, it is fair to say that Muslim scholars, traditional or modern, are those who have the authority to reinterpret and amend Islamic law. However, the problem would be that Muslim jurists who hardly are involved in governments and even judiciaries of various Muslim countries are not involved with practical necessities of modern Westphalian state order. Except for very recent decades (particularly since the early 1980s) there have not been many debates in Islamic *fiqh* in relation to freedom of expression and opinion. The limited legal principles, developed in *fiqh* in relation to freedom of thought and expression, are more concerned with the obligation of Muslims to preserve their religion and to avoid expressing opinions inconsistent with principles of the Sharia.

Apostasy and blasphemy are the areas which have developed in *fiqh* and are concerned with freedom of expression. Both the English terms and legal concepts of blasphemy and apostasy are articulated in a category entitled *Al-Raddah* or *Irtidad* in the *fiqh*. Practically, there is not much difference between apostasy (*Irtidad*) and blasphemy (*sabb al-nabi*). However, the latter is more concerned with insulting the Prophet, his household, or the Quran. Blasphemy can be carried out by Muslims and non-Muslims whereas apostasy can only be committed by a Muslim.

Irtidad is defined as 'abandonment of Islam by Muslims and returning to *Kofr* (any belief system other than Islam)'.[55] Under traditional Islamic *fiqh*, *Irtidad* includes changing religion, denying any principles of Sharia, which is accepted by majority of Muslims. It also includes insulting or ridiculing the Prophet Mohammad or any other prophet, insulting or ridiculing the Quran or the Sunna, claiming to have divine inspiration or undermining God's names or rules.[56] The latter, in Western legal tradition, is dealt with under the category of blasphemy. However, under Islamic law there are no major differences between apostasy and blasphemy.

The punishment of *Irtidad* in the Quran is only the hellfire.[57] It can be said that the Quran has treated changing religion as a personal matter that individuals are able to choose without any legal sanctions by the Islamic state.

However, based on some narrated traditions (cited above) and selected practices of the Prophet and his early companions, a majority of traditional Muslim jurists prescribed the death penalty for *Irtidad* of a man but have different views on the punishment of *Irtidad* in relation to a woman. According to the Hanafi School of jurisprudence, a woman who becomes an apostate should be imprisoned until she repents or dies in prison.[58] The Shia School, similar to the *Hanafi* School, makes a distinction between a man and a woman and requires a woman not to be executed but imprisoned until she repents. Further, the Shia school makes a distinction between an apostate who is born Muslim and an apostate who converted to Islam and then abandoned Islam. For the latter case the apostate would be given some time to repent.[59]

The traditional position of Islamic jurisprudence, in relation to the expression of opinion concerning principles of the Sharia, is reinterpreted by some well-known Muslim scholars in recent centuries. These scholars, similar to traditional

[55] S Sayyed Sabeq, *Fiqh al-sunna [The Sunni Jurisprudence]*, 2nd edn, vol 2 (Beirut, Darelfk, 1998) 301.

[56] Ibid 304.

[57] The Quran: 2:217 'and whoever who turns back from their religion and become disbelievers their good deeds would give no fruit in this world and in here after and they will be residents of the hell forever'.

[58] Sabeq, *Fiqh al-sunna* (n 55) 305.

[59] M Helli, *Sharay al-Islam [the Laws of Islam]* (Beirout, Dar al-Adhwa, 1983) 183–84.

jurists, base their argument on the Quran and the Sunna sources of Islam as well as other sources. Muhammad Abdu, and Allama Muhammad Iqbal[60] are amongst two twentieth-century Muslim scholars who emphasise the freedom of thought and expression as prevailing views within the Sharia against the traditional restrictive views, adhered to by traditional jurists (*foqaha*). In view of modern interpretation of the primary sources of law related to freedom of thought and expression, these scholars argue that punishment prescribed for *Irtidad* at early stages of Islam took place because the apostasy at the time had an element of treason in it and it was not a mere expression of opinion.[61] In line with this interpretation more contemporary jurists argue for compatibility of freedom of opinion and expression and religious beliefs in Islam.[62] Mohaghegh Damad has strongly argued that based on the various *Quranic* verses and historical contexts, including the tradition of the Prophet, his companion and early Islamic societies, freedom of thought and religion was tolerated greater than many other societies including the European societies up until the eighteenth century.[63]

There is a number of thematic reasoning advanced by contemporary Muslim scholars in relation to modern revisions of *Irtidad*. First, there is no punishment provided for apostasy in the Quran. Secondly, the tradition of the Prophet does not strongly support punishing apostasy and blasphemy in all circumstances. Finally, apostasy must be analysed and interpreted in the social and political context of the time.[64]

Some contemporary scholars such as Hallaq believe that 'apostasy is in some way equivalent to high treason in the modern nation state'.[65] Further, Rahman, Tariq Ramadan and Kamali have argued that the mere change of religion may not result in commission of the offence of apostasy and blasphemy.[66] Abd al-Mutaal Saidi, an early twentieth-century Muslim scholar, has written a book on freedom of religion in Islam in which he argues against capital punishment for apostates.[67] He cites Ibrahim Ibn Yazd al-Nakhai (died 718 AD), one of the early high-profile scholars of *hadiths* and Islamic jurisprudence, who required that an apostate should not be punished by death; rather, they should be asked to repent forever.[68] He argues that, based on the Quran, Muslims only have the obligation of inviting apostates to return to Islam.[69]

[60] M Iqbal, *The Reconstructions of Religious Thought in Islam*, 2nd edn (Lahore, Iqbal Academy Pakistan Institute of Islamic Culture, 1989) 87.

[61] See Black et al, *Modern Perspectives on Islamic Law* (n 48) 270–71.

[62] M Kadivar, An Introduction to the Public and Private Debate in Islam (2003) 70 *Social Research* 3, 559.

[63] SM Muhaghigh Damad, *Rowshangari Dini [Religious Enlightenment]*, vol 2 (Tehran, Ettelaat Press, 2005) 125–41.

[64] Black et al (n 48) 270.

[65] WB Hallaq, *Sharia: Theory, Practice, Transformations* (Cambridge, Cambridge Press, 2009) 319.

[66] A Black et al (n 48) 270; Kamali (n 34) 93.

[67] Abd al-Mutaal Saidi, *Al-Hurriyah al-diniyah fi al-Islam* (Dār al-fikr al-'Arabī, Cairo, no date, but probably 1960s).

[68] Ibid 72, 148, 156.

[69] For a thorough discussion of Saidi's view, and further discussion on apostasy in Islam, see R Peters and GJJ De Vries, 'Apostasy in Islam' (1976–77) 17 *Die Welt Des Islams* 1.

Abdullahi Ahmed An-Na'im, while acknowledging that the majority of Muslim jurists have categorised apostasy as a *hadd* offence, punishable by death, argues that such classification violates the fundamental right of freedom of religion.[70] He further states

> to remove all constitutional and human rights objections, the legal concept of apostasy and all its serial and criminal consequences must be abolished. Whatever Sunna authority may exist for penal and other legal consequences of apostasy should be taken as transitional and no longer applicable.[71]

Under the Shia school of law, one of the greatest Shia scholars of the thirteenth century, Muhaqiq Helli, whose writings have been the official textbooks of Shia seminaries for several centuries, treats *Irtidad* as *Tazir* punishment and hence it is left up to the state to regulate the offence of apostasy and blasphemy.[72] In recent times, Ayatollah Hossein Ali Montazeri of Qom, Iran (died 2009) issued a *fatwa* stating that apostasy does not include the action of those who change their religion based on research and investigations without any animosity and confrontation. This means that committing apostasy can only be subject of criminal sanctions if it is committed alongside other offences such as treason or violent uprising against the state (*Hirabeh*). The Grand Ayatollah Yosuf Sanei, of Qom Seminary, argues that the death penalty shall not be applied to an apostate for three reasons: First, apostasy is a *Tazir* offence and hence the state must prescribe punishment based on expediency and for protection of the society similar to prescribing punishment for any other offences. Secondly, even if apostasy is a *hadd* punishment, according to the view of some Muslim scholars, *Hudud* punishments cannot be applied except under authority of the Imam (or the Prophet). Finally, even if apostasy is a *hadd*, and *hudud* are applicable in the contemporary world, then according to the principle of 'removal of *hududs* based on reasonable doubt', apostasy should not be the subject of criminal sanctions, least of all, the death penalty"[73]

B. Freedom to Criticise (*Hurriyyat Al-Muaradah*)

Based on primary sources of Islamic law, the Quran and the Sunna, and the practice of Muslim states, particularly immediately after the Prophet Mohammad, a principle has been developed, in Islamic jurisprudence. This principle is known as *Hurriyyat al-Muaradah*, which can be translated as 'freedom to criticise', particularly the government and state authorities.[74] A number of Quranic principles,

[70] AA An-Na'im, *Toward an Islamic Reformation: Civil Liberties, Human Rights, and International Law* (New York, Syracuse University Press, 1990) 109.

[71] Ibid 109.

[72] M Helli, *Sharay al-Islam [The Laws of Islam]* (Beirut, Dar al-Adhwa, 1983) 183–86.

[73] Grand Ayatollah Saanei's Official Website, Questions and Answers on Apostasy',http://saanei.xyz/.

[74] Muhammad Sadiq Afifi, *Al Mojtama Al Islami v Usul Al Hokm [Islamic Society and Governing Principles)* (Cairo, Darr Al Etsam, 1980) 93–96.

inter alia the doctrines of *Hisbah* and *Shura*, have already been examined. The Sunna and practice of the Prophet, and his companions, particularly shows that the freedom to criticise the authorities is a well-established principle of the Sharia. A leading *hadith* on this matter is narrated that the Prophet of Islam said 'the highest jihad (struggle for faith) is to express a word of truth to a tyrannical ruler'.[75] The history of Islam relating to early successors of the Prophet Mohammad, known as the Righteous Caliphate, shows numerous examples where the caliphs and state authorities were criticised, and it was accepted that criticism of the authorities is part of the Sharia. For example, the first caliph of Islam, Abu Bakr, in his inaugural address, said that 'I have been given authority to rule you (by the council of Muslims) but I am not the best of you. I need your help if I am right, and you shall correct me when I am wrong'.[76] This tradition derived from the practices of the first rightly guided caliph of Islam, Abu Bakr, and is widely considered to authorise constructive criticism of states and governments, and encourages Muslim individuals to remain aware and concerned regarding the activities of political leaders in society.[77] There have been many other examples of the practice of the early caliphs of Islam applying the principle of *al-Muaradah*. These include a number of incidents where the second caliph of Islam, Omar Ibn Khattab, encouraged and confirmed evaluation and critical assessment of his rule.[78] Muslim scholars argue that these precedents in the early history of Islam show that Islam gives the citizens the right to monitor government activities, and the right to express their views and opinions.[79] Perhaps one of the best examples of the sunna supporting this proposition of a *hadith*, wherein as already noted above, the Prophet commended speaking out the truth in the face of tyranny and tyrannical rule.[80]

C. Freedom of Expression (*Hurriyyat Al-Ray*)

The word *Ray*, in Arabic, means some kind of knowledge which is based on evidence and reasoning. In Persian, *Ray* refers to votes as well as decisions of the courts. Under Islamic jurisprudence, the sources of law include the two sacred texts (the Quran and the Sunna), which include the practice of the Prophet Mohammad, *Ijma* (the consensus of the majority of Muslim jurists of the time)

[75] Ibn Majah, *Sunan*, Kitab al-Fitan, *Hadith* no 4011.

[76] Abu Habib, Darasah, at 727 as discussed in Kamali (n 34) 50–51.

[77] Ibid 51.

[78] It is well-narrated in the history of Islam, as well as in Islamic jurisprudence, that in his inaugural speech, the second caliph invited members of the community to rectify him if he was wrong in administering the public affairs of Muslims. A man from the audience told the newly elected caliph that if they saw any deviation from the Quran or the tradition of the Prophet, they would rectify it by their swords: Abu Zahrah, al-Jarimah *wa'l-Uqubah fi'l-Fiqh al-Islami [Punishments in Islamic Jurisprudence]* (Cairo, Daralfikr, no date) 160.

[79] For a thorough discussion of the principle of *al-Muaradah* and scholarly debates around this, see Kamali (n 34) 51–52.

[80] Ibn Majah, Sunan, Hadith no 4011.

and *Qias* (analogical reasoning). This means there is no role for the doctrine of *Ray* as a source of law in traditional Islamic law. However, given that both the Quran and the Sunna only cover a limited area of law within the modern practice of legal systems, it is arguable that in the absence of any principles in the major sources of the Sharia, *Ray* (reasoning) can be a source of law or an acceptable method of interpretation of sources of law. In other words, as long as *Ray*, or people's freedom to express their opinion, is not inconsistent with principles of Sharia, it must be protected. Further, there is considerable evidence within the Quran, the Sunna and the practice of the Prophet and his companions, that validates the protection of *Ray* under Islamic jurisprudence. Those Quranic verses and *hadiths* that have been previously cited in favour of certain doctrines, such as *Hisbah* and *Shura*, can also be used to justify protection of the *Ray* under Islamic law.

The position of Islamic jurisprudence, *fiqh*, can be summarised as follows. First, under the *Sharia*, apostasy, which includes the modern concept of blasphemy, is a *hadd* offence with fixed punishment, alongside several other offences. Secondly, unlike some other fixed punishments, such as punishment for stealing (*Sirqah*) and slander (*Qadhf*), which are prescribed by the Quran, the punishments provided for apostasy and blasphemy are not sanctioned by the Quran, but under the Sunna of the Prophet Mohammad. Under Shia School, and according to a few leading jurists, notably Mohaqiq Helli, apostasy is a discretionary offence (*tazir* not a *hadd*) and its regulation is left to the relevant state and the society. Finally, a significant number of modern scholars (both traditional and modern thinkers) argue that apostasy can only be subject of punishment if it is equated to treason.

VIII. Legal Restrictions on Freedom of Expression

Like any other legal system, there are restrictions and limitations on freedom of expression under Islamic law. Apart from apostasy, which has a special significance under Islamic jurisprudence, other limitations are similar to any other legal system. In modern common law and civil law systems, defamation, insults and sedition are the areas in which freedom of expression may be limited. There are also laws prohibiting blasphemous comments in modern legal systems.[81] Kamali cites a large number of criminal offences under the Sharia, which may restrict the practice of freedom of expression. According to him:

> Under the *Sharia*, violations of the freedom of speech occur either in the form of particular offences—such as slanderous accusations (*qadhf*), blasphemy, sedition (*fitnah*), insult

[81] RW Lee, 'The Law of Blasphemy' (1918) 16 *Michigan Law Review* 149; KAE Jacob, 'Defending Blasphemy: Exploring Religious Expression Under Ireland's Blasphemy Laws' (2012) 44 *Case Western Reserve Journal of International Law* 803; J Patrick, 'The Curious Persistence of Blasphemy' (2011) 23 *Florida Journal of International Law* 187; R Sandberg and N Doe, 'The Strange Death of Blasphemy' (2008) 71 *Modern Law Review* 971; BD Inglis, 'Religious Freedom and the Modern Law of Blasphemy' (1956–58) 2 *Victoria University of Wellington Law Review* 229.

> (*sabb*) and cursing (*l'an*), attribution of lies or calumny (*iftira*) and the labelling of others as disbelievers (*tafkfir*)—or they may take the form of a contempt for, or a denial of, the accepted norms and principles of Islam, which may fall under the general headings of infidelity or disbelief (*kufr*), and heresy (*bid'ah*). Some of these are criminal offences and carry specific penalties, whereas other are not so well defined and tend to evoke moral condemnation only.[82]

As already stated, many of the examples stated by Kamali are also limitations on free speech and expression in modern legal systems, such as defamation and sedition. However, some of those examples are specific to the legal system of Islam.

Accusation of slander (*qadhf*) is a Quranic offence which provides a specific punishment for people who accuse others of a specific slander (adultery or *zina*) without providing strict evidences for their claim. According to the Quran, 'And those who launch a charge against chaste women, and produce not four witnesses (to support their allegations), flog them with eighty stripes; and reject their evidence ever after: for such men are wicked transgressors'.[83]

In many modern legal systems, adultery is not a crime; hence, accusing other people of adultery may not be legally prohibited. However, under Islamic law, sexual slander is prohibited and attracts the *hadd* punishment. It is notable that the *qadhf* can be established only if a person accuses another person of actual unlawful intercourse (*zina*). Other accusations may still be subject to punishment, but only the *tazir* punishment, and not the *hadd* punishment. Providing this fundamental punishment for accusations of inchastity by the Quran has created a culture in Muslim societies that goes beyond the limit of law. This means that making accusations, labelling people, or insulting other people for inchastity and sexual offences and misbehaving is taken very seriously. As a result, Muslim societies do not tolerate any expression involving accusations of inchastity and foul language, which involves a sexual nature. In Western countries, while the use of foul sexual language and accusations are not welcomed in public, people who use such language are not charged with an offence. Western societies are more tolerant of this type of language, to the extent that while it is not socially acceptable, such language is not legally prohibited. Therefore, when Salman Rushdie used some of this language in his novel *Satanic Verses*, in relation to the Prophet Muhammad and his wives, the reaction among Muslims was significant.

One of the restrictions to freedom of expression under Islamic law may be insult or *sabb*, particularly against the Prophet of Islam. The meaning and scope of the word '*sabb*', or 'insult', are not clear. However, it seems that words and expressions or gestures which humiliate the dignity of people are prohibited in Islam. However, insulting the Prophet and sacred personalities and values of Islam is significant, and may be subject to the offence of blasphemy. Therefore, insulting the Prophet or the denigration of Allah and the Quran, are subject to blasphemy, which is a serious offence and can attract the death penalty. Again, while there are many verses of the Quran which generally prohibit Muslims from insulting others,

[82] Kamali (n 34) 166–67.
[83] The Quran 24:4.

there is no specific punishment prescribed for blasphemy in the Quran. As noted already, the punishment for blasphemy, like apostasy, is provided by the Sunna.

It is notable that the scope of restrictions on freedom of expression under Islamic law is probably too wide. For example, the principle that criticising or rejecting any undisputed legal principle of Islam may be subject to apostasy may limit legal scholars in Muslim societies from examining, analysing and reforming the Islamic legal system. It also may unreasonably restrict freedom of expression and speech. Having said that, the spirit of Islamic law, and the Quran, is compatible with the principles of freedom of expression and speech. As articulated by An-Na'im, Islamic culture, religion and law can be sustained and promoted by principles of freedom of expression and not by violation of it.[84] The Quran clearly admires people who listen to different views and expressions, and follow the best views.[85]

This is not to say that Islamic law and Muslim culture should be completely changed, and similarly to Western societies, must accept unlimited freedom in relation to sacred texts and people. However, legal principles which regulate the lives and private relationships of people, as well as political structures which may administer the public affairs of people, should not be immune from critical evaluation by all members of any society. The social, political and legal structures of the world have changed, and are changing, and Islamic law and Muslim societies have no other options but to re-evaluate and change their systems. According to new developments, this requires freedom of expression, opinion and speech, which is indeed a universal principle of human rights and international law.

IX. Conclusions

As shall be argued in the next chapter, the internationally established freedom of expression represents one of the fundamental principles of human rights and liberal philosophy. It is also anchored within many legal, political and cultural systems. While the spirit of the Islamic culture and sources of law, and many legal principles of Islam, is compatible with aspects of the principle of freedom of expression as developed under international human rights law, there are some significant challenges in modern Muslim state practices and in Muslim communities around the world. A number of high-profile legal and political cases since the early 1980s, as well as some violent and extremist incidents in recent years, have raised considerable questions in relation to the status of tolerance and freedom of speech

[84] AA An-Na'im, 'The Contingent Universality of Human Rights: The Case of Freedom of Expression in African and Islamic Contexts' (1997) 11 *Emory International Law Review* 29, 42.

[85] 'Give the good news to those who listen to different views and perspectives (*qawl*), and follow the best of [those views] … those are the ones whom God has guided, and those are the ones who are indeed people of wisdom (*ulul al-bab*)': The Quran 39:17–18.

within Muslim societies and under Islamic law. This chapter, whilst considering these cases, has also highlighted the emergent legal and political complexities.

A large number of Quranic verses, as well as legal maxims developed in the Quran such as the doctrines of *Hisbah* and *Shura*, strongly protect and promote freedom of expression and speech. Further, there is no punishment prescribed for either apostasy or blasphemy in the Quran. In other sources of Islamic law such as the Sunna of the Prophet Muhammad (his sayings and practice), while there are sporadic sayings that provide punishment for certain examples of blasphemy and apostasy, there are many other sayings and practices which support and promote freedom of speech and expression. In addition, in Islamic jurisprudence, which consists of Islamic legal principles, a large number of legal maxims, doctrines and principles have been developed, which may well adopt the principle of freedom of speech, as developed in modern legal systems and under international human rights law. Criminalising apostasy and blasphemy in a relatively broad scope is an area of Islamic jurisprudence which may, in some instances, be inconsistent with the principle of freedom of speech under international laws. However, Islamic jurists who, like common law senior judges, have the role of developing new and innovative legal principles, have expressed various views in the interpretation of Islamic law which can accommodate the principle of freedom of expression. Islamic law, like any other legal system, has restrictions on freedom of expression, which are relatively broad. However, these restrictions are not part of the fundamentals of the Sharia, and can be reinterpreted and refined.

6

Freedom of Expression and Freedom of Religion: Conflict or Convergence?

I. Introduction

The preceding discussion has established the value of the rule of law and in so doing highlighted the nexus between freedom of expression and the rule of law. This chapter begins with the broad, yet strong underlying statement that freedom of expression is the fulcrum upon which democracy and the rule of law rotates.[1] The umbilical relationship between rule of law, democracy and the freedom of expression is self-evident: freedom of expression is the foundational stone of all free and democratic societies.[2] Freedom of expression remains a vital tool in criticism of government and holding political figures to account for their actions. Freedom of expression and speech is also an established venue for self-fulfilment and allows an opportunity for autonomy and articulation. It allows for intellectual development, self-belief and human understanding. Freedom of expression also represents a fundamental right within international law.[3] Freedom of expression provides oxygen for other activities and rights including the right to freedom of religion or belief.

Expression partakes of a special right in claiming immunities from regulations because of its unique value for society.[4] As considered in this chapter, it has many advocates–utilitarians, democrats and self-autonomists amongst others and has been defended through multifarious ways.[5] That said, and notwithstanding the virtuous nature of free expression, criticisms abound. There are many critics and

[1] The term 'freedom of expression' is used interchangeably with 'freedom of speech'.

[2] See Human Rights Committee, General Comment No 34 (Article 19: Freedom of Opinion and Expression) CCPR/C/GC/34 (12 September 2011) para 2.

[3] The right to opinion and expression is most prominently crystallised in Art 19 ICCPR, International Convention on the Elimination of All Forms of Racial Discrimination, New York, 7 March 1966, 660 U.N.T.S. Parallel rights are contained in Art 19 of the Universal Declaration of Human Rights, 1948, Universal Declaration of Human Rights, GA Res 217A (III), UN Doc A/810 at 71 (1948); Art 10 of the European Convention on Human Rights (as amended) www.echr.coe.int/Documents/Convention_ENG.pdf and Art 13 of the American Convention on Human Rights 'Pact of San Jose, Costa Rica' (B-32) O.A.S. Treaty Series No 36, 1144 U.N.T.S. 123.

[4] See E Barendt, *Freedom of Speech* (Oxford, Oxford University Press, 2005) 7.

[5] Ibid. See also the consideration in Ch 5 above.

doubters of the value of this right. An unbridled right to freedom of expression is unacceptable. But even with the requisite constraints and limitations, freedom of expression is not necessarily a panacea for a perfect existence.

There are further, as yet, unresolved questions: in the eventuality of a conflict, should free expression trump other equally fundamental rights such as right to freedom of religion or belief? If there are to be restraints and restrictions, who are to be the ultimate arbitrators of such choices?[6] As this part of the study elaborates, religious expressions themselves–in a variety of manner–challenge human rights standards (including some requiring curbs on expression). If a religion or religious ideology is adamant on gender, racial or religious discrimination should limits be drawn on such expression?[7] If a religious-political campaign champions in its cause objectives that include bringing an end to democratic processes themselves, should it be allowed?[8] Can religions be allowed to enjoy special immunities or prerogatives? Whilst religious doctrinal expressions can include criticism of various cultural, political and social practices, can religions themselves claim immunity from criticism or ridicule? The tussle on the limits of freedom of expression in the context of religious rights represents a deeper challenge for international law. The deeper challenge is about the nature and scope of international human rights law in which there are perceived tensions between freedom of expression and claims advanced by followers of religions seeking protection and rights for religions and religious ideologies.[9]

This chapter analyses the various facets of the right to freedom of expression vis-à-vis the right to freedom of religion or belief to assess the potential conflicts between these rights. A central point of contention is the extent to which freedom of expression can make allowances for the protection of religions or religious ideologies. Do constitutional practices or international laws suggest the existence of a norm whereby insults or defamation of a religion per se is prohibited? In the context of this study, state practices emergent from Muslim majority countries retain a particular relevance. Through the legislative, constitutional and political practices of Pakistan, this, chapter assesses the legitimacy and validity of laws

[6] L Alexander, *Is there a Right to Freedom of Expression?* (Cambridge, Cambridge University Press, 2005) 138.

[7] L Alexander, 'Liberals in Religion and the Unity of Epistemology' (1993) 30 *San Diego Law Review* 763; L Alexander 'Good God, Garvey! The Inevitability and Impossibility of a Religious Justification of Free Exercise Exemptions' (1998) 47 *Drake Law Review* 35; S Fish, 'Mission Impossible' (1997) 97 *Columbia Law Review* 2255.

[8] See the *Refah Partisi* case, whereby the ECtHR majority (4-3) upheld the dissolution of the Welfare Party on the grounds that its policies were contrary to the secularist nature of the Turkish state. The Court upheld the ban since the Party's aims included the introduction of Islamic law, which would threaten the fundamental character of the Turkish state and would endanger the right to freedom of religion or belief, a Convention right; *Refah Partisi (the Welfare Party) and Others v Turkey* (2002) 35 EHRR 3; (2003) 37 EHRR 1. See K Boyle, 'Human Rights, Religion and Democracy: The Refah Party Case' (2004) 1 *Essex Human Rights Review* 1.

[9] See RC Blitt, 'Defamation of Religion: Rumors of its Death are Greatly Exaggerated' (2011) 62 *Case Western Reserve Law Review* (2011) 347, 351.

that protect religions, religious personalities and symbols (and in some cases impose serious penal sanctions for blasphemy). In examining the practice of anti-blasphemy laws as applied in Pakistan, the study analyses the challenges to the right to freedom of expression and also the wider impact of such laws and norms upon individual and collective rights.

II. The Nexus between Freedom of Expression and Freedom of Religion

There is a significant nexus between freedom of expression and the right to freedom of religion or belief. Freedom of expression, including the right to hold opinions, engages significantly with the right to freedom of religion or belief. In the context of the right to freedom of religion, an uninhibited and absolute right to have or adopt a religion–the *forum internum*–is protected by the provisions ensuring the right to hold or form opinions. The *forum internum* protected by the rights to hold or form opinions, is guaranteed as an absolute right within international law.[10] The Human Rights Committee has decisively asserted that any criminalisation of holding opinions, regardless of the nature of the opinion, remains incompatible with the right to freedom of expression.[11] The applicability of criminal sanctions for holding of religious opinions is therefore impermissible and incompatible with the fundamental precepts of the right to freedom of opinion and expression as expressed in Article 19 of the ICCPR. Similarly any coercion to influence the holding or not holding of religious opinions is prohibited by the ICCPR within international law.[12] It is thus impermissible to criminalise holding of religious opinions nor is it acceptable to deploy 'harassment, intimidation or stigmatization of a person including arrest, detention, trial or imprisonment for reasons of the opinions they may hold'.[13] Exercise of religion or religious beliefs and sentiments have such significant nexus with freedom of

[10] See Human Rights Committee, General Comment No: 22 (Article 18) The right to freedom of thought, Conscience and Religion CCPR/C/21Rev.1/Add.4 (27 September 1993) in which the 'Committee observes that the freedom to "have or to adopt" a religion or belief necessarily entails the freedom to choose a religion or belief, including, inter alia, the right to replace one's current religion or belief with another or to adopt atheistic views, as well as the right to retain one's religion or belief. Article 18(2) bars coercions that would impair the right to have or adopt a religion or belief, including the use of threat of physical force or penal sanctions to compel believers or non-believers to adhere to their religious beliefs and congregations, to recant their religion or belief or to convert. Policies or practices having the same intention or effect, such as for example those restricting access to education, medical care, employment or the rights guaranteed by article 25 and other provisions of the Covenant are similarly inconsistent with article 18(2). The same protection is enjoyed by holders of all beliefs of a non-religious nature'; ibid para 5.

[11] See Human Rights Committee General Comment No: 34 (n 2) para 9.

[12] Ibid para 10.

[13] Ibid para 9.

expression that without the latter, the right to freedom of religion or belief is rendered vacuous and incomplete. As the Rabat Plan of Action emphasises

> The freedom to exercise or not one's religion or belief cannot exist if the freedom of expression is not respected as free public discourse depends on respect for the diversity of deep convictions which people may have. Likewise, freedom of expression is essential to creating an environment in which a constructive discussion about religious matters could be held. Indeed, free and critical thinking in open debate is the soundest way to probe whether religious interpretations adhere to, or rather distort the original values that underpin religious belief.[14]

Religious expressions may be manifested either individually or in a community and in private and in public.[15] Such forms of expression encompass worship, observance, practice and teaching. Concepts of worship include ritual and ceremonial acts giving direct expression to belief as well as various practices integral to such acts, including the building of places of worship and observance of holidays and rest.[16] The observance and expression of religion or belief includes not only ceremonial acts but also includes customs and traditions in the nature of observance of dietary regulations, the wearing of distinctive clothing or head coverings, participation in rituals associated with certain stages of life and the use of a particular language customarily spoken by a group.[17] The practice and teaching of religion or belief includes such essential activities as the freedom to choose religious schools and the freedom to prepare and distribute religious text or publications.

In all of the aforementioned, religious expressions take a variety of forms including express words, writings and forming images, paintings, dress code, rituals, ceremonial actions and behaviours. Manifestations of religions are also conveyed through such exercises as conversions, proselytisation or preaching and in this process some forms of expression are adjudged impious, heretical, lewd, profane or, as shall be examined in the chapter, outright blasphemous. According to international human rights law, restrictions are permissible upon religious expressions or the freedom to manifest religion or belief only if the law prescribes limitations and these restrictions are necessary to protect public safety, order,

[14] Rabat Plan of Action on the prohibition of advocacy of national, racial or religious hatred that constitutes incitement to discrimination, hostility or violence: Conclusions and recommendations emanating from the four regional expert workshops organised by OHCHR, 2011, and adopted by experts in Rabat, Morocco on 5 October 2012, para 10. See UNCHR, Annual Report of the United Nations Commissioner for Human Rights, Addendum, 'Report of the United Nations Commissioner for Human Rights on expert workshops on the Prohibition of incitement to national, racial or religious hatred' A/HRC/22/17/Add.4 (11 January 2013) www.ohchr.org/Documents/Issues/Opinion/Seminar-Rabat/Rabat_draft_outcome.pdf.

[15] See Art 18(1) ICCPR.

[16] For the Muslims, the annual pilgrimage to Mecca (*Zil-Hajj*) in Saudi Arabia constitutes an essential tenet of faith. Similarly, financial and material support including building of places of worship (*Masajid*) is a high priority religious act.

[17] Muslim rituals include fasting during the holy month of Ramadan; the wearing of hijab for women and the ritual sacrifice of an animal, the *Qurbani* on the 10th, 11th and 12th of Zil-Hajj.

health or morals, or the fundamental rights and freedoms of others.[18] As shall be considered in greater detail, forms of religious expression that lead to advocacy of national, racial or religious hatred constitute incitement to discrimination, hostility or violence and are also to be prohibited by law.

III. Freedom of Expression, Democracy and Government

Freedom of expression, including the freedom to form and hold opinions, is often treated as a segment of rule of law and pathway to democratic governance. Freedom of expression forms the basis of the citizen's rights to participatory democracy. It is critical for the 'prosperity of a pluralistic culture'[19] and remains crucial for controlling governmental abuse and corruption.[20] The rights of citizens to participatory democracy has been the raison d'etre of the first amendment to the United States Constitution,[21] Article 5 of the German Constitution (1949),[22] Article 10 of the European Convention on Human Rights (1950)[23] and Article 21 of the Japanese constitution (1946).[24]

An uninhibited right to form opinions, including those driven by religious ideologies or religious morality, and the prerogative to exchange ideas forms an essential platform for understanding of state structures, the law-making apparatus and the content of laws. As Allen notes, without the freedom of speech, conscience, religion and association and without the capability to criticise governments, the moral justification for following laws would be lost:

> The rights to receive information and to exchange and debate ideas, whenever such information and ideas concern the content of the laws and the nature of government actions and policies, are integral features of the constitutional interpretation of the rule of law. These rights, along with the associated liberties of conscience and association, both protect and foster rational criticism of government and enable the citizen to determine the moral justification for compliance with its rules or orders. It would make no sense to require the conformity of laws to a conception of the common good, and invite the citizen to acknowledge their claim to his obedience on the basis of that conception, if liberties of speech, conscience and association were denied. It would be inconsistent with a view of legal obligation grounded in moral responsibility towards the common good

[18] See Art 18(3) ICCPR.

[19] See J Raz, 'Free Expression and Personal Identification' (1991) 11 *Oxford Journal of Legal Studies* 303, 324.

[20] Ibid 324.

[21] First Amendment (Amendment I) to the US Constitution (adopted on 15 December 1791).

[22] Art 5: Freedom of expression, arts and sciences, Basic Law for the Federal Republic of Germany, 23 May 1949, www.refworld.org/docid/4e64d9a02.html.

[23] Art 10: Freedom of Expression, ECHR (as amended) www.echr.coe.int/Documents/Convention_ENG.pdf.

[24] Art 21, Constitution of Japan, 3 November 1946, www.refworld.org/docid/3ae6b4ee38.html.

> to deny the citizen knowledge of reasons which may exist for disobedience; and it is only the freedom to express his dissent which enables the conscientious citizen, if he resorts to civil disobedience, to distinguish himself from the common criminal who, without questioning the justice of the laws, seeks to evade them for purely personal gain.[25]

The utilitarian argument therefore is that since free expression sustains democracy, it is in the public good.[26] Freedom of expression, however, is a core fundamental right for individuals since it allows individuals the path towards individual self-fulfilment, intellectual development and the opportunity to express one's values and beliefs. It is, in other words, the essential medium for the articulation of one's entire existence. The denial of this right of expression is therefore the denial of individual existence. In further broadening this paradigm, Ronald Dworkin argues for a constitutional conception of democracy whereby political institutions respect the rights of all citizens including minorities and marginalised groups.[27] In making a case for group rights, Dworkin pursues the claim that all minorities are entitled to engage in public discourse expressing and articulating their religious, cultural, sociological and political values as a prerequisite to the constitutional conception of democracy and claims of equal participation before the law.[28] Similarly, according to Dworkin, within this liberal composite, minority rights cannot be surrendered nor can majorities deny minorities their essential freedoms including the freedom of expression and the freedom of religion or belief. Our consideration in Chapter 5 suggests that this matrix of liberal democracy cannot be applied to modern Muslim majority states such Saudi Arabia and Iran. Furthermore, as this chapter elaborates, minority rights are denied within the legislative and political framework of Pakistan and notions of free expression are curbed through arbitrary and politically mandated anti-blasphemy laws.

In his analysis, Professor Joseph Raz has a position not dissimilar to that of Professor Ronald Dworkin. Raz makes the claim that freedom of expression provides validation of the relevant ways of life of members within each society.[29] This freedom of expression therefore is a recognition as well as a validation of the ways of life of various groups including minority groups. Therefore, in the wider scheme, censoring or criminalising expression is not merely a condemnation of the expression of opinion, but also a censorship of 'whole style of life of which they are a part'.[30] Freedom of expression, according to Raz, validates and supports diversity whereas censorship is an insult and an undue restriction.[31] Raz's

[25] TSR Allen, 'The Rule of Law as the Rule of Reason: Consent and Constitutionalism' (1999) 115 *Law Quarterly Review* 221, 238 (footnotes omitted).

[26] Raz, 'Free Expression and Personal Identification' (n 19) 309. For Joseph Raz, freedom of expression is in the public good, not merely because it supports individual freedom but because it sustains democracy which is in the public good. Ibid 309.

[27] See R Dworkin, *Freedom's Law* (New York, Oxford University Press, 1996) 15–26.

[28] Ibid.

[29] See Raz (n 19) 303, 309–11.

[30] Ibid 310.

[31] Ibid 321–23.

sentiment is graphically illustrated through the anti-blasphemy laws targeting Ahmadiyyas of Pakistan. Although these laws aim to silence the Ahmadiyyas, they are in effect a decisive condemnation and censorship of the entire lifestyle of this community.

The argument supporting a universal right of free expression no doubt carries great relevance. What is possibly more contentious is the desirability of the right to complete uninhibited expression. Free expression, it is argued, leads to forming of opinions and discovery of the truth. The discovery of truth, especially religious truth, however is by no means an objective undertaking. The pointers to truth have different variants and can be transmitted through a range of equally valid interpretations. Therefore, it is a naive assumption that pristine truth would flow automatically from uninhibited or unrestrained freedom of expression. Critics of freedom of speech have even questioned the wisdom of the judgement that free, uninhibited expression inevitably leads to truth. Attempts at establishing the truth within religions confirms the futility of such an exercise.

If the objective of advocating a right to freedom of expression is to establish facts and to reach to the truth, then this goal is premised on the basis that reaching out to the truth is a fundamentally positive attribute and is also in the common good. However, getting to know the truth–as Barendt examines–is not necessarily always in the common good. Knowledge of some truths can be dangerous and socially and politically divisive.[32] The knowledge of truths behind the phenomena of slavery, slave trade, colonialism, racial or religious imperialism has led to bitterness and fragmentation within societies. In the context of Islam, attempts to establish truths within the Sunni or Shia movements have been painfully evident: the 1400 years old Sunni-Shia bloody confrontation is the most direct example of the futility of efforts for the ultimate truth.

A further, more complex question relates to the content of permissible forms of expression and its conflicts with other values, such as religious morality. Liberal democratic paradigms would envision a licence for all forms of expressions, including literary and artistic discourses. The inherent liberalism would allow for incorporation of non-political expressions including commercial expressions and hard-core pornography. If there are to be any regulations, these are to be of a low threshold, allowing maximum space and allowance for expression. Thus, for Ronald Dworkin, extreme speech including defamatory attacks on government officials as well as hate speech is to be tolerated and the state cannot determine the boundaries of acceptable speech. Dworkin draws a broad umbrella of freedom of expression including sexually explicit materials which must be tolerated in a democratic society, even at the expense of undermining the religious or moral value of the majority population.[33]

[32] See Barendt, *Freedom of Speech* (n 4) 8.

[33] See Dworkin, (n 27) 214; R Dworkin, 'Is there a Right to Pornography' (1981) 1 *Oxford Journal of Legal Studies* (1981) 177.

IV. Challenges and Potential Conflicts with the Right to Freedom of Religion or Belief

Despite its acknowledgement, societies and states differ radically in granting the right to free expression. There is a wide divergence in drawing parameters, which are based on historic social, ethical, cultural, political, moral and religious backgrounds. Religions and religious morality strongly feature in defining the nature of expression and placing limitations on expression. An examination of international and comparative laws provides woefully inadequate guidelines on engagement of conflict between the right to expression vis-à-vis the right to freedom of religion or belief. Religious morality can influence speech, actions and behaviour of various segments of the society, for example those of women, religious minorities and transgendered communities.[34] Religious restrictions are placed on women in many societies; dress codes, codes of morality and sexual behaviours are all forms of expression and women often have their expression limited or restrained.[35] Sexual minorities, have, in many societies, also found their rights, including right to expression, restricted and undermined. Religious minorities are also frequently at the receiving end of restrictive laws and regulations imposed by the state apparatus.[36] Depending on the ideological bases and approaches adopted by the majority populations, there are limits set on the behaviour, speech, dress code and physical expression of minorities: overstepping these limits can prove costly leading to denunciations, recriminations and penal sanctions. The ultimate act of sacrilege is manifested in charges of blasphemy or apostasy. Although (as considered in the context of Islamic law in Chapter 5 above) blasphemy is not exclusively a misdemeanour conducted by religious minorities, religious and political dissenters are frequently made the victims.

Latest available figures suggest that strict state-controlled criminally sanctioned anti-blasphemy laws are currently applied in nearly a quarter of all of the world's states.[37] Anti-blasphemy laws are applied in 70 per cent of states from the MENA region, 18 per cent from Asia-Pacific states and 31 per cent of the Americas. There are other states from Africa, namely Nigeria, Somalia and Sudan that apply strict penal sanctions for blasphemy. Anti-blasphemy laws remain on

[34] See J Rehman and E Polymenopoulou, 'Is Green a Part of the Rainbow? *Sharia* and Homosexuality in the Muslim World' (2013) 37 *Fordham International Law Journal* (2013) 1; J Rehman, 'The *Sharia*, Islamic Family Laws and International Human Rights Law' (2007) 21 *International Journal of Law, Family and Policy* 108.

[35] See J Rehman, *International Human Rights Law* (London, Longman, 2010) 511–55.

[36] See S El Feki and J Rehman 'Faith in the Flesh' in K Lalor, E Mills, A Sánchez García and P Haste (eds), *Gender, Sexuality and Social Justice: What's Law Got to Do with It?* (Kent, Institute of Development Studies, 2016) 43–49.

[37] Pew Research Centre, 'Which Countries Still Outlaw Apostasy and Blasphemy?' (28 May 2014) www.pewresearch.org/fact-tank/2016/07/29/which-countries-still-outlaw-apostasy-and-blasphemy/.

the statute books and are applied within the South-Asian states of Pakistan, India and Bangladesh. Blasphemy is also captured by the laws of several European states including Greece, Austria, Denmark, Finland and Ireland. As considered earlier, the common law offence of blasphemy and blasphemous libel within England and Wales was abolished in 2008.[38] This broad overview confirms that anti-blasphemy laws are a global phenomenon and not the domain of one particular region or prerogative of a religious mind-set. In the realm of Islam, one specific form of religious expression is viewed with particular contempt, namely the offence of apostasy, the ultimate act of religious expression of abandoning one's faith and converting to another faith or becoming a non-believer. As examined in Chapter 5, there are possibilities of a fine dividing line between apostasy and blasphemy within the Islamic legal traditions. Serious penal sanctions are provided for apostates in several states, including 60 per cent of the MENA region, 10 per cent of Asia-Pacific and 8 per cent of Sub-Saharan Africa. In addition, there is a wide variant of domestic defamation of religions and hate speech laws across the globe. Defamation of religion laws persist in 15 out of 20 states of the MENA region, 13 out of 48 in Sub-Saharan Africa and 6 out of 35 states of the Americas including Brazil and Canada.[39]

With this disturbing situation at the national level, it is necessary to look at guidelines from the international and regional laws. The ICCPR, the most widely accepted international civil and political rights instrument, deals with the right to freedom of expression in Articles 19 and 20, as well as in Articles 17, 18, 25 and 27. Articles 19 and 20 provide as follows:

> Article 19
>
> 1. Everyone shall have the right to hold opinions without interference.
>
> 2. Everyone shall have the right to freedom of expression; this right shall include freedom to seek, receive and impart information and ideas of all kinds, regardless of frontiers, either orally, in writing or in print, in the form of art, or through any other media of his choice.
>
> 3. The exercise of the rights provided for in paragraph 2 of this article carries with it special duties and responsibilities. It may therefore be subject to certain restrictions, but these shall only be such as are provided by law and are necessary:
>
> (a) For respect of the rights or reputations of others;
> (b) For the protection of national security or of public order (ordre public), or of public health or morals.

[38] The Criminal Justice and Immigration Act 2008 provides for the abolition of the common law offences of blasphemy and blasphemous libel. According to s 79(1), 'The offences of blasphemy and blasphemous libel under the common law of England and Wales are abolished'; see Criminal Justice and Immigration Act 2008, www.opsi.gov.uk/acts/acts2008/ukpga_20080004_en_1 See also pt II above.

[39] Pew Research Centre, 'Which Countries Still Outlaw Apostasy and Blasphemy?' (n 37).

Article 20

1. Any propaganda for war shall be prohibited by law.

2. Any advocacy of national, racial or religious hatred that constitutes incitement to discrimination, hostility or violence shall be prohibited by law.

The Human Rights Committee has engaged with and commented upon state practices relating to the challenges emanating from religious expression and the potential conflict between freedom of expression vis-à-vis freedom of religion or belief in three of its four mechanisms: the compulsory reporting mechanisms, General comments interpreting and explaining the ICCPR provisions and the individual complaints procedure.[40] In its various activities the Committee has highlighted and elaborated upon the relationship between freedom of expression and freedom of religion or belief as well as the relationship between the provisions of Article 19 and Article 20 of the Covenant. Article 19 has also been the subject of a general comment, in which the Committee has specifically engaged with matters related to freedom of religion or belief including the validity of anti-blasphemy laws.[41]

In its General Comment 34 (para 48) the Human Rights Committee notes:

> Prohibitions of displays of lack of respect for a religion or other belief system, including blasphemy laws, are incompatible with the Covenant, except in the specific circumstances envisaged in article 20, paragraph 2, of the Covenant. Such prohibitions must also comply with the strict requirements of article 19, paragraph 3, as well as such articles as 2, 5, 17, 18 and 26. Thus, for instance, it would be impermissible for any such laws to discriminate in favour of or against one or certain religions or belief systems, or their adherents over another, or religious believers over non-believers. Nor would it be permissible for such prohibitions to be used to prevent or punish criticism of religious leaders or commentary on religious doctrine and tenets of faith.[42]

In highlighting the relationship between Article 19 and Article 20 of the Covenant, the Committee makes the following observations:

> Articles 19 and 20 are compatible with and complement each other. The acts that are addressed in article 20 are all subject to restriction pursuant to article 19, paragraph 3. As such, a limitation that is justified on the basis of article 20 must also comply with article 19, paragraph 3.[43]

[40] On the work of the Committee, see A De Zayas, J Möller and T Opsahl, 'Application of the International Covenant on Civil and Political Rights under the Optional Protocol by the Human Rights Committee' (1985) 28 *German Yearbook of International Law* 9; PR Ghandhi, *The Human Rights Committee and the Right of Individual Communication: Law and Practice* (Aldershot, Ashgate, 1998); D McGoldrick, *The Human Rights Committee: Its Role in the Development of the International Covenant on Civil and Political Rights* (Oxford, Clarendon Press, 1991).

[41] Human Rights Committee General Comment No: 34 (n 2) para 48.

[42] Ibid para 48.

[43] Ibid para 50.

> What distinguishes the acts addressed in article 20 from other acts that may be subject to restriction under article 19, paragraph 3, is that for the acts addressed in article 20, the Covenant indicates the specific response required from the State: their prohibition by law. It is only to this extent that article 20 may be considered as *lex specialis* with regard to article 19.[44]

> It is only with regard to the specific forms of expression indicated in article 20 that States parties are obliged to have legal prohibitions. In every case in which the State restricts freedom of expression it is necessary to justify the prohibitions and their provisions in strict conformity with article 19.[45]

V. The Boundaries of Freedom of Expression, Freedom of Religion or Belief and Anti-blasphemy Laws

As has been noted above, the Human Rights Committee has declared anti-blasphemy laws incompatible with freedom of expression, unless these are targeted at prohibiting by law advocacy of religious hatred that constitutes incitement to discrimination, hostility or violence. Anti-blasphemy laws also must not discriminate in favour of or against a particular religion or the followers of any particular religion.[46] Similarly it is not permissible for anti-blasphemy laws to prevent or indeed to punish criticisms of religious leaders or institute punishments for criticisms of religious doctrines or the tenets of faith.[47]

The Covenant and the Committee suggest the illegality of anti-blasphemy laws that purport to prohibit lack of respect for a particular religion or criticism of a tenet of faith or ridiculing of its religious leaders except in the specific circumstances of Article 20(2). Thus, even religious offensive comments, insults or ridicule of religion do not authorise restriction through the introduction of anti-blasphemy laws. While there appears to be clarity in theory, in practice there is considerable confusion while dealing with anti-blasphemy laws, defamation of religion laws and incitement to religious hatred laws. Therefore, notwithstanding a robust approach adopted by the Human Rights Committee, the *Realpolitik* appears to be much sterner. Substantial campaigns have been launched to protect religions from insults, ridicule and offensive comments thereby sanctifying and justifying anti-blasphemy laws. The defenders of anti-blasphemy laws or defamation of religion laws are plentiful in governments, within civil societies and even

[44] Ibid para 51.
[45] Ibid para 52.
[46] Ibid para 48.
[47] Ibid.

in the human rights community. One such strong proponent of inducting laws to prevent and punish blasphemy is the former Special Rapporteur on Contemporary forms of Racism, Racial Discrimination and Xenophobia and related Intolerance, Doudou Diène. In his official capacity as the Special Rapporteur on Contemporary forms of Racism, Racial Discrimination and Xenophobia and related Intolerance, Doudou Diène lent support to measures to prevent blasphemy, for in his view, blasphemy or defamation of religion provides

> the intellectual justification and legitimizing discourse that support all forms of discrimination. Without it, institutionalized and physical violence cannot be sustained. When defamatory discourse meets with enabling political, intellectual and media-related local conditions, including socio-economic exclusion of religious minorities, it resonates in society and gains strength. Therefore, fighting religious discrimination in general requires a strong focus on preventing the direct and indirect consequences of defamation of religions, including its role in legitimizing racist and discriminatory discourse.[48]

For Diène, insults to religion or blaspheming a religion itself is unacceptable since it instutionalises discrimination, ostracisation and physical violence of the religious minorities. In this view, blasphemy or insults to religions must be prohibited in order to eradicate religious discrimination. He appears to suggest that it is the combination of defamatory discourses alongside other forms of socio-economic exclusions that lead to institutionalised discrimination and physical violence. Religious discrimination and violence against minorities is so inextricably linked with defamation of religions that without the removal of such blasphemous environment it would not be possible to eradicate discrimination or violence against minorities. Social and political context are clearly relevant for minorities and in an environment that is hostile to their religion and their religious tenets, individuals belonging to these minorities are unlikely to prosper.

The arguments advanced by Diène may well be appealing if laws are installed to protect religious minorities and their faith from the blasphemy or defamation of their religions committed by the majority populations. However, Diène's arguments are flawed in contexts where at the constitutional and domestic levels, the majority population establishes laws to capture and punish expressions made by religious minorities that are not in conformity with the wishes of the powerful majority. Contrary to Doudou Diène's assertions defamation of religious laws or anti-blasphemy laws, in general, are about preserving the status quo and domination of the predominant faith and not necessarily about protecting religious minorities. Anti-blasphemy laws have tended to be politically motivated

[48] 'Racism, Racial Discrimination, Xenophobia and Related forms of Intolerance: Follow-up to Implementation of the Durban Declaration and Programme of Action' Report of the Special Rapporteur on Contemporary forms of racism, racial discrimination, xenophobia and related forms of Intolerance: Doudou Diène, on the manifestation of defamation of religions and in particular on the serious implications of Islamophobia on the enjoyment of all rights, A/HRC/6/6 (21 August 2007) para 13.

and in many instances led to abuse of minority rights. As the former UN Special Rapporteur on the Prevention of Discrimination and Protection of Minorities, Arcot Krishnaswami, has emphasised

> [t]he laws against blasphemy have been framed in such a manner that they characterize any pronouncement not in conformity with the predominant faith as blasphemous. Under such laws, censorship of books, pamphlets and newspapers, as well as control of the media of mass communications such as films, radio, television and the like, have sometimes been used to limit unduly—or even to prohibit altogether—the dissemination of beliefs other than those of the predominant religion or philosophy.[49]

It is the case that in the present context Diène has a narrow focus: xenophobia and related forms of intolerance and, in particular, Muslim minorities and Islamophobia in the west. In his campaigns, he urges the criminalisation of Islamophobia and argues for the establishment of the norm prohibiting defamation of Islam. Diène controversially points to the 'explicit defamation of Islam'[50] and thereby blurs the boundaries between Islamophobic statements which target Muslim minorities and legitimate intellectual criticism of Islam or Islamic practices. Diène emphatically asserts that

> Islamophobic statements have been falsely claimed to be scientific or scholarly, in order to give intellectual clout to arguments that link Islam to violence and terrorism. Furthermore, the manipulation and selective quoting of sacred texts, in particular the Koran, as a means to deceptively argue that these texts show the violent nature of Islam has become current practice.[51]

Diène's arguments are flawed in that human rights norms can only successfully operate if allowed to engage, challenge and question religions and religious beliefs. Criticisms of a religion–including ridicule and insult–cannot be consigned to criminal sanctions so long as it does not incite religious hatred or leads to imminent violence. Asma Jahangir, the former Special Rapporteur on Freedom of Religion or Belief, makes the point that '[f]reedom of religion primarily confers a right to act in accordance with one's religion but does not bestow a right for believers to have their religion itself protected from all adverse comment'.[52] An additional factor is that while speech which incites others to hatred or damages the reputation of others may be limited under Article 20(2) ICCPR, this cannot be extended past groups and individuals to protect 'religions'.

[49] See A Krishnaswami, *Study of Discrimination in the Matter of Religious Rights and Practices* (New York, United Nations, 1960, www2.ohchr.org/ENGLISH/ISSUES/RELIGION/docs/Krishnaswami_1960.pdf, at 41.

[50] A/HRC/6/6, para 23.

[51] Ibid para 23.

[52] 'Report of the Special Rapporteur on freedom of religion or belief, Asma Jahangir, and the Special Rapporteur on contemporary forms of racism, racial discrimination, xenophobia and related intolerance' Doudou Diène, further to Human Rights Council decision 1/107 on incitement to racial and religious hatred and the promotion of tolerance A/HRC/2/3 (20 September 2006) para 37.

Asma Jahangir has further argued that

> [t]he right to freedom of expression can legitimately be restricted for advocacy that incites to acts of violence or discrimination against individuals on the basis of their religion. Defamation of religions may offend people and hurt their religious feelings but it does not necessarily or at least directly result in a violation of their rights, including their right to freedom of religion.[53]

She would appear to further build her case by suggesting that while the difference between criticism of a religion and incitement against the adherents of the same religion might be minimal, if criticism crosses this line, it is prohibited by Article 20(2) ICCPR and, therefore, does not require a further layer of protection through blasphemy laws or criminalisation of defamation of religions.

The human rights arguments as advanced by the former Special Rapporteur Asma Jahangir and the Human Rights Committee point to objective standards of assessing conduct that amounts to advocacy of national, racial or religious hatred constituting incitement to discrimination, hostility or violence. Given the political environment in which much of blasphemy laws operate, in practice, however, these are extremely difficult standards to establish and their appropriate implementation is unlikely. As this study establishes through the case of Pakistan, making objective judgments as to the conduct that amounts to incitement to religious hatred is an almost impossible task. In a societal fabric that is submerged in and biased against other beliefs, it becomes impossible to make objective decisions regarding conduct that amounts to advocacy of religious hatred. The system itself is heavily politicised and judicial officers are frightened or coerced. While investigating the cases emerging from Pakistan, many examples can be provided: subjectivity and prejudice was apparent in the leading case of *Zahiruddin*, where Pakistan's Supreme Court took the approach that it was natural for Muslims to be incited and cause breach of peace in instances when things are said against their Prophet. According to the Court

> It is the cardinal faith of every Muslim to believe in every Prophet and praise him. Therefore, if anything is said against the Prophet, it will injure the feelings of a Muslim and may even incite him to the breach of peace, depending on the intensity of the attack.[54]

Having considered some of the teachings of the leader of the Ahmadiyyas, Mirza Ghulam Ahmad, the Court noted

> Can then anyone blame a Muslim if he loses control of himself on hearing, reading or seeing such blasphemous material as has been produced by Mirza Sahib?[55]

Barendt's prediction is an accurate one as Pakistan's courts are inevitably drawn towards accepting the subjective interpretations and claims of offence caused to the sentiments of the orthodoxy. He notes that

[53] Ibid para 37.
[54] *Zaheeruddin v the State* (1993) SCMR 1718, para 83.
[55] Ibid para 84.

> [t]here is a risk that courts would simply accept the subjective claims of outrage or hurt made by particular religious communities. The result would be the proscription of speech which other groups would cheerfully tolerate or find only mildly offensive when comparable remarks were about them.[56]

VI. Applicability and Impact of Blasphemy: The Case of Pakistan

The continued applicability of anti-blasphemy laws among many jurisdictions raise deeply troubling issues. The absence of an agreed definition of blasphemy alongside political manipulation as an instrument of abuse and exploitation represents historic as well as modern concerns.[57] Pakistan presents a contemporary example of politicisation and manipulation of anti-blasphemy laws. As this discussion highlights, there are serious curbs on religious expression, which include restrictions on the articulation of minority views but which also contain restraints on expression that deviate from the state-sponsored and state-approved religious and ideological narrative.[58] Furthermore, the vague nature of the blasphemy laws and their arbitrary application has produced a culture of religious intolerance, bigotry and fanaticism. There is an environment which inculcates a sense of fear; any criticism of the arbitrariness in the system is often perceived as an attack on Islam, the Sharia and the Islamic system of governance. The situation is so difficult and venomous that even recommendations to reconsider the existence of blasphemy laws evoke risk of serious recriminations and therefore any official proposal of repeal appears unlikely.[59] The mayhem leading to the paralysis of the Federal capital, Islamabad in 2016 in the aftermath of the execution of Mumtaz Qadri–the killer

[56] Barendt (n 4) 191–92.

[57] See J Rehman and S Berry, 'Is "Defamation of Religions" Passé? The United Nations, Organisation of Islamic Cooperation, and Islamic State Practices: Lessons from Pakistan' (2012) 44 *George Washington International Law Review* 431.

[58] See J Rehman, 'The *Sharia*, International Human Rights Law and the Right to Hold Opinions and Expression' in M-L Frick and AT Müller (eds), *Islam and International Law* (Leiden, Martinus Nijhoff, 2013) 244–68; J Rehman 'Minority Rights and the Constitutional Dilemmas of Pakistan' (2001) 19 *Netherlands Quarterly of Human Rights* 417–43.

[59] Over the years there have been significant recommendations for repeal or modifications of the anti-blasphemy laws. During the latest round of the Universal Periodic Review (October 2012) Pakistan received 7 recommendations related to anti-blasphemy laws. For details of these recommendations, see Human Rights Council, Pakistan: Report of the Working Group on the Universal Periodic Review, A/HRC/22/12 (26 December 2012) https://documents-dds-ny.un.org/doc/UNDOC/GEN/G12/190/31/PDF/G1219031.pdf?OpenElement; Human Rights Council, Pakistan: Views on conclusions and/or recommendations, voluntary commitments and replies presented by the State under review A/HRC/22/12/Add.1 (13 March 2013) https://documents-dds-ny.un.org/doc/UNDOC/GEN/G13/118/51/PDF/G1311851.pdf?OpenElement; the former Special Rapporteur on Freedom of Religion or Belief, Heiner Bielefeldt also strongly recommended repeal of blasphemy laws noting that 'States should repeal any criminal law provisions that penalize apostasy, blasphemy and proselytism as they may prevent persons belonging to religious or belief minorities from fully enjoying their

of Punjab Governor, Salman Taseer–confirms not only the power of the religious zealots, but also the vulnerability of the administration to maintain law and order when challenged by fanatical mobs. The late Governor of Punjab, Salman Taseer was campaigning for the release of Aasia Bibi, a Christian woman sentenced to death under section 295-C of the Pakistan Penal Code.[60] The Governor had also condemned the blasphemy laws, as 'black laws', and was supporting a private member's bill in parliament, to amend section 295-C provisions with a view to reducing the prospects of miscarriages of justice and removal of the punishment of the death penalty.[61]

Those protesting at the streets of the Federal capital, Islamabad in March 2016 proclaimed Mumtaz Qadri a national and religious hero and their

> demands included the unconditional release of all Sunni clerics and leaders booked on various charges, including terrorism and murder; the recognition of Mumtaz Qadri as a martyr and the conversion of his Adiala Jail cell into a national heritage site; assurances that the blasphemy laws will not be amended; and the removal of Ahmadis and other non-Muslims who had occupied key posts. They also demanded the execution of blasphemy accused Aasia Bibi, the woman former Punjab Governor Salmaan Taseer was killed for defending.[62]

VII. Rationale behind Anti-blasphemy Laws

The original intent of the British instigated anti-blasphemy law as contained in the Indian Penal Code (1860) had been the maintenance of public order in a multi-religious and religiously sensitive society.[63] This was manifest through the specific provisions enshrined in the Penal Code.[64] In pursuit of its objectives, the Indian Penal Code introduced section 295 (intentional damage or defilement of a place or object of worship), section 296 (disturbing religious ceremonies or gatherings) and section 298 (intentionally insulting an individual's religious feelings).

freedom of religion or belief' 'Report of the Special Rapporteur on freedom of religion or belief'; H Bielefeldt (24 December 2012) UN Doc A/HRC/22/51, para 66. 'Report of the Special Rapporteur on the independence of judges and lawyers, Addendum: Mission to Pakistan, Gabriela Knaul' HRC/23/43/Add.2 (4 April 2013) para 117, www.refworld.org/docid/51b9a0794.html. Also note the detailed study by the International Commission on Jurists on Pakistan's Blasphemy law and the Commission's recommendation, *On Trial: The Implementation of Pakistan's Blasphemy Laws* (Geneva, ICJ, 2015) 57–61.

[60] See 'Pakistan Minorities Minister Shabaz Bhatti Shot Dead' *BBC News* (2 March 2011) www.bbc.co.uk/news/world-south-asia-12617562.

[61] Pakistan Penal Code (Act XLV of 1860).

[62] See Y Yasin, 'Laiquat Bagh to D–Chowk–A Trail of Destruction' (28 March 2016) www.dawn.com/news/1248357.

[63] See the Indian Penal Code (Act No 45 of 1860).

[64] See O Siddique and Z Hayat, 'Unholy Laws and Holy Speech: Blasphemy Laws in Pakistan—Controversial Origins, Design Defects and Free Speech Implications' (2008) 17 *Minnesota Journal of International Law* 303, 307.

In 1927, a further section, section 295-A was inserted, criminalising 'deliberate and malicious acts intended to outrage religious feelings of any class by insulting its religion or religious believers'. The induction of section 295-A was the legislative response to the blasphemous act ensued through the publication of the so-called 'Rangila Rasool' pamphlet.[65] Section 295-A, was intended to criminalise acts that were intended to outrage religious feelings of believers.

Although broadly defined as 'Offences Relating to Religion' within the Penal Code, these offences characterised certain common features. First, these offences were directed at the protection of all religions and were applicable to followers of all faiths without discrimination. Secondly, *mens rea* or intent to commit the crime was integral to the charge, with the prosecution having to satisfy the application of the criminal standard of the crime having taken place, beyond reasonable doubt. Thirdly, the drafting of the provisions of offences was precise, laying out essential criteria for the prosecution to establish, before convictions could be secured.

Since the objective of anti-blasphemy laws was to maintain public order, without prioritising one religion over the other, as judicial arbiters, domestic courts were, on the whole, able to take a more objective stance to minimise abuse emanating from the laws. This remained the position even after the creation of an independent Pakistan in August 1947, with courts requiring the prosecution to fully establish all the ingredients of the charge including the necessity of establishing a deliberate, malicious intent involved in blasphemy charge. Thus, for example, in relation to section 295-A, the Lahore High Court decided in 1960 that

> [T]hings may be said or written which will outrage the religious feelings of followers of other religions. When a person does that, the law will presume that he intended to insult the religious beliefs of the followers of other religions. But even so the ingredients of Section 295-A of the [PPC] will not have been satisfied because they can be satisfied only *if it is established that the intention to insult the religious beliefs was deliberate and malicious.*[66]

It is therefore intriguing to contrast the further additions to blasphemy laws into the Pakistan Penal Code, their rationale and results upon the minority communities. These provisions are as follows: section 295-B (Defiling, etc, of Holy Quran); section 295-C (Use of derogatory remarks, etc, in respect of the Holy Prophet); section 298-A (Use of derogatory remarks, etc, in respect of holy personages); section 298-B (Misuse of epithets, descriptions and titles, etc, reserved for certain holy personages or places); and section 298-C (Person of Quadiani group, etc, calling himself a Muslim or preaching or propagating his faith). The objective of these additional sections of anti-blasphemy laws was not the maintenance of public order but to promote religious orthodoxy, politicise religion and in the

[65] International Commission of Jurists, *On Trial: The Implementation of Pakistan's Blasphemy Laws* (n 59) 8.

[66] *The Punjab Religious Book Society v State* (1960) 12 PLD 629 (Lah) at 638 (emphasis added); also see *Muhammad Khalil v State* (1962) 13 PLD 850 (Lah).

process curb freedom of expression and freedom of religion of minorities.[67] More specifically, the anti-blasphemy provisions within Pakistan's Penal Code relating to Islam are a product of the *Nizam-e-Mustafa movement* (movement for the implementation of the Sharia) during the dictatorial regime of General Zia-ul-Haq (1977–88).[68] These provisions are not aimed at protecting all faiths, but related specifically to blasphemy against Islam and the mainstream Muslim belief. Unlike the colonial implants, these laws were drafted in a manner to relieve the prosecution of the requirement of *mens rea* or criminal intent for the commissioning of the offence. The vagueness and arbitrary construction of these laws rendered great uncertainty in the criminal law and implementation of the penal code.

VIII. Natural Justice, Rule of Law and the Crime of Blaspheming

The prosecution of blasphemy impinges upon freedom of expression and the right to freedom of religion or belief. However, in this process it also tramples over many of the cardinal principle of natural justice, the rule of law and fundamental rights provisions of the Constitution of Pakistan 1973, including the right to freedom of religion or belief, freedom of expression as well as the right to fair trial.[69] Sensing risks from injudicious domestic laws and arbitrary practices, in 2012, the Supreme Court of Pakistan confirmed that the same meaning and content is to ascribed to the right to fair trial in the context of Pakistan as is '[b]roadly universally recognized'.[70] In associating the right to a fair trial with the fundamental right of access to justice, the Supreme Court noted that this right '[s]hould be read in every statute even if not expressly provided for it'.[71] In its more recent jurisprudence, whilst reaffirming the nexus between the right to fair trial and the rule of law, the Lahore High Court emphasised that '[t]he right of fair trial is essential right in all countries respecting the rule of law'.[72] The Court then highlighted what it termed as the 'basic ingredients of fair trial' as:

(i) the Court/Tribunal be independent, impartial and established under the law,
(ii) all persons shall be equal before the courts and Tribunal in the determination of their right and obligations;

[67] JT Temperman, 'Blasphemy, Defamation of Religions and Human Rights Law' (2012) 26 *Netherlands Quarterly of Human Rights* 517, 522.
[68] On the politicised nature of these anti-blasphemy laws, see J Rehman, 'Freedom of Expression, Apostasy and Blasphemy within Islam' (2010) 79 *Criminal Justice Matters* 4.
[69] International Commission of Jurists (n 59) 5–8.
[70] *Suo Moto Case No 4 of 2010 [Contempt Proceedings against Syed Yousaf Raza Gillani, the Prime Minister of Pakistan regarding non-compliance of the Court's Order dated 16-12-2009] Criminal Orignal Petition No 6 of 2012 in Suo Moto Case No 4 of 2010, decided on 26 April, 2012*, PLD 2012 SC 553, para 33.
[71] Ibid para 26.
[72] *Bilal Akbar Bhatti v Election Tribunal etc.* PLD 2015 Lahore 272, para 13.

(iii) every one shall be entitled to a fair hearing within reasonable time;
(iv) every one shall have a right of counsel;
(v) right of public hearing if not prohibited by law;
(vi) the procedure of trial as provided by the statute to be followed and
(vii) the statute must provide a remedy of appeal.[73]

The structure, content and manner of the prosecution of anti-blasphemy laws falls foul not only of the aforementioned injunctions of the Pakistani legal jurisprudence, but also contravenes the cardinal principles of rule of law and natural justice. A key prerequisite of natural justice and the right to fair trial, according to the International Commission of Jurists, is

> that criminal offences must be prescribed by law and must conform to the principle of legality. This means that the laws proscribing acts or omissions as criminal must be formulated clearly and precisely to ensure individuals can regulate their conduct accordingly ... Crimes must be classified and described in precise and unambiguous language that narrowly defines the punishable offense. This means that there must be a clear definition of the criminalized conduct, that establishes its elements and the factors that distinguish it from conduct that is permissible. Vague laws undermine the rule of law because they leave the door open to selective prosecution and interpretation, based on discriminatory policies of government officials and the personal predilections of judges ... The principle of legality, as well as the presumption of innocence, also requires that the prosecution prove each element of the crime to the required legal standard (in criminal cases beyond a reasonable doubt).[74]

The essence of natural justice is the applicability of presumption of innocence for every individual unless and until proven guilty, with the prosecution having the burden of proving the commission of offence beyond reasonable doubt. However, in the case of prosecuting anti-blasphemy laws within Pakistan, the prosecution is not only not required to prove its case beyond reasonable doubt, many of these offences are deemed by the courts as procedurally strict liability offences. Therefore, as strict liability offences, the prosecution does not need to establish any specific intention to blaspheme on the part of the defendant. Section 295-C, which was inserted by the Criminal Law (Amendment) Act, III of 1986 and was part of the wider agenda of Islamisation of Pakistan under General Zia-ul-Haq, provides a problematic proof of the application of strict liability to offences that now carry a statutory punishment of death. Although originally designed as an alternative form of punishment, the death penalty was deemed mandatory after the Federal Shariat Court ruled in 1990 that the alternative punishment of life imprisonment was repugnant to the injunction of Islam.[75] However, within the same judgment, the Federal Shariat Court also made the following pronouncements:

> 295-C should be amended to make 'the same acts or things when said about other Prophets, also an offence with the same punishment as suggested above'; and Blasphemy

[73] Ibid para 13.

[74] International Commission of Jurists (n 59) 18–19 (footnotes omitted); see the *Constitution of the Islamic Republic of Pakistan* (1973) as amended; Ch 1: Fundamental Rights, www.na.gov.pk/publications/constitution.pdf.

[75] *Muhammed Isamail Queshi v Pakistan* PLD 1991 FSC 10.

under section 295-C was an 'intentional or reckless wrong', and required the requisite *mens rea* of 'intention, purpose, design, or at least foresight'.[76]

Since the government took no action in response to the judgment of the Federal Shariat Court, this Court's interpretation of section 295-C remains binding upon all courts of Pakistan. Regrettably, while the alternative punishment of imprisonment is no longer valid, Pakistani courts have decided to shed the Federal Shariat Court's explicit injunction of the necessity of establishing 'intention, purpose, design, or at least foresight' and wholly treat the offence under section 295-C as pertaining to the realm of strict liability. There are additional overarching flaws in the system of prosecuting anti-blasphemy laws. As the United States Commission for Religious Freedom has pointed out, accusations of blasphemy can be launched spuriously with the accusers not being legally required to present actual evidence of blasphemy.[77] The system, as such, does not carry penalties for false accusations of blasphemy, encouraging allegations based on personal vendettas, enmities or pure and simple hatred for non-Muslims.[78] As noted, the heavily politicised nature of the anti-blasphemy laws also presents a very serious concern owing to their inherent ambiguity and lack of specificity; the prosecution of offences under section 295-C provides a significant example of vague provisions that are being misapplied with convictions leading to the death penalty. Section 295-C provides as follows:

Use of derogatory remarks, etc., in respect of the Holy Prophet:

Whoever by words, either spoken or written, or by visible representation or by any imputation, innuendo, or insinuation, directly or indirectly, defiles the sacred name of the Holy Prophet Muhammad (peace be upon him) shall be punished with death, or imprisonment for life, and shall also be liable to fine.

Criminal sanctions within the Penal Code based upon terminology such as 'words, either spoken or written, or by visible representation or by any imputation, innuendo, or insinuation, directly or indirectly' provide considerable ambiguity of legal language. Similarly, the meaning of the term 'defile' is vague and uncertain. As the International Commission of Jurists has pointed out

[t]he vague and overbroad wording of section 295-C of the Pakistan Penal Code, which criminalizes words, representations, imputations, innuendos, or insinuations, which directly or indirectly, defile 'the sacred name of the Holy Prophet', has allowed prejudices, religious leanings and personal predilections of judges to shadow their judgments, calling into question their impartiality. This bias is apparent in the conduct of judges during blasphemy proceedings, and also their judgments. These concerns are magnified further by the requirement under Pakistani law that judges presiding over first instance trials in

[76] Ibid.

[77] United States Commission on International Religious Freedom (Washington, USCIRF, 2016) 114.

[78] Ibid 114.

> 295-C cases be Muslim. The provision, when coupled with the vagueness of the law, all but invites the types of partiality … and is inconsistent with the rights to trial before an independent and impartial court.[79]

As considered in this chapter, the nature of these laws has opened up an opportunity for manipulative segments within society to target vulnerable individuals leading to considerable miscarriages of justice. There have been convictions by trial courts and death sentences awarded where the accused was engaged in academic or intellectual debate[80] or alleged statements were made by mentally unstable or physically handicapped persons[81] or indeed, most commonly, as a response to localised, land, business or resource disputes. Examples abound as the history of spurious claims leading to convictions is long and protracted. In the now infamous case of Aasia Bibi, Ms Bibi was working as a farmhand in Ittan Wali, a village 60 miles west of Lahore. During her work in the fields she was asked by a landlord to fetch water. She complied, but the other women she was working with–all Muslims–refused to touch the water bowl and drink the water: as it had been touched by a Christian, it was considered to be 'unclean'.[82] Subsequently, a Muslim mob was initiated in Sheikhupura, Ms Bibi was taken to the police station, and blasphemy charges were framed against her: she was prosecuted under section 295-C of the Pakistan Penal Code for insulting the Prophet and, on the 7 November 2010, she was sentenced to death (hanging) by the local court of Sheikhupura.[83] A few days later, the Lahore High Court restrained both the Pakistan President Zardari and the late Punjab Governor, Salman Taseer, from pardoning her or from taking part in any activity aimed at securing pardon for her. Further, on 6 December 2010, the Lahore High Court dismissed a petition that sought a direction to parliament to desist from amending the blasphemy provisions of the Penal Code and confirmed the death sentence. On 8 December 2010, Yousuf Quershi, Imam of Mohabat Khan mosque in Peshawar, pronounced a reward of Rs. 500,000 for anyone who killed Bibi if the verdict was not applied.[84] Already, during the 1990s, Pakistan's reputation was

[79] International Commission of Jurists (n 59) 34.

[80] See Y Sheikh, 'Blasphemy: My Journey through Hell' (2004) https://mm-gold.azureedge.net/Articles/Younus_Sheikh/blasphemy.html (2004).

[81] International Commission of Jurists (n 59) 34.

[82] See Human Rights Commission of Pakistan (HRCP) Report, *State of Human Rights in 2010*, Lahore, 2011 at 55, 134; 'Asia Bibi, Pakistan Blasphemy Case Defendant, Death Sentence Handed Down' *Huffington Post* (25 May 2011) www.huffingtonpost.com/2010/11/11/asia-bibi-pakistan-blasph_n_782297.html; F Hassan, *Blasphemy in Pakistan* (January–March 2012) 28(1) *Peace Magazine* 19.

[83] J Perlez, 'Pakistani Sentenced to Death May Get a Pardon' *New York Times* (22 November 2010) www.nytimes.com/2010/11/23/world/asia/23pstan.html; 'Christian woman sentenced to death in Pakistan for blasphemy' *The Telegraph* (9 November 2010) www.telegraph.co.uk/news/religion/8120142/Christian-woman-sentenced-to-death-in-Pakistan-for-blasphemy.html; F La Rue, *Report of the Former UN Special Rapporteur on Freedom of Expression* (27 May 2011) A/HRC/17/27/Add.1, 1753. See BBC, 'Fear for Pakistan's death row Christian woman' *BBC News* (6 December 2010) www.bbc.co.uk/news/world-south-asia-11923701.

[84] According to the HRCP Report (n 82) Qureshi said, 'No president, no parliament and no government has the right to interfere in the tenets of Islam. Islamic punishment will be implemented at all

marred by a series of section 295-C convictions including those involving Rahmat Masih, Manzoor Mashi and Salamat Masih.[85] In 1993, Rahmat Masih, Manzoor Masih and Salamat Masih (after a dispute with local Muslims) were accused of writing blasphemous remarks against the Prophet. Salamat was 11 years old and illiterate at the time when he was alleged to have committed those offences. All three accused were shot at in front of the Lahore High Court in March 1994, an attack which caused the death of Manzoor. The remaining two were sentenced to death in February 1995, a verdict that generated international condemnation, with Benazir Bhutto, the then Prime Minister, openly expressing her unhappiness at this outcome. On appeal to the Lahore High Court in 1995, the Court found that both Rahmat Masih and Salamat Masih could not possibly have written the name of Allah in Arabic as they were unfamiliar with the Arabic language. They were acquitted by the High Court, and, once released, fled to Germany.[86] Unfortunately, one of the Lahore High Court Judges, Justice Arif Iqbal Bhatti, who had acquitted the two Christians Salamat and Rahmat Massih, was subsequently murdered. His murderers have not been apprehended, although it is widely believed that the murder was committed by religious extremists.[87]

Further evidence of the vague constitution of the anti-blasphemy laws is provided by the so-called Anti-Islamic Activities of the Quadiani Group, Lahore Group and Ahmadis (Prohibition and Punishment) Ordinance XX of 1984 (inserting section 298-B and section 298-C). According to section 298-B:

> Misuse of epithets, descriptions and titles, etc., reserved for certain holy personages or places:
>
> (1) Any person of the Quadiani group or the Lahori group (who call themselves 'Ahmadis' or by any other name who by words, either spoken or written, or by visible representation-
>
> (a) refers to or addresses, any person, other than a Caliph or companion of the Holy Prophet Muhammad (peace be upon him), as 'Ameer-ul-Mumineen', 'Khalifatul- Mumineen', 'Khalifa-tul-Muslimeen', 'Sahaabi' or 'Razi Allah Anho';
>
> (b) refers to, or addresses, any person, other than a wife of the Holy Prophet Muhammad (peace be upon him), as 'Ummul-Mumineen';

costs [...] We will strongly resist any attempt to repeal laws which provide protection to the sanctity of Holy Prophet Muhammad. Anyone who kills Aasia will be given Rs. 500,000 in reward from Masjid Mahabat Khan [...] We expect her to be hanged and if she is not hanged then we will ask the *mujahideen* and the Taliban to kill her'.

[85] Dawn, www.dawn.com/news/589587/high-profile-blasphemy-cases-in-the-last-63-years (8 December 2010).

[86] See 'Boy Escapes Hanging in Pakistan *The Times* (24 February 1995); 'Boy 14: Escapes Death Sentence' *The Guardian* (24 February 1995).

[87] See Amnesty International, *Annual Report 1998* (London, Amnesty International, 1999) 4; Christian Solidarity Worldwide, *Former High Court Judge Associated with the famous Blasphemy 1995 Trial Murdered in Lahore* (London, Christian Solidarity Worldwide, 10 October 1997).

(c) refers to, or addresses, any person, other than a member of the family 'Ahle-bait' of the Holy Prophet Muhammad (peace be upon him), as 'Ahle-bait'; or
(d) refers to, or names, or calls, his place of worship a 'Masjid';

shall be punished with imprisonment of either description for a term which may extend to three years, and shall also be liable to fine.

(2) Any person of the Quadiani group or Lahori group (who call themselves 'Ahmadis' or by any other name) who by words, either spoken or written, or by visible representation refers to the mode or form of call to prayers followed by his faith as 'Azan', or recites Azan as used by the Muslims, shall be punished with imprisonment of either description for a term which may extend to three years, and shall also be liable to fine.[88]

Section 298-B restricts the practice and manifestation of the Ahmadiyya religion in a variety of ways. The Ahmadiyyas commit an offence if by 'spoken or written, or by visible representation' they address any of their holy personalities with the title of 'Ameer-ul-Mumineen', 'Khalifatul- Mumineen', 'Khalifa-tul-Muslimeen', 'Sahaabi' or 'Razi Allah Anho'.[89] Ahmadiyyas are prevented from questioning the finality of the Prophet Mohammed (PBUH);[90] from calling their place of worship a 'Masjid';[91] and from referring to prayers or reciting Azan.[92] Further section 298-C states

> Any person of the Quadiani group or the Lahori group (who call themselves 'Ahmadis' or by any other name), who directly or indirectly, poses himself as a Muslim, or calls, or refers to, his faith as Islam, or preaches or propagates his faith, or invites others to accept his faith, by words, either spoken or written, or by visible representations, or in any manner whatsoever outrages the religious feelings of Muslims shall be punished with imprisonment of either description for a term which may extend to three years and shall also be liable to fine.

The vagueness and arbitrary character of the aforementioned provisions is self-evident in deploying terms such as 'directly or indirectly, poses himself as a Muslim'[93] or 'preaches or propagates his faith, or invites others to accept his faith, by words, either spoken or written, or by visible representations, or in any manner whatsoever outrages the religious feelings of Muslims'.[94] Ahmadiyyas have been targeted for using such terms as *Aslam-o-Alikum* (Muslim form of greetings) or for reciting verses from the Muslim Holy Book (Quran). These pieces of legislation opened the way for the intimidation and harassment of the Ahmadiyya community by members of the general public. Ahmadiyyas have been forced to ensure that that none of their activities, be they religious, social or cultural, could

[88] Pakistan Constitution (Second Amendment) Act 1974 (Act XLIX of 1974).
[89] Pakistan Penal Code, s 298-B(1).
[90] Ibid s 298-B(1)(a).
[91] Ibid s 298-B(1)(d).
[92] Ibid s 298-B(2).
[93] Ibid s 298-C.
[94] Ibid.

in any sense be associated with those of the mainstream Muslims, lest they be prosecuted for having 'indirectly or directly posed as a Muslim'. The Ahmadiyyas have become irrelevant and their physical existence inconsequential.[95] As noted above, a number of criminal proceedings have been brought against Ahmadiyyas, for various activities such as offering *Azan*[96] or having displayed religious scriptures such as *Kalima Tayyaba*,[97] through to wearing Muslim traditional dress, offering prayer or even sporting a beard.[98] Therefore, by censoring and criminalising all forms of Ahmadiyya expression, there has been a censorship of their existence and lifestyle.

In order to seek justice, religious minorities have turned to the judiciary. However, there is great disappointment as even senior judges have too often been either fearful or heavily politicised to uphold the rule of law and international human rights standards. *Zaheerudin v State*[99] remains the leading case and has already been referred to. In *Zaheerudin*, the Supreme Court of Pakistan in trivialising the importance of Ahmadiyya religious sentiments compared their practices with trade mark infringement, and in so doing adopted the position that an Islamic state has the right to protect the sanctity of religious terms, and prevent their manifestation and usage by other groups. The Court also went on to note the negative impact of Ahmadiyya religious practices on the majority Muslims, the *Ummah*. In particular, the Court noted that the Ahmadiyya use of epithets, as prohibited under section 298-B of the anti-blasphemy laws, appears 'in a manner which to the Muslim mind looks like a deliberate and calculated act of defiling and desecration of their holy personages'.[100]

Furthermore, and as noted already, the Court was explicit that Ahmadiyyas (through their pretence and in particular by pretending to be Muslims) are themselves responsible for inciting violence. If Muslims do react in a violent manner, and are provoked then the state cannot take responsibility for the safety of Ahmadiyyas. As the Court proclaimed '[i]t is like creating a Rushdie out of him. Can the administration in that case guarantee his life, liberty and property, and if so at what cost?'[101] The Supreme Court, in the cases challenging the anti-blasphemy laws, can be seen to protect members of the majority from minority religious practices that are perceived to be blasphemous under the pretext that they may lead to civil unrest or incitement to violence. Nevertheless, by shielding

[95] See Raz (n 19) 310.

[96] Arabic, meaning: Islamic call for prayers. For a catalogue of recent cases and discussion, see *Bulletins* produced by the Ahmadiyya Muslim Association (UK), www.ahmadiyya.org.uk.

[97] Arabic, meaning: there is no God but Allah and Prophet Mohammad (PBUH) is His Messenger.

[98] According to Ahmadiyya Muslim Community during April 1984 and December 2015, over 500 prosecutions were brought against Ahmadiyyas for 'posing as Muslim', www.thepersecution.org/facts/summary.html.

[99] *Zaheerudin v State*, 26 SCMR 1718 (S.Ct 1993) (Pak.) For analysis and critique of the case, see M Lau, 'Pakistan—*Zaheer-ud-din v. State*: Islam and Fundamental Rights in Pakistan, The Case of *Zaheer-ud-din v. State* and its Impact on the Fundamental Right to Freedom of Religion' (1994) 1 *Yearbook of Islamic and Middle Eastern Law* 565.

[100] *Zaheerudin v State* (n 99) 1765.

[101] *Dard v Pakistan* No 149/89 (Sup Ct of Pak, 3 July1993).

the majority not only from direct insult but also from minority religious practices that they may find insulting, the anti-blasphemy laws have perpetuated intolerant attitudes towards minority religions and favoured the religion of the majority. It is also, unfortunately, the case that intolerance of religious minorities has been institutionalised in Pakistan,[102] as evidenced through the operations of state institutions particularly the judiciary and the police force.[103] Therefore the net result as predicted by Dobras is that '[e]ven if no violence could result, Pakistan's blasphemy laws allow the [state] to punish minorities for merely preaching their own faith, since such an action can be deemed to be an affront to Islam'.[104]

IX. Anti-blasphemy Laws and Religiously Motivated Violence and Intolerance

The narrative of blasphemy has strengthened the spirit of intolerance and physical violence. Religious minorities are an obvious target, but intimidation, harassment and violence has increasingly been deployed against all vulnerable sections of the community. There is a direct linkage of extreme speech and hatred preached by such groups as Al-Qaeda, Pakistani Taliban (representing the Pakistani version of Taliban) and recently the ISIS (also known as Da'esh)[105] inspired groups operating in Pakistan. All these groups, although opposed to each other, share a very similar outlook on issues of expression, religious minorities and women. Their version of *Jihad* also allows them to justify fighting and killing of fellow Muslims, who do not share their ideology of hate and violence for religious minorities.[106] The Pakistan armed forces are currently engaged in an armed conflict with militant groups in Waziristan and certain border regions, though with serious and substantial ramifications in the entire state. These radical groups have retaliated, targeting all communities though religious communities have been a regular subject of organised non-state attacks. Recently, according to the spokesperson of the Pakistani Taliban, during 2015 alone, the group had carried out 136 physical acts of violence

[102] IH Malik, *Religious Minorities in Pakistan* (London, Minority Rights Group, 2002) 21.

[103] RJ Dobras, 'Is the United Nations Endorsing Human Rights Violations?: An Analysis of the United Nations' Combating Defamation of Religious Resolutions and Pakistan's Blasphemy Laws' (2009) 37 *Georgia Journal of International and Comparative Law* 339, 357.

[104] Ibid 355.

[105] ISIS (Islamic State of Syria and Iraq) also called as ISIL 'Islamic State of Iraq and the Levant'. It has taken the name of 'the Islamic State'. This entity is also known in the Arabic language as *ad-Dawlah al-Islāmiyah fī 'l- 'Irāq wa-sh-Shām*, resulting in the acronym Da'esh, Da'ish, Da'eesh, or DAESH. On 29 June 2014, ISIS announced the establishment of a worldwide caliphate and Aub Bakr al-Baghdadi appointed himself its caliph. For further analysis, see G Wood, 'What ISIS Really Wants', www.theatlantic.com/magazine/archive/2015/03/what-isis-really-wants/384980/ (March 2015).

[106] SR Valentine, *The Thehrik-i-Taliban Pakistan: Ideology and Beliefs* (Bradford, Pakistan Security Research Unit, 2009) Brief Number 49, 7.

that resulted in the death of 680 persons.[107] The Christian community is frequently associated with the West and, therefore, regrettably treated by insurgent groups as a legitimate target in the 'war on terror'. Retribution is frequently meted out to the Christian minority for any religiously offensive act committed in the West: for example, a number of churches were attacked in 2010 in response to a Florida Church burning a Quran.[108] Perpetrators of these crimes are rarely brought to justice, indicating institutional support (or at least acquiescence).[109] However, Muslim minority communities have also been subject to violent attacks. The Shias of Pakistan have also increasingly become a target of radical organisations.[110] These instances display not only intolerance of non-Muslim religious minorities but intolerance of difference. The failure of the Pakistani government to react to instances of violence and incitement with appropriate measures indicates the extent to which the extremists influence opinion in Pakistan.[111] One recent example of brutality was witnessed in the mass killings of men, women and children in April 2016 through a suicide bombing. The intended target was Christian children celebrating Easter in a park in Lahore, though the callous attack also led to other innocent civilian deaths. It is estimated that over 70 people died with several dozen seriously injured.[112] The tragic instances of violence have become far too frequent to be recounted in this study, however, there are glimpses of state complicity or at least impunity in targeting certain groups such as the Ahmadiyyas. Thus, in Lahore during May 2010, militants attacked two Ahmadiyya mosques using guns and grenades. At least 93 Ahmadiyya were reported to have been killed.[113] Notable for its absence was the provincial and federal governments' condemnation of the attacks on the Ahmadiyyas from within Pakistan.[114] Similarly, in the numerous attacks against the Shia minority community, there is a noticeable lack of enthusiasm to investigate, apprehend and convict the culprits involved. The failure of successive Pakistani governments to undertake appropriate action indicates either support from within the state establishment for the fanatical organisations or more probably political weakness to take firm action to protect the rights of religious minorities against extremists.

[107] US Department of State, *International Religious Freedom Report for 2015* (Washington, 2016) 116.

[108] US Commission on International Religious Freedom, *Annual Report: 2011* (Washington, 2012) 114.

[109] DF Forte, 'Apostasy and Blasphemy in Pakistan' (1994) 10 *Connecticut Journal of International Law* 27, 67.

[110] See Home Office, *Country Information Guidance: Pakistan: Shia Muslims* (Independent Chief Inspector of Borders and Immigration, London, 2015).

[111] Ibid.

[112] R Tanveer, 'Nation in mourning after suicide blast in Lahore kills 72, including 29 children' *The Express Tribune* (27 March 2016).

[113] US Commission on International Religious Freedom, *Annual Report: 2011* (n 108) 114.

[114] D Walsh, 'Ahmadi massacre silence is dispiriting' *The Guardian* (7 June 2010) www.guardian.co.uk/commentisfree/belief/2010/jun/07/ahmadi-massacre-silence-pakistan.

The expression of violence is also played out and witnessed in the intimidation and harassment of women, in particular women belonging to religious minorities. The recently published report by the All Party Parliamentary Group on Freedom of Religion or Belief makes the point that

> [w]omen from religious minorities across Pakistan are 'doubly discriminated' against, at systematic risk of becoming victims of abductions, extortion, hijacking and being held for ransom, trafficking, rape, forced marriages, forced conversions and allegations of blasphemy. Women and girls face discrimination and marginalization and are targeted simply because they are minorities. Hindu girls in Sindh and Christian girls in Punjab, for example, are abducted, raped and forced to convert to Islam, facing extreme pressure including threats to themselves and their families from the abductor and his family. The majority of the Christian women are illiterate and do menial jobs, working in factories or as domestic servants with a risk of sexual harassment, physical abuse forced conversion and marriage and even death.[115]

There are many instances of abduction of non-Muslim women, forced conversions and marriages to Muslim men. In 2014, a leading women's rights organisation, *Aurat Foundation* reported that every year, around 1000 girls were forcibly converted to Islam through marriage or bonded labour. There is inadequate interest on the part of the police to investigate such crimes and to punish these heinous crimes against mostly Hindu or Christian women.[116]

The injustices evident in the implementation of anti-blasphemy laws are also reflected in many ostensibly religious laws that impact women and religious minorities. These laws include the *Hudood* Ordinances, the application of which has seriously undermined and victimised vulnerable communities. Notwithstanding the state's commitment to non-imposition of an exclusively Islamic code on non-Muslims, these Ordinances for the most part also control the activities of non-Muslims alongside the majority Muslims. Religious minorities under these Ordinances remain liable to suffer from punishments such as physical amputations, whipping etc for various offences related to theft, whipping for having committed *zina* and death or whipping in case of *zinabiljabar* and *Qazf*. The imposition of the *Hudood* Ordinances, an exclusively Islamic code, on non-Muslims is also discriminatory in the manner of its application. For the application of the *hadd* conviction, strict evidentiary requirements must be complied with: in accordance with these requirements, while Muslims can give evidence against non-Muslims, non-Muslims are barred from giving evidence against an accused who happens to be a Muslim. Attempts have been made to modify the *Hudood* ordinances and to eradicate some injustice created through the application of these laws. One such noticeable effort was made during the time of General Pervaiz Musharraf through

[115] See All Parties Parliamentary Group for International Freedom of Religion or Belief, *Freedom of Religion or belief in Pakistan and UK Governmental Policy: Parliamentary Inquiry*, https://freedomdeclared.org/in-parliament/pakistan-report, 47.

[116] US Department of State, *International Religious Freedom Report for 2015* (Washington, 2016) 115.

the introduction of the Protection of Women (Criminal Law Amendment) Act 2006. Under this legislation, while both adultery and rape remained criminal offences, rape cases were removed from the *Hudood* Ordinances and reverted to criminal laws as applied under the Pakistan Penal Code. The removal from the *Hudood* Ordinances also meant the removal of the *hudd* evidential requirement of four witnesses. Convictions could be based on criminal evidence including the use of circumstantial and forensic evidence.[117] However, the Criminal Law (Amendment) Act 2006 has been the subject of intense legal and political debate. In 2013, the Council of Islamic Ideology determined that the Criminal Law (Amendment) Act 2006 was contrary to the provisions of Islamic law and therefore recommended that it should be held void under the constitutional provisions. Whilst the future of the Criminal Law (Amendment) Act 2006 remains uncertain, much of criminal justice system is directed against religious minorities and women.

X. Conclusions

As examined in this study, freedom of expression is a firmly entrenched right in the constitutions of the world as well as within international law. Its value to society and democratic governance has also been fully endorsed. Expression forms the basis of exercising many other rights including the right to freedom of religion or belief and many arguments can be made in respect of the critical nature of the right to free expression for ensuring pluralism and democracy. Expression in its broader, true, sense is much more than mere physical expression; the right to expression mandates and validates the entire existence of individuals, communities or societies. Repressing expression equates to non-recognition and coercion; censorship and condemnation of expression leads to rejection and closure of the path of sustenance and vitality.

Commentators, such as Temperman, have argued that in reality there is no conflict between the right to freedom of expression and the right to freedom of religion. He claims that

> [t]here is no abstract 'clash' between freedom of expression and freedom of religion or belief. The portrayal of the two discussed fundamental rights–the right to freedom of expression and the right to freedom of religion or belief–as being somehow perpetually at odds, as inevitably 'clashing' whenever being implemented, is a flawed and hazardous one.[118]

According to this perspective, the most appropriate mechanism to combat incitement is through criminalisation of any advocacy of religious hatred without

[117] See All Parties Parliamentary Group on Freedom of Religion or Belief, *Freedom of Religion or Belief in Pakistan and UK Governmental Policy* (n 115) 48.

[118] Temperman, 'Blasphemy, Defamation of Religions and Human Rights Law' (n 67) 545.

having the need to rely upon anti-blasphemy laws. Such an approach, whilst following established international law doctrines, also operates on the assumption that there are practical objective mechanisms for disentangling permissible insults or criticism of religions from the impermissible incitement to religious hatred. The former Special Rapporteur on Freedom of Religion or Belief, Asma Jahangir, also appears to be pointing towards objective assessments. She notes:

> [T]he question as to whether criticism, derogatory statements, insults or ridicule of one religion may actually negatively affect an individual's right to freedom of religion or belief *can only be determined objectively* and, in particular, by examining whether the different aspects of the manifestation of one's right to freedom of religion are accordingly negatively affected.[119]

It may well be that in liberal societies, with established democratic legal and judicial frameworks, objective assessments can be made. However, in the context of societies influenced and dependent on a particular brand of religious orthodoxy and in the absence of an independent judiciary it is nigh on impossible to anticipate objectivity and impartiality on matters of religion. Instead, in such environments, the police as well as the judicial officers may be keen to reaffirm their commitment and religious loyalty at the expense of objectivity. The case of Pakistan provides an unfortunate example whereby the anti-blasphemy laws have been deployed not only to curb the right to free expression, but also as an instrument of repression and undermining religious minorities. Blasphemy trials, as noted by the International Commission of Jurists, often turn into an odyssey of theology and religious prowess rather than interpretation and application of law. Thus, in one case,

> the Lahore High Court appeared to base its reasoning more on the 'faith of the court' than the law: It is the absolute faith of the court that none in this world can undermine the respect, honour, sanctity, inviolability and piety of the Holy Prophet … whosoever … has any doubt regarding His supremacy as the last Prophet … is none but an infidel.[120]

Within this argument of faith versus objectivity, it is faith that inevitably comes out victorious.

[119] 'Report of the Special Rapporteur on freedom of religion or belief, Asma Jahangir, and the Special Rapporteur on contemporary forms of racism, racial discrimination, xenophobia and related intolerance' (n 52) para 39.

[120] *Manzar-ul-Haq Shah Jahan v the State*, Criminal Appeal No 608 of 2012, Lahore High Court (10 June 2015.

7

Islamic Law, International Dimensions in Freedom of Expression

I. Introduction

The previous chapter has examined the conceptual challenges with freedom of expression exemplifying the disjointed and botched efforts to curb expression through the application of anti-blasphemy laws. As already noted, the chameleon-like presence of blasphemy and offences against religion are pervasive in many parts of world.[1] In exploring actions to curb free speech, this chapter focuses on Muslim majority state practices individually as well as under the umbrella of the OIC. The approach of the OIC towards the application of the principles of rule of law has already been examined in Part II of this study. A further examination of the practices of this organisation in the present context can be justified for a variety of reasons. As noted already, the OIC represents the world's largest organisation after the United Nations. The raison d'etre of the organisation is to forge unity amongst the Muslim *Ummah*.[2] The Organisation is premised to revive Islamic unity and Muslim symbolism that had been dismembered after the formal dissolution of the Ottoman Caliphate at the end of the First World War.[3] These ideological commitments are evident in both the original[4] as well as the revised OIC Charter (adopted in 2008)[5] whereby the organisation pledges a commitment to not only 'safeguard

[1] See Ch 6.

[2] J Rehman, *Islamic State Practices, International Law and the Threat from Terrorism: A Critique of the 'Clash of Civilizations' in the New World Order* (Oxford, Hart Publishing, 2005) 27; H Moinuddin, *The Charter of the Islamic Conference and Legal Framework of Economic Cooperation Among its Member States: A Study of the Charter, the General Agreement for Economic, Technical and Commercial Co-operation and the Agreement for Promotion, Protection and Guarantee of Investments Among Member States of the OIC* (Oxford, Clarendon Press, 1987).

[3] See C Skutsch 'Organization of the Islamic Conference (OIC)' in J Ciment (ed), *Encyclopaedia of Conflicts Since World War II* (London, Routledge, 1999) 185.

[4] The OIC Charter was approved and adopted at the third Islamic Conference of Foreign Ministers held in Jeddah in March 1972. The Charter was registered in conformity with Art 102 of the UN Charter on 1 February 1974. For the text of the OIC Charter (1972) Text, see http://Arabian-union.org/reference/oic_charter_text.htm. The Charter was revised and adopted in 2008; for the text of the revised Charter of the Organisation of Islamic Cooperation, adopted on 14 March 2008, see www.oic-oci.org/english/charter/OIC%20Charter-new-en.pdf; see also P Sands and P Klein, *Bowett's Law of International Institutions* (London, Sweet and Maxwell, 2001) 148.

[5] See Charter of the Organisation of Islamic Cooperation, adopted on 14 March 2008; see www.oic-oci.org/english/charter/OIC%20Charter-new-en.pdf.

and protect the common interests and support the legitimate causes of the Member States and coordinate and unify the efforts of the Member States in view of the challenges faced by the Islamic world in particular and the international community in general'[6] but also to 'protect and defend the true image of Islam, to combat defamation of Islam and encourage dialogue among civilisations and religions'.[7] This study also confirms that as the international discourse on freedom of expression has developed especially since the adoption of Human Rights Council Resolution 16/18, the subject and context of Resolution 16/18 has become 'the jealous preserve'[8] of the OIC on the one hand and 'the West' on the other.

As considered in this study, several organisations can potentially have a stake in representing transnational Islamic state practices: these include inter alia private organisations such as the Islamic Council of Europe[9] as well as the regional organisations of the Arab League,[10] ASEAN,[11] SAARC[12] and the African Union.[13] Whilst

[6] OIC Charter, Art 1(2). Ibid.

[7] OIC Charter, Art 1(12). Ibid.

[8] M Limon, N Ghanea and H Power, 'Combating Global Religious Intolerance: The Implementation of Human Rights Council Resolution 16/18' (Policy Report) (London, Universal Rights Group, 2014) 20.

[9] Although potentially relevant, the work of Islamic Council of Europe (ICE) does not appear to have a major contemporary impact. The Islamic Council of Europe is a private organisation, and formally established in London in 1973 but with strong affiliations with the Muslim World League (a conservative, state-led Saudi organisation). ICE is accredited with drafting 2 constitutional and human rights instruments: The Universal Islamic Declaration of Human Rights (UIDHR) adopted in 1981, www.alhewar.com/ISLAMDECL.html and A Model of an Islamic Constitution (MIC) produced in 1983, www.salaam.co.uk/knowledge/islamic_constitution_part1.pdf. Ostensibly, UIDHR provides rights that parallel the provisions of UDHR and provides an Islamic response to Western, secularised human rights. Closer examination of the 2 documents, however, reveals significant differences. There are also differences in the English and the Arabic versions. The considerable equivocation and ambiguity in the various provisions of the document have allowed critics to suggest that the drafters of the Declaration were not able to agree on many of the provisions and therefore sought to resort to ambiguous terminology. Amidst the numerous ambiguous provisions, none are more problematic than those relating to freedom of expression. The UIDHR, in engaging with the right to freedom of expression, conflates this right with the other rights and freedoms such as the freedom of belief. The provisions vividly capture the ideology and mentality of the architect of the right to freedom of expression within UIDHR. Everyone, according to the Declaration, has the right to free expression so long as the expression is within the remit of legal limits which is prescribed by the public authorities. In making it impermissible to 'hold in contempt or ridicule the religious beliefs of others' the UIDHR represents the initial though significant steps towards legitimising the criminal offence of anti-blasphemy laws within domestic legislations. Although initially the work of private actors, the UIDHR was subsequently embraced by several Islamic states, including Pakistan, Saudi Arabia and Egypt as a document symbolising human rights within Islam. For further analysis, see AE Mayer, *Islam and Human Rights: Tradition and Politics* (Oxford, Westview Press, 1995) 22; J Rehman, *International Human Rights Law* (London, Longman, 2010) 362.

[10] See Charter of the League of Arab States, 22 March 1945, 70 U.N.T.S 241; Arab Charter on Human Rights, 12 *International Human Rights Reports* (2005) 893; entered into force 15 March 2008.

[11] ASEAN Charter (2007) http://asean.org/asean/asean-charter/.

[12] See Charter of the South Asian Association for Regional Cooperation, http://saarc-sec.org/saarc-charter.

[13] See Constitutive Act of the African Union, Togo, 11 July 2000 OAU Doc CAB/LEG/23.15 and the African [Banjul] Charter on Human and Peoples' Rights, adopted 27 June 1981, OAU Doc CAB/LEG/67/3 rev. 5, 21 I.L.M. 58 (1982).

the aforementioned organisations share membership of states with those of the OIC, the latter organisation is the self-proclaimed mouthpiece for the Muslim nations. The contemporary and exclusive focus of the OIC on Islamic cooperation and upon 'Islamic values' emanating from the Muslim majority state practices and the deep, longstanding involvement of the organisation with the issue of freedom of expression necessitates a detailed and focused examination.

II. Freedom of Expression and the Evolution of the OIC

Founded upon a summit held in Rabat, the Kingdom of Morocco, on 12 Rajab 1389 H (25 September 1969), the OIC's establishment was a direct reaction against an arson attack upon *Al-Aqsa* mosque in occupied Jerusalem on 21 August 1969. Motivated to defend the faith and integrity of the Muslim people, a large group of states united by this common cause, covenanted in their first meeting held in Rabat to liberate Jerusalem and *Al-Aqsa* from occupation.[14] With a revised Charter adopted by the Eleventh Islamic Summit held in Dakar, 13–14 March 2008, the OIC now exists as an inter-governmental organisation comprising 57 states. The OIC continues to pool its resources and efforts in its endeavour to present a unified voice and protect the interests of Muslim peoples and the Muslim world community.

A unified Islamic narrative in defining the parameters of acceptable forms of expression has been a fundamental characteristic of the OIC as an international organisation. This position is highlighted by the revised Charter's commitment to 'protect ... and defend the true image ...' of Islam.[15] The practical manifestation of the commitment has been evident in OIC's response to all cases of cross-jurisdictional and international acts of blasphemy including the blasphemous writings of Salman Rushdie in his novel, *Satanic Verses*,[16] the *Jyllands-Posten* Mohammad cartoons controversy emergent after the publication of cartoons of Prophet Mohammad in Denmark and republished in other parts of the world,[17] or

[14] For a background of the OIC, see www.oic-oci.org; Moinuddin, *The Charter of the Islamic Conference and Legal Framework of Economic Cooperation Among its Member States* (n 2).

[15] OIC Charter, Art 1(12).

[16] See Ch 5 above; although disagreements emerged in relation to the validity of Imam Khomeni's *fatwa* condemning Salman Rushdie to the death sentence, on 16 March 1989, the OIC nevertheless roundly condemned Rushdie. His book was comprehensively labelled as blasphemy and Rushdie was denounced as an apostate. See Mayer, *Islam and Human Rights* (n 9) 155–56; see also J Rehman 'Freedom of Expression, Apostasy and Blasphemy within Islam: *Sharia*, Criminal Justice Systems and Modern Islamic State Practices' (2010) 79 *Criminal Justice Matters* 4, 4.

[17] OIC Secretary General reiterated his Concerns on the Dangerous Implications of Inciting Hatred against Islam and Muslims (6 April 2008) www.oic-oci.org/oicv3/topic/?t_id=921&ref=434&lan=en; OIC Expresses Dismay at Danish Court Decision on Offensive Cartoons of Prophet Muhammad (22 June 2008) www.oic-oci.org/oicv3/topic/?t_id=1156&ref=538&lan=en; OIC Islamophobia Observatory Spokesman Condemns Reprint of Blasphemous Cartoon by Swedish Newspapers (11 March 2011) www.oic-oci.org/oicv3/topic/?t_id=3475&ref=1492&lan=en.

the more recent high-profile cases of blasphemy including the 14-minute trailer, entitled *Innocence of Muslims* (2012).[18]

The narrative on freedom of expression was initially articulated in the OIC's primary human rights declaration, the Cairo Declaration on Human Rights in Islam (CDHRI).[19] The OIC adopted the CDHRI in 1990, which continues to represent the guiding principles on human rights for the OIC member states.[20] The Declaration was adopted and issued at the 19th Islamic Conference of Foreign Ministers by 45 foreign ministers in Cairo on 5 August 1990. The primary objective of CDHRI was that its provisions should serve as the guiding principles in issues of human rights, providing an alternative Islamic response to the Universal Declaration of Human Rights (1948).[21] Although the Declaration represents non-binding guiding principles for members of the OIC, it nevertheless constitutes an important document in the armoury of members of the OIC.[22] According to CDHRI, in ensuring human rights within Islamic constitutional systems, the exclusive yardstick is the Islamic Sharia as 'the only source of reference'.[23] More specifically, the CDHRI is a document immersed in ambiguity and confusion, evident in its appearance and revealing in its psyche.

The Declaration positively asserts a right to free expression, although this right is tied to the prerequisite that those views 'would not be contrary to the principles of *Sharia*'[24]—presumably the Islamic state being the adjudicator of the limit and appropriateness of these views. Furthermore, this right is accompanied by a right to 'advocate what is right, and propagate what is good and warns against what is wrong and evil according to the norms of Islamic *Sharia*'.[25] Whilst it is acknowledged that '[i]nformation is a vital necessity to society', such exchanges

[18] OIC Group in New York Condemns the Release of the Anti-Muslim Video and Calls for Collective Action against Provocations and Systematic Incitement to Hatred (22 September 2012) www.oic-oci.org/oicv3/topic/?t_id=7189&ref=2951&lan=en.

[19] Cairo Declaration on Human Rights in Islam, 5 August 1990, UN GAOR, World Conf on Hum Rts, 4th Sess, Agenda Item 5, UN Doc A/CONF.157/PC/62/Add.18 (1993); the text of the Declaration is also available at: www.fmreview.org/sites/fmr/files/FMRdownloads/en/FMRpdfs/Human-Rights/cairo.pdf.

[20] Note the recognition accorded to CDHRI by the OIC Permanent Human Rights Commission, 'Statute of the OIC Independent Human Rights Commission' adopted by the 38th Session of the Council of Foreign Ministers (CFM) held in Astana, Kazakhstan (28–30 June 2011) available at www.oic-iphrc.org/en/data/docs/about/Statute/IPHRC%20Statute%20EV.pdf.

[21] A Tadjdini, 'The Organisation of Islamic Cooperation and Regional Challenges to International Law and Security' (2012) 4 *Amsterdam Law Forum* 36, 45; A al-Ahsan, 'Law, Religion and Human Dignity in the Muslim World Today: An Examination of OIC's Cairo Declaration of Human Rights' (2008–09) 24 *Journal of Law and Religion* 569, 573.

[22] On the OIC Independent Permanent Human Rights Commission, see below.

[23] CDHRI, Art 25; See M Baderin, 'Identifying Possible Mechanisms within Islamic Law for the Promotion and Protection of Human Rights in Muslim States' (2004) 22 *Netherlands Quarterly of Human Rights* 329, 345. This restrictiveness also presents the dangerous signal of 'self-containedness' that displaces the application of customary rules codified by Art 31(3)(c) of the VCLT (1961) as well as established norms of customary international law and human rights law. See I Cismas, 'Introductory Note to the Statute of the OIC Independent Permanent Human Rights Commission' (2011) 50 *International Legal Materials* 1148, 1148.

[24] CDHRI, Art 22(a).

[25] Ibid Art 22(b).

of information '[m]ay not be exploited or misused in such a way as may violate sanctities and the dignity of Prophets, undermine moral and ethical Values or disintegrate, corrupt or harm society or weaken its faith'.[26]

These provisions provide for troubling reading: political authorities are the ultimate arbiters of morality, ethical values and are protectors of sanctity and dignity of Prophets. On this basis, anti-blasphemy laws are authorised in cases, which, according to the state authorities violate the sanctities and dignity of the Prophets. Censorship is also sanctioned for acts which state officials view as corrupting the society, undermining ethical and moral values or attempts to weaken the Islamic faith.[27]

CDHRI also advances a problematic and awkward alternative to Article 20(2) ICCPR in that while it is impressible to '[e]xcite nationalistic or doctrinal hatred or to do anything that may be an incitement to any form or racial discrimination'[28] no reference is made to religious discrimination.[29] Ostensibly, therefore, the Declaration both sanctifies discrimination on the basis of religion and condones incitement based on religious grounds. The penultimate Article of CDHRI, Article 24, further restricts the ambit of the rights through subjecting all rights and freedoms to the Islamic Sharia. The content of the Sharia is imprecise and its application in Muslim majority states has been politically motivated. CDHRI is an unfortunate licence to OIC member states to deploy the rhetoric of the Sharia for political gains.

The concluding article, Article 25 declares Islamic Sharia as 'the only source of reference for the explanation or clarification of any of the articles of this Declaration'. The Declaration appears rather vague in its position in respect of an absolute freedom of religion. Article 10 provides that

> Islam is the religion of true unspoiled nature. It is prohibited to exercise any form of pressure on man or to exploit his poverty or ignorance in order to force him to change his religion to another religion or to atheism.

The CDHRI fails to provide answers in the context of the most profound forms of religious expression–the inherent rights of individuals to convert to another religion or belief in instances where there is no exploitation or ignorance involved. The Declaration is unable to draw distinctions between the *forum internum* and *forum externum* of the right to freedom of thought, conscience and religion.[30] The *forum internum* constitutes the private and internal realm of the person, in which everyone has freedom of thought, conscience, religion or belief, as well as freedom of choice in having, maintaining or adopting another religion or belief.

[26] Ibid Art 22(c).
[27] Ibid Art 22(c).
[28] Ibid Art 22(d).
[29] ICCPR, Art 20(2) provides as follows: 'Any advocacy of national, racial or religious hatred that constitutes incitement to discrimination, hostility or violence shall be prohibited by law'.
[30] See J Rehman 'What is Article 18 and what is it not?' in M Evans (ed), *Article 18: An Orphaned Rights–A Report of the All Parliamentary Group on International Religious Freedom* (London, APPG on Religious Freedom or Belief, 2013) 10–17, 12.

Article 10 makes an express reference to Islam but the failure to acknowledge *forum internum* represents a substantial omission in this document; the explicit provisions of the Universal Declaration on Human Rights as regards absolute freedom of religion and including the freedom of the individual to change his religion or belief are absent from CDHRI.[31] From a plain and literal reading of Article 10 and given the Islamic bias of the document, it might appear legitimate to suggest that all conversions from Islam are a consequence of compulsion and exploitation.[32] CDHRI similarly portrays nervousness over *forum externum*, an avenue for the outward manifestations and expressions of one's religion or belief. International human rights instruments, including the UDHR and the ICCPR, acknowledge that *forum externum* can be made the subject of legitimate restrictions.[33] However, the boundaries drawn by international human rights are both narrowly construed and driven by the objective criterion. Sharia law as the only source of reference raises problematic concerns as to whether other competing religions or beliefs can have a meaningful and wholesome manifestation within a Muslim state. It is certain that the inherent ambiguities embedded in CDHRI, not least in its substantive provisions relating to freedom of expression (and limits associated with this freedom), have rendered the Declaration imbecilic, ineffective and also unreliable.

III. Countering and Combating 'Defamation of Religions'

The OIC's narrative on the limits on freedom of expression and the efforts by its individual members to institute an associated international norm of criminalisation of 'defamation of religions' was played out in divisive struggles within the

[31] The risks inherent in CDHRI were evident and highlighted by the Secretary General of the International Commission of Jurists, Adama Dieng, when he noted inter alia that (1) it gravely threatens the inter-cultural consensus on which the international human rights instruments are based; (2) it introduces, in the name of the defence of human rights, an intolerable discrimination against both non-Muslims and women; (3) it reveals a deliberately restrictive character in regard to certain fundamental rights and freedoms, to the point that certain essential provisions are below the legal standards in effect in a number of Muslim countries; (4) it confirms, under cover of the 'Islamic Sharia (Law)', the legitimacy of practices, such as corporal punishment, which attack the integrity and dignity of the human being; Press Release (Geneva, 5 December 1991). E.CN.4/1992/SR.20, paras. 17–20; cited in D Littman, 'Universal Human Rights and "Human Rights in Islam"' Midstream (New York) February/ March 1999, www.dhimmitude.org/archive/universal_islam.html.

[32] See Mayer (n 9) 159–60.

[33] See Art 18 UDHR Universal Declaration of Human Rights, GA Res 217A (III), UN Doc A/810 at 71 (1948) and Art 18(3) ICCPR, International Convention on the Elimination of All Forms of Racial Discrimination, New York, 7 March 1966, 660 U.N.T.S.

United Nations for several years. Armed with the banner of banning 'defamation of religions', several resolutions were introduced by the members of the OIC. Although the roots of the OIC's campaign for criminalisation of insults and blasphemy of Islam are historic, the first formal exercise to introduce the defamation of Islam resolution within the then Human Rights Commission was conducted in 1999. Accordingly, this initial effort was entitled 'Defamation of Islam'.[34] This draft was heavily criticised and rejected for not only its exclusive focus on Islam but for also introducing an ambiguous concept within international law.[35] The rationale for the draft resolution 1999/82 was–in the words of its sponsor to counter–'new manifestations of intolerance and misunderstanding, not to say hatred, of Islam and Muslims in various parts of the world'.[36] The agreed draft that was introduced and adopted as Resolution 1999/82 focuses upon issues of inter alia: 'the negative stereotyping of religions';[37] the association of Islam with human rights violations and terrorism;[38] the role of the media in inciting 'acts of violence, xenophobia or related intolerance and discrimination towards Islam and any other religion';[39] and the need for states to take 'measures to combat hatred, discrimination, intolerance and acts of violence, intimidation and coercion motivated by religious intolerance'[40] The provisions of Human Rights Commission Resolution 1999/82

[34] See Commission on Human Rights, Draft Res 1999/L40, Racism, Racial Discrimination, Xenophobia and All Forms of Discrimination (20 April 1999) UN Doc E/CN.4/1999/L40; see also UN ESCOR, 55th Sess, 61st mtg at 1 (29 April, 1999) UN Doc E/CN.4/1999/SR.61 ('Mr. Akram (Pakistan) introducing draft Res E/CN.4/1999/L.40 on behalf of the States Members of the United Nations that were members of the Organization of the Islamic Conference [Cooperation], said that, in the past few years, there had been new manifestations of intolerance and misunderstanding, not to say hatred, of Islam and Muslims in various parts of the world. … No other religion received such constant negative media coverage. That defamation campaign was reflected in growing intolerance towards Muslims').

[35] Mr Höynck (Germany) said that, despite intensive consultations on the draft resolution itself and on the amendments contained in document E/CN.4/1999/L.90, it had unfortunately been impossible to find common ground. Comm. HR, Draft Resolution on Racism, at 9. The trend of focusing on Islam, however, continued with 'Defamation of Religions' Resolutions adopted by the HRC, see eg HRC 4/9 on Combating Defamation of Religions (adopted by a vote of 24 to 14 with 9 abstentions). While presenting this on behalf of the OIC, Pakistan's representative Tehmina Janjua made the observation that 'it was Islam that was being targeted. There was a clear recognition of the existence of the phenomenon. The manifestations of Islamophobia had extensively been documented by three Special Rapporteurs. In a post 9/11 world, Muslims had suffered from discrimination. There were numerous instances reflecting the defamation of Islam, not only in law and judicial practices but also through Islamophobia. Therefore, the draft resolution was presented. The profiling of Muslims constituted racism and was a human rights violation. The resolutions would compel the international community to address the phenomenon of the defamation of religions and the consequence it had on individuals'. Human Rights Council Adopts Seven Resolutions and Two Decisions, including Text on Darfur, 30 March 2007, www.ohchr.org/EN/NewsEvents/Pages/DisplayNews.aspx?NewsID=2509&LangID=E.

[36] UN Economic and Social Council, Commission on Human Rights, Summary Record of the 61st meeting, UN Doc.E/CN.4/1999/SR 61, 55th Sess (1999), 1.

[37] Commission on Human Rights Resolution 1999/82 (30 April 1999) UN Doc E/CN.4/Res 1999/82, para 1.

[38] Ibid para 2.

[39] Ibid para 3.

[40] Ibid para 4.

represent a conflation of Islamophobia and xenophobia combined with efforts to condemn any insult of religions and association of Islam with human rights violations.

Human Rights Commission Resolution 1999/82 introduced a considerable trend which gained significant currency in subsequent years. The United Nations bodies adopted no fewer than 20 resolutions on the subject of 'Defamation of Religions'.[41] Sponsored by the OIC, these resolutions were adopted by the UNCHR (and subsequently UNHRC)[42] and the UN General Assembly.[43] In addition, the various UN Special Rapporteurs as well as the High Commissioner for Human Rights and the United Nations General Secretary wrote nearly 30 reports highlighting the gravity of the subject.[44] The campaign to establish a norm criminalising the 'defamation of religions' presented serious but unique challenges. 'Defamation of Religions' as a term had not been used in a UN resolution prior to the adoption of Human Rights Commission Resolution 1999/82 and lacked meaning. The expansion of the scope of the Resolution to include religions more generally, also resulted in a stance inconsistent with the vocabulary of international human rights law: the focus of the Resolution remained religions (as opposed to religious groups or minorities) though religions per se cannot derive protection from the human rights regime. Indeed, attempts to deploy the cover of international human rights law to protect religions subsequently became

[41] See RC Blitt, 'Defamation of Religion: Rumors of its Death are Greatly Exaggerated' (2011) 62 *Case Western Reserve Law Review* 347, 349.

[42] See Commission on Human Rights Resolutions: UN Commission on Human Rights Resolution 'Defamation of Religions' Res 2000/84 (26 April 2000) UN Doc E/CN.4/Res/2000/84; Commission on Human Rights Resolution 'Combating Defamation of Religions as a Means to Promote Human Rights, Social Harmony and Religious and Cultural Diversity' Res 2001/4 (18 April 2001) UN Doc/E/CN. Res 2001/4; Commission on Human Rights Resolution 'Combating Defamation of Religions' Res 2002/9 (15 April 2002) UN Doc/E/CN. Res 2002/9; Commission on Human Rights Resolution 'Combating Defamation of Religions' Res 2003/4 (14 April 2003) UN Doc/E/CN. Res 14 April 2003; Commission on Human Rights Resolution 'Combating Defamation of Religions' Res 2004/6 (13 April 2004) UN Doc/E/CN. Res 2004/6; Commission on Human Rights Resolution 'Combating Defamation of Religions' Res 2005/3 (12 April 2005) UN Doc/E/CN. Res 2005/3; followed by HRC Resolutions: A/HRC/RES/4/9 'Combating defamation of religions' (30 March 2007) A/HRC/RES/4/9; A/HRC/RES/7/19 'Combating defamation of religions' (27 March 2008) A/HRC/RES/7/19; A/HRC/RES/10/22 'Combating defamation of religions' (26 March 2009) A/HRC/RES/10/22; A/HRC/RES/13/16 'Combating defamation of religions' (25 March 2010) A/HRC/RES/13/16.

[43] See eg, UN Doc A/RES/60/150, 'Combating defamation of religions' GA Res 60/150 (16 December 2005) UN Doc A/RES/60/150; UN Doc A/RES/61/164 'Combating defamation of religions' GA Res 61/164 (19 December 2006) UN Doc A/RES/61/164; UN Doc A/RES/62/154 'Combating defamation of religions' GA Res 62/154 (18 December 2007) UN Doc A/RES/62/154; UN Doc A/RES/62/154'Combating defamation of religions' GA Res 61/164 (19 December 2006) UN Doc A/RES/61/164; UN Doc A/RES/63/171 'Combating defamation of religions' GA Res 63/171 (18 December 2008) UN Doc A/RES/63/171; UN Doc A/RES/64/156 'Combating defamation of religions' GA Res 64/156 (18 December 2009) UN Doc A/RES/64/156; UN Doc A/RES/65/224 'Combating defamation of religions' GA Res 65/224 (21 December 2010) UN Doc A/RES/65/224.

[44] See Blitt, 'Defamation of Religion (n 41) 349.

the subject of considerable criticism from human rights experts[45] and UN mandate holders.[46]

The state sponsors, of the 'defamation of religions' resolutions, aimed at introducing a prohibition on any form of insult and adverse comment against Islam in the form of an international norm, directly analogous to national blasphemy laws. Members of the OIC were well aware of the exceptional and extraordinary nature of the concept of 'defamation of religions' and the consequent undesirability of introducing such a discourse within international human rights law. In light of the obvious difficulties in persuading the international community towards establishing an international crime of defamation of Islam, a strategic path was devised to conflate issues of discrimination and hatred against Muslim minorities in the West (Islamophobia) with hate speech against Islam. It is hence no surprise that the prohibition of 'defamation of religions' resolutions sponsored by the OIC are couched in the language of human rights and non-discrimination.

After the official launch of the movement within the UN in 1999, and in order to garner greater support from UN member states, it became a pattern of 'defamation of religions' resolutions to highlight concerns over inter alia 'the ethnic and religious profiling of Muslim minorities';[47] 'physical attacks and assaults on businesses, cultural centres and places of worship of all religions, in particular

[45] For analysis, see AG Belnap, 'Defamation of Religions: A Vague and Overbroad Theory that Threatens Basic Human Rights' (2010) *Brigham Young University Law Review* 635–86; GL Bennett, 'Defamation of Religions: The End of Pluralism?' (2009) 23 *Emory International Law Review* 69; M Grinberg, 'Defamation of Religions v. Freedom of Expression: Finding the Balance in a Democratic Society' (2006) 18 *Sri Lanka Journal of International Law* 197; R Dobras, 'Is the United Nations Endorsing Human Rights Violations?: An Analysis of the United Nations' Combating Defamation of Religions Resolutions and Pakistan's Blasphemy Laws' (2008–09) 37 *Georgia Journal of International and Comparative Law* 339; D Petrova, '"Smoke and Mirrors": The Durban Review Conference and Human Rights Politics at the United Nations' (2009) 10 *Human Rights Law Review* 129; LA Leo, FD Gaer and EK Cassidy, 'Protecting Religions from "Defamation" A Threat to Universal Human Rights Standards' (2011) 34 *Harvard Journal of Law and Public Policy* 769; S Parmar, 'The Challenge of "Defamation of Religions" to Freedom of Expression and the International Human Rights System' [2009] *European Human Rights Law Review* 353; M Evans, 'Advancing Freedom of Religion or Belief: Agendas for Change' (2011) 1 *Oxford Journal of Law and Religion* 5.

[46] 'Report of the Special Rapporteur on freedom of religion or belief, Asma Jahangir, and the Special Rapporteur on contemporary forms of racism, racial discrimination, xenophobia and related intolerance' Doudou Diène, further to Human Rights Council decision 1/107 on incitement to racial and religious hatred and the promotion of tolerance A/HRC/2/3 (20 September 2006); Joint statement by Mr. Githu Muigai, Special Rapporteur on contemporary forms of racism, racial discrimination, xenophobia and related intolerance, Ms Asma Jahangir, Special Rapporteur on freedom of religion or belief and Mr Frank La Rue, Special Rapporteur on the promotion and protection of the right to freedom of opinion and expression, 'Freedom of expression and incitement to racial or religion hatred' OHCHR side event during the Durban Review Conference, Geneva (22 April 2009) 1–2.

[47] Commission on Human Rights Resolutions: 2002/9, para 3; 2003/4, para 4; 2004/6, para 6; 2005/3, para 3; HRC Resolutions 4/9, para 3; 7/9, para 3; GA Resolutions: A/RES/60/150, para 3; A/RES/61/164, para 3; A/RES/62/154, para 6; A/RES/ 63/171, para 5; A/RES/64/156, para 5; A/RES/ 65/225, para 5.

of Muslims in many parts of the world';[48] hatred and discrimination;[49] 'laws or administrative measures that have been specifically designed to "control" and "monitor" Muslim and Arab minorities';[50] and the 'deliberate stereotyping of religions, their adherents and sacred persons in the media and by political parties and groups in some societies'.[51] The unfortunate events of 9/11 and the inevitable backlash upon Muslim minorities was seized upon to highlight Islamophobia and an assault upon the otherwise peaceful values of Islam.[52] The resolutions adopted after 11 September 2001 whilst highlighting increasing discrimination and hostility towards Muslim minorities aimed to establish a nexus between defamation of Islam and persecution of Muslims. The campaign led by the OIC and its allies was played out for many years within the United Nations General Assembly as well as in the United Nations Human Rights Council. As already noted, the ideal of the universal prohibition of defamation of religions was also supported by various United Nations Special Rapporteurs and UN bodies to the extent that every year numerous resounding resolutions were passed upholding the principle of the prohibition of defamation of religions. The high-water mark of this phenomenon can be envisaged by the United Nations General Assembly Resolution 65/224, entitled 'Combating Defamation of Religions' and adopted on 21 December 2010. In this resolution, the General Assembly inter alia:

> 2. *Expresses deep concern* at the negative stereotyping of religions and manifestations of intolerance and discrimination in matters of religion or belief still evident in the world;
>
> 5. *Notes with deep concern* the intensification of the overall campaign of vilification of religions, and incitement to religious hatred in general, including the ethnic and religious profiling of religious minorities;
>
> …

[48] Commission on Human Rights Resolutions: 2002/9, para 7; 2003/4, para 9; 2004/6, para11; 2005/3, para 2; HRC Resolutions 4/9, para 6; 7/19, para 7; GA Resolutions: A/RES/60/150, para 2; A/RES/ 61/164, para 2; A/RES/ 62/154, para 3.

[49] Commission on Human Rights Resolutions: 2002/9, para 6; 2003/4, para 7; 2004/6, para 9; 2005/3, para 10; HRC Resolutions 4/9, para 8; 7/19, para 9; 10/22, para 13; GA Resolutions: A/RES/60/150 para 10; A/RES/61/164, para 11; A/RES/62/154, para 12; A/RES/63/171, para 16; A/RES/64/156, para 16; A/RES/65/225, para 16.

[50] HRC Resolution 4/9, para 5.

[51] HRC Resolution 7/19, para 4.

[52] See D Diène, 'Situation of Muslim and Arab peoples in various parts of the world' (23 February 2004) UN Doc E/CN.4/2004/19; D Diène, 'Defamation of Religions and Global Efforts to Combat Racism: Anti-Semitism, Christianophobia and Islamophobia' (13 December 2004) UN Doc. E/CN.4/2005/18/Add.4, 7–11; 'Racism, Racial Discrimination, Xenophobia and Related forms of Intolerance: Follow-up to Implementation of the Durban Declaration and Programme of Action' Report of the Special Rapporteur on Contemporary forms of racism, racial discrimination, xenophobia and related forms of Intolerance: Doudou Diène, on the manifestation of defamation of religions and in particular on the serious implications of Islamophobia on the enjoyment of all rights (21 August 2007) A/HRC/6/6; J Rehman, Islamophobia after 9/11: International Terrorism, Sharia and Muslim Minorities in Europe–The Case of the United Kingdom (2003–04) 3 *European Yearbook of Minority Issues* 217.

> *7. Expresses deep concern*, in this respect, that Islam is frequently and wrongly associated with human rights violations and terrorism;
>
> ...
>
> *9. Deplores* the use of the print, audio-visual and electronic media, including the Internet, and any other means to incite acts of violence, xenophobia or related intolerance and discrimination against any religion, as well as the targeting and desecration of holy books, holy sites, places of worship and religious symbols of all religions;
>
> *16. Urges* all States to provide, within their respective legal and constitutional systems, adequate protection against acts of hatred, discrimination, intimidation and coercion resulting from vilification of religions, and incitement to religious hatred in general;

To fully appreciate the contents of Resolution 65/224, it is important to be aware of its context and background. This Resolution was adopted at a time when many member states of the United Nations were active in the domestic application of anti-blasphemy laws. As noted already, OIC–the primary proponent of establishing a global norm on the prohibition of 'defamation of religions'–had in its revised charter of 2008 committed the organisation to 'combating defamation of Islam' as one of its primary objectives.[53] By 2009, the OIC and its member States had been emboldened to make a declaration that prohibition of 'defamation of religions' as a norm had:

> Repeatedly been observed to command support by a majority of the UN member states–a support that transcended the confines of the OIC Member States. The succession of UNGA and UNHRC resolutions on the defamation of religions makes it a standalone concept with international legitimacy. It should not be made to stand out by creating the impression that it somehow encroaches upon freedom of expression.
>
> ...
>
> [Accordingly, a]ny denial of these facts constitutes a contradiction of the established position of the international community, the international legitimacy and above all the main provisions of international law and international humanitarian law.[54]

As referred to earlier, the OIC member states had also been embroiled in a number of controversies surrounding defamation of religions. This included the continuing fallout from the *Jyllands-Posten* Mohammad cartoons controversy emergent after the publication of cartoons of Prophet Mohammad in Denmark and republished in other parts of the world,[55] the naming of non-humans

[53] According to Art 1: 'The objectives of the Organisation of the Islamic Conference shall be ... to protect and defend the true image of Islam, to combat defamation of Islam and encourage dialogue among civilisations and religions' (Art 1(12) of the Charter of the Organisation of Islamic Conference, 14 March 2008) www.oicun.org/2/24/20140324031549266.html.

[54] Second Rep of the OIC Observatory on Islamophobia, 36th Sess, 23–25 May 2009, 4–5, OIC.Doc. OIC-CS-2nd OBS-REP-FINAL (10 May 2009).

[55] See eg J Klausen, *The Cartoons that Shook the World* (New Haven, Yale University Press, 2009); D Keane, 'Cartoon Violence and Freedom of Expression' (2008) 30 *Human Rights Quarterly* 845; 'France Boost Embassy Security after Muhammad Cartoons' *CBC News* (19 September 2012) www.cbc.ca/news/world/story/2012/09/19/france-embassies-cartoon-muhammad.html.

after holy personalities[56] and desecration or destruction of holy scriptures or documents.[57] OIC members such as Pakistan had invoked international criticism for draconian punishments for anti-blasphemy laws as exemplified by the Aasia Bibi case.[58] As considered in earlier chapters of this study, in November 2010, the case of Aasia Bibi, a Christian woman, gained international attention after she was sentenced to death for blasphemy under section 295-C of the Pakistan Penal Code for insulting the Prophet Mohammad. The impact of this incident had been dramatic since both the Punjab Governor, Salman Taseer and Shahbaz Bhatti, the Christian Federal Cabinet Minister of Minority Affairs, who defended her case and campaigned for the reform of Pakistan's blasphemy laws, were assassinated.[59]

IV. Resolution 16/18 and Beyond

Notwithstanding the substantial emphasis of members of the OIC on anti-blasphemy laws to curb freedom of expression domestically, the official campaign within the UN to fully develop an international norm on the prohibition of defamation of religion came to a hiatus in 2011. The most potent explanation for such a development is the exhaustion engendered by a debate that was unlikely to be resolved within the corridors of United Nations. The membership of the United States in 2009 to the Human Rights Council was also a signal of a changing political environment within the Council as well as in the United Nations. It was equally the case that despite the assertive language and furore of Resolution 65/224 (adopted by the General Assembly in 2010) the concept of 'defamation of religions' had in fact been in decline for some time.[60] Indeed, ever since 2008, the combined strength of those abstaining and those voting against had exceeded those states that voted in favour of the 'defamation of religions' resolutions within the General Assembly.[61] During the 2011 session, it became patently obvious to the OIC member states that the global and geo-political momentum had shifted

[56] See eg 'Reports: Sudan Arrests UK Teacher for Teddy Bear Blasphemy' *CNN* (26 November 2007) edition.cnn.com/2007/WORLD/africa/11/26/sudan.bear/index.html.

[57] See eg 'Pentagon urges controversial Florida Pastor to Stop Qur'an Burning Plans' *The Guardian* (20 April 2012) www.guardian.co.uk/world/2012/apr/20/pentagon-florida-pastor-quran-burning; 'Nigeria Teacher Dies "Over Koran"' *BBC News* (21 March 2007) news.bbc.co.uk/1/hi/6477177.stm.

[58] See J Rehman and E Polymenopoulou, 'The Case of Aasia Bibi' (2012–13) 16 *Asian Yearbook of International Law* 136.

[59] Salman Taseer was assassinated by his own guard for defending her case and as a punishment for his campaign to reform Pakistan's blasphemy laws, as it was the case 2 months later also for Shahbaz Bhatti, the Christian Federal Cabinet Minister of Minority Affairs. See also N Pillay, 'UN Human Rights Chief Condemns Pakistan Assassination, Urges Reform of Blasphemy Laws' (2 March 2011) www.ohchr.org/en/NewsEvents/Pages/DisplayNews.aspx?NewsID=10784&LangID=E.

[60] See KLH Samuel, *The OIC, the UN, and Counter-Terrorism Law-Making: Conflicting or Cooperative Legal Orders?* (Oxford, Hart Publishing, 2013) 312; Leo, Gaer and Cassidy, 'Protecting Religions from "Defamation"' (n 45) 770.

[61] See Samuel, *The OIC, the UN, and Counter-Terrorism Law-Making* (n 60) 312.

firmly against the political rhetoric of banning 'defamation of religions': any further induction of such resolutions was certain to be defeated by the Western block led by the United States. Within this environment, intense efforts were made by the United States administration to reach a consensus on a subject where both the OIC and its Western adversaries felt unable to secure an outright and complete victory.

In a background of reconciliation led by the UN as well as the OIC Secretary General, the HRC adopted (without a vote) Resolution 16/18 entitled 'Combating intolerance, negative stereotyping and stigmatization of, and discrimination, incitement to violence and violence against, persons based on religion or belief'.[62] The UN General Assembly followed suit with substantively similar resolutions in the years that followed.[63] These resolutions appear to focus on the protection of individuals rather than protection of religions. For example, while the 'defamation of religions' resolutions raise the issue of 'the negative stereotyping of religions',[64] HRC Resolution 16/18 '*[e]xpresses deep concern* at the continued serious instances of derogatory stereotyping, negative profiling and stigmatization of persons based on their religion or belief'.[65] Further, Resolution 16/18

> *Recognizes* that the open public debate of ideas, as well as interfaith and intercultural dialogue, at the local, national and international levels can be among the best protections against religious intolerance and can play a positive role in strengthening democracy and combating religious hatred, and convinced that a continuing dialogue on these issues can help overcome existing misperceptions.[66]

Resolution 16/18 recognises that stifling legitimate criticism of religions does not protect religious groups and instead the open discussion of contentious issues is to

[62] HRC Resolution, 'Combating intolerance, negative stereotyping and stigmatization of, and discrimination, incitement to violence, and violence against persons based on religion or belief', A/HRC/RES/16/18 (adopted 24 March 2011, without a vote). Note, subsequent Human Rights Council Resolutions: 19/25 of 23 March 2012, 'Combating intolerance, negative stereotyping and stigmatization of, and discrimination, incitement to violence and violence against, persons based on religion or belief', A/HRC/19/L.7 (adopted 23 March 2012, without a vote); 22/31 of 22 March 2013 'Combating intolerance, negative stereotyping and stigmatization of, and discrimination, incitement to violence and violence against, persons based on religion or belief', A/HRC/22/L.40 (adopted 22 March 2013, without a vote); 25/34 of 26 March 2014 'Combating intolerance, negative stereotyping and stigmatization of, and discrimination, incitement to violence and violence against, persons based on religion or belief' A/HRC/25/L.41 (adopted 28 March 2014, without a vote).

[63] See GA Resolution 66/167 of 19 December 2011 'Combating intolerance, negative stereotyping, stigmatization, discrimination, incitement to violence and violence against persons, based on religion or belief' GA Res 66/167 (19 December 2011) UN Doc A/RES/66/167; GA Res 67/178 of 20 December 2012, 'Combating intolerance, negative stereotyping, stigmatization, discrimination, incitement to violence and violence against persons, based on religion or belief' GA Res 67/178 (20 December 2012) UN Doc A/RES/67/178; GA Res of 18 December 2013 'Combating intolerance, negative stereotyping, stigmatization, discrimination, incitement to violence and violence against persons, based on religion or belief' GA Res 68/169 (18 December 2013) UN Doc A/RES/68/169.

[64] Commission on Human Rights Resolution 1999/82 (30 April 1999) UN Doc E/CN.4/Res 1999/82. para 1.

[65] HRC Resolution 16/18, para 1 (*emphasis added*).

[66] Ibid para 4.

be encouraged as a method of protecting individuals and minorities from religious intolerance. By legitimising 'open public debate of ideas', the HRC moved away from the controversial concept of 'defamation of religions' which restricted freedom of expression in order to protect religions from criticism. With the adoption of Human Rights Council Resolution 16/18 (which omitted any explicit references to the defamation of religions), the United States and a number of Western liberal democracies were able to claim 'historic'[67] success followed by the 'pledge to protect the freedom of religion for all while also protecting freedom of expression'.[68]

Subsequent to the adoption of Resolution 16/18, a series of meetings (involving various multiparty actors) were conducted under the auspices of the 'Istanbul Process'. The 'Istanbul Process' was officially triggered through a ministerial meeting held on 15 July 2011, hosted by Ekmeleddin İhsanoğlu, the then Secretary General of the OIC and attended by the then US Secretary of State Hillary Clinton and Catherine Ashton, European Union (EU) Foreign Representative alongside foreign ministers and officials from 28 states. The meeting resulted broadly in a twofold pledge to institute a 'process of sustained and structured engagement' on implementation.[69] Such an engagement would be conducted, first, through the process of convening a series of expert meetings to reflect upon and document best practices for the implementation of the action plan as set out in the provisions of Human Rights Council Resolution 16/18. Secondly, the commitment was that the progress on implementation mechanisms was to be 'underwritten and monitored by the Human Rights Council through available reporting mechanisms'.[70]

The Istanbul Process formally commenced with the first meeting to assess the implementation of Resolution 16/18 in December 2011 in Washington DC and hosted by the US State Department. OIC and EU representatives as well as 26 states participated in these discussions with the general tenor that Resolution 16/18 provided an acceptable compromise between the proponents of defamation of religions and those in opposition to it. Hillary Clinton made the concluding observations that:

> Now this year, the international community in the Human Rights Council made an important commitment. And it was really historic, because before then, we had seen the international community pit against one another freedom of religion and freedom of

[67] Hilary Rodham Clinton, Secretary of State, 'Remarks at the Istanbul Process for Combating Intolerance and Discrimination Based on Religion or Belief' (Washington DC, December 2011) www.state.gov/secretary/20092013clinton/rm/2011/12/178866.htm; the Danish Institute for Human Rights considers Resolution 16/18 as 'one of the most important thematic texts ever adopted by the Council'. See H Power and MJ Petersen 'Informal Report of the 5th Meeting of the Istanbul Process: From Resolution to Realisation–How to Promote Effective Implementation of Human Rights Council Resolution 16/18', www.universal-rights.org/wp-content/uploads/2015/02/URG-DIHR-Report-on-the-5th-Meeting-of-the-Istanbul-Process-Jeddah-2015.pdf.

[68] Ibid.

[69] See Proceeding of the Ministerial meeting held on 15 July at IRCICA in Istanbul, Turkey.

[70] Power and Petersen 'Informal Report of the 5th Meeting of the Istanbul Process: From Resolution to Realisation–How to Promote Effective Implementation of Human Rights Council Resolution 16/18' (n 67) 5.

expression. And there were those in the international community who vigorously and passionately defended one but not the other. And our goal in the work that so many nations represented here have been doing, with the adoption of Resolution 16/18 and then again last month in the General Assembly's Third Committee, was to say we all can do better. And this resolution marks a step forward in creating a safe global environment for practicing and expressing one's beliefs. In it, we pledge to protect the freedom of religion for all while also protecting freedom of expression. And we enshrined our commitment to tolerance and inclusivity by agreeing to certain concrete steps to combat violence and discrimination based on religion or belief. These steps, we hope, will help foster a climate that respects the human rights of all.[71]

As envisaged by Hillary Clinton, the Washington Conference focused upon prohibiting discrimination based on religion or belief. There was also an emphasis upon 'training of officials on religious and cultural awareness', consideration of outreach strategies with 'enforce[ement] of laws that prohibit discrimination on the basis of religion or belief'.[72] The conference reiterated the need for security operations to work within the framework of established human rights, highlighting the negative impact of such tactics as profiling on the basis of religion or ethnicity.[73] The second meeting within the process took place in London in December 2012. Jointly convened by UK and Canada, the focus of this session was upon the action plan of Resolution 16/18 namely 'overcoming obstacles to the equal participation of all groups in society', 'combating intolerance through education', and 'developing collaborative networks between government and civil society'.[74]

The third meeting, held in Geneva (June 2013) and convened by the OIC, covered three panel debates on the provisions of HRC Resolution 16/18: speaking out against intolerance (paragraph 5(e)); adoption measures to criminalise incitement (paragraph 5(f)) and the positive role that an open, constructive and respectful debate of ideas can play in combating intolerance (paragraph 5(h)])[75] The fourth meeting of the 'Istanbul Process' was held in Doha, Qatar (March 2014) and hosted by the OIC and the Doha International Centre for Interfaith Dialogue. The meeting focused on paragraph 5(h) of the Human Rights Council Resolution 16/18 namely

[r]ecognizing that the open, constructive and respectful debate of ideas, as well as interfaith and intercultural dialogue at the local, national and international levels, can play a positive role in combating religious hatred, incitement and violence.

[71] Clinton, 'Remarks at the Istanbul Process for Combating Intolerance and Discrimination Based on Religion or Belief' (n 67).

[72] The Istanbul Process for Combating Intolerance and Discrimination Based on Religion or Belief' Implementing Human Rights Council (HRC) Resolution 16/18, December Expert Level Meeting, Background note, US Department of State, Diplomacy in Action, www.humanrights.gov.

[73] Ibid.

[74] Foreign and Commonwealth Office, Conference on Freedom of Religion or Belief, Foreign and Commonwealth Office (4 December 2012) www.gov.uk/government/news/conference-on-freedom-of-religion-or-belief.

[75] UN Watch, 'No Such thing as Islamic Terrorism' (12 July 2013) http://blog.unwatch.org/index.php/category/defamation-of-religion/.

According to the Doha-based International Centre for Interfaith Dialogue,

> [b]y bringing interfaith community experts together with relevant experts in government, this Istanbul Process meeting contributed significantly to the advancement of religious tolerance and freedom and the formation of collaborative partnership between government and civil society in promoting those goals.[76]

The fifth meeting within the process was conducted in Jeddah, Saudi Arabia and convened at the General Secretariat, 3–4 June 2015, with the most recent meeting agreed to be held in Singapore (2016). The Jeddah meeting entitled 'From Resolution to Realisation–How to Promote Effective Implementation of Human Rights Council Resolution 16/18' addressed inter alia the following themes: (1) potential areas of tension between communities and promotion of understanding through dialogue; (2) countering and combating advocacy to religious hatred that constitute incitement to discrimination, hostility or violence through affirmative action; (3) understanding the need to combat denigration, negative religious stereotyping of persons and incitement to religious hatred through adopting measures to criminalise incitement to imminent violence based on religion or belief.[77]

V. The 'Istanbul Process': Limitations and Shortcomings

Notwithstanding the intelligent and relevant 'action-oriented' nature of Resolution 16/18, the practical impact of this Resolution has been limited. At the substantive level Resolution 16/18 does not fit well with existing structures of international human rights law. The overly broad provisions of Resolution 16/18 do not relate with the non-discriminatory articles within the international bill of rights or the more specific treaty provisions. In reiterating this point Parmar notes that the 'Istanbul Process' covers

> a broad range of discriminatory behaviour, namely 'intolerance, negative stereotyping and stigmatization of, and discrimination … and violence against persons based on religion or belief' and is not tied to the international legal framework, particularly under article 20(2) of the ICCPR.[78]

Serious limitations have also emerged in relation to implementation of the provisions of Resolution 16/18. As was agreed at the ministerial conference of July 2011,

[76] DICID, Report for the Doha Meeting for Advancing Religious Freedom through Interfaith Collaboration Istanbul Process 16/18 for Combating Intolerance and Discrimination Based on Religion or Belief (24–25 March 2014) 5, www.universal-rights.org/wp-content/uploads/2015/02/Doha-Meeting-final.pdf.

[77] Power and Petersen (n 67) 16.

[78] S Parmar, 'The Rabat Plan of Action: A Global Blue Print for Combating "Hate Speech"' [2014] *European Human Rights Law Review* 21, 24.

the provisions of the Resolution can only be meaningful with a full and effective implementation at domestic level. Therefore, there have been calls for

> [s]tates and other relevant stakeholders to move up a gear and implement HRC resolution 16/18 in a comprehensive and holistic manner, addressing obstacles, bad practices and the needed reforms at the domestic level.[79]

Regrettably, the implementation pledge has been marred by either non-implementation or highly selective implementation of the provisions of Resolution 16/18. Particular difficulties have been evidenced in inter alia encouraging the creation of collaborative networks (paragraph 5(a)); speaking out against intolerance, including advocacy of religious hatred that constitutes incitement to discrimination, hostility or violence (paragraph 5(e)); recognising the value of open, constructive and respectful debate of ideas and interfaith dialogue (paragraph 5(h)); understanding the need to combat denigration and negative religious stereotyping of persons (paragraph 5(g)); states to foster religious freedom and pluralism by promoting religious communities to manifest their religion, and to contribute openly and on equal footing to society (paragraph 6(b)); and states to encourage representation and meaningful participation of individuals irrespective of their religion, in all sectors of society (paragraph 6(c)). The most contentious and challenging proposition–the repercussions of which shall be analysed in subsequent sections–is contained in paragraph 5(f); a provision that has retained the potential of 'holding hostage'[80] all other parts of the Resolution 16/18 plan.

A further serious drawback in the 'Istanbul Process' action plan has been the failure of states to report on implementation. The few states that have submitted reports reflect generally superficial content, providing summaries of pre-existing policies. It has been estimated that only around 15 per cent of states have submitted implementation information.[81] The overall limitations of the 'Istanbul Process' have also become increasingly obvious: it is principally an inter-governmental system, with a lack of transparency, that has made it difficult to scrutinise the progress or achievements of the process. The Doha meeting, the fourth in the cycle of 'Istanbul Process' was the first occasion in which non-state actors and members of the civil society could make a noticeable contribution to the proceedings.

As the 'Istanbul Process' progressed, disagreement appeared in the understanding of objectives and goals of this project. In particular, fault lines and cracks emerged between the OIC members and the Western states. The veneer of consensus over the terminology of Human Rights Council Resolution 16/18 was

[79] Fidh, Fifth Session of the Istanbul Process: OIC General Secretariat, Jeddah, Saudi Arabia (3–4 June 2015) (Written Submission).

[80] Power and Petersen (n 67) 21.

[81] Universal Rights Group, 'Combating Religious Intolerance: The Implementation of Human Rights Council' Resolution 16/18; A/HRC/28/47 Report of the United Nations High Commissioner for Human Rights (19 January 2015).

short-lived as serious dissensions resurfaced. The divisions and disagreements, it would appear, are not so much on the deployment of certain terminology, for example, 'advocacy' of 'religious hatred' that forms 'incitement' to violence.[82] On the other hand, there is a fundamental lack of consensus over the meaning of the terms and the permissible boundaries between expression of ideas and 'advocacy' of 'religious hatred' that results in incitement. In other words, the disagreement is evident in the understanding, nature and threshold of Article 20(2) ICCPR.[83] Ambassador Michael G Kozak, Acting Principal Deputy Assistant Secretary for Democracy, Human Rights and Labor, who represented the United States at the third 'Istanbul Process' meeting made the pertinent comment in the Geneva meeting that

> I feel compelled to express disappointment that much of the debate we have had here on 'incitement' was essentially the same debate we have witnessed during the years before 16/18 was passed, involving the same parties and many of the same individuals ... The narrative in terms reminiscent of the Cold War pits 'the West' against 'the rest'. Religious intolerance throughout the world is attributed to the failure of the West to either endorse or enforce more sweeping criminal prohibitions on speech. It is never explained how prohibiting media in the West from reporting on people who wrongly appropriate to themselves the term 'jihadis' would somehow result in better treatment for Christians in Egypt or Shia in Pakistan. Nor is it explained how the application of anti-Semitism laws to anti-Muslim expression would result in better outcomes for Muslims in Europe when we are seeing an increase in anti-Semitism that parallels the growth in anti-Muslim expression—most often from the same groups of haters. Nor is there any examination of why those countries that have expansive restrictions on religious expression also have even higher degrees of religious violence and intolerance than those that do not. Instead, it is just presumed that getting the so-called 'West' to adopt a defamation of religions resolution or now a broader interpretation of Article 20 of the ICCPR than either the Human Rights Committee or the OHCHR workshops have found warranted would somehow be the silver bullet that fixes all problems[84]

As noted by Ambassador Michael G Kozak, one major source of such divisions is that the OIC member states continue to insist upon setting limits upon expression, opposing the Western view that rejects revisiting the agreed terms of Human Rights Council Resolution 16/18 action plan (paragraph 5(f)). OIC members have also insisted on the sanctity of religions and insist that Islam must be immune from insults and criticisms. These tensions were evident in the views advanced

[82] See para 5(e) of the Human Rights Council Resolution 16/18.

[83] See New York City Bar Association, United Nations Resolutions on Religious Hate Speech: The Impact on Freedom of Expression (New York, 2014) www2.nycbar.org/pdf/report/uploads/20072724-UNResolutionsonReligiousHateSpeech--ImpactonFreedomofExpression.pdf.

[84] Statement by Ambassador Michael G Kozak, Acting Principal Deputy Assistant Secretary for Democracy, Human Rights and Labor, Istanbul Process for Combating Intolerance, Discrimination and Incitement to Hatred and/or violence on the Basis of Religion or Belief (Geneva, 21 June 2013).

by His Excellency Iyad Ameen Madani, Secretary General of the OIC at the 4th Istanbul Process Meeting convened in Doha in 2014, as he noted:

> There are those who are ready to speak out against intolerance and discrimination but are clearly not ready to determine the threshold between freedom of expression and hate speech and least to even discuss its criminalization. Lack of such clarity or even an effort to delineate or discuss this important shortcoming continues to be a source of concern for many. Consensus on Res. 16/18 would thus remain fragile unless it stands the test of full and effective implementation through open and candid discussions to determine where freedom of expression ends and incitement to religious hatred begins. Freedom of expression is not an absolute right. OIC's position is firmly grounded in Article 19 and 20 of the International Covenant on Civil and Political Rights (ICCPR), which provide clear limitations, including the duty of the State to prohibit by law, 'any advocacy of national, racial or religious hatred that constitutes incitement to discrimination, hostility or violence'. In this spirit, the OIC has been active in engaging in constructive debates at the international level to further delineate boundaries between the free speech and the hate speech, including incitement to violence. It is also important to highlight that OIC has always upheld the principle of openly discussing all ideas, values or beliefs in an environment of tolerance and respect. Its position on the need to protect the sanctity of religions and their symbols is not to accord exceptional protection to a particular set of values, but to avoid defamatory stereotyping and insults that result in negative profiling of their adherents and lead to undue discrimination, hostility and violence against them. Distinguished Participants, Islam like other religions recognizes the role of critical thinking. However, there must be a distinction between criticism or constructive discussion, which is a legitimate part of freedom of expression, and sheer disrespect, defamation, insult and negative stereotyping that falls into the category of inciting religious hatred. This is a very important aspect of the larger discourse that requires careful consideration. In many societies religious convictions or spiritual values constitute an essential part of individuals' daily lives and is the backbone of their individual and communitarian identities. Hence, an attack on their religion or disrespect of their religious beliefs is an attack on their individual and collective identity and dignity. It is essential to draw a line between free speech and hate speech. While interfaith and intercultural dialogue can help better understanding, it must also be complemented with integrated international efforts to combat incitement to religious intolerance, discrimination and hatred through effective legal means.[85]

The Jeddah meeting witnessed the resurfacing of historical divisions that had besieged the freedom of expression debates during 'defamation of religions' resolutions. The Jeddah meeting was also an occasion where OIC states and their western counterparts traded 'rhetorical blows about selectivity, double standards and hypocrisy'.[86] At this meeting, a delegate from Pakistan went so far as to assert that

[85] Statement by His Excellency Iyad Ameen Madani, Secretary General of the OIC at the 4th Istanbul Process Meeting on the follow-up of Implementation of HRC Resolution 16/18 (24 March 2014) www.oic-oci.org/oicv3/topic/?t_id=8945&ref=3590&lan=en.

[86] Limon, Ghanea and Power, 'Combating Global Religious Intolerance: The Implementation of Human Rights Council Resolution 16/18' (n 8) 20.

the criminalisation of defamation of religions constitutes a norm of customary international law. In support of his arguments he cited several UN resolutions and existing blasphemy laws in some European states.[87] While such an assertion was immediately rebuffed by Western states the argument persists as to whether there now exists an international or at least regional norms that sanctions prohibition of defamation or insults of religions. Overt or implicit prohibition on defamation of religions are applied in several OIC member states.[88] As noted earlier in this study, surveys establish that anti-blasphemy laws are applicable in 14 out of 20 (nearly 70 per cent) of all states from the Middle-East and North Africa as well 9 out of 50 states from Asia Pacific. Nigeria and Somalia also have anti-blasphemy laws. With the rise of domestic application of all laws to curb religious expressions, it is anticipated that anti-blasphemy laws continue to exist in nearly a quarter of all of the world's states.[89]

Conversely, there is also the view that if criminalisation of defamation of religions has not matured into a norm of international law, there is equally no prohibition of installing anti-blasphemy laws within customary international law. Not only is this position advanced by many jurists in the Muslim world, but there is also a body of commentators in the West with similar views. Cox, whilst echoing these sentiments, makes the following observations:

> It can be strongly argued that laws against blasphemy or defamation of religion do not represent a violation of international human rights law (either as it *is* or *should* be interpreted), but merely unsettling for western States which had assumed that their views of such matters were empirically correct and that their approaches warranted international status. … It is [] an argument that no contemporary international norm which *is* genuinely international in nature can systematically exclude or ignore the views of nearly a quarter of the world's population.[90]

Outside of the General Assembly and the Human Rights Council, OIC member states have been engaged in developing norms combating defamation of religions and xenophobia. One significant avenue has been through the proceedings of the Ad Hoc Committee on the Elaboration of Complementing Standards. The Ad Hoc Committee owes its existence to the Durban Declaration and Programme of Action (adopted in 2001 at the World Conference against Racism, Racial Discrimination, Xenophobia and Related Intolerance) according to which a recommendation was made that the then Human Rights Commission 'prepare complementary

[87] Power and MJ Petersen (n 67) 20.

[88] RC Blitt, 'The Bottom up Journey of "Defamation of Religion" from Muslim States to the United Nations: A Case Study of the Migration of Anti-Constitutional Ideas' in A Sarat (ed), *Special Issue Human Rights: New Possibilities/New Problems* (Studies in Law, Politics and Society, vol 56) (Bingley, Emerald Group Publishing Limited, 2011) 121–211.

[89] Pew Research Centre, 'Which Countries Still Outlaw Apostasy and Blasphemy?' (28 May 2014) www.pewresearch.org/fact-tank/2014/05/28/which-countries-still-outlaw-apostasy-and-blasphemy.

[90] N Cox, 'The Freedom to Publish "Irreligious" Cartoons' (2016) 16 *Human Rights Law Review* 195, 207.

international standards to strengthen and update international instruments against racism, racial discrimination, xenophobia and related intolerance in all their aspects'.[91] The assignment was initially tasked to an Intergovernmental Working Group on the effective Implementation of the Durban Declaration and Programme of Action. The Working Group in its 2006 report made the recommendations on issues of procedural and substantive gaps respectively:

> (a) the Committee on the Elimination of Racial Discrimination (CERD) to conduct a further study on possible measures to strengthen implementation through additional recommendations or the update of its monitoring procedures;
>
> (b) that OHCHR select, in close consultation with regional groups, five highly qualified experts to study the content and scope of the substantive gaps in the existing international instruments to combat racism, racial discrimination, xenophobia and related intolerance.

Following the Working Group's recommendation, reports were procured by the five experts focusing on existing gaps in international standards.[92] The Committee on the Elimination of All Forms of Racial Discrimination also submitted a report on possible mechanism for strengthening implementation.[93] After having considered the two studies, the Human Rights Council established the Ad Hoc Committee and assigned this Committee 'for commencing its process of elaborating complementary standards, and that one of its main priorities be to ensure that the draft instrument(s) is/are produced for negotiations'. The Ad Hoc Committee had its first session in 2008 and has since that time met for an annual session, concluding its eighth session.

In its campaigns, the OIC conflated the subject of incitement to religious hatred with defamation of religions and argued for the adoption of some sort of additional protocol or universal declaration for codifying freedom of expression in the context of human responsibilities. It may be called an additional protocol or universal declaration on 'freedom of expression and human responsibilities' … a comprehensive framework is needed for analysing national laws as well as understanding their provisions. This could then be compiled in a single universal document as guidelines for legislation—aimed at countering 'defamation of or incitement to religious hatred and violence'.[94]

91 www.ohchr.org/EN/Issues/Racism/AdHocCommittee/Pages/AdHocIndex.aspx.

92 See Report on the study by the five experts 'On the content and scope of substantive gaps in the existing international instruments to combat racism, racial discrimination, xenophobia and related intolerance' (A/HRC/4/WG.3/6).

93 See Study by the Committee on the Elimination of Racial Discrimination 'On possible measures to strengthen implementation through optional recommendations or the update of its monitoring procedures' (A/HRC/4/WG.3/7).

94 Transcript of the Concluding Session of the Seminar on Articles 19 and 20, Organized By the Office of High Commissioner for Human Rights, Geneva, Switz, 2 October 2008, Remarks by Mojtaba Amiri Vahid, Deputy of the Permanent Observer Missions of the OIC to the UN Office in Geneva, 3.

This deliberately orchestrated conflation is evidenced in many campaigns made by individual OIC members or those by the organisation as a whole before the Ad Hoc Committee. Thus:

> addressing the theme of "[d]iscrimination based on religion or belief' within the Ad Hoc Committee, the OIC called for, *inter alia*, criminal liability for those 'who commit, instigate, or aid
>
> and abet … directly or indirectly' the following:
>
> (d) … *public insults and defamation* threats against a person or a grouping of persons on the grounds of their … religion
>
> …; [and]
>
> (e) … *publication of material that negatively stereotypes, insults, or uses offensive language on matters regarded by followers of any religion or belief as sacred* or inherent to their dignity as human beings, with the aim of protecting their fundamental human rights.[95]

In the continuation of the project to criminalise defamation of Islam, OIC member states have remained insistent that freedom of religion or belief of individuals incorporates adverse expressions upon their religions or beliefs. Implicit in these assertions is also the failure to appreciate the boundaries drawn and the high threshold provided by Article 20(2). This consciousness of high threshold had led the former Special Rapporteur on Freedom of Religion or Belief Asma Jahangir to take the view that 'expressions should only be prohibited under Article 20 *if they constitute incitement to imminent acts of violence or discrimination against a specific individual or group*'.[96]

The Special Rapporteur further warned

> [a]gainst confusion between a racist statement and an act of defamation of religion. The elements that constitute a racist statement are not the same as those that constitute a statement defaming a religion. To this extent, the legal measures, and in particular the criminal measures, adopted by national legal systems to fight racism may not necessarily be applicable to defamation of religion.[97]

The Ad Hoc Committee has continued with its work, although its sessions have not been without controversy. At the same time, the OIC campaigns to institute new norms of international law. The larger challenge in this debacle is about preserving the sanctity of traditional notions of international human rights law

[95] A/HRC/AC.1/2/2, Human Rights Council, Ad Hoc Comm on the Elaboration of Complementary Standards, Outcomes Referred to in Paragraph 2(D) of the Road Map on the Elaboration of Complementary Standards at A/HRC/AC.1/2/2 (26 August 2009) para 27.

[96] 'Report of the Special Rapporteur on freedom of religion or belief, Asma Jahangir, and the Special Rapporteur on contemporary forms of racism, racial discrimination, xenophobia and related intolerance' Doudou Diène, further to Human Rights Council decision 1/107 on incitement to racial and religious hatred and the promotion of tolerance A/HRC/2/3 (20 September 2006) (emphasis added) para 47.

[97] Ibid para 49.

which only protect the rights of the individuals and render all religions or religious ideologies open to offensive comments and assertions.[98]

VI. Rabat Plan of Action

In order to overcome the various lacunae in the Istanbul Process, a parallel process, the Rabat Plan of Action was deployed. The Rabat Plan of Action represents a series of OHCHR-led workshops characterised by a regional focus and the participation of a number regional experts. These workshops culminated in the final production of a document in Rabat, Morocco on 4 and 5 October 2012. The Plan of Action adopted on 5 October 2012, brought together conclusions and recommendations of a series of workshops organised by OHCHR in 2011. The planned consultative meetings (leading to the adoption of the Rabat Plan of Action) were guided by the relevant UN Special Rapporteurs: these were Frank La Rue Special Rapporteur on Freedom of Opinion and Expression; Heiner Bielefeldt, Special Rapporteur on Freedom of Religion or Belief, Adama Dieng, registrar of the UN International Criminal Tribunal for Rwanda; Mutuma Ruteere, UN Special Rapporteur on Racism, Racial Discrimination, Xenophobia and Related Intolerance. The process also involved non-governmental organisations such as Article XIX and as many as 45 experts from various legal and cultural backgrounds.[99] The workshops took place in Europe (Vienna, 9–10 February 2011), Africa (Nairobi, 6–7 April 2011), Asia and the Pacific (Bangkok, 6–7 July 2011), the Americas (Santiago, 12–13 October 2011) and Africa (Rabat, 4–5 October 2011).

According to the High Commissioner on Human Rights,

> [t]he principal aim of the whole exercise was to conduct a comprehensive assessment of the implementation of legislation, jurisprudence and policies regarding advocacy of national, racial or religious hatred that constitutes incitement to discrimination, hostility or violence at the national and regional levels, while encouraging full respect for freedom of expression, as protected by international human rights law.[100]

The plan aims to clarify state obligations under Article 20 of the ICCPR and in so doing sets out a comprehensive assessment of implementation of legislation, jurisprudence and policies on advocacy of hatred constituting incitement to violence and discrimination. The plan recommends the adoption of comprehensive anti-discrimination legislation, with a view to undertake preventative action to

[98] Blitt (n 41) 351.

[99] United Nations, Human Rights: www.ohchr.org/EN/NewsEvents/Pages/TheRabatPlanofAction.aspx (United Nations Human Rights, Office of the High Commissioner: Geneva).

[100] United Nations Commissioner for Human Rights, 'Annual Report of the United Nations Commissioner for Human Rights, Addendum, Report of the United Nations Commissioner for Human Rights on expert workshops on the Prohibition of incitement to national, racial or religious hatred' (11 January 2013) A/HRC/22/17/Add. para 6.

combat incitement to hatred. It recommends that there should be distinctions on three types of expression:

> [e]xpression that constitutes a criminal offence; expression that is not criminally punishable but may justify a civil suit or administrative sanctions; expression that does not give rise to criminal, civil or administrative sanctions but still raises a concern in terms of tolerance, civility and respect for the rights of others.[101]

A further recommendation emerging from the Rabat Plan of Action is that having regard to the relationship between Article 19 and 20 of the ICCPR, domestic laws should be expressly guided by Article 20 provisions and that states should incorporate domestic legislation to provide robust and precise definitions of key terms including hatred, discrimination, violence and hostility, and therefore to move away from ambiguity encountered inter alia in the anti-blasphemy laws.[102] It follows naturally that the Rabat Plan of Action to recommend the repeal of anti-blasphemy laws or laws prohibiting defamation of religions: the major premise is that such laws stifle and unduly inhibit both the right to freedom of expression as well as the right to freedom of religion or belief.[103] The role of the media, national institutions as well as the judiciary is critical. In order to promote equality, national human rights institutions (with large competencies on social dialogue to deal with incidents of incitement to hatred) should be established. Furthermore, the Action Plan recommends that an independent judiciary should adjudicate on matters pertaining to incitement to hatred cases, including assessment of comprehensive threshold test. There should be a high threshold for criminal sanction with states to apply alternative measures in preventing incitement to hatred, including inter alia inter cultural dialogue and pluralism ensuring respect for diversity and minority groups. An independent and objective media can play a critical role in developing a pluralistic environment.

The Rabat Plan of Action also takes note of the high threshold for placing limitations on freedom of expression, and for defining incitement to hatred and in so doing the application of Article 20 of the Covenant. In order to make an assessment of the applicability of Article 20, it lays out a number of tests with criteria. These represent, according to the Rabat Plan of Action, a six-part threshold test for expression that is criminally prohibited and are based on the following:

— Context: Context is of great importance when assessing whether particular statements are likely to incite to discrimination, hostility or violence against the target

[101] 'Rabat Plan of Action on the prohibition of advocacy of national, racial or religious hatred that constitutes incitement to discrimination, hostility or violence: Conclusions and recommendations emanating from the four regional expert workshops organised by OHCHR, 2011, and adopted by experts in Rabat, Morocco on 5 October, 2012'. UNCHR, Annual Report of the United Nations Commissioner for Human Rights, Addendum, *Report of the United Nations Commissioner for Human Rights on expert workshops on the Prohibition of incitement to national, racial or religious hatred* A/HRC/22/17/Add.4 (11 January 2013) www.ohchr.org/Documents/Issues/Opinion/SeminarRabat/Rabat_draft_outcome.pdf, para 20.

[102] Ibid.

[103] Ibid.

group and it may have a bearing directly on both intent and/or causation. Analysis of the context should place the speech act within the social and political context prevalent at the time the speech was made and disseminated

— Speaker: The position or status of the speaker in the society should be considered, specifically the individual's or organisation's standing in the context of the audience to whom the speech is directed.
— Intent: Article 20 of the ICCPR requires intent. Negligence and recklessness are not sufficient for an article 20 situation which requires 'advocacy' and 'incitement' rather than mere distribution or circulation. In this regard, it requires the activation of a triangular relationship between the object and subject of the speech as well as the audience.
— Content or form: The content of the speech constitutes one of the key foci of the court's deliberations and is a critical element of incitement. Content analysis may include the degree to which the speech was provocative and direct, as well as a focus on the form, style, nature of the arguments deployed in the speech at issue or in the balance struck between arguments deployed, etc
— Extent of the speech: This includes elements such as the reach of the speech, its public nature, magnitude and the size of its audience. Further elements are whether the speech is public, what the means of dissemination are, considering whether the speech was disseminated through one single leaflet or through broadcasting in the mainstream media or internet, what was the frequency, the amount and the extent of the communications, whether the audience had the means to act on the incitement, whether the statement (or work of art) was circulated in a restricted environment or widely accessible to the general public.
— Likelihood, including imminence: Incitement, by definition, is an inchoate crime. The action advocated through incitement speech does not have to be committed for that speech to amount to a crime. Nevertheless some degree of risk of resulting harm must be identified. It means the courts will have to determine that there was a reasonable probability that the speech would succeed in inciting actual action against the target group, recognising that such causation should be rather direct.[104]

Notwithstanding, the wisdom apparent from the Rabat Plan of Action, its practical utility has not become obvious. In addition, as has been pointed out, there is a substantial gap of understanding between the 'Istanbul process' and the Rabat Plan of Action.[105] This Action Plan has engaged significantly with the relationship between freedom of speech and hate speech and in so doing targeted anti-blasphemy laws as negative and ineffective. The Action Plan analyses and considers the obligations of a range of actors including the United Nations and state obligations. On the other hand, and as considered already, the 'Istanbul process' has largely been a state-led process and has as yet failed to deal with difficult topics such as anti-blasphemy laws: serious tension persists on the boundaries in

[104] Ibid para 29.
[105] Parmar, 'The Rabat Plan of Action' (n 78) 24.

which freedom of expression can be made permissible. Furthermore, the 'Istanbul process' has not been inclusive of communities and there remains a significant need to involve civil society and faith based or non-faith based organisations. The ultimate success of the Rabat Plan of Action as well as that of the 'Istanbul process' is dependent on their effective implementation which is still less than satisfactory.

In this context, the recent 'Beirut Declaration on '"Faith for Rights" (F4R)' of March 2017[106] deserves mentioning. It openly addresses the problem of lack of respect and implementation of the core human rights of freedom of religion and freedom of expression. The Declaration was elaborated by faith-based and civil society actors working in the field of human rights in culmination of a trajectory of meetings initiated by the Office of the United Nations High Commissioner for Human Rights (OHCHR) in the elaboration for the Rabat Plan of Action of 2012 and continued thereafter.[107] In the Declaration, the undersigning faith-based and civil society actors express their conviction that 'faith and rights should be mutually reinforcing spheres', 'that individual and communal expression of religions or beliefs thrive and flourish in environments where human rights, based on the equal worth of all individuals, are protected', but that, similarly, 'human rights can benefit from deeply rooted ethical and spiritual foundations provided by religion or beliefs'.[108] The subscribers have agreed to 18 commitments on 'Faith for Rights', which include 'to stand up and act for everyone's right to free choices and particularly for everyone's freedom of thought, conscience, religion or belief', 'to prevent the use of the notion of "State religion" to discriminate against any individual or group', 'to monitor interpretations, determinations or other religious views that manifestly conflict with universal human rights norms and standards', and 'to leverage the spiritual and moral weight of religions and beliefs with the aim of strengthening the protection of universal human rights and developing preventative strategies'.[109]

The Beirut Declaration and the 18 commitments on 'Faith for Rights' are a promising signal and show that the protection of religion is not in opposition to the protection of human rights, as is sometimes seen, but that they can be mutually beneficial to each other. Under the rule of law premise, the dedication and actions of governments are required to reflect this insight in addition to faith-based and civil society actors.

[106] See the document as published by the OHCHR on 29 March 2017, www.ohchr.org/Documents/Press/21451/BeirutDeclarationonFaithforRights.pdf, reprinted in app III below.

[107] Ibid. The meetings after 2012 were held in Geneva (February 2013), Amman (November 2013), Manama (2014), Tunis (October 2014 and April 2015), Nicosia (October 2015), Beirut (December 2015) and Amman (January 2017).

[108] Beirut Declaration on 'Faith for Rights' (F4R) (n 106) para. 1

[109] See the document as published by the OCHCR on 29 March 2017, 18 Commitments on 'Faith for Rights' (n 106).

VII. OIC Agenda and the Future of Freedom of Expression

Whilst the shift in semantics after the adoption of Resolution 16/18 was laudable, the reality has been considerably grim: the analysis of the approach adopted in Human Rights Council Resolution 16/18 (and subsequent related resolutions in the Council and in the General Assembly) suggests more a diplomatic veneer than a growth in international consensus. As already noted, the OIC group as well as its adversaries claimed victory in the aftermath of Resolution 16/18: with the adoption of the Resolution 16/18, the United States and its primarily Western allies heralded the closure of an era of 'false divide that pit[ted] religious sensitivities against freedom of expression'[110] with international community being in pursuit of 'a new approach based on concrete steps to fight intolerance wherever it occurs'.[111] On the other hand, the OIC–led by Muslim majority states such as Pakistan–continued to interpret Resolution 16/18 and subsequent resolutions as an endorsement of the organisation's efforts of prohibition of 'defamation of religions'.[112]

HRC Resolution 16/18 was presented by Pakistan on behalf of the OIC. The sponsoring state, Pakistan, was–and is clearly–of the view that Resolution 16/18 does not replace the previously adopted resolutions on 'defamation of religions'. After the adoption of Resolution 16/18 on 24 March 2011, Pakistan's Ambassador and representative to the OIC, Mr Zamir Akram made an unequivocal assertion that '[t]his resolution does not replace the OIC's earlier resolutions on combating defamation of religions which were adopted by the Human Rights Council and continue to remain valid'.[113] Similar views were echoed by other members of the OIC.[114]

Since the adoption of Resolution 16/18, the OIC–at an organisational level–has consistently adopted numerous resolutions confirming the organisation's position on defamation of religions. In his statement at the High Level Segment of the sixteenth session of the Human Rights Council, the then Secretary General of the OIC noted that '[the organisation] has a principled position against defamation of any religion'[115] reiterating his call from the fifteenth session of the Council

[110] HR Clinton, US Secretary of State, Remarks at the OIC High Level Meeting on Combating Religious Intolerance (15 July 2011) www.humanrights.gov/dyn/secretary-clintons-remarks-at-the-oic-meeting-on-combating-religious-intolerance.html.

[111] Ibid.

[112] See Blitt (n 41).

[113] P Goodenough, 'U.N. Religious "Defamation" Resolution is not Dead, Says Islamic Bloc' *CNS. Newscom* (30 March 2011) http://cnsnews.com/news/article/un-religious-defamation-resolution-not-dead-says-islamic-bloc.

[114] Ibid.

[115] Statement by His Excellency Ekmeleddin İhsanoğlu, Secretary General of the Organisation of the Islamic Conference, at the High Level Segment of the 16th Session of the Human Rights Council Geneva (1 March 2011).

for the '[e]stablishment of an Observatory of the High Commissioner to monitor acts of defamation of all religions or incitement to hatred or violence on religious grounds as a first step towards concerted action at the international level'.[116] In the OIC's Astana Declaration adopted in June 2011, the organisation called upon '[t]he international community to take effective measures to combat the defamation of religions'.[117] The Astana Declaration is reinforced by a Resolution No 35/38-POL of the OIC entitled 'Combating Defamation of Religions' in which the OIC Council of Foreign Minsters '[e]xpress deep concern at the intensification of the overall campaign of defamation of Islam'.[118]

> Resolution No 35/38-POL
>
> [a]ppreciates the efforts of the OIC Working Groups on Human Rights in New York and Geneva towards sustaining support for the resolution on Combating Defamation of Religions and for facilitating the adoption by consensus of the HRC resolution 16/18 on Combating Intolerance, Violence Against Persons Based on Religion or Belief and requests the two groups to intensify their efforts to coordinate position and continue to explore options with regard to broadening support for the resolution on defamation of religions as well as other resolutions of importance to the OIC.[119]

In effectively downgrading HRC Resolution 16/18, Resolution No 35/38-POL urged the OIC Secretary-General to '[t]ake appropriate steps to evolve and sustain an effective mechanism towards maintaining and broadening the support base for the OIC sponsored resolution on combating defamation of religions'.[120] While '[u]rging all member states to continue to support the Resolution No. 35/38-POL "on bloc in favour"'[121] of a Resolution [on Defamation of Religions], it degraded Resolution 16/18 as one of the 'alternative approaches' open for further consideration.[122] In another resolution adopted at the same time–Resolution No 34/38-POL–the OIC Council of Foreign Ministers called for expediting the 'implementation process of its decision on developing "a legally binding instrument to prevent intolerance, discrimination, prejudice and hatred on the grounds of religion and defamation of religions and to promote and ensure the respect of all religions"'.[123]

[116] Ibid.

[117] OIC, OIC Astana Declaration: Peace, Cooperation and Development (Adopted by the thirty-eighth session of the OIC Council of Foreign Ministers) Astana Republic of Kazakhstan, done on 30 June 2011.

[118] OIC, Resolution No 35/38-POL on Defamation of Religions, OIC/CFM-38/2011/POL/FINAL, 1.

[119] Ibid para.14.

[120] Ibid para 16.

[121] Ibid para 15.

[122] Ibid para 15.

[123] OIC, Resolution No.34/38-POL on Combating Islamophobia and Eliminating hatred and Prejudice against Islam (Adopted by the thirty-eighth session of the OIC Council of Foreign Ministers) (Session of Peace, Cooperation and Development) OIC/CFM-38/2011/POL/FINAL held in Astana, Republic of Kazakhstan from 26–28 June Rajab 1432 H (28–30 June 2011) para 12.

Furthermore the resolution provided for concrete and practical steps for the adoption of a legally binding instrument, as it is decided to set up '[o]ne open-ended Intergovernmental Group of Legal and Political Experts to develop and examine the legal and political elements of such an instrument for its submission to the next session of the CFM for adoption'.[124] The OIC Secretary General was required to further strengthen the Islamophobia Observatory with the submission of an annual report on defamatory acts against Islam and the OIC inter-parliamentary group of the OIC states are required to take appropriate measures to combat all forms and manifestation of defamation of Islam.[125] The cumulative effect of Resolution No 35/38-POL and Resolution No 34/38-POL is that the OIC views HRC Resolution 16/18 as nothing more than an approach open for future consideration. However, in the meantime the organisation remains intent on formalising internationally legally binding instruments banning or criminalising any form of defamation of Islam–an objective, as noted already, that is stated and reaffirmed in the revised Charter of the OIC.[126] Furthermore and as considered already, even within the context of the 'Istanbul Process' the OIC secretariat and its individual members have insisted upon a clear distinction between what is 'legitimate' freedom of expression as opposed to disrespect, insult or defamation of religions.[127] The historic disagreements and divisions between the OIC and the Western world have resurfaced and were evident in the proceedings of the Geneva (2013), Doha (2014) and Jeddah (2015) meetings.

The potential value of the OIC's Independent Permanent Human Rights Commission (IPHRC) for advancing the rule of law principles was examined in Part II of this study. The institutional and regulatory reforms in the organisation, in particular, the establishment of the IPHRC deserve a brief, tentative examination in the present context.[128] From a human rights and freedom of expression perspective, the establishment of the IPHRC is a welcome development within the framework of the OIC's 'Ten-Year Programme of Action', in 2005.[129] However, notwithstanding the enthusiasm associated with the establishment of a Commission focused on human rights issues, the Constitution, composition and powers of IPHRC reflect inherent limitations. Unlike other regional bodies, IPHRC is envisaged as a purely consultative body of the OIC Council of Foreign Ministers. It is

[124] Ibid para 14.

[125] Ibid para 15.

[126] www.oicun.org/2/24/20140324031549266.html.

[127] See Statement by His Excellency Iyad Ameen Madani, Secretary General of the OIC at the 4th Istanbul Process (n 85).

[128] See www.oic-iphrc.org/en/about/.

[129] In order to meet the challenges of the 21st century, the Islamic Summit called upon member states to take joint actions within the framework of the OIC 'to revive the Muslim Ummah's pioneering role as a fine example of tolerance and enlightened moderation and a force for international peace and harmony'. See Ten-Year Programme of Action to Meet the Challenges Facing the Muslim Ummah in the 21st Century, www.oic-iphrc.org/en/data/docs/legal_instruments/OIC%20Instruments/TYPOA-%20AEFV/TYPOA-EV.pdf.

devoid of any independent monitoring powers. Its composition does not reflect the desired level of autonomy; the independence of the members is likely to be compromised as members of IPHRC are elected by the OIC Council of Foreign Ministers. The structural limitations and concerns of lack of independence are reinforced by its operations and practices which, thus far, have been equivocal and unconvincing. At one level, there has been greater involvement and cooperation with the international human rights institutions; there is certainly an increase in sharing and appearing on the global rights platform. As noted in Part II, specifically on issues pertaining to freedom of expression, the IPHRC organised a thematic debate on 'Freedom of Expression and Hate Speech' in November 2015.[130] The thematic debate included a number of key participants including contributions from UN Special Rapporteur on Freedom of Expression, Mr David Kay (via video link) and the former UN Special Rapporteur on Racism, Mr Doudou Diène. At another level, there continue to remain huge insurmountable ideological differences. These differences are illustrative of the positions adopted by the OIC vis-à-vis their Western adversaries. Thus, the Outcome document, a product of the thematic debates on freedom of expression and hate speech conducted in November 2015, reflects such tensions and disagreements. The Outcome Document commences by acknowledging that freedom of expression is a key human right, which is vital for development of stable, peaceful and progressive democratic societies.[131] It also emphasises that the freedom of expression is not 'absolute' but that its exercise is subject to 'special duties and corresponding responsibilities' based on 'avoidance of harm to others' to ensure societal cohesion. The document asserts that in Islam freedom of expression is guaranteed, but that Islam 'makes distinction between criticism or constructive discussion and sheer disrespect, defamation, insult and negative stereotyping that fall into the category of inciting religious hatred'.[132]

The Outcome Document calls upon the '[n]eed for responsible use of freedom of expression to ensure protection of the rights of others, respect the right of privacy and personal dignity and maintenance of socio-cultural harmony'. It goes on to repeat the orthodox OIC position emphasising

> [t]he need to protect the sanctity of religions and their symbols is not to accord exceptional protection to the particular set of values but to avoid defamatory stereotyping and insults that result in negative profiling of their adherents leading to undue discrimination, hostility and violence against them. Hence, the beneficiary remains the individual of targeted religion, a legitimate subject of international human rights law.

[130] See above Ch 2; IPHRC '8th Session: Outcome Document of Thematic Debate on "Freedom of Expression and Hate Speech"', 23 November 2015, www.oic-iphrc.org/data/sessions/8th_iphrc_thematic_debate_outcome_en.pdf; for text see app I.

[131] Ibid.

[132] Ibid.

The document then conflates acts of terrorist groups and organisations such as Da'esh and Boko Haram with '[p]rinting of senseless caricatures of Prophet Mohammad (PBUH)'. The document

> [c]ondemn[s] acts of incitement to hatred resulting in devastating and despicable killing of non-Muslims by terrorist groups such as Daesh and Boko Haram etc.; printing of senseless caricatures of Prophet Mohammad (PBUH); appalling treatment of Rohingya Muslims in Myanmar; desecration of holy scriptures and sites in different parts of the world, that have all resulted in promoting a culture of discrimination and violence leading to loss of innocent lives and wider sense of alienation, rejection, and polarization among affected communities.

Such statements are, however, not only equivocal, ambiguous and misconceived: the linkages drawn between acts of Da'esh and Boko Haram and printing of the Prophet's caricatures in the same sentence appears to suggest that the printing of despicable caricatures and other unacceptable forms of expression is somehow a matter of equal gravity to the killings and horrible acts of terrorism and torture conducted by Boko Haram and Da'esh. Furthermore, if the statement wishes to highlight incitement to religious hatred as the major concern, there are double standards deployed: whilst the appalling atrocities committed by Da'esh and Bako Haram are noted as is the unacceptable treatment endured by Rohingya Muslims in Myanmar, no reference is made of the equally serious violations of rights by Muslim dictatorial regimes (for example Syria, Iraq, Bahrain, Yemen etc) resulting in equally substantial human rights violations.

As regard Resolution 16/18 of the Human Rights Council, the Outcome Document expresses its:

> confidence in OIC sponsored HRC Resolution 16/18 (entitled Combating intolerance, negative stereotyping and stigmatization of, and discrimination, incitement to violence and violence against persons based on religion or belief), repeatedly adopted by the Human Rights Council and UN General Assembly by consensus, which includes substantive, administrative, political and legislative actions to be taken at the national and international levels to address the concerns relating to incitement to religious hatred and discrimination.[133]

The Outcome Document urges states to implement the action plan provided by Resolution 16/18, emphasising on the need to regularly report these mechanisms. While some solace could be achieved through this document's recognition of the inclusive approaches provided in 'Rabat Plan of Action on the prohibition of advocacy of national, racial or religious hatred that constitutes incitement to discrimination, hostility or violence', the over-emphasis on limiting freedom of expression and the inability to appreciate the high threshold approved by the Rabat plan of Action remains problematic. In summary, as the premier flagship instrument representing the OIC's vision on freedom of expression, the Outcome Document does not augur as a beacon of hope and optimism.

[133] Ibid.

That said, there may be some causes for optimism: the Outcome Document makes a recommendation that the OIC commissions a study that analyses the existing legal practices used to combat hate speech and incitement to hatred in different parts of the world. Such a study, however, would only prove meaningful if it works within the standards established by international human rights law, in particular Article 20(2) of the ICCPR. The Council of Ministers at its forty-second meeting in 2015 mandated the IPHRC to Review the Cairo Declaration on Human Rights in Islam (1990).[134] The Commission formed a committee that met in February 2016 for the first time and formulated preliminary suggestions. Such a review would be a welcome development, although it would be wholly optimistic in the current political environment to anticipate wholesale revision to either the CDHRI (1990) or the Covenant on the Rights of the Child in Islam–two of the foundational documents of the IPHRC.

VIII. Conclusions

As examined already, within the UN Human Rights Council, members belonging to the OIC have vociferously continued to champion the implementation of paragraph 5(f) of Resolution 16/18. In all of the OIC hosted meetings (Geneva, Doha and Jeddah) the 'defamation of Islam' has returned to the agenda in the guise of paragraph 5(f). During the Geneva meeting, the then OIC Secretary General repeatedly asserted that the aim of the 'Istanbul Process' was to provide a response to the 'alarming increase in intolerance and discrimination against Muslims'[135] particularly through identification of a threshold for criminalisation of incitement. Zamir Akram, Pakistan's Ambassador, argued that there should be defined boundaries of freedom of expression and was critical of the double standards when expression was curtailed on holocaust denial.[136]

Within their practices, it seems certain that the OIC member states perceive HRC Resolution 16/18 as a package. Individual states, as well as the organisation, view the international debate on freedom of expression with substantial and fortified limitations especially around criticism of religion, religious beliefs but also around treatment of minorities. OIC member states have suggested that legal measures (in the West) against Islamophobia should be brought to the same levels as anti-semitism and have campaigned for an international monitoring

[134] See Resolution on Legal Affairs adopted by 42nd Session of the Council of Foreign Ministers (Session of Joint Vision to strengthen Tolerance and Reject Terrorism) Kuwait, State of Kuwait (27–28 May 2015) para 12. OIC/CFM-42/2015/LEG/RES/FINAL, www.oic-oci.org/subweb/cfm/43/en/docs/fin/43cfm_res_leg_en.pdf.

[135] Remarks of the OIC Secretary General, Opening Session of the third Istanbul Process, Geneva Meeting (19 June 2013).

[136] Comments made during the third Istanbul Process meeting, Geneva (19 June 2013).

mechanism, for example, an Islamophobia observatory, in order to protect Muslim minorities based in Europe and North America. However, the OIC and individual member states such as Pakistan, Egypt and Saudi Arabia have been equally assertive in persisting with their domestic policies which seriously undermines freedom of expression through anti-blasphemy and anti-apostasy laws.

Having regard to the positions adopted by the OIC as well as the practices of its individual Islamic states,[137] it is hardly credible to accept that a greater understanding has emerged subsequent to HRC Resolution 16/18. On the other hand, Blitt's comment appears convincing that

> even if defamation of religion per se is on hiatus from the UN, absent additional measures–including a decisive repudiation of the concepts' validity–further international effort to implement measures for combating intolerance risk enabling an alternative framework in which governments continue justifying, in the name of protecting religious belief, domestic measures that punish the exercise of freedom of expression and freedom of thought, conscience, and religion or belief.[138]

[137] eg since 2011, charges have brought, and conviction secured against Nabil Karoui, *Tunisia* (for insulting a recognised religion) (Tunisian Penal Code, Art, 48) for representation of God as imagined from a child's point of view, www.voanews.com/policy/editorials/africa/A-Question-Of-Freedom-Of-Expression-153797455.html (24 May 2012); Adel Imam, charged in *Egypt* (accused of offending Islam, including beards and Jilbab) /www.bbc.co.uk/news/world-middle-east-17832703(25 April 2012); Alex Aan (prosecuted for creating a Facebook page in support of atheism in *Indonesia*) www.guardian.co.uk/world/2012/may/03/indonesia-atheists-religious-freedom-aan (3 May 2012); Hamza Kashgari (*Saudi* national charged with writing his wish not to bow before Prophet Mohammad but to shake his hands as equals do) www.bbc.co.uk/news/world-asia-17001900; Mansor Almaribe, an Australian citizen punished with 75 lashes in *Saudi Arabia* for quoting out of a book which insulted Prophet Mohammad's companion, www.theaustralian.com.au/news/nation/mansor-almaribe-who-was-imprisoned-for-blasphemy-in-saudi-arabia-has-returned-home-to-melbourne/story-e6frg6nf-1226243204214 (13 January 2012); in May 2014, the blogger Raif Badawi was sentenced by the Saudi Arabian government to 10 years in prison and 1000 lashes. He has been kept in detention since that time, while some of the 1000 lashes have already been dispensed. See Amnesty International Report, 'Saudi Arabia: A year of bloody repression since flogging of Raif Badawi' (6 January 2016) www.amnesty.org/en/press-releases/2016/01/saudi-arabia-a-year-of-bloody-repression-since-flogging-of-raif-badawi.

[138] Blitt (n 41) (abstract).

Part V

Conclusions

8

Concluding Reflections

This study has drawn its origins and primary inspiration from the work of the International Law Association's Committee on International Law and Islamic Law. For nearly a decade, the authors of this work, in their capacity as Co-Rapporteurs, have been engaged in arguments strengthening the relationship between the rule of law, freedom of expression and Islamic law.[1] This research has engaged in identifying the extent to which the right to freedom of expression is significant for the appropriate application of rule of law. It has also explored whether, notwithstanding conceptual and inherent ambiguities, the core values of the rule of law reflect principles inherited from all the major world traditions and civilisations. This examination has been done from a comparative legal perspective and has also included interdisciplinary thoughts. The research was undertaken from civil law, common law and international law perspectives and included Shiite and Sunni approaches, complemented by references to legal philosophy.

The present book, as the result of the joint endeavour, identified that the Sharia–the normative framework of Islam–articulates many of the modern principles of rule of law. While there is substantial lacuna of practical implementation, the constitutional affirmation of rule of law principles by Muslim majority states presents cause for optimism. At the transnational level, the OIC (representing the interests and values of Muslim states) has also endorsed the values inherent in the rule of law. The revisions in the OIC Charter in 2008 and the more recent establishment of the IPHRC in 2012 can be taken as evidence of this organisation's commitment to strengthen the implementation of the rule of law and human rights.

The core challenge of the present topic was to distinguish carefully between theory and practice, on the one hand, but also to understand their mutual influence on the other. In addition, the importance of historical and political realities needed to be considered as well as that of economic circumstances. As a predominantly legal research project–as opposed to a study of social science or economy–the present project started from a normative analysis of the regulatory framework. Having identified the normative basis, its system and methodology, the practice of states in conformity or not with the framework was analysed. It is certainly the discrepancy between theory and practice that needed to be addressed and its ways and means of improvement to be identified. As regards the particular

[1] See Ch 1 above.

quality of Islamic law as a normative system based on religious texts, the analysis of state practice is, however, not sufficient. The opinions and actions of the members of society are equally relevant and important. In this respect, it was important to highlight that Islamic law is a normative system that is regarded as all-encompassing, containing legal, religious and moral norms pertaining to all aspects of private and public life. Legal and religious rights and obligations are not always clearly separable. However, it has to be noted that rules of different normative quality also influence the behaviour of Western societies. It is necessary to endeavour in a thoughtful and well-informed engagement with religion, broadly defined, as it is put by An-Na'im, because of its strong influence on human behaviour, regardless of the formal characterisation of the relationship between religion and the state.[2] For a proper implementation of the law, and in particular human rights, it is necessary that the citizens of a state accept and agree that legal rights and obligations are compatible with their religious beliefs. Ideally, religious, moral and legal norms, even if formally separated, are not in contradiction to each other, both in Muslim and in Western societies.

I. Future Perspectives on Islamic Law, the Rule of Law and Freedom of Expression

Traditional and classical Islamic law has not had an effective framework comparable to modern legal systems. As discussed in Chapter 2, independent judicial institutions in the position to control the power of government developed in Europe from the late seventeenth century alongside liberalism and were based on previous developments from the thirteenth century.[3] In this vein, the modern concept of the rule of law is closely linked to the doctrine of the separation of powers and constitutional government developed in Europe.

Under Islamic legal tradition, 'law' has certain characteristics which are fundamentally different from the Western conceptions of law.[4] In Islam, unlike in Western legal traditions, 'law' is not a product of social contract; rather, legal principles are based on religious texts and their interpretation by highly qualified Muslim jurists. In traditional Islamic thought, 'law' is considered divine and not produced through political processes or by sovereign authorities. This may reduce

[2] AA An-Na'im, 'Islam and Human Rights: Introductory Remarks and Reflections' in H Elliesie (ed), *Beiträge zum Islamischen Recht VII. Islam and Human Rights* (Frankfurt, Peter Lang, 2010) 41.

[3] On classical, medieval and modern roots and theories on liberalism, see generally B Tamanaha, *On the Rule of Law: History, Politics and Theory* (Cambridge, Cambridge University Press, 2004).

[4] H Esmaeili, 'The Rule of Law in the Middle East' in J Sikenat, J Hickey Jr and P Barenboim (eds), *The Legal Doctrines of the Rule of Law and the Legal State (Rechtstaat) vol 38* (Berlin, Springer, 2014) 315–29, 317.

the possibility of critical examination by scholars and by the general public. That said and as discussed in Chapter 3, Islamic law has certain characteristics which suggest that it can accommodate modern principles of the rule of law. Concepts in Islamic public law such as *shura* (consultation), *biat* (voting and allegiance), *ijtihad* (personal interpretation of religious texts) and *maslahah* (expediency) are of significant potential in this respect. Furthermore, Islamic jurisprudence, known as *fiqh*, puts significant emphasis on developing legal principles and rules, in many instances in reflection of new circumstances and situations. Therefore, there is considerable potential that Islamic law can accommodate modern concepts and principles of law including the rule of law. This study has analysed rationalist and reformist approaches to Islamic law in the work of past Muslim jurists and scholars such as Ghazali and Mawardi (eleventh century), Ibn Khaldun (fourteenth century), Shah Wali Allah (eighteenth century) and Allamah Mohammad Iqbal (twentieth century). However, it has also been shown that the reformist and pluralistic approaches towards the Sharia and Islamic law have been weakened since the rise and growth of political Islam in the 1960s up until now. This study highlights that the Sharia must regain its previous rational and pluralistic tradition in order to overcome the modern challenges the Muslim world faces today.

As regards freedom of expression, it is submitted that the modern concepts and principles of the right to freedom of thought, expression and opinion are products of Western liberal philosophy and international human rights law. The doctrine of liberalism, according to which individuals should be free from governmental interference and coercion, developed in the mid-nineteenth century in Europe. While the Islamic legal system recognises aspects of freedom of thought and expression, rules of traditional Islamic law and culture do not support the wide-ranging presence of rights based on such principles. That said, it is argued that Islam, its legal system, its culture and civilisation has embraced diversity and tolerance and provides some recognition of freedoms including freedom of religion, thought and expression. Islam and its civilisation is not a monolithic system (legal, social, political, cultural etc). The Islamic civilisation originated from Arabian society of the seventh century and further expanded into the Middle East, Africa, Asia and parts of Europe within several centuries. The extensive diversity of people, schools of thought, philosophies, sects, legal systems, cultures and politics feature the existing tolerance and freedoms within the religion of Islam, the Sharia and Islamic law. Furthermore, it has been argued that the spirit of the Quran is consistent with freedom of thought and expression. Various verses in the Quran support freedom of thought, expression and exchange of ideas. Certain legal concepts and maxims, such as the doctrine of *hisbah*, are based upon freedom of expression.

While aspects of freedom of expression could be found embedded in Islam and in Islamic law, it nevertheless remains necessary to discuss the permissible limitations. Even Western and liberal legal philosophy as well as international human rights recognise that the freedom of expression is not absolute and that its exercise may be subject to restrictions. Such restrictions may be necessary to preserve the rights and freedoms of other members of society or general public interests.

As Immanuel Kant has put it, the freedom of one person needs to be restricted where it infringes the freedom of the other.[5]

It is exactly on this point where the importance of the rule of law becomes paramount. The restrictions which are imposed by the state must satisfy criteria that are sufficiently precise, publicly promulgated, equally applied by institutions that are accountable and consistent with human rights standards. These 'strands of the rule of law', as highlighted and analysed in Chapter 2, have to be respected in the exercise of state power restricting the freedom of expression of individuals. The present study thus engaged in an analysis as to whether these criteria are accepted in Islamic law (or are at least not incompatible with it). It turned out that, in this respect, there are still significant hurdles, not only in the practice but also in the theory of Islamic law, which are not entirely easy to overcome. The main controversy is situated around the extent to which it is permissible to restrict the freedom of expression for combatting blasphemy and apostasy.

Apostasy in Islam is regarded a serious crime and as a *hadd* crime considered to be a crime against God. In addition, it is mentioned as a crime in the Quran, a primary source with highest authority in Islamic law. This makes it particularly difficult to abrogate, suppress or even ignore this offence. However, this study has also highlighted that, while the Quran prohibits apostasy, it does not prescribe punishment for either apostasy or blasphemy. This important fact is often overlooked. All too easily Muslims are ready to accept, what has in fact been the result of subsequent Islamic jurisprudence (*fiqh*), that apostasy must be punished by the death penalty. But a suspicion should arise from the fact that the different schools of law, including Sunni and Shia schools, have interpreted this punishment differently depending on whether the accused was a man or a woman, a believer or a non-believer, and on the readiness of the accused to repent. Depending on the case, a number of lashes could be considered as sufficient. However, even punishment by lashes would be flagrantly incompatible with the requirement under the rule of law premise that restrictions of the freedom of expression must be compatible with human rights standards.[6]

The study, in this respect, turned towards the interpretation suggested by learned Islamic scholars allowing for a flexible application of the required punishment for *irtidad* (apostasy and blasphemy), in particular because the Quran does not prescribe a particular punishment. It can thus be argued that no punishment is required whatsoever by state authorities for the *hadd* crime of apostasy in this worldly life but the exercise of justice is postponed to the hereafter.

[5] I Kant, 'The Metaphysics of Morals' (1797) in H Reiss (ed), *I Kant, Political Writings* (Cambridge, Cambridge University Press, 2nd edn, 1991) 131, 134.

[6] See the case of the blogger Raif Badawi who was sentenced by the Saudi Arabian government to 10 years in prison and 1000 lashes in 2014. He has been kept in detention since that time, while some of the 1000 lashes have already been dispensed. See Amnesty International Report, 'Saudi Arabia: A year of bloody repression since flogging of Raif Badawi' (6 January 2016) www.amnesty.org/en/press-releases/2016/01/saudi-arabia-a-year-of-bloody-repression-since-flogging-of-raif-badawi/.

Nevertheless, several Muslim majority states do not follow this interpretation but instead implement an interpretation suggested by one of the Islamic schools of law (*fiqh*), including the imposition of the death penalty for the crimes of apostasy and blasphemy. In addition, the punishment for the crime of apostasy, which is inherently directed towards Muslim believers with the purpose of deterring their change of religion, is also applied to non-Muslims, such as adherents of religious minorities.[7] This disturbing situation is the result of a lack of distinction between apostasy and blasphemy under Islamic law and is thus rather widespread in the Muslim world. This approach raises serious concerns under the rule of law premise: treating unequal things equally is the opposite of equal application of the law.

The existence of anti-blasphemy laws and the severe punishments prescribed for *irtidad* (apostasy and blasphemy) substantially restrict the freedom of expression. Not only do they have implications for the freedom of expression from a legal perspective they have also become part of Muslim culture, politics and society even in modern relatively democratic societies, such as Indonesia.[8] Muslim societies need to return to the spirit of Islam and the Quran by flexing these rigid principles developed in Islamic jurisprudence (*fiqh*) by Muslim jurists over the last centuries in order to adapt and adjust Islamic law to meet the requirements of the rule of law.

In 2007, a distinguished Middle Eastern jurist claimed that 'none of the Middle Eastern jurisdictions has reached the critical mass on which I am comfortable describing it as a state where the rule of law prevails'.[9] A decade later, the situation in the Middle East and the wider Muslim world has hardly changed: in some major Muslim majority countries, such as Egypt and Turkey, the practice of the rule of law has even deteriorated. However, certain aspects of the rule of law, such as independent judicial institutions, recognition of human rights, elections, federalism, parliamentarism and accountability of government, exist in a few Muslim countries.[10] The World Justice Project (WJP) in 2011 assessed the extent to which countries and regions of the world observe the rule of law.[11] Certain principles and elements of the rule of law, such as limitation of governmental powers, human rights, open government, access to civil justice, absence of corruption, existence of security and order as well as effective criminal justice were

[7] See Chs 6 and 7 above.

[8] In mid-April 2017, the first non-Muslim governor of Jakarta lost the re-election and is now fighting to stay out of jail for commenting on the interpretation of Quran which was considered by some Muslims in Indonesia as blasphemous: see B Henschke, 'Ahok trial: The blasphemy case testing Indonesian identity' *BBC Online* (14 February 2017) www.bbc.com/news/world-asia-38902960.

[9] C Mallat, *Introduction to Middle Eastern Law* (Oxford, Oxford University Press, 2007) 6; see also M Tessler and E Gao, 'Gauging Arab Support for Democracy' (2005) 16 *Journal of Democracy* 83–97, 84.

[10] eg in Turkey, Jordan, Kuwait, Qatar, the United Arab Emirates and Iran parliamentary and other elections are regularly held. In Bangladesh, Pakistan, Indonesia and Malaysia relatively independent judiciaries and other legal institutions, such as legal profession associations, exist.

[11] MD Agrast, JC Botero and A Ponce, *The World Justice Project Rule of Law Index 2011* (2011) http://worldjusticeproject.org/rule-of-law-index.

analysed. Thus, Pakistan was rated low for its level of government accountability, weak justice system and poor security situation particularly in relation to terrorism and crime. However, the country was rated strong for having an independent court system and due process in administrative proceedings. Iran was rated weak in government accountability and problems were noted with respect to political interference with the court system.[12] Nevertheless, the country was considered to have relatively strong law enforcement and a fairly efficient judiciary. Indonesia was in the top half of the rankings (amongst low-middle income countries in most dimensions) including freedom of opinion and open government, but was ranked high in relation to corruption. Most of the Muslim majority states rated average (to below average) for many elements of the rule of law. As discussed in Chapter 7, some Muslim majority states, individually and under the umbrella of the OIC, pursue policies and laws against blasphemy and apostasy which seriously undermine freedom of expression as recognised under international law. Furthermore, there are also other significant restrictions provided in the domestic law of most Muslim majority countries, such as restrictions on criticising the government or restrictions on artistic expression. To the extent that these restrictions cannot be based on fundamentals of the Sharia and Islamic law they may be reinterpreted and refined. It is thus essentially a matter of political will, influence and power to remove or reformulate them.

II. International Obligations and the Future Direction of the Right to Freedom of Expression

The present study has shown–as also indicated in the table of ratifications reprinted in Appendix II–that OIC members have ratified the ICCPR and other international human rights instruments without specific reservations relating to the right to freedom of expression.[13] The fact that Muslim majority states are able to accept these international obligations of granting freedom of expression confirms that (at least in principle) these states do not envisage incompatibility or irreconcilable differences between the Sharia and the applicability of this right.

Various factors point to the right to freedom of expression binding upon OIC members. Treaty obligations contained within the ICCPR (and related instruments) point to the voluntary action now binding these states within international law through treaty ratifications. Indeed, the absence of specific reservations pertaining to freedom of expression points to a consensus amongst these states as accepting obligations to ensure this right within their constitutional frameworks.

[12] Ibid.
[13] See app II below.

On the other hand, broad generalised declarations of incompatibility or interpretative declarations based on the Sharia or domestic laws cannot absolve states of specific undertakings of fundamental rights including respect for the right to freedom of expression. In fact, Muslim majority state practices point towards an established moral and legal obligation to no longer place reservations restricting the right to freedom of expression as provided by Article 19 and Article 20 of the ICCPR. This is exemplified by the case of Pakistan. In 2010, Pakistan a Muslim majority state and a key member of the OIC, entered reservations inter alia to Article 19 upon ratification of the ICCPR.[14] This ensued considerable opposition from other states parties to the treaty, principally on grounds of incompatibility with the objects and purposes of this convention. In the face of considerable moral, political and economic pressure, Pakistan had ultimately to withdraw from this reservation. This withdrawal also confirmed that the Sharia is not envisaged as the stumbling block in accepting international obligations pertaining to the right to freedom of expression. A survey of the contemporary constitutional laws also affirms the legislative recognition of the right to freedom of expression: all Muslim majority states positively enshrine the right to freedom of expression within their respective constitutions. It can therefore be asserted with some certainty that whilst there are disagreements as to the boundaries of freedom of expression, there is an agreement within the Muslim world that these rights exist within international and constitutional laws. It also is the case that equivocation and discord over the scope of the right to freedom of expression is a global phenomenon and cannot be attributed as an exclusive weakness of the Muslim world. The Western world is besieged by freedom of expression issues including the controversy surrounding the denials of holocaust and the limits to pornography.[15]

III. International Human Rights Law and Permissible Limits to Freedom of Expression

It has been noted that neither the ICCPR nor general international law contains provisions to accommodate respect for religions, religious dogmas or beliefs. Incorporating protection for religions or beliefs within human rights law is inconsistent with the established international legal framework. International human rights law is designed to protect human rights and does not encompass protection for beliefs and ideologies.[16] Such attempts to add protection in the form of

[14] See J Rehman and S Berry, 'Is "Defamation of Religions" Passé? The United Nations, Organisation of Islamic Cooperation, and Islamic State Practices: Lessons from Pakistan' (2012) 44 *George Washington International Law Review* (2012) 431; Ch 6 above.

[15] See E Barendt, *Freedom of Speech* (Oxford, Oxford University Press, 2005) 7.

[16] See Rehman and Berry, 'Is "Defamation of Religions" Passé?' (n 14).

criminalising defamation of religions has incurred considerable opposition from various states, human rights experts and the United Nations mandate-holders. As examined by this study, while not according any specific protection to religions or beliefs, international human rights law does prohibit in absolute terms advocacy of religious hatred which constitutes violence and hostility or leads to discriminatory approaches. Accordingly, Article 20(2) of the ICCPR prohibits by law 'any advocacy of national, racial or religious hatred that constitutes incitement to discrimination, hostility or violence'.[17] The Human Rights Committee has noted that advocacy of inter alia religious hatred leading to violence establishes a specific instance where states parties are obliged to respond.[18] They are required to take action to enact 'prohibition by law'[19] and '[i]t is only to this extent that article 20 may be considered as *lex specialis* with regard to article 19'.[20] Furthermore, according to the Committee,

> [i]t is only with regard to the specific forms of expression indicated in article 20 that States parties are obliged to have legal prohibitions. In every case in which the State restricts freedom of expression it is necessary to justify the prohibitions and their provisions in strict conformity with article 19.[21]

It is accepted that the distinction between the insult of a religion and the insult and hatred for the followers of a religion can sometimes be a difficult exercise. However, international human rights law is only engaged when criticism and insults reach the threshold of advocacy of 'religious hatred that constitutes incitement to discrimination, hostility or violence'. It therefore needs to be emphasised that while the difference between ridiculing a religion and incitement against the adherents of the same religion might involve difficult subjective assessments, if criticism or ridicule crosses this established threshold, it is prohibited by Article 20(2) of the ICCPR and therefore does not require a further layer of protection as the proponents of defamation of religions have suggested. Attempts to conflate race and religion in this context are equally flawed: thus to argue that, since international human rights law prohibits criticisms, insults and ridicule of a race or racial characteristics, similar prohibitions of criticisms need to apply to religions and followers of religious beliefs or ideologies is highly problematic.[22] The discussion over racial superiority is not considered to have any merit or positive effect owing to the immutable nature of race, whereas religion, because it can be changed, and adherents to religions or beliefs can alter the manner in which they practise their faith or values, can be subject to legitimate debate and criticism. Such a debate and analysis (if conducted in a constructive manner) may result in

[17] See Art 20(2) ICCPR, considered in Ch 6 above.
[18] Human Rights Committee, General Comment No 34, para 51.
[19] Ibid para 51.
[20] Ibid para 51.
[21] Ibid para 52.
[22] See Ch 6 above.

open discussion of religious beliefs and lead to possible reform.[23] Freedom and the ability to question, criticise and reform religious and ideological tenets also represent a core element of democracy and rule of law. The late Professor Ronald Dworkin has eloquently made the point that:

> It is often said that religion is special, because people's religious convictions are so central to their personalities that they should not be asked to tolerate ridicule of their beliefs, and because they might feel a religious duty to strike back at what they take to be sacrilege … [w]e cannot make an exception for religious insult if we want to use law to protect the free exercise of religion in other ways. If we want to forbid the police from profiling people who look or dress like Muslims for special searches, for example, we cannot also forbid people from opposing that policy by claiming, in cartoons or otherwise, that Islam is committed to terrorism, however misguided we think that opinion is. Certainly we should criticize the judgment and taste of such people. But religion must observe the principles of democracy, not the other way around. No religion can be permitted to legislate for everyone about what can or cannot be drawn any more than it can legislate about what may or may not be eaten. No one's religious convictions can be thought to trump the freedom that makes democracy possible.[24]

IV. Freedom of Expression and Freedom of Religion

Muslim majority states, have, for a considerable period, felt uncomfortable with expressions which are deemed offensive towards the religion of Islam or Islamic doctrines. This study has highlighted various instances of clashes and confrontation between the Muslim world and Western society. This discord stretches from the historic and infamous Rushdie affair to the recent killings in Paris at the *Charlie Hebdo* offices. Domestically, Muslim majority states have strenuously attempted to resist expression that is allegedly blasphemous and in the process targeted certain individuals and communities. This study has examined, inter alia, the cases of Mahmoud Muhammad Taha, Taslima Nasrin, Abu Zayd and Aasia Bibi–individuals who have been accused, charged or convicted of the crimes of apostasy or blasphemy.[25] Religious communities and minority groups have been victimised through draconian laws, including anti-blasphemy laws. As shown in this study, Muslim majority state practices (individually as well as under the umbrella of the OIC) evidence significant policies and laws targeting blasphemy

[23] Therefore, as Eric Barendt has argued, '[l]imits on freedom of expression should not be upheld as necessary to prevent offence to religious groups, for this is often a thin disguise for the imposition of restriction on the open discussion of religious truths and beliefs'. See E Barendt, 'Religious Hatred Laws: Protecting Groups or Belief?' (2011) 17 *Res Publica* 41, 53.

[24] R Dworkin, 'The Right to Ridicule' *The New York Review of Books* (23 March 2006) www.nybooks.com/articles/2006/03/23/the-right-to-ridicule/.

[25] See Chs 4, 5 and 6 above.

and apostasy: these policies, laws and practices seriously undermine freedom of expression and opinion as recognised under international law. Furthermore, the presence of highly ambiguous and artificially created blasphemy offences results in gross breach of natural justice in implementing such laws.[26] Chapter 6 of this study has explored the highly damaging consequences of the ill-conceived and arbitrary anti-blasphemy laws as currently operational within Pakistan. The tragic effect of these dangerous policies (and efforts of their implementation) has wider implications. Moves to restrict freedom of expression by state authorities within Muslim jurisdictions have been treated with scepticism by the international community, since these restrictions are frequently driven by ulterior motives. Political leaders from these states express determination to retain such laws, ostensibly to prevent disrespect for Islam and to protect the Muslim faith. In practice, a number of patterns emerge. With the politicisation of Islam, the criminal justice systems in several Muslim majority states have been manipulated to empower the political elite (often working in conjunction with religious clerics).[27] As noted in an earlier section, anti-blasphemy laws form part of the wider agenda to curb free thinking and free speech. In many instances the enforcement of these draconian laws has provided an excuse for the elimination of political opponents or moderate reformers. Laws restricting freedom of expression have been manipulated to marginalise religious minorities or vulnerable communities. The induction and application of these laws are visible in the backdrop of a corrupt and degenerating criminal justice system, politicisation of Islam with political capital being gained from repression of domestic opposition or marginalisation, ostracisation and exclusion of vulnerable groups. Such determination to criminalise disrespect for Islam is reflected within the international fora: Muslim majority states have continued with the rhetorical assertions relating to the defamation of religion. As examined in this study, although officially on hiatus, the urge to impose a prohibition on defamation of religion remains visible: the commitment 'to combat defamation of Islam' and 'to protect and defend the true image of Islam' is also contained in the revised OIC Charter of 2008, albeit combined with the duty to 'encourage dialogue among civilisations and religions'.[28] The dedication to combat insults of Islam is ingrained in the psyche of many of the debates taking place within this organisation. The deeper malaise within OIC and its members regrettably is producing a highly damaging impact upon all liberal values including a positive affirmation of the right to freedom of expression.

The study has identified the presence and manner of implementation of anti-blasphemy laws as retrograde and damaging. The judicial sanctioning of physical violence (eg in the form of executions or whipping) to curb forms of expression

[26] See eg 'Kuwaiti Jailed for 10 Years for Twitter "Blasphemy"' *BBC News* (4 June 2012) www.bbc.co.uk/news/world-middle-east-18322418.

[27] See eg the cases of Iran, Pakistan and Afghanistan.

[28] See Charter of the Organisation of Islamic Cooperation, adopted on 14 March 2008, www.oicun.org/2/24/20140324031549266,html Art 1(12).

has nourished and strengthened the spirit of intolerance: religious minorities become an obvious target, but such intolerance has led to violence against women, children, the elderly and those with differing sexual orientation and gender identities. Furthermore, the presence of violence and repression of free expression are inextricably linked; societies that curb freedom of expression are also likely to encounter social violence and intolerance. One manifestation of intolerance and violence has been the mushrooming of non-state actors, the self-styled and righteous promoters of a backward oriented Islamic identity. These include groups such as the Da'esh (ISIS), Al-Qaeda, Al-Shabab or the Taliban. Although differing widely in their perspectives of the Sharia and world visions, they all share a similar outlook in opposing the liberal democratic right of freedom of expression.

These non-state actors (alongside some traditional religious scholars in various Muslim societies) pursue a superficial interpretation of Islamic texts and strongly oppose tolerance and individual freedom. At the same time, many governments and rulers in Muslim majority states for the reasons noted earlier, also rely on traditional interpretation of religious texts to give legitimacy to their actions. They try to attract popular support by invoking traditional understandings of Islamic texts. It is arguably now up to the Muslim jurists, intellectuals and the media to challenge repressive and illiberal interpretation of Islamic law that promote punishment for blasphemy and apostasy. The recent Beirut Declaration and 18 Commitments on 'Faith for Rights' (F4R)[29] formulated by faith-based and civil society actors working in the field of human rights can be regarded as one step in the right direction. As has been demonstrated, both the Quran and the Sunna of the Prophet of Islam, prohibit compulsion in religion and allow Muslims to participate in social and political affairs which require freedom of expression and thought.

[29] Reprinted in Annex III.

Appendix I: IPHRC 8th Session: Outcome Document of Thematic Debate on 'Freedom of Expression and Hate Speech'

23 November 2015

The OIC Independent Permanent Human Rights Commission (IPHRC) held a thematic debate on "Freedom of Expression and Hate Speech" during its 8th Regular Session, on 23rd November 2015. H.E. Iyad Ameen Madani, Secretary General of OIC and IPHRC Chairperson Amb. Ilham Ahmed inaugurated the debate. Key panelists for the thematic discussion were Dr. Abdul Salam Al Abadi, Secretary General of International Islamic Fiqh Academy (Fiqh Academy), Mr. David Kaye, UN Special Rapporteur on Freedom of Expression (participated through video link) and Mr. Doudou Diene, former UN Special Rapporteur on Racism. Ms. Pansy Tlakula, Special Rapporteur on Freedom of Expression from the African Commission on Human and Peoples Rights also sent a special message for the debate that was read by one of her colleagues. Besides Commission Members, representatives of OIC Member and Observer States actively participated in the debate.

After going through a rich, intense and inclusive discussion among panelists, Commission Members and Member States on the subject that covered almost all aspects of this important debate including its philosophical and legal basis, importance of its promotion and strengthening in all societies (religious and secular alike), differing views on how best to identify incitement to hatred and hate speech as well as possible measures to combat its misuse through legal and non legal measures including role of various stakeholders in this regard, the Commission adopted the following:

Acknowledged that freedom of expression is a key human right, which is vital for development of stable, peaceful and progressive democratic societies. However, the scope of freedom of expression as provided in the Holy Quran, Article 22 of the Cairo Declaration on Human Rights in Islam, Article 19 of Universal Declaration of Human Rights (UDHR), Article 10 of European Convention on Human Rights, Article 13 of American Convention on Human Rights, Article 9 of African

Charter on Human and Peoples' Rights and Articles 19 & 20 of the International Covenant on Civil and Political Rights (ICCPR) stipulate that this human right is not 'absolute' rather its exercise is subject to 'special duties and corresponding responsibilities' based on 'avoidance of harm to others' to ensure societal cohesion.

Highlighted that freedom and equality are fundamental precepts of Islam wherein it recognizes humans (both men and women) as free and equal beings. Islam, guarantees freedom of expression and like other religions recognizes the role of critical thinking. However, it makes distinction between criticism or constructive discussion and sheer disrespect, defamation, insult and negative stereotyping that fall into the category of inciting religious hatred.

Further highlighted that whereas freedom of expression has been one of the key factors for creation of modern day inclusive, tolerant and multicultural societies, the hate speech motivated by racism, xenophobia and intolerance, coupled with impunity for perpetrators create a climate of fear and social exclusion of the targeted persons and groups, which is anathema to the ideals of pluralism and democracy. Hence, the need for responsible use of freedom of expression to ensure protection of the right of others, respect the right of privacy and personal dignity and maintenance of socio-cultural harmony.

Recalled that although not all hateful messages result in actual hate crimes, these crimes rarely occur without prior stigmatization and dehumanization of targeted groups and incitement to hatred fuelled by religious or racial bias. Hence the promotion and protection of freedom of expression must go hand in hand with efforts to combat intolerance, discrimination and incitement to hatred. To this end, it also called upon UN Special Procedures to present balanced reporting by paying equal attention to both issues.

Expressed serious concerns over the rising trend of violence using incitement to hatred and discrimination based on race or religion and squarely condemned all related acts of violence that resulted in killing and maiming of thousands of innocent people. It also condemned acts of incitement to hatred resulting in devastating and despicable killing of non-Muslims by terrorist groups such as Daesh and Boko Haram etc.; printing of senseless caricatures of Prophet Mohammad (PBUH); appalling treatment of Rohingya Muslims in Myanmar; desecration of holy scriptures and sites in different parts of the world, that have all resulted in promoting a culture of discrimination and violence leading to loss of innocent lives and wider sense of alienation, rejection, and polarization among affected communities.

Further expressed concern over the growing incidents of Islamophobia that are clear manifestations of incitement to hatred and discrimination against Muslims and their pristine religion Islam. Appreciated the role of Islamophobia Observatory of the OIC General Secretariat and encouraged it to continue working in close cooperation with relevant regional and international organizations to aptly highlight the blight of Islamophobia.

Reiterated its position on freedom of expression, which provides limitations in accordance with Articles 19 & 20 of the ICCPR, including the duty of the State to prohibit, by law, "any advocacy of national, racial or religious hatred that constitutes incitement to discrimination, hostility or violence". It was explained that the need to protect the sanctity of religions and their symbols is not to accord exceptional protection to the particular set of values but to avoid defamatory stereotyping and insults that result in negative profiling of their adherents leading to undue discrimination, hostility and violence against them. Hence, the beneficiary remains the individual of targeted religion, a legitimate subject of international human rights law.

Further expressed confidence in OIC sponsored HRC Resolution 16/18 (entitled Combating intolerance, negative stereotyping and stigmatization of, and discrimination, incitement to violence and violence against persons based on religion or belief), repeatedly adopted by the Human Rights Council and UN General Assembly by consensus, which includes substantive, administrative, political and legislative actions to be taken at the national and international levels to address the concerns relating to incitement to religious hatred and discrimination. To this end, urged Member States to address the implementation gaps and provide regular reports on its implementation to the Human Rights Council as well as rededicate to the agreed ideals in a comprehensive manner involving inclusive approaches provided in 'Rabat Plan of Action on the prohibition of advocacy of national, racial or religious hatred that constitutes incitement to discrimination, hostility or violence'.

Observed that there is a need to build consensus on the threshold of freedom of expression where it converts into hate speech and incitement to hatred needing criminalization as provided in Article 20 of the ICCPR and para 7(f) of the Res.16/18, which calls for "adopting measures to criminalize incitement to imminent violence based on religion or belief". To this end it referred to the well established legal provision based on Article 29 of UDHR, which provides that the exercise of all rights and freedoms is subject to limitations set by law that include purposes such as recognition and respect for the rights and freedoms of others as well as General recommendation No. XV on Article 4 of International Convention on the Elimination of All Forms of Racial Discrimination by ICERD Committee clearly stating that "prohibition of the dissemination of all ideas based upon racial superiority or hatred is compatible with the right to freedom of opinion and expression".

Stressed the need to avoiding double standards in application of universal standards of freedom of expression and while working to find common ground to define hate speech, suggested that existing legal practices used by different countries to address hate crimes, incitement to hatred, discrimination and violence based on race or religion must be applied universally to provide equal protection to all targeted groups and individuals.

Upheld that while legal response involving affirmative punitive action is of key importance, a 'multilayered approach', which promotes human rights and tolerance, encourages dialogue and understanding among different groups and builds the capacity of national authorities, including security officials as well as media, thus creating an environment conducive to preventing acts of incitement to hatred, is of vital significance.

Underlined the need to depoliticize the international discourse on the subject by moving away from an ideological debate to a legal, moral and ethical discussion within the human rights framework. To that end urged adoption of an intellectual, moral and ethical strategy in both the West and the Muslim world to bridge the gulf of misunderstanding or 'clash of ignorance' by countering the increasingly negative political rhetoric and biased media coverage.

Further underlined the importance of human rights education as an effective tool to combat hatred and promote better understanding of diversity, hence the need for its wider application and integration into national human rights plans of action, educational plans and other relevant national plans of action to foster universally recognized human rights values and to promote a culture of peace that helps achieving sustainable development.

Noted the crucial role of religious leaders in (i) speaking out against acts and expressions of inter and intra religious hatred and intolerance, (ii) defeating intolerance, discrimination and violence committed in the name of religion by providing a counter-narrative that highlights the correct religious teachings of tolerance and peaceful co-existence thus strengthening the resilience of societies against extremist and intolerant views; (iii) raising awareness among masses on their right to seek legal recourse against religious intolerance and discrimination and (iv) promoting religious norms and values that strengthen socio-cultural and religious understanding among various segments of society.

Further noted the important role being played by young people in every field of human endeavour and the fact that they are the future of mankind, encouraged Member States to invest in capacity building of their youth through comprehensive strategies that would help them know, respect and develop the cultural heritage of their own and that of all mankind, thus promoting a culture of peace, mutual respect and understanding that would help combat culture of intolerance and strengthen peace and security.

Acknowledged the strength of social media in quickly disseminating views and forming opinions as well as its misuse by terrorist and extremist groups for fomenting hatred and intolerance as well as new recruitment in their ranks. Encouraged Member States to pay special attention and raise awareness about this phenomenon as well as monitor its misuse for incitement to hatred, discrimination and violence.

Called upon media to (i) abide by the standards of responsible journalism, (ii) avoid biased and unfounded reporting leading to stereotyping and incitement to hatred against specific groups and communities and (iii) promote respect for diversity and socio-cultural and religious sensitivities of different segments of society that are vital for building inclusive, peaceful and pluralistic societies.

Further called upon all States to take firm actions to avoid misuse of religion for inciting hatred, discrimination and violence and to pursue introspective approaches on improving/ repealing laws with regards to rights of religious and other minorities to bring in conformity with their respective international human rights obligations.

Recommended that OIC may commission a study that analyzes the existing legal practices used to combat hate speech and incitement to hatred in different parts of the world with a view to suggesting parameters for hate speech and incitement to hatred based on one's race or religion as well as practical steps, in accordance with international human rights law, to combat such hateful expressions that include both legal action such as proscription when needed and other inclusive approaches as defined in Res 16/18 and Rabat Plan of Action.

Further recommended full and effective implementation of Res. 16/18 and the Rabat Plan of Action at all levels and in this context stressed the importance of political commitment at the highest level. It also encouraged States to strengthen and rationalize numerous expert mechanisms working on the issue of incitement to hatred to better interpret and implement existing international obligations including the use of Universal Periodic Review, relevant Treaty Bodies and UN Special Procedures as well as establishment of a mechanism under the Office of the High Commissioner for Human Rights to follow up its implementation.

Recognized the commendable scholarly work done by the Fiqh Academy in the field of human rights and emphasized the need to develop collaborative linkages among the OIC, IPHRC, Fiqh Academy and ISESCO for promoting better understanding of human rights perspective of Islam in a coordinated manner including through the use of media.

Appendix II

OIC Member States Status of Ratification of International Human Rights Treaties

	ICCPR	ICESCR	CEDAW	CRC	CAT
Afghanistan	**1983 a** dec: Art. 48(1) + (3) contradict international character of treaty as not all states can join	**1983 a** dec: Art. 26(1) + (3) contradict international character of treaty as not all states can join	**2003**	**1994** dec: reserves right to make reservations concerning Sharia law	**1987** res: Art. 20, 30(1)
Albania	**1991 a**	**1991 a**	**1994 a**	**1992**	**1994 a**
Algeria	**1989** dec: Art. 1 not impairing right to self determination, State of dependence of certain territories is contrary to purposes and principles of the UN; Art. 22 interpreted as making the law framework for State actions; Art. 23(4) does not impair essential foundations of the Algerian legal system.	**1989** dec: Art. 1 not impairing right to self determination; Art. 1(3), Art. 14 State of dependence of certain territories is contrary to purposes and principles of the UN; Art. 8 interpreted as making the law framework for State actions; Art. 13(3) + (4) don't impair right to freely organise educational system	**1996 a** res: Art. 2, 15(4), 16, 29(1) provisions may not contradict the Algerian Family Code	**1993** dec: Art. 14(1) + (2), 13, 16, 17 constitution and national law	**1989** dec: Art. 21, 22 recognition state parties and individuals communications to committee

(continued)

OIC Member States Status of Ratification of International Human Rights Treaties					
	ICCPR	**ICESCR**	**CEDAW**	**CRC**	**CAT**
Azerbaijan	**1992 a**	**1992 a**	**1995 a**	**1992 a**	**1996 a** dec: recognition of individual complaints procedure
Bahrain	**2006 a** res: Art. 3, 18, 23 Sharia Law; Article 9(5), 14(7) national law of Bahrain; SG did not accept reservation due to objections by other States	**2007 a** dec: Art. 8(1)(d) does not prejudice right to prohibit strikes	**2002 a** res: Art. 2, 9(2), 15(4), 16, 29(1)	**1992 a**	**1998 a** res: Art. 30(1); *Art. 20* (withdrawn 1998)
Bangladesh	**2000 a** res: Art. 14(3)(d) national law; dec: Art. 10(3), 11, 14(6) regarding financial constraints and municipal law	**1998 a** dec: Art. 1 right of self-determination applies in historical context, Art. 2, 3, 7, 8 Constitution and national law; Art. 10, 13 progressive realisation	**1984 a** res: Art. 2, 16(1)(c); *Art. 13(a), 16(1)(f)* (withdrawn 1997)	**1990** res: Art. 14(1), 21	**1998 a** dec: Art. 14(1) national law
Benin	**1992 a**	**1992 a**	**1992**	**1990**	**1992 a**
Brunei-Darussalam			**2006 a** gen res: Islamic law, constitution; res: Art. 9(2), 29(1)	**1995 a** gen res: constitution, Islam; res: Art. 14, 20(3), 21(b) + (c) + (d) + (e); *Art. 20(1) + (2), 21(a)* (withdrawn 2015)	Sig. 2015 dec: reserves right to reservations and declarations upon ratification

OIC Member States Status of Ratification of International Human Rights Treaties

	ICCPR	ICESCR	CEDAW	CRC	CAT
Burkina-Faso	**1999 a**	**1999 a**	**1987 a**	**1990**	**1999 a**
Cameroon	**1984 a**	**1984 a**	**1994**	**1993**	**1986 a** dec: recognition of state-parties communication to committee if states have made a similar declaration at least 12 months before the communication, recognition of individual complaints procedure
Chad	**1995 a**	**1995 a**	**1995 a**	**1990**	**1995 a**
Comoros	Sig. 2008	Sig. 2008	**1994 a**	**1993**	Sig. 2000
Cote D'Ivoire	**1992 a**	**1992 a**	**1995**	**1991**	**1995 a**
Djibouti	**2002 a**	**2002 a**	**1998 a**	**1990** *gen res: religion and traditional values* (withdrawn 2009)	**2002 a**
Egypt	**1982** gen dec: Sharia	**1982** gen dec: Sharia	**1981** res: Art. 2, 16 Sharia; 29(1)	**1990** *res: Art. 20, 21* (withdrawn 2003)	**1986 a**

(continued)

OIC Member States Status of Ratification of International Human Rights Treaties					
	ICCPR	**ICESCR**	**CEDAW**	**CRC**	**CAT**
Gabon	**1983 a**	**1983 a**	**1983**	**1994**	**2000**
Gambia	**1979 a** res: Art. 14(3)(d) financial aid for capital offences only	**1978 a**	**1993**	**1990**	Sig. 1985
Guinea	**1978** Art. 48(1) contrary to the principle of the universality of international treaties	**1978** Art. 26(1) contrary to the principle of the universality of international treaties; Art. 1(3), 14 contrary to granting independence to colonial countries and people	**1982**	**1990 a**	**1989**
Guinea-Bissau	**2010**	**1992 a**	**1985**	**1990**	**2013** Art. 21, 22 recognition state parties and individuals communications to committee
Guyana	**1977** dec: Art. 14(3)(d), (6) full application cannot be guaranteed	**1977**	**1980**	**1991**	**1988**

OIC Member States Status of Ratification of International Human Rights Treaties					
	ICCPR	ICESCR	CEDAW	CRC	CAT
Indonesia	**2006 a** dec: Art. 1 self determination does not allow secession	**2006 a** dec: Art. 1 self determination does not allow secession	**1984** res: Art. 29(1)	**1990** *res: constitution, Art. 1, 14, 16, 17, 21, 22, 29* (withdrawn 2005)	**1998** dec: Art. 20(1)(2) (3) implemented in compliance with principles of sovereignty and territorial integrity; res: Art. 30(1)
Iran	**1975**	**1975**		**1994** res: Sharia, international legislation	
Iraq	**1971** dec: no recognition of and obligations towards Israel; no entry to OP-ICCPR	**1971** dec: no recognition of and obligations towards Israel	**1986 a** res: Art. 2(f) + (g), 16, 29(1); dec: no recognition of Israel	**1994 a** res: Art. 14(1)	**2011 a**
Jordan	**1975**	**1975**	**1992** res: Art. 9(2), 16(1)(c) + (d) + (g); *Art. 15(4)* (withdrawn 2009)	**1991** res: Art. 14, 20, 21	**1991 a**
Kazakhstan	**2006**	**2006**	**1998 a**	**1994**	**1998 a** Art. 21, 22 recognition state parties and individuals communications to committee

(continued)

OIC Member States Status of Ratification of International Human Rights Treaties					
	ICCPR	**ICESCR**	**CEDAW**	**CRC**	**CAT**
Kuwait	**1996 a** dec: Art. 2(1), (3), Art. 23 Sharia and national law; res: Art. 25(b) national law regarding armed forces or police	**1996 a** dec: Art. 2(2), 3 national law; Art. 9 social security provisions apply only to nationals; res: Art. 8(1)(d)	**1994 a** res: Art. 9(2), 16(1)(f), 29; *Art. 7(a)* (withdrawn 2005)	**1991** res: Sharia, local statutes; dec: Art. 7 citizenship for children with unknown parents; Art. 21 adoption not approved as abandoning Islam is forbidden	**1996 a** res: Art. 20, 30(1)
Kyrgyzstan	**1994 a**	**1994 a**	**1997 a**	**1994 a**	**1997 a**
Lebanon	**1972 a**	**1972 a**	**1997 a** res: Art. 9(2), 16(1)(c) + (d) + (f) + (g), 29(1)	**1991**	**2000 a**
Libya	**1970 a** dec: no recognition of Israel	**1970 a** dec: no recognition of Israel	**1989 a** res: Art. 2, Art. 16(1)(c) + (d)	**1993 a**	**1989 a**
Malaysia			**1995 a** gen res: Sharia; res: Art. 9(2), 16(1)(a) + (c) + (f) + (g), dec: Art. 11 interpreted as prohibition of discrimination on the basis of equality between men and women only	**1995 a** res: Art. 2, 7, 14, 28(1)(a), 37; *Art. 22, 28(1)(b) + (c) + (d) + (e), 28(2) + (3), 40(3) + (4), 44, 45* (withdrawn 1996) dec: 28 (1)(a) compulsory primary education, monetary aid for those eligible	

OIC Member States Status of Ratification of International Human Rights Treaties					
	ICCPR	**ICESCR**	**CEDAW**	**CRC**	**CAT**
Maldives	**2006 a** res: Art. 18 Constitution of Maldives	**2006 a**	**1993 a** res: Art. 16 (Sharia), gen res: Sharia, constitutional and national law	**1991** gen res: all provisions relating to adoption; res: Ar. 14, 21	**2004 a**
Mali	**1974 a**	**1974 a**	**1985**	**1990** res: Art. 16	**1999 a**
Mauritania	**2004 a** res: Art. 18, 23(4) Sharia	**2004 a**	**2001 a** gen res: Sharia; withdrawn 2014; res: 13(a), 16	**1991** gen res: Islam;	**2004 a** res: Art. 20, 30(1)
Morocco	**1979**	**1979**	**1993 a** dec: Art. 2 Sharia, rules of succession; Art. 15(4) Moroccan Code of Personal Status; res: Art. 29(1)	**1993** dec: Art. 14(1) constitution and national law; *res: Art. 14* (withdrawn 2006)	**1993** res: Art. 30(1)
Mozambique	**1993 a**		**1997 a**	**1994**	**1999 a**
Niger	**1986 a**	**1986 a**	**1999 a** res: Art. 2(d) + (f), 5(a), 15(4), 16(1)(c) + (e) + (g), 29(1); dec: Art. 5(b) family education, compliance with Art. 17 ICCPR	**1990**	**1998 a**
Nigeria	**1993 a**	**1993 a**	**1985**	**1991**	**2001**

(continued)

OIC Member States Status of Ratification of International Human Rights Treaties					
	ICCPR	**ICESCR**	**CEDAW**	**CRC**	**CAT**
Oman			**2006 a** gen res: Sharia, national legislation; res: Art. 9(2), 15(4), 16 especially (a) + (c) + (f), 29(1)	**1996 a** gen res: application limited by material resources; res: Art. 14; *Art. 7, 9, 21, 30* (withdrawn 2011)	
Pakistan	**2010** *res: Articles 3, 6, 7, 12, 13, 18, 19, 25, 40* (withdrawn 2011) dec: self-determination	**2008** dec: progressive realisation, in keeping with economic conditions and development plans	**1996 a** dec: Constitution; res: Art. 29(1)	**1990** *gen res: Sharia* (withdrawn 1997)	**2010** res: Art. 8, 28, 30; *Art. 3, 4, 6, 12, 13, 16* (withdrawn 2011)
Palestine	**2014 a**	**2014 a**	**2014 a**	**2014 a**	**2014 a**
Qatar			**2009 a** res: Art. 2(a), Art. 9(2), Art. 15(1) + (4); 16(1)(a) + (c) + (f), 29(1); dec: Art. 1 not encouraging relationships outside legitimate marriage, Art. 5(9) not encouraging women to abandon role of mother and undermine structure of family	**1995** *gen res: Sharia* (withdrawn 2009); res: Art. 2, 14 (Sharia)	**2000 a** res: Art. 1, 16; *Art. 21, 22; gen res: Sharia* (withdrawn 2012)
Saudi Arabia			**2000** gen res: Sharia; res: Art. 9(2), 29(1)	**1996 a** gen res: Sharia	**1997 a** res: Art. 20, 30(1)

OIC Member States Status of Ratification of International Human Rights Treaties					
	ICCPR	**ICESCR**	**CEDAW**	**CRC**	**CAT**
Senegal	**1978** dec: recognizes only those communications to the HRC of states which recognize the competence of the committee—12 month time limit	**1978**	**1985**	**1990**	**1986** Art. 21, 22 recognition state parties and individuals communications to committee
Sierra Leone	**1996 a**	**1996 a**	**1988**	**1990**	**2001**
Somalia	**1990 a**	**1990 a**		**2015** res: Art. 14, 20, 21 + all provisions contrary to Sharia	**1990 a**
Sudan	**1986 a**	**1986 a**		**1990**	Sig. 1986
Suriname	**1976 a**	**1976 a**	**1993 a**	**1993**	
Syrian Arab Republic	**1969 a** dec: no recognition of Israel; Art. 48(1) incompatible with purpose of treaty as not all states can join	**1969 a** dec: no recognition of Israel; Art. 26(1) incompatible with purpose of treaty as not all states can join	**2003 a** res: Art. 2, 9(2), 15(4), 16(1)(c) + (d) + (f) + (g), 16(2), 29(1); no recognition of Israel	**1993** gen res: Sharia, national legislation; res: Art. 14; *Art. 20, 21* (withdrawn 2012)	**2004 a** res: Art. 20; dec: no recognition of Israel
Tajikistan	**1999 a**	**1999 a**	**1993 a**	**1993 a**	**1995 a**

(continued)

OIC Member States Status of Ratification of International Human Rights Treaties

	ICCPR	ICESCR	CEDAW	CRC	CAT
Togo	**1984 a**	**1984 a**	**1983 a**	**1990**	**1987** Art. 21, 22 recognition state parties and individuals communications to committee
Tunisia	**1969** dec:recognizes only those communications to the HRC of states which recognize the competence of the committee—12 month time limit	**1969**	**1985** dec: constitution, *Art. 15(4)*; res: *9(2), 16(c) + (d) + (f) + (g) + (h), 29(1)* (withdrawn 2014)	**1992** dec: not impeding national legislation concerning abortion; *implementation limited to available means; Art. 40(2)(b) + (v)* (withdrawn 2002); *constitution; Art. 2, 7* (withdrawn 2008)	**1988** Art. 21, 22 recognition state parties and individuals communications to committee
Turkey	**2003** gen. dec: diplomatic relations + where legal order of Turkey applies; res: Art. 27 constitution + treaty of Lausanne	**2003** gen. dec: diplomatic relations + where legal order of Turkey applies; res: Art. 13(3), (4) constitution	**1985 a** res: Art. 29(1); Art. *15(2) + (4), 16(1)(c) + (d) + (f) + (g)* (withdrawn 1999); *Art. 9(1)* (withdrawn 2008)	**1995** res: Art. 17, 29, 30 constitution + treaty of Lausanne	**1988** res: Art. 30(1); dec: Art. 21, 22 recognition state parties and individuals communications to committee
Turkmenistan	**1997 a**	**1997 a**	**1997 a**	**1993 a**	**1999 a**

OIC Member States Status of Ratification of International Human Rights Treaties					
	ICCPR	**ICESCR**	**CEDAW**	**CRC**	**CAT**
Uganda	**1995 a**	**1987 a**	**1985**	**1990**	**1986 a** Art. 21 recognition state parties communications to committee if state has made dec under Art. 21 as well
United Arab Emirates			**2004 a** res: Art. 2(f), 9, 15(2), 16, 29(1)	**1997 a** res: Art. 7, 14, 17, 21	**2012 a** res: Art. 20, 30(1); dec: lawful sanctions under national law ≠ torture
Uzbekistan	**1995 a**	**1995 a**	**1995 a**	**1994 a**	**1995 a**
Yemen	**1987 a** dec: no recognition of Israel	**1987 a** dec: no recognition of Israel	**1984 a** res: Art. 29(1)	**1991**	**1991 a**

Appendix III: Beirut Declaration on 'Faith for Rights' (F4R)

"There are as many paths to God as there are souls on Earth." (Rumi)[1]

1. We, faith-based and civil society actors working in the field of human rights and gathered in Beirut on 28–29 March 2017, in culmination of a trajectory of meetings initiated by the Office of the United Nations High Commissioner for Human Rights (OHCHR),[2] express our deep conviction that our respective religions and beliefs share a common commitment to **upholding the dignity and the equal worth of all human beings**. Shared human values and equal dignity are therefore common roots of our cultures. Faith and rights should be mutually reinforcing spheres. Individual and communal expression of religions or beliefs thrive and flourish in environments where human rights, based on the equal worth of all individuals, are protected. Similarly, human rights can benefit from deeply rooted ethical and spiritual foundations provided by religion or beliefs.

2. We understand our respective religious or belief convictions as a source for the protection of the **whole spectrum of inalienable human entitlements**—from the preservation of the gift of life, the freedoms of thought, conscience, religion, belief, opinion and expression to the freedoms from want and fear, including from violence in all its forms.

— *"Whoever preserves one life, is considered by Scripture as if one has preserved the whole world." (Talmud, Sanhedrin, 37,a).*
— *"Someone who saves a person's life is equal to someone who saves the life of all." (Qu'ran 5:32)*
— *"You shall love the Lord your God with all your heart, all your soul, all your strength, and with your entire mind; and your neighbour as yourself." (Luke 10:27)*
— *Let them worship the Lord of this House who saved them from hunger and saved them from fear." (Sourat Quraish, verses 3,4)*

[1] All quotations from religious or belief texts were offered by participants of the Beirut workshop in relation to their own religion or belief and are merely intended to be illustrative and non-exhaustive.

[2] OHCHR organized related international meetings, expert seminars and regional workshops, including in Geneva (October 2008), Vienna (February 2011), Nairobi (April 2011), Bangkok (July 2011), Santiago de Chile (October 2011), Rabat (October 2012), Geneva (February 2013), Amman (November 2013), Manama (2014), Tunis (October 2014 and April 2015), Nicosia (October 2015), Beirut (December 2015) and Amman (January 2017).

- *"A single person was created in the world, to teach that if anyone causes a single person to perish, he has destroyed the entire world; and if anyone saves a single soul, he has saved the entire world."* (*Mishna Sanhedrin 4:5*)
- *"Let us stand together, make statements collectively and may our thoughts be one."* (*Rigveda 10:191:2*)
- *"Just as I protect myself from unpleasant things however small, in the same way I should act towards others with a compassionate and caring mind."* (*Shantideva, A Guide to the Bodhisattva's Way of Life*)
- *"Let us put our minds together to see what life we can make for our children."* (*Chief Sitting Bull, Lakota*)

3. Based on the above, among many other sources of faith, we are convinced that our **religious or belief convictions are one of the fundamental sources** of protection for human dignity and freedoms of all individuals and communities with no distinction on any ground whatsoever. Religious, ethical and philosophical texts preceded international law in upholding the oneness of humankind, the sacredness of the right to life and the corresponding individual and collective duties that are grounded in the hearts of believers.

4. We pledge to disseminate the **common human values that unite us**. While we differ on some theological questions, we undertake to combat any form of exploitation of such differences to advocate violence, discrimination and religious hatred.

- *"We have designed a law and a practice for different groups. Had God willed, He would have made you a single community, but He wanted to test you regarding what has come to you. So compete with each other in doing good. Every one of you will return to God and He will inform you regarding the things about which you differed."* (*Qu'ran 5, 48*)
- *"Ye are the fruits of one tree, and the leaves of one branch."* (*Bahá'u'lláh*)

5. We believe that freedom of religion or belief does not exist without the **freedom of thought and conscience** which precede all freedoms for they are linked to human essence and his/her rights of choice and to freedom of religion or belief. A person as a whole is the basis of every faith and he/she grows through love, forgiveness and respect.

6. We hereby solemnly launch together from Beirut the **most noble of all struggles, peaceful but powerful**, against our own egos, self-interest and artificial divides. Only when we as religious actors assume our respective roles, articulate a shared vision of our responsibilities and transcend preaching to action, only then we will credibly promote mutual acceptance and fraternity among people of different religions or beliefs and empower them to defeat negative impulses of hatred, viciousness, manipulation, greed, cruelty and related forms of inhumanity. All religious or belief communities need a resolved leadership that unequivocally dresses that path by acting for equal dignity of everyone, driven by our shared humanity and respect for the absolute freedom of conscience of every human being. We pledge

to spare no effort in filling that joint leadership gap by protecting freedom and diversity through "faith for rights" activities.

— *"We perfected each soul within its built in weakness for wrong doing and its aspiration for what is right. Succeeds he or she who elevate to the path of rightness." (Qu'ran 91, 7–9)*

7. The present declaration on "Faith for Rights" **reaches out to persons belonging to religions and beliefs in all regions of the world**, with a view to enhancing cohesive, peaceful and respectful societies on the basis of a common action-oriented platform agreed by all concerned and open to all actors that share its objectives. We value that our declaration on Faith for Rights, like its founding precedent the Rabat Plan of Action on incitement to discrimination, hostility or violence (October 2012), were both conceived and conducted under the auspices and with the support of the United Nations that represents all peoples of the world, and enriched by UN human rights mechanisms such as Special Rapporteurs and Treaty Body members.

8. While numerous welcomed initiatives attempted over time to link faith with rights for the benefit of both, none of these attempts fully reached that goal. We are therefore convinced that **religious actors should be enabled**, both nationally and internationally, to assume their responsibilities in defending our shared humanity against incitement to hatred, those who benefit from destabilising societies and the manipulators of fear to the detriment of equal and inalienable human dignity. With the present F4R Declaration, we aim to join hands and hearts in building on previous attempts to bring closer faith and rights **by articulating the common grounds** between all of us and **define ways in which faith can stand for rights** more effectively so that both enhance each other.

— *"Mankind is at loss. Except those who believe in doing righteous deeds, constantly recommend it to one another and persist in that vein." (Qu'ran 103, 3)*

9. Building on the present declaration, we also intend to **practice what we preach** through establishing **a multi-level coalition**, open for all independent religious actors and faith-based organisations who genuinely demonstrate acceptance of and commitment to the present F4R declaration by implementing projects on the ground in areas that contribute to achieving its purpose. We will also be charting a roadmap for concrete actions in specific areas, to be reviewed regularly by our global coalition of Faith for Rights.

10. To achieve the above goal, we pledge as believers (whether theistic, non-theistic, atheistic or other[3]) to fully adhere to **five fundamental principles**:

a) Transcending traditional inter-faith dialogues into **concrete action-oriented Faith for Rights (F4R) projects at the local level.** While dialogue is important,

[3] See UN Human Rights Committee, general comment no. 22 (1993), UN Doc. CCPR/C/21/Rev.1/Add.4, para. 2.

it is not an end in itself. Good intentions are of limited value without corresponding action. Change on the ground is the goal and concerted action is its logical means.

— *"Faith is grounded in the heart when it is demonstrated by deeds."* (*Hadith*)

b) **Avoiding theological and doctrinal divides** in order to act on areas of shared inter-faith and intra-faith vision as defined in the present F4R declaration. This declaration is not conceived to be a tool for dialogue among religions but rather a joint platform for common action in defence of human dignity for all. While we respect freedom of expression and entertain no illusion as to the continuation of a level of controversy at different levels of religious discourse, we are resolved to challenge the manipulation of religions in both politics and conflicts. We intend to be a balancing united voice of solidarity, reason, compassion, moderation, enlightenment and corresponding collective action at the grassroots level.

c) **Introspectiveness** is a virtue we cherish. We will all speak up and act first and foremost on our own weaknesses and challenges within our respective communities. We will address more global issues collectively and consistently, after internal and inclusive deliberation that preserves our most precious strength, i.e. integrity.

d) **Speaking with one voice**, particularly against any advocacy of hatred that amounts to inciting violence, discrimination or any other violation of the equal dignity that all human beings enjoy regardless of their religion, belief, gender, political or other opinion, national or social origin, or any other status. Denouncing incitement to hatred, injustices, discrimination on religious grounds or any form of religious intolerance is not enough. We have a duty to redress hate speech by remedial compassion and solidarity that heals hearts and societies alike. Our words of redress should transcend religious or belief boundaries. Such boundaries should thus no longer remain a free land for manipulators, xenophobes, populists and violent extremists.

e) We are resolved to **act in a fully independent manner**, abiding only by our conscience, while seeking partnerships with religious and secular authorities, relevant governmental bodies and non-State actors wherever Faith for Rights (F4R) coalitions are freely established in conformity with the present declaration.

11. Our **main tool and asset is reaching out to hundreds of millions of believers** in a preventive structured manner to convey our shared convictions enshrined in this F4R declaration. Speaking up in one voice in defence of equal dignity of all on issues of common challenges to humanity equally serves the cause of faith and rights. Human beings are entitled to full and equal respect, rather than mere tolerance, regardless of what they may believe or not believe. It is our duty to uphold this commitment within our respective spheres of competence. We will also encourage all believers to assume their individual responsibilities in the

defence of their deeply held values of justice, equality and responsibility towards the needy and disadvantaged, regardless of their religion or belief.

— *"People are either your brothers in faith, or your brothers in humanity." (Imam Ali ibn Abi Talib)*
— *"On the long journey of human life, Faith is the best of companions" (Buddha)*

12. We aim to achieve that goal in a concrete manner that matters **for people at the grassroots level** in all parts of the world where coalitions of religious actors choose to adhere to this declaration and act accordingly. We will support each other's actions, including through a highly symbolic annual Walk of Faith for Rights in the richest expression of our unity in diversity each 10th of December in all parts of the world.

13. Articulating through the present declaration a common vision of religious actors, on the basis of the Rabat Plan of Action of 2012 and follow-up meetings, would provide the tipping point for **disarming the forces of darkness**; and help dismantling the unholy alliance in too many hearts between fear and hatred. Violence in the name of religion defeats its basic foundations, mercy and compassion. We intend to transform the messages of mercy and compassion into acts of solidarity through inter-communal social, developmental and environmental faith-based projects at the local, national, regional and global levels.

14. We **fully embrace the universally recognised values** as articulated in international human rights instruments as common standards of our shared humanity. We ground our commitments in this F4R declaration first and foremost in our conviction that religions and beliefs share common core values of respect for human dignity, justice and fairness. We also ground these commitments in our acceptance of the fact that "***Everyone has duties*** *to the community in which alone the free and full development of his personality is possible*".[4] Our duty is to practice what we preach, to fully engage, to speak up and act on the ground in the defence of human dignity long before it is actually threatened.

— *"Oh you believers, why don't you practice what you preach? Most hateful for God is preaching what you don't practice." (Qu'ran 61:2–3)*
— *"Speak up for those who cannot speak for themselves, for the rights of all who are destitute. Speak up and judge fairly; defend the rights of the poor and needy." (Proverbs 31:8–9)*

15. Both **religious precepts and existing international legal frameworks** attribute responsibilities to religious actors. Empowering religious actors requires actions in areas such as legislation, institutional reforms, supportive public policies and training adapted to the needs of local religious actors who often are one of the main sources of education and social change in their respective areas of action. International conventions and covenants have defined key legal terms such

[4] Article 29, paragraph 1, of the Universal Declaration of Human Rights (1948).

as genocide, refugee, religious discrimination and freedom of religion or belief.[5] All these concepts have corresponding resonance in different religions and beliefs. In addition, numerous declarations and resolutions[6] provide elements of religious actors' roles and responsibilities that we embrace and consolidate in this F4R declaration.

16. We agree as human beings that **we are accountable to all human beings** as to redressing the manner by which religions are portrayed and too often manipulated. We are responsible for our actions but even more responsible if we do not act or do not act properly and timely.

— *"We will ask each of you about all what you have said and done, for you are accountable" (Quran, Assaafat, 24)*
— *"Every man's work shall be made manifest." (Bible, 1 Corinthians iii. 13)*

17. While States bear the primary responsibility for promoting and protecting all rights for all, individually and collectively to enjoy a dignified life free from fear and free from want and enjoy the freedom of choice in all aspects of life, we as religious actors or as individual believers do bear a distinct responsibility to **stand up for our shared humanity and equal dignity of each human being** in all circumstances within our own spheres of preaching, teaching, spiritual guidance and social engagement.

— *"Whoever witnesses an injustice or wrong doing should change its course by his hand. If He or she cannot do that, they by his words. If he or she is unable to do that then by their hearts. This would be the weakest of acts of faith" (Hadith).*

[5] These include the Convention on the Prevention and Punishment of the Crime of Genocide (1948); Convention Relating to the Status of Refugees (1951); International Convention on the Elimination of All Forms of Racial Discrimination (1965); International Covenant on Civil and Political Rights (1966); International Covenant on Economic, Social and Cultural Rights (1966); Convention on the Elimination of All Forms of Discrimination against Women (1979); Convention against Torture and Other Cruel, Inhuman or Degrading Treatment or Punishment (1984); Convention on the Rights of the Child (1989); International Convention on the Protection of the Rights of All Migrant Workers and Members of Their Families (1990); Convention on the Rights of Persons with Disabilities (2006); and International Convention for the Protection of All Persons from Enforced Disappearance (2006).

[6] These include the Universal Declaration of Human Rights (1948); Declaration on the Elimination of All Forms of Intolerance and Discrimination Based on Religion or Belief (1981); Declaration on the Rights of Persons Belonging to National or Ethnic, Religious and Linguistic Minorities (1992); Principles of Conduct for the International Red Cross and Red Crescent Movement and NGOs in Disaster Response Programmes (1994); UNESCO Declaration on Principles of Tolerance (1995); Final Document of the International Consultative Conference on School Education in Relation to Freedom of Religion or Belief, Tolerance and Non-Discrimination (2001); Toledo Guiding Principles on Teaching about Religions and Beliefs in Public Schools (2007); United Nations Declaration on the Rights of Indigenous Peoples (2007); The Hague Statement on "Faith in Human Rights" (2008); Camden Principles on Freedom of Expression and Equality (2009); Human Rights Council resolution 16/18 on Combating Intolerance, Negative Stereotyping and Stigmatization of, and Discrimination, Incitement to Violence and Violence against, Persons Based on Religion or Belief (and Istanbul Process, 2011)s; Rabat Plan of Action on the prohibition of advocacy of national, racial or religious hatred that constitutes incitement to discrimination, hostility or violence (2012); Framework of Analysis for Atrocity Crimes (2014); Secretary-General's Plan of Action to Prevent Violent Extremism (2015); as well as the Fez Declaration on preventing incitement to violence that could lead to atrocity crimes (2015).

18. **Religious communities, their leaders and followers** have a role and bear responsibilities independently from public authorities both under national and international legal instruments. By virtue of article 2(1) of the 1981 UN Declaration on the Elimination of all Forms of Intolerance and of Discrimination Based on Religion of Belief, "no one shall be subject to discrimination by any State, institution, group of persons or person on the grounds of religion or belief". This provision establishes direct responsibilities of religious institutions, leaders and even each individual within religious or belief communities.

19. As much as the notion of effective control[7] provides the foundation for responsibilities of non-State actors in times of conflict, we see a similar legal and ethical justification in case of religious leaders who exercise a **heightened degree of influence over the hearts and minds of their followers** at all times.

20. Speech is fundamental to individual and communal flourishing. It constitutes one of the most crucial **mediums for good and evil sides of humanity.** War starts in the minds and is cultivated by a reasoning fuelled by often hidden advocacy of hatred. Positive speech is also the healing tool of reconciliation and peace-building in the hearts and minds. Speech is one of the most strategic areas of the responsibilities we commit to assume and support each other for their implementation through this F4R declaration on the basis of the thresholds articulated by the Rabat Plan of Action.

21. Under the International Covenant on Civil and Political Rights (article 20, paragraph 2), States are obliged to prohibit any advocacy of national, racial or religious hatred that constitutes incitement to discrimination, hostility or violence. This includes **incitement to hatred by some religious leaders in the name of religion.** Due to the speaker's position, context, content and extent of sermons, such statements by religious leaders may be likely to meet the threshold of incitement to hatred. Prohibiting such incitement is not enough. Remedial advocacy to reconciliation is equally a duty, including for religious leaders, particularly when hatred is advocated in the name of religions or beliefs.

22. The clearest and most recent guidance in this area is provided by the 2012 Rabat Plan of Action[8] which articulates **three specific core responsibilities of religious leaders:** (a) Religious leaders should refrain from using messages of intolerance or expressions which may incite violence, hostility or discrimination; (b) Religious leaders also have a crucial role to play in speaking out firmly and promptly against intolerance, discriminatory stereotyping and instances of hate speech; and (c) Religious leaders should be clear that violence can never be tolerated as a response to incitement to hatred (e.g. violence cannot be justified by prior provocation).

[7] Under certain circumstances, in particular when non-State actors exercise significant/effective control over territory and population (e.g. as *de facto* authorities), they are also obliged to respect international human rights as duty bearers (see UN Docs. CEDAW/C/GC/30, para. 16; A/HRC/28/66, paras. 54–55).

[8] See UN Doc. A/HRC/22/17Add.4, annex, appendix, para 36.

Appendix IV: The Text of the Madina (Medina) Charter

The original text can be found in Ibn Hisham's Al-Sirat al-Nabawiyyah [Biography of the Prophet], written in 9th century AD)

English Translation is taken from Muhammad Hamidullah, *The First Written Constitution in the World* (first published 1941).

In the name of God, the Beneficent and the Merciful.

(1) This is a prescript of Muhammad, the Prophet and Messenger of God (to operate) between the faithful and the followers of Islam from among the *Quraish* and the people of Madina and those who may be under them, may join them and take part in wars in their company.

(2) They shall constitute a separate political unit (*Ummat*) as distinguished from all the people (of the world).

(3) The emigrants from the *Quraish* shall be (responsible) for their own ward; and shall pay their blood-money in mutual collaboration and shall secure the release of their own prisoners by paying their ransom from themselves, so that the mutual dealings between the believers be in accordance with the principles of goodness and justice.

(4) And *Banu 'Awf* shall be responsible for their own ward and shall pay their blood-money in mutual collaboration, and every group shall secure the release of its own prisoners by paying their ransom from themselves so that the dealings between the believers be in accordance with the principles of goodness and justice.

(5) And *Banu Al-Harith-ibn-Khazraj* shall be responsible for their own ward and shall pay their blood-money in mutual collaboration and every group shall secure the release of its own prisoners by paying their ransom from themselves, so that the dealings between the believers be in accordance with the principles of goodness and justice.

(6) And *Banu Sa'ida* shall be responsible for their own ward, and shall pay their blood-money in mutual collaboration and every group shall secure the release of its own prisoners by paying their ransom from themselves, so that the dealings between the believers be in accordance with the principles of goodness and justice.

(7) And *Banu Jusham* shall be responsible for their own ward and shall pay their blood-money in mutual collaboration and every group shall secure the release of its own prisoners by paying their ransom so that the dealings between the believers be in accordance with the principles of goodness and justice.

(8) And *Banu an-Najjar* shall be responsible for their own ward and shall pay their blood-money in mutual collaboration and every group shall secure the release of its own prisoners by paying their ransom so that the dealings between the believers be in accordance with the principles of goodness and justice.

(9) And *Banu ʿAmr-ibn-ʿAwf* shall be responsible for their own ward and shall pay their blood-money in mutual collaboration and every group shall secure the release of its own prisoners by paying their ransom, so that the dealings between the believers be in accordance with the principles of goodness and justice.

(10) And *Banu-al-Nabit* shall be responsible for their own ward and shall pay their blood-money in mutual collaboration and every group shall secure the release of its own prisoners by paying their ransom so that the dealings between the believers be in accordance with the principles of goodness and justice.

(11) And *Banu-al-Aws* shall be responsible for their own ward and shall pay their blood-money in mutual collaboration and every group shall secure the release of its own prisoners by paying their ransom, so that the dealings between the believers be in accordance with the principles of goodness and justice.

(12) (a) And the believers shall not leave any one, hard-pressed with debts, without affording him some relief, in order that the dealings between the believers be in accordance with the principles of goodness and justice.

(b) Also no believer shall enter into a contract of clientage with one who is already in such a contract with another believer.

(13) And the hands of pious believers shall be raised against every such person as rises in rebellion or attempts to acquire anything by force or is guilty of any sin or excess or attempts to spread mischief among the believers; their hands shall be raised all together against such a person, even if he be a son to any one of them.

(14) And no believer shall kill another believer in retaliation for an unbeliever, nor shall he help an unbeliever against a believer.

(15) And the protection of God is one. The humblest of them (believers) can, by extending his pro-tection to any one, put the obligation on all; and the believers are brothers to one another as against all the people (of the world).

(16) And that those who will obey us among the Jews, will have help and equality. Neither shall they be oppressed nor will any help be given against them.

(17) And the peace of the believers shall be one. If there be any war in the way of God, no believer shall be under any peace (with the enemy) apart from other believers, unless it (this peace) be the same and equally binding on all.

(18) And all those detachments that will fight on our side will be relieved by turns.

(19) And the believers as a body shall take blood vengeance in the way of God.

(20) (a) And undoubtedly pious believers are the best and in the rightest course.

(b) And that no associator (non-Muslim subject) ahall give any protection to the life and property of a *Quraishite*, nor shall he come in the way of any believer in this matter.

(21) And if any one intentionally murders a believer, and it is proved, he shall be killed in retaliation, unless the heir of the murdered person be satisfied with blood-money. And all believers shall actually stand for this ordinance and nothing else shall be proper for them to do.

(22) And it shall not be lawful for any one, who has agreed to carry out the provisions laid down in this code and has affixed his faith in God and the Day of Judgment, to give help or protection to any murderer, and if he gives any help or protection to such a person, God's curse and wrath shall be on him on the Day of Resurrection, and no money or compensation shall be accepted from such a person.

(23) And that whenever you differ about anything, refer it to God and to Muhammad (ﷺ).

(24) And the Jews shall share with the believers the expenses of war so long as they fight in conjunction.

(25) And the Jews of *Banu 'Awf* shall be considered as one political community (*Ummat*) along with the believers—for the Jews their religion, and for the Muslims theirs, be one client or patron. He, however, who is guilty of oppression or breach of treaty, shall suffer the resultant trouble as also his family, but no one besides.

(26) And the Jews of *Banu-an-Najjar* shall have the same rights as the Jews of *Banu 'Awf.*

(27) And the Jews of *Banu-al-Harith* shall have the same rights as the Jews of *Banu 'Awf.*

(28) And the Jews of *Banu Sa'ida* shall have the same rights as the Jews of *Banu 'Awf.*

(29) And the Jews of *Banu Jusham* shall have the same rights as the Jews of *Banu 'Awf.*

(30) And the Jews of *Banu al-Aws* shall have the same rights as the Jews of *Banu 'Awf.*

(31) And the Jews of *Banu Tha'laba* shall have the same rights as the Jews of *Banu 'Awf.* Of course, whoever is found guilty of oppression or violation of treaty, shall himself suffer the consequent trouble as also his family, but no one besides.

(32) And *Jafna*, who are a branch of the *Tha'laba* tribe, shall have the same rights as the mother tribes.

(33) And *Banu-ash-Shutaiba* shall have the same rights as the Jews of *Banu 'Awf*; and they shall be faithful to, and not violators of, treaty.

(34) And the *mawlas* (clients) of *Tha'laba* shall have the same rights as those of the original members of it.

(35) And the sub-branches of the Jewish tribes shall have the same rights as the mother tribes.

(36) (a) And that none of them shall go out to fight as a soldier of the Muslim army, without the per-mission of Muhammad (ﷺ).

(b) And no obstruction shall be placed in the way of any one's retaliation for beating or injuries; and whoever sheds blood shall be personally responsible for it as well as his family; or else (i.e., any step beyond this) will be of oppression; and God will be with him who will most faithfully follow this code (sahifdh) in action.

(37) (a) And the Jews shall bear the burden of their expenses and the Muslims theirs.

(b) And if any one fights against the people of this code, their) i.e., of the Jews and Muslims) mutual help shall come into operation, and there shall be friendly counsel and sincere behaviour between them; and faithfulness and no breach of covenant.

(38) And the Jews shall be bearing their own expenses so long as they shall be fighting in conjunction with the believers.

(39) And the Valley of *Yathrib* (*Madina*) shall be a *Haram* (sacred place) for the people of this code.

(40) The clients (*mawla*) shall have the same treatment as the original persons (i.e., persons accepting clientage). He shall neither be harmed nor shall he himself break the covenant.

(41) And no refuge shall be given to any one without the permission of the people of the place (i.e., the refugee shall have no right of giving refuge to others).

(42) And that if any murder or quarrel takes place among the people of this code, from which any trouble may be feared, it shall be referred to God and God's Messenger, Muhammad (ﷺ); and God will be with him who will be most particular about what is written in this code and act on it most faithfully.

(43) The *Quraish* shall be given no protection nor shall they who help them.

(44) And they (i.e., Jews and Muslims) shall have each other's help in the event of any one invading *Yathrib*.

(45) (a) And if they (i.e., the Jews) are invited to any peace, they also shall offer peace and shall be a party to it; and if they invite the believers to some such affairs, it shall be their (Muslims) duty as well to reciprocate the dealings, excepting that any one makes a religious war.

(b) On every group shall rest the responsibility of (repulsing) the enemy from the place which faces its part of the city.

(46) And the Jews of the tribe of *al-Aws*, clients as well as original members, shall have the same rights as the people of this code: and shall behave sincerely and faithfully towards the latter, not perpetrating any breach of covenant. As one shall sow so shall he reap. And God is with him who will most sincerely and faithfully carry out the provisions of this code.

(47) And this prescript shall not be of any avail to any oppressor or breaker of covenant. And one shall have security whether one goes out to a campaign or remains in *Madina*, or else it will be an oppression and breach of covenant. And God is the Protector of him who performs the obligations with faithfulness and care, as also His Messenger Muhammad (ﷺ).

Select Bibliography

Books

Abi Abdullah Al-qortbi, *Al-Jame Li Ahkam Al-Qubran, Dar Alam Al-Kitab [Comprehensive Verses Providing Rules]* (Riyadh, Dar Alam Al-Kitab, 2003).

——, *Al-Jame Li Ahkam Al-Qubran [Comprehensive Verses Providing Rules]* (Riyadh, Dar Alam Al-Kitab, 2003).

Abiad, N, *Sharia, Muslim States and International Human Rights Treaty Obligations: A Comparative Study* (London, BIICL, 2008).

Abou-El-Fadl, K, *Rebellion and Violence in Islamic Law* (Cambridge, Cambridge University Press, 2001).

——, K, *Speaking in God's Name: Islamic Law, Authority and Women* (London, Oneworld Press, Oxford, 2001).

——, *The Place of Tolerance in Islam* (Boston, Beacon Press, 2002).

——, *Islam and the Challenge of Democracy* (Princeton, Princeton University Press, 2004).

——, *The Great Theft: Wrestling Islam from the Extremists* (San Francisco, Harper Collins, 2005).

——, *The Search for Beauty in Islam: Conference of the Books* (Lanham, Rowman & Littlefield Publishers, Inc, 2006).

——, *Reasoning with God: Reclaiming Sharia in the Modern Age* (Lanham, Rowman & Littlefield Publishers, Inc, 2014).

——, Cohen, J and Chasman, D (eds), *Islam and the Challenge of Democracy: A Boston Review Book* (Princeton, Princeton University Press, 2004).

Abu Zahrah, *al-Jarimah wa'l-Uqubah fi'l-Fiqh al-Islami [Crimes and Punishments in Islamic Jurisprudence]* (Cairo, Dar al-Fikr, no date) 160.

Abul Ala Maududi, S, *Human Rights in Islam* (Leicester, Islamic Foundation, 1976).

Adams J, *A Defence of the Constitutions of Government of the United States of America*, vol I (London, 1787).

Afifi, M, *Al Mojtama Al Islami v Usul Al Hokm [Islamic Society and Governing Principles]* (Cairo, Darr Al Etsam, 1980).

Agrama, HA, *Questioning Secularism, and the Rule of Law in Modern Egypt* (Chicago, University of Chicago Press, 2012).

Agrast, MD, Botero, JC and Ponce, A, *The World Justice Project Rule of Law Index 2011* (2011) <http://worldjusticeproject.org/rule-of-law-index.>.

Ahmad, Z, *The Epistemology of Ibn Khaldun* (London, Routledge, 2003).

Al Jaziri, A, *Kital al Fiq Ala al Madahib al Arba'a [Book of Jurisprudence according to four Juristic Schools]* vol 5 (Beirut, Darelfkr, 1999).

Ala Maududi A, *Political Theory of Islam* (Lahore, Islamic Publications, 1985).

Alexander, L, *Is there a Right to Freedom of Expression?* (Cambridge, Cambridge University Press, 2005).

Al-Ghazali, M, *The Socio-Political Thought of Shah Wali Allah* (Delhi, Adams Publishers and Distributors, 2001).
Al-Mutaal Saidi, A, *Al-Hurriyah al-diniyah fi al-Islam* (Cairo, Dār al-fikr al-ʻArabī, circa 1960s).
Al Sabiq, S, *Fiqh Al Sunna [The Sunni Jurisprudence]*, vol 2 (Beirut, Darelfk, 1998).
Al-Tirmidhi, *Sunan al-Tirmidhi*, IV, 213.
An-Na'im, AA, *Toward an Islamic Reformation: Civil Liberties, Human Rights and International Law* (Syracuse, Syracuse University Press, 1990).
——, *Human Rights in Cross-Cultural Perspectives: A Quest for Consensus* (Philadelphia, University of Pennsylvania Press, 1992).
——, *African Constitutionalism and the Role of Islam* (Philadelphia, University of Pennsylvania Press, 2006).
——, *Islam and the Secular State: Negotiating the Future of Sharia* (Cambridge Massachusetts, Harvard University Press, 2010).
——, *Islam and Human Rights: Selected Essays of Abdullahi An-Na'im* (Aldershot, Ashgate Publishing Limited, 2010).
——, *Muslims and Global Justice* (Philadelphia, University of Pennsylvania Press, 2011).
Anderson, J, *Law Reform in the Muslim World* (London, Athlone Press 1976).
Arabi, O, *Studies in Modern Islamic Law and Jurisprudence* (Leiden/Boston, Brill, 2001).
Attia, GE, *Towards Realization of the Higher Intents of Islamic Law: Maqāsid al-Sharia: A Functional Approach* (London, The International Institute of Islamic Thought, 2007).
Azara, A and Hudsom, W (eds), *Islam Beyond Conflict, Indonesian Islam and Western Political Theory* (Aldershot, Ashgate, 2008).
Baderin, M, *International Human Rights and Islamic Law* (Oxford, Oxford University Press, 2003).
—— (ed), *International Law and Islamic Law* (Aldershot, Ashgate, 2008).
Barendt, E, *Freedom of Speech* (Oxford, Oxford University Press, 2005).
Bassiouni, MC (ed), *The Islamic Criminal Justice System* (London, Oceana, 1982).
Beatson, J and Cripps, Y (eds), *Essays in Honour of Sir David Williams* (Oxford, Oxford University Press, 2002).
Bellamy, R (ed), *The Rule of Law and the Separation of Powers* (Aldershot, Ashgate, 2005).
Bingham, T, *The Rule of Law* (London, Penguin, 2010).
Black, A, Esmaeili, H and Hosen, N, *Modern Perspectives on Islamic law* (Cheltenham, Edward Elgar, 2013).
Boucher, D (ed), *The Social Contract from Hobbes to Rawls* (London, Routledge, 1994).
Brown, N, *The Rule of Law in the Arab World* (Cambridge, Cambridge University Press, 1997).
——, *Constitutions in a Non-constitutional World: Arab Basic Laws and the Prospects for Accountable Government* (New York, State University of New York Press, 2001).
Bunzl, J (ed), *Islam, Judaism, and the Political Role of Religions in the Middle East* (Florida, Florida University Press 2004).
Carothers T (ed), *Promoting the Rule of Law Abroad: In Search of Knowledge* (Washington DC, Brookings Institution Press, 2006).
Cass, R, *The Rule of Law in America* (Baltimore and London, Johns Hopkins University Press, 2001).
Charpin, D, *Writing, Law, and Kingship in Old Babylonian Mesopotamia* (Chicago, University of Chicago Press, 2010).
Ciment, J (ed), *Encyclopaedia of Conflicts Since World War II* (London, Routledge, 1999).

Costa P and Zolo, D (eds), *The Rule of Law. History, Theory and Criticism* (Dordrecht and others, Springer, 2007).
Cotran E and Sherif, AO (eds), *Democracy, Rule of Law and Islam* (Leiden, Brill, 1999).
—— and Yamani, M (eds), *The Rule of Law in the Middle East and the Islamic World. Human Rights and the Judicial Process* (New York, IB Tauris, 2000).
Coulson, N, *A History of Islamic Law* (Edinburgh, Edinburgh University Press, 1964).
Dicey, AV, *Introduction to the Study of the Law of the Constitution* (London and New York, Macmillan and Co, 1885).
——, *Introduction to the Study of the Law of the Constitution* (London, Macmillan and Co, 1964).
Donnelly, J, *Universal Human Rights in Theory and Practice* (Ithaca, New York, Cornell University Press, 2003).
Dworkin, R, *Freedom's Law* (New York, Oxford University Press, 1996).
Ellisie, H (ed), *Beiträge zum Islamischen Recht VII. Islam and Human Rights* (Frankfurt, Peter Lang, 2010) 35.
Emon, AM, Ellis, MS and Glahn, B (eds), *Islamic Law and International Human Rights Law: Searching for Common Ground?* (Oxford, Oxford University Press, 2012).
Enayat, H, *Law, State, and Society in Modern Iran: Constitutionalism, Autocracy and Legal Reform, 1906–1941* (New York, Palgrave Macmillan, 2013).
Engineer, AA (ed), *Islam and Revolution* (Delhi, Ajanta Books International, 1984).
Evans M (ed), *Article 18: An Orphaned Rights–A Report of the All Parliamentary Group on International Religious Freedom* (London, APPG on Religious Freedom or Belief, 2013).
Farrior S (ed), *Equality and Non-Discrimination under International Law* (Oxford, Routledge, 2015).
Finnis, J, *Natural Law and Natural Rights* (Oxford, Oxford University Press, 2011).
Frick, M-L and Müller, AT (eds), *Islam and International Law: Engaging Self-Centrism from a Plurality of Perspectives* (Leiden, Martinus Nijhoff, 2013).
Gazzali, M, *Kimiya-e Saadat [The Alchemy of Happiness]*, rev edn (Kuala Lumpur, Islamic Book Trust, 2007).
Ghandhi, PR, *The Human Rights Committee and the Right of Individual Communication: Law and Practice* (Aldershot, Ashgate, 1998).
Ghunaimi, MT, *The Muslim Conception of International Law and the Western Approach* (The Hague, Martinus Nijhoff, 1968).
Gleeson, M, *The Rule of Law and the Constitution* (Sydney, NSW, ABC Books, 2000).
Gowder, P, *The Rule of Law in the Real World* (New York, Cambridge University Press, 2016).
Grote, R and Röder T, *Constitutionalism in Islamic Countries: Between Upheaval and Continuity* (Oxford, Oxford University Press 2011).
Guha, R, *Makers of Modern India* (Cambridge, Massachusetts, Harvard University Press, 2011).
Guillaume, A, *Islam* (London, Penguin, 1954).
Hafiz Al-Mundhiri, *Mukhtasar Sahih Muslim* (Dar al-Salam, Li Al-Nashr v Al-Tuzi, 16, *Hadith* no.34).
Hallaq, WB (ed), *The Formation of Islamic Law* (Aldershot, Ashgate Publishing Limited, 2004).
——, *An Introduction to Islamic Law* (Cambridge, Cambridge University Press, 2009).
——, *Sharia: Theory, Practice, Transformations* (New York, Cambridge Press, 2009).
Hamidullah, M, *The First Written Constitution in the World* (Lahore, Kazi Publications, 1986).

Hammer, S and Husein, F (eds), *Religious Pluralism and Religious Freedom: Religions, Society and the State in Dialogue. Contributions to the Australian-Indonesian Dialogue* (Yogyakarta, Center for Religious and Cross-Cultural, 2013).

Harris, D et al (eds), *Law of the European Convention on Human Rights*, 3rd edn (Oxford, Oxford University Press, 2014).

Hart HLA, *The Concept of Law*, 3rd edn (Oxford, Clarendon Press, 2012).

Hatcherd, J, Ndulo, M and Slinn, P, *Comparative Constitutionalism and Good Governance in the Commonwealth: An Eastern and Southern African Perspective* (Cambridge, Cambridge University Press, 2004).

Hayek, F, *Law, Legislation and Liberty* (Chicago, Chicago University Press, 1978).

Heath, JM, (ed), *The Creator as Critic. And Other Writings by E M Foster* (Toronto, Dundurn Press, 2008).

Helli, M, *Sharay al-Islam [the Laws of Islam]* (Beirout, Dar al-Adhwa, 1983).

Herdegen, M, *Principles of International Economic Law* (Oxford, Oxford University Press, 2013).

Hodgson, M, *The Venture of Islam* (Chicago, The University of Chicago Press, 1974).

Hosen, N, *Sharia & Constitutional Reform in Indonesia* (Singapore, Institute of Southeast Asian Studies, 2007).

Hulsman, C (ed), *The Sharia as the Main Source of Legislation?* (Marburg, Tectum, 2012).

Ibn Majah, *Sunan, Kitab al-Fitan, Hadith no 4011.*

Ibn Qudamah, *Al-Mughni [Complete (Rules of Islam)]* vol VIII (Riyadh, Dar al-elam Al-Kotob).

Imam Abu Hamid Mohammed Ghazali, *Al Mustafa Min Il Al-Usul* vol 1, 139–40 (Cairo, al-Maktabah al-Tijariyyah, 1937).

Iqbal, AM, *The Reconstruction of Religious Thought in Islam* (Islamabad, Institute of Islamic Culture, 1986).

Iqbal, M, *Six Lectures on the Reconstruction of Religious Thought in Islam* in M Saeed Sheikh (ed), (Islamabad, Institute of Islamic Culture, 1996).

Jayasuriya, K (ed), *Law, Capitalism and Power in Asia: The Rule of Law and Legal Institutions* (Oxford, Routledge, 1999).

Kamali, MH, *Freedom of Expression in Islam* (Cambridge, Islamic Texts Society, 1997).

——, *Principles of Islamic Jurisprudence* (Cambridge, The Islamic Texts Society, 2003).

——, *Sharia Law: An Introduction (Foundations of Islam)* (London, One World Publications, 2008).

Kayaoglu T, *The OIC's Independent Permanent Human Rights Commission: An Early Assessment* (Copenhagen, The Danish Institute for Human Rights, 2015).

——, *The Organization of Islamic Cooperation: Politics, Problems, and Potential* (Copenhagen, The Danish Institute for Human Rights, 2015).

Keping, Y (ed), *Democracy and the Rule of Law in Contemporary China* (Leiden/Boston, Brill, 2010).

Khatami, M, *Islam, Liberty and Development* (Binghamton, Global Academic Publishing, 1998).

Klausen, J, *The Cartoons that Shook the World* (New Haven, Yale University Press, 2009).

Kriegel, B, *The State and the Rule of Law* (Princeton, Princeton University Press, 1995).

Lalor, K, Mills, E, Sánchez García A and Haste P (eds), *Gender, Sexuality and Social Justice: What's Law Got to Do with It?* (Kent, Institute of Development Studies, 2016).

Levy, L, *Blasphemy: Verbal Offences Against the Sacred: from Moses to Salman Rushdie* (Chapel Hill, University of North Carolina Press, 1993).

Linz, J, *Totalitarian and Authoritarian Regimes* (Boulder, Lynne Rienner Publishers, 2000).
Mahiou, A (ed), *L'Etat de droit dans le monde arabe* (Paris, CNRS, 1997).
Malik, IH, *Religious Minorities in Pakistan* (London, Minority Rights Group, 2002).
Mallat, C, *Introduction to Middle Eastern Law* (Oxford, Oxford University Press, 2007).
Martin, V, *Creating an Islamic State: Khomeini and the Making of a New Iran* (London/ New York, Tauris, 2003).
Masud, MK et al, *Mufties, Fatwas, and Islamic Legal Interpretation* (Cambridge, Harvard University Press, 1996).
Mathis-Moser, U (ed), *Responsibility to Protect. Peacekeeping, Diplomacy, Media, and Literature Responding to Humanitarian Challenges* (Innsbruck, Innsbruck University Press, 2012).
Mayer, AE, Islam and Human Rights: Tradition and Politics (Oxford, Westview Press, 1995).
——, *Islam and Human Rights. Tradition and Politics*, 5th edn (Oxford, Westview Press, 2013).
McGoldrick, D, *The Human Rights Committee: Its Role in the Development of the International Covenant on Civil and Political Rights* (Oxford, Clarendon Press, 1991).
Mikhail, H, *Politics and Revelation: Mawardi and After* (Edinburgh, Edinburgh University Press, 1995).
Mill, JS, *On Liberty* (London, John Parker, 1859).
Mirza Yusuf Moustashar Al-Douleh Tabrizi, *Yek Kalama [One Term]* Sadeq Sajjadih (ed), (1985).
Moinuddin, H, *The Charter of the Islamic Conference and Legal Framework of Economic Cooperation Among its Member States: A Study of the Charter, the General Agreement for Economic, Technical and Commercial Co-operation and the Agreement for Promotion, Protection and Guarantee of Investments Among Member States of the OIC* (Oxford, Clarendon Press, 1987).
Mojtahed Shabestari, M, *Naqdi bar Qara'at Rasmi az Din [Examination of Prophetic Reading of Religion]* (Tehran, Tarh No, 2002).
Moustafa, T and Ginsburg T (eds), *Rule by Law. The Politics of Courts in Authoritarian Regimes* (Cambridge, Cambridge University Press, 2008).
Muhaghigh Damad, SM, *Rowshangari Dini [Religious Enlightenment]*, vol 2 (Tehran, Ettelaat Press, 2005).
Mumtaz, A (ed), *State, Politics, and Islam* (Indianapolis, American Trust Publications, 1986).
Najeebabadi, A, *The History of Islam, vol 1* (Riyadh, Dar-us salam, International Publications, 2000).
Nasr Hamid Abu Zayd, *Al-Ittijah al-'Aqli fi al-Tafsir: ditasa fi qadiyyat al-magaz fi'l Qur'an 'ind'l Mu'tazilah [The Rational Trend in Exegesis: a Study of the Problem of Metaphor in the Qur'an by the Mu'tazilites]* (Beirut, Al Markaz Al Tahaqafi Al Arabi, 1998).
Nasr, S, *The Heart of Islam: Enduring Values for Humanity* (San Francisco, Harper One, 2002).
Nowak, M, *U.N. Covenant on Civil and Political Rights. CCPR Commentary* (Kehl, NP Engel, 2005).
Perry-Kessaris, A (ed), *Law in the Pursuit of Development: Principles into Practice?* (New York, Routledge, 2010).
Peters, R, *Crime and Punishment in Islamic Law* (Cambridge, Cambridge University Press, 2005).
Petersen, MJ, *Islamic or Universal Human Rights? The OIC's Independent Permanent Human Rights Commission* (Copenhagen, DIIS Report, 2012).

Popper, K, *The Open Society and Its Enemies, Volume I: The Spell of Plato* (New York, Routledge, 2002, reprint of 1945).

Rahman, F, *Islam* (London, Weidenfeld and Nicolson, 1966).

——, 'The Principle of Shura and the Role of Umma in Islam' in M Ahmed (ed), *State, Politics, and Islam* (Illinois, American Trust Publications, 1986).

Ramcharan, B, *United Nations Protection of Humanity and its Habitat. A New International Law of Security and Protection* (Leiden, Boston, Brill Nijhoff, 2016).

Rawls, J, *A Theory of Justice* (Cambridge, Massachusetts, Harvard University Press 1999).

Rehman, J, *Islamic State Practices, International Law and the Threat from Terrorism: A Critique of the 'Clash of Civilizations' in the New World Order* (Oxford, Hart Publishing, 2005).

——, *International Human Rights Law* (London, Longman, 2010).

—— and Breau, S (eds), *Religion, Human Rights and International Law* (Leiden, Brill/Nijhoff, 2007).

Reiss, H (ed), *Kant. Political Writings* (Cambridge, Cambridge University Press, 1991).

Rothwell, D et al (eds), *International Law. Cases and Materials with Australian Perspectives*, 2nd edn (New York, Cambridge University Press, 2014).

Sabeq, S, *Fiqh al-sunna [The Sunni Jurisprudence]*, 2nd edn (Beirut, 1998).

Saeed, A, *Islamic Thought: An Introduction* (Oxford, Routledge, 2006).

Samuel, KLH, *The OIC, the UN, and Counter-Terrorism Law-Making: Conflicting or Cooperative Legal Orders?* (Oxford, Hart Publishing, 2013).

Sands, P and Klein, P, *Bowett's Law of International Institutions* (London, Sweet and Maxwell, 2001).

Sarat, A (ed), *Special Issue Human Rights: New Possibilities/New Problems* (Studies in Law, Politics and Society, vol 56) (Bingley, Emerald Group Publishing Limited, 2011).

Saunders, C and Roy, KL (eds), *The Rule of Law* (Sydney, The Federation Press, 2003).

Schacht, J, *An Introduction to Islamic Law* (Oxford, The Clarendon Press, 1964).

—— and Bosworth, C (eds), *The Legacy of Islam* (Oxford, Oxford University Press 1979).

Schulte-Schlemmer S and Tung Ko-Yung (eds), *Liber Amicorum Ibrahim F.I. Shihata: International Finance and Development Law* (The Hague, Kluwer Law International, 2001).

Sellers, M and Tomaszewski, T (eds), *The Rule of Law in Comparative Perspective* (Dordrecht, Springer, 2010).

Shabestari, M, *Hermenutik, Kitab va Sunnat [Hermeneutics, the Book (the Quran) and Tradition]* (Tehran, Tarhe Now, 1996).

Shaltut, M, *Al-Islam, Aqida wa-Sharia [Islam: Belief and Sharia]* (Cairo, Al-Azhar Press, 1959).

Shapiro, I, *The Rule of Law* (New York, New York University Press, 1994).

Silkenat, JR, Hickey Jr, JE and Barenboim, PD (eds), *The Legal Doctrines of the Rule of Law and the Legal State (Rechtsstaat)* (Dordrecht, Springer, 2014).

Soroush, A, Bast Tajrobeh Nabavi *[The Expansion of Prophetic Experience]* (Tehran, Serat Publishers 2006); English trans: A Soroush, *The Expansion of Prophetic Experience: Essays on Historicity, Contingency and Plurality in Religion* (N Mobasser ed, F Jahanbakhsh trans (Leiden, Brill Publishers, 2009).

Taha, M, *The Second Message of Islam [Contemporary Issues in the Middle East]* trans A An Na'im (Syracuse, Syracuse University Press, rev edn, 1996).

Taji-Farouki S (ed), *Modern Muslim Intellectuals and the Qur'an* (Oxford, Oxford University Press, 2004).

Tamanaha, BZ, *On the Rule of Law: History, Politics and Theory* (Cambridge, Cambridge University Press, 2004).

Thierstein, J and Kamalipour Y (eds), *Religion, Law, and Freedom: A Global Perspective* (Westport, CT, Greenwood, 2000).

Van Dijk, P, Van Hoof, F, Van Rijn, A and Zwaak, L (eds), *Theory and Practice of the European Convention on Human Rights* (Antwerp/Oxford, Intersentia, 2006).

Vogel, FE, *Islamic Law and Legal System: Studies of Saudi Arabia* (Leiden/Boston, Brill, 2000).

Vogt, K, Larsen, L and Moe, C (eds), *New Directions in Islamic Thought: Exploring Reform and Muslim Tradition* (London, IBTauris, 2008).

Walles, D, Mosher, M and Rahe, P (eds), *Montesquieu's Science of Politics: Essays on the Spirit of Laws* (Maryland, Rowman and Littlefield, 2001).

Watt, WM, *Muhammad at Medina* (Oxford, Clarendon Press, 1956).

——, *Muslim Intellectual: A Study of Al-Ghazali* (Edinburgh, Edinburgh University Press, 1963).

Weiss, B, *The Spirit of Islamic Law* (Georgia, University of Georgia Press, 2006).

Articles

Abou El Fadl, K, 'Soul Searching and the Spirit of Sharia: A Review of Bernard Weiss's The Spirit of Islamic Law' (2002) 1 *Washington University Global Studies Law Review* 553.

——,'Islam and the Challenge of Democratic Commitment' (2003) 27(1) *Fordham International Law Journal* 2.

Al-Ahsan, A., 'Law, Religion and Human Dignity in the Muslim World Today: An Examination of OIC's Cairo Declaration of Human Rights' (2008–09) 24 *Journal of Law and Religion* 569.

Alexander, L, 'Liberals in Religion and the Unity of Epistemology' (1993) 30 *San Diego Law Review* 763.

Alexander, L, 'Good God, Garvey! The Inevitability and Impossibility of a Religious Justification of Free Exercise Exemptions' (1998) 47 *Drake Law Review* 35.

Ali-Karamali, S and Dunne F, 'The Ijtihad Controversy' (1994) 9 *Arab Law Quarterly* 238.

Allen, TSR, 'The Rule of Law as the Rule of Reason: Consent and Constitutionalism' (1999) 115 *Law Quarterly Review* 221.

Anderson, J, 'Recent Developments in Sharia Law' (1950) 40 *The Muslim World* 244.

An-Na'im, AA, 'The Islamic Law of Apostasy and its Modern Applicability' (1986) 16(3) *Religion* 197.

——, 'A Kinder, Gentler Islam?' (1991) 52 *Transition* 4.

——, 'Human Rights in the Arab World: A Regional Perspective' (2001) 23 *Human Rights Quarterly* 701.

——, 'The Contingent Universality of Human Rights: The Case of Freedom of Expression in African and Islamic Contexts' (1997) 11 *Emory International Law Review* 29, 42.

Arjomand, S, 'The Constitution of Medina: A Sociolegal Interpretation of Muhammad's Acts of Foundation of the Umma' (2009) 41(4) *International Journal of Middle East Studies* 555.

Arzt, D, 'Religious Human Rights in Muslim States in the Middle East and North Africa' (1996) 10 *Emory International Law Review* 139.

Baderin, M, 'Identifying Possible Mechanisms within Islamic Law for the Promotion and Protection of Human Rights in Muslim States' (2004) 22 *Netherlands Quarterly of Human Rights* 329.

Barendt, E, 'Religious Hatred Laws: Protecting Groups or Belief?' (2011) 17 *Res Publica* 41.

Belén Soage, A, '*Shura* and Democracy: Two Sides of the Same Coin?' (2014) 8(3) *Religion Compass* 90.

Belnap, AG, 'Defamation of Religions: A Vague and Overbroad Theory that Threatens Basic Human Rights' (2010) *Brigham Young University Law Review* 635–86.

Bennett, GL, 'Defamation of Religions: The End of Pluralism?' (2009) 23 *Emory International Law Review* 69.

Berween M, 'Al-Watiqah: The First Islamic Constitution' (2003) 23 *Journal of Muslim Minority Affairs* 103.

Blitt, RC, 'Defamation of Religion: Rumors of its Death are Greatly Exaggerated' (2011) 62 *Case Western Reserve Law Review* (2011) 347.

——, 'Defamation of Religion: Rumors of its Death are Greatly Exaggerated' *Legal Studies Research Paper* 182 (April 2012).

Boyle, K, 'Human Rights, Religion and Democracy: The Refah Party Case' (2004) 1 *Essex Human Rights Review* 1.

Cavallaro, J and Brewer, S, 'Re-evaluating Regional Human Rights Litigation in the Twenty-First Century: The Case of the Inter-American Court' (2008) 102 *American Journal of International Law* 768.

Chakravorty, P, 'Rushdie Incident as Law-and-Literature Parable, The [Notes]' (1995) 104(8) *Yale Law Journal* 2213.

Chase A, 'Legal Guardians: Islamic Law, International Law, Human Rights Law, and the Salman Rushdie Affair'(1996) 11(3) *American University Journal of International Law and Policy* 375.

Chi, M, 'China's Participation in WTO Dispute Settlement over the Past Decade: Experiences and Impacts' (2012) 1 *Journal of International Economic Law* 29.

Cismas, I, 'Introductory Note to the Statute of the OIC Independent Permanent Human Rights Commission' (2011) 50 *International Legal Materials* 1148.

Crawford, J, 'International Law and the Rule of Law' (2003) 24 *Adelaide Law Review* 4.

Crouch, M, 'Law and Religion in Indonesia: The Constitutional Court and Blasphemy Law' (2012) 7 *Asian Journal of Comparative Law* 1.

Cox, N, 'The Freedom to Publish "Irreligious" Cartoons' (2016) 16 *Human Rights Law Review* 195.

De Zayas, A, Möller J and Opsahl, T, 'Application of the International Covenant on Civil and Political Rights under the Optional Protocol by the Human Rights Committee' (1985) 28 *German Yearbook of International Law* 9.

Denny, F, 'Umma in the Constitution of Medina' (1977) 31(1) *Journal of Near Eastern Studies* 39.

Detmold, MJ, 'The Unity of Law and Morality: A Refutation of Legal Positivism' (2004) *Cambridge Law Journal* 65.

Dobras, RJ, 'Is the United Nations Endorsing Human Rights Violations?: An Analysis of the United Nations' Combating Defamation of Religious Resolutions and Pakistan's Blasphemy Laws' (2008–09) 37 *Georgia Journal of International and Comparative Law* 339.

Dupret, B, 'La chari'a est la source de la législation': interprétations jurisprudentielles et théories juridiques' in A Mahiou (ed), *L'Etat de droit dans le monde arabe* (Paris, CNRS, 1997) 125.

Dworkin, R, 'Is there a Right to Pornography' (1981) 1 *Oxford Journal of Legal Studies* (1981) 177.

——, 'The Right to Ridicule' *The New York Review of Books* (23 March 2006) www.nybooks.com/articles/2006/03/23/the-right-to-ridicule/.

Esmaeili H, 'Islamic Law Across Cultural Borders: The Involvement of Western Nationals in Saudi Murder Trials' (2001) 28 *Denver Journal of International Law and Policy* 145.

——, 'On a Slow Boat Towards the Rule of Law: The Nature of Law in the Saudi Arabian Legal System' (2009) 26 *Arizona Journal of International and Comparative Law* 1.

——, 'The Nature and Development of Law in Islam and the rule of law Challenge in the Middle East and the Muslim World' (2011) 26(2) *Connecticut Journal of International Law* 329.

Evans, M, 'Advancing Freedom of Religion or Belief: Agendas for Change' (2012) 1 *Oxford Journal of Law and Religion* 5.

Falk R, 'Religion and Global Governance: Harmony or Clash' (2002) 19 *International Journal of World Peace* 3.

Fish, S, 'Mission Impossible' (1997) 97 *Columbia Law Review* 2255.

Forte, D, 'Apostasy and Blasphemy in Pakistan' (1994) 10 *Connecticut Journal of International Law* 27.

Foster N, 'Islamic Perspectives on the Law of Business Organisations I: an Overview of the Classical Sharia and a Brief Comparison of the Sharia Regimes with Western-Style Law' (2010) 11 *European Business Organization Law Review* 3.

——, 'Islamic Perspectives on the Law of Business Organisations II: the Sharia and Western-style Business Organisations' (2010) 11 *European Business Organization Law Review* 273.

Fuller, LL, 'The Morality of Law' (1973) 40(2) *Indiana Law Review* 270.

Gosalbo-Bono, R, 'The Significance of the Rule of Law and its Implications for the European Union and the United States' (2010) 72 *University of Pittsburgh Law Review* 229.

Grinberg, M, 'Defamation of Religions v. Freedom of Expression: Finding the Balance in a Democratic Society' (2006) 18 *Sri Lanka Journal of International Law* 197.

Hallaq, WB, 'Was the Gate of Ijtihad Closed?' (1984) 16 *International Journal of Middle East Studies* 3.

Harpaz, MD, 'Sense and Sensibilities of China and WTO Dispute Settlement' (2010) 6 *Journal of World Trade* 1155.

Hart, HLA, 'Positivism and the Separation of Law and Morals' (1958) 71 *Harvard Law Review* 593.

Howard-Hassmann, R, 'The Charlie Hebdo Murders and Freedom of Speech' (2015) 2(2) *The Indonesian Journal of International & Comparative Law* 467.

Inglis, BD, 'Religious Freedom and the Modern Law of Blasphemy' (1956–58) 2(4) *Victoria University of Wellington Law Review* 229.

Jacob, AE, 'Defending Blasphemy: Exploring Religious Expression Under Ireland's Blasphemy Laws' (2012) 44(3) *Case Western Reserve Journal of International Law* 803.

Jenco, L, '"Rule by Man"' and "Rule by Law" in Early Republican China: Contributions to a Theoretical Debate' (2010) 69 *Journal of Asian Studies* 181.

Jennings WI, 'Review of Law of the Constitution (9th edn)' (1940) 2 *Modern Law Review* 321.

Juss, S, 'Burqua-Bashing and the *Charlie Hebdo* Cartoons' (2015) 26(1) *King's Law Journal* 27.

Kadivar, M, 'An Introduction to the Public and Private Debate in Islam' (Fall 2003) 70(3) *Social Research* 559.

Kausikan B, 'Asia's Different Standard' (1993) 92 *Foreign Policy* 24.

——, 'An Asian Approach to Human Rights' (1995) 89 *Proceedings of the American Society of International Law* 146.

Keane, D, 'Cartoon Violence and Freedom of Expression' (2008) 30 *Human Rights Quarterly* 845.

Keith K, 'The International Rule of Law' (2015) 28 *Leiden Journal of International Law* 403.

Kelly, MJ, 'Islam & International Criminal Law: A Brief (In)Compatability Study' (2010) *Pace International Law Review Online Companion* 17.

Kennedy, C, 'Islamization and Legal Reform in Pakistan, 1979–1989' (1990) 63(1) *Pacific Affairs* 62.

——, 'Repugnancy to Islam–Who Decides? Islam and Legal Reform in Pakistan' (1992) 41(4) *International and Comparative Law Quarterly* 769.

Khadduri, M, 'Islam and the Modern Law of Nations' (1956) 50 *American Journal of International Law* 358.

Khan, M and Mirakhor, A, 'Islamic Banking: Experiences in the Islamic Republic of Iran and in Pakistan' (1990) 38(2) *Economic Development and Cultural Change* 353.

Klock, K, 'Resolution of Domestic Disputes Through Extra-Judicial Mechanisms in the United States and Asia: Neighbourhood Justice Centers, the Panchayat, and the Mahalla' (2001) 15 *Temple International and Comparative Law Journal* 275.

Kramer, M, 'On the Moral of the Rule of Law' (2004) 63 *Cambridge Law Journal* 65.

Lasse, L et al, 'The Muhammad Cartoons Controversy in Comparative Perspective' (2009) 9(3) *Ethnicities* 291.

Lau, M, 'Pakistan—*Zaheer-ud-din v. State*: Islam and Fundamental Rights in Pakistan, The Case of *Zaheer-ud-din v. State* and its Impact on the Fundamental Right to Freedom of Religion' (1994) 1 *Yearbook of Islamic and Middle Eastern Law* 565.

Lee, RW, 'The Law of Blasphemy' (1918) 16(3) *Michigan Law Review* 149.

Leo, LA, Gaer FD and Cassidy EK, 'Protecting Religions from "Defamation" A Threat to Universal Human Rights Standards' (2011) 34 *Harvard Journal of Law and Public Policy* 769.

Lyombe E and Berkowitz D, 'Le Monde, French Secular Republicanism and the Mohammed Cartoons Affair' (2009) 71(3) *The International Communication Gazette* 181.

Mahmoud, M, 'Mahmud Muhammad Taha and the Rise and Demise of the Jumhuri Movement' (2001) 23(1) *New Political Science* 65.

Marboe, I, 'The Rule of Law in the Islamic Legal System' (2011) 7 *Journal of Islamic State Practices in International Law* 1.

Mayer, AE, 'Law and Religion in the Muslim Middle East' (1987) 35(1) *The American Journal of Comparative Law* 127.

Miller, F, 'Plato and the Rule of Reason' (2005) 43 *Southern Journal of Philosophy* 50.

Mir-Hosseini, Z, 'How the Door of *Ijtihad* Was Opened and Closed: A Comparative Analysis of Recent Family Law Reforms in Iran and Morocco' (2007) 64 *Washington and Lee Law Review* 1499.

Modood T et al, 'The Danish Cartoon Affair: Free Speech, Racism, Islamism and Integration' (2006) 44(5) *International Migration* 3.

Najjar, FM, 'Islamic Fundamentalism and the Intellectuals: The Case of Nasr Hamid Abu Zayd' (2000) 27(2) *British Journal of Middle Eastern Studies* 177.

O'Flaherty M, 'Freedom of Expression: Article 19 of the International Covenant on Civil and Political Rights and the Human Rights Committee's General Comment No 34' (2012) 12 *Human Rights Law Review* 627.

O'Sullivan, D, 'The Death Sentence for Mahmoud Muhammad Taha: Misuse of the Sudanese Legal System and Islamic Sharia Law?' (2001) 5(3) *The International Journal of Human Rights* 45.

——, 'Egyptian Cases of Blasphemy and Apostasy Against Islam: Takfir al-Muslim' (2011) 7 *The International Journal of Human Rights* 97.

——, 'Egyptian Cases of Blasphemy and Apostasy Against Islam: Takfir al-Muslim' (2011) 7(2) *The International Journal of Human Rights* 97.

——, 'The Rabat Plan of Action: A Global Blue Print for Combating "Hate Speech"' [2014] *European Human Rights Law Review* 21.

Patrick, J, 'The Curious Persistence of Blasphemy' (2011) 23(2) *Florida Journal of International Law* 187.

Peerenboom, R, 'Beyond Universalism and Relativism: The Evolving Debates about "Values in Asia"' (2003–04) 14 *Indian International and Comparative Law Review* 1.

Peters, R, 'The Islamization of Criminal Law: a Comparative Analysis' (1994) 34(2) *Die Weld des Islams* 246.

——, 'Humanity as the A and Ω of Sovereignty' (2009) 20 *European Journal of International Law* 513.

—— and De Vries, J, 'Apostasy in Islam' (1976–77) 17(1) *Die Welt Des Islams* 1.

Petrova, D, '"Smoke and Mirrors": The Durban Review Conference and Human Rights Politics at the United Nations' (2009) 10 *Human Rights Law Review* 129.

Porter, A, 'Words Can Never Hurt Me? Sticks, Stones and Section 18C' (2015) 40(2) *Alternative Law Journal* 86.

Quane H, 'The Significance of an Evolving Relationship: ASEAN States and the Global Human Rights Mechanisms' (2015) 15 *Human Rights Law Review* 283.

Radin, MJ, 'Reconsidering the Rule of Law' (1989) 69 *Boston University Law Review* 781.

Raz, J, 'The Rule of Law and Its Virtue' (1977) 93 *Law Quarterly Review* 195.

——, 'Free Expression and Personal Identification (1991) 11 *Oxford Journal of Legal Studies* 303.

Rehman, J, 'Minority Rights and the Constitutional Dilemmas of Pakistan' (2001) 19 *Netherlands Quarterly of Human Rights* 417.

——, 'Islamophobia after 9/11: International Terrorism, Sharia and Muslim Minorities in Europe–The Case of the United Kingdom' (2003–04) 3 *European Yearbook of Minority Issues* 217.

——, 'The *Sharia*, Islamic Family Laws and International Human Rights Law' (2007) 21 *International Journal of Law, Family and Policy* 108.

——, 'Freedom of Expression, Apostasy and Blasphemy within Islam' (2010) 79 *Criminal Justice Matters* 4.

—— and Berry, S, 'Is "Defamation of Religions" Passé? The United Nations, Organisation of Islamic Cooperation, and Islamic State Practices: Lessons from Pakistan' (2012) 44 *George Washington International Law Review* 431.

—— and Polymenopoulou E, 'Justice after Democracy in the Arab World: Islamic Law Perspectives on Accountability' (2012) 54 *German Yearbook of International Law* 53.

—— and Polymenopoulou, E, 'The Case of Aasia Bibi' (2012–13) 16 *Asian Yearbook of International Law* 136.

—— and Polymenopoulou, E, 'Is Green a Part of the Rainbow? *Sharia* and Homosexuality in the Muslim World' (2013) 37 *Fordham International Law Journal* (2013) 1.

Rishmawi, M, 'The League of Arab States. Human Rights Standards and Mechanisms' (2005) *Open Society Foundations and Cairo Institute for Human Rights Studies* 43.

——, 'The Revised Arab Charter on Human Rights: A Step Forward?' (2005) 5 *Human Rights Law Review* 361.

——, 'The Arab Charter on Human Rights and the League of Arab States: An Update' (2010) 10 *Human Rights Law Review* 169.
Sachedina, A, 'Guidance or Governance? A Muslim Conception of "Two Cities"' (2000) 68 *George Washington Law Review* 1079.
Sandberg R and Doe, N, 'The Strange Death of Blasphemy' (2008) 71(6) *Modern Law Review* 971.
Seniawski, B, 'Riba Today: Social Equity, the Economy, and Doing Business under Islamic Law' (2001) 39 *Columbia Journal of Transnational Law* 701.
Sfeir, G, 'Basic Freedoms in a Fractured Legal Culture: Egypt and the case of Nasr Hamid Abu Zayd' (1998) 53 *The Middle East Journal* 402.
Shamsul Alam, S, 'Women in the Era of Modernity and Islamic Fundamentalism: The Case of Taslima Nasrin of Bangladesh' (1998) 23 *University of Chicago Press* 429.
Shavit, U, 'Is *Shura* a Muslim Form of Democracy? Roots and Systemisation of a Polemic' (2010) 46(3) *Middle Eastern Studies* 349.
Sidahmed, A, 'Freedom of Religion, Apostasy and Human Rights: An Appraisal' (2000) 4 *The Mediterranean Journal of Human Rights* 139.
Siddique O and Hayat, Z, 'Unholy Laws and Holy Speech: Blasphemy Laws in Pakistan–Controversial Origins, Design Defects and Free Speech Implications' (2008) 17 *Minnesota Journal of International Law* 303.
Slaughter, MM, 'The Salman Rushdie Affair: Apostasy, Honor, and Freedom of Speech' (1993) 79 *Virginia Law Review* 153.
Sturges, P, 'Limits to Freedom of Expression? The Problem of Blasphemy' (2015) 41(2) *International Federation of Library Associations and Institutions* 112.
Syariat, P, 'Islam Di Provinsi Ace' (2014) 2(2) *International Multidisciplinary Journal* 61.
Tadjdini, A, 'The Organisation of Islamic Cooperation and Regional Challenges to International Law and Security' (2012) 4 *Amsterdam Law Forum* 36.
Temperman, JT, 'Blasphemy, Defamation of Religions and Human Rights Law' (2012) 26 *Netherlands Quarterly of Human Rights* 517.
Tessler M and Gao, E, 'Gauging Arab Support for Democracy' (2005) 16(3) *Journal of Democracy* 83.
Waldron J, 'Are Sovereigns Entitled to the Benefit of the International Rule of Law?' (2011) 22 *European Journal of International Law* 317.
Walters, MD, 'Dicey on Writing the Law of the Constitution' (2012) 32 *Oxford Journal of Legal Studies* 21.

Other Documents

Akbar Gangi, *Rowshanfekriy Faqihaneh [Jurisprudential Intellectualism]* (unpublished manuscript] (on file).
Kadivar, M, 'Reconstruction of Wisdom: A Condition for Reconciling Religion and Human Rights' (16 May 2007) (unpublished paper presented at the Human Rights Conference, Mofid University, Qom, Iran, on file).
Limon, M, Ghanea N and Power H, 'Combating Global Religious Intolerance: The Implementation of Human Rights Council Resolution 16/18' (Policy Report) (London, Universal Rights Group, 2014).
Valentine, SR., *The Thehrik-i-Taliban Pakistan: Ideology and Beliefs* (Bradford, Pakistan Security Research Unit) Brief Number 49.

Glossary

Ahkam—Rules
Akhlaq—Moral principles of Islam
Al-kafirun—Non-believers
Amr be al-marouf v Nahy an al-monkar—Inviting people (including the state) to do good and warning others to avoid what is wrong
Ansar—Literally means helpers. It refers to the people of Medina who accepted Islam and supported the Prophet and Muslims
Ayat al-ahkam—Verses in the Quran which prescribe binding rules (including legal principles)
Azan—Islamic call for prayers
Bab or kitab—Book, door, sections, chapter of book
Baqarah—A cow. Also the title of the largest chapter of the Quran
Din—Religion
Fatwa—A legal or juristic view of a Muslim authority (*Moftir* or *Mojtahid*) on an area of Sharia
Fiqh—The study of Sharia and Islamic law
Fitnah—Sedition
Foqaha—Plural of faqih. Muslim jurists
Hadd—(Singular to Hudud/Hudood) Literally means the limit(s). Under Islamic law punishments for a number of offences are mandated and fixed by God
Hadidth—The sayings of the Prophet Muhammad
Hajj—Pilgrimage and performing of duties around the Kabah
Haram—Forbidden
Hayat al-Amre be al-Marouf v Nahy An al-Monkar—The Commission for the Promotion of Virtue and Prevention of Vice
Hedayah—Guidance from darkness to light and salvation
Hijab—Cover. The Islamic dress code
Hijaz—An area within the Arabian Peninsula (current Saudi Arabia)
Hirabeh—Armed uprising against the state
Hisbah—Accountability
Hoquq—Plural of *haq*. Law or laws. In some contexts it may refer to rights
Hukm al-qanun—Rule of law
Hurriyyat al-Muaradah—Freedom to criticise or argue
Hurriyyat al-Ra'y—Freedom of expression or view
Ibadat—Rituals
Iftira—Defamation
Ijma—Source of law based on the consensus of Muslim jurists
Ijtihad—Process of personal interpretation of religious texts
Iman—Faith

Irfan—Theosophy
Istihsan—Equity or juristic preference (not as a system under common law but as a concept)
Istinbat—Inferring binding rules from original sources (the Quran and the Sunna)
Istishab—Presumptions of continuity
Kabah—The cube structure in the centre of Islam's holiest Mosque in Mecca
Kalima Tayyaba—There is no God but Allah and Prophet Mohammad (PBUH) is His Messenger
Khatamiat—The concept that the prophet of Islam is the last Prophet of God
Khmar—Alcoholic drinks
Klam—Theology
Kofr—Literally means covering the truth. It refers to non-believers
L'an—Cursing
Madhhab—Religion, sect, school of thought, school of law
Makruh—Disliked
Mamlouks—Property (it refers to slaves under Abbasid who later became part of the army of Muslims)
Mohajerin—Migrants
Marouf—Acceptable, good, right
Masalal mursalah—Public policy (consideration of public interest)
Maslahah— Expediency as a source of law
Masajid—Places of worship
Moamilat—Commercial and personal transactions including family relations
Motezalah—An Islamic school of thought which based its legal theory on rationalism (eighth to tenth centuries)
Mubah—Permitted indifference
Mufti— Person who issues a *fatwa*
Munker—Forbidden, wrong
Mustahabb or Mamdoub—Recommended
Najran—An area within current Saudi Arabia
Qadhf (Qazf)—Unsubstantiated accusation of adultery
Qanun—Canon, Law, Rule
Qiyas—Analogical reasoning
Qual—Views, Perspectives and Sayings
Quisas—Retaliation. An eye for an eye
Qurash—The tribe of the Prophet
Qurbani—Ritual sacrifice of an animal
Rida—Conscious rejection of Islam by a Muslim including conversion from Islam to other religions or becoming an atheist
Sabb—Insult
Sabb al-nabi—Insulting the Prophet
Sadd al-dharai—Blocking the means
Shura—Consultation
Siasah—Policy, punishment
Sirqah—Stealing. There is a prescribed punishment (*Hadd*) for *sirqah*
Tafkfir—Labelling and accusing of others as non-believers
Tazir—All crimes and punishments which are not specifically prescribed by the Quran and the Sunna

Ulul al-bab—People of wisdom
Ummah—The community of believers in Islam
Uqubat—Punishments and criminal law
Urf—Common practice/custom
Ustadh—Professor
Wahy—Devine revelation from God to the Prophet of Islam
Wajib—Obligatory
Yathrib—The ancient name for the city of Medina in Saudi Arabia
Zina—Adultery
Zinabiljabar—Rape

INDEX

Note: Alphabetical arrangement is word-by-word, where a group of letters followed by a space is filed before the same group of letters followed by a letter, eg 'free speech' will appear before 'freedom'. Page numbers followed by the letter 'n' refer to footnotes on the quoted pages. In determining alphabetical arrangement, initial articles and prepositions are ignored.

www.ingramcontent.com/pod-product-compliance
Lightning Source LLC
LaVergne TN
LVHW052253200926
848481LV00002B/355